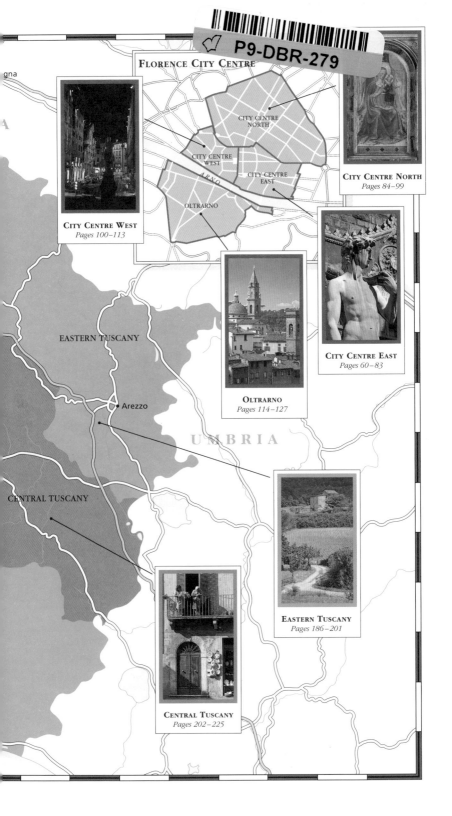

P9-DBR-279

FLORENCE CITY CENTRE

CITY CENTRE NORTH

CITY CENTRE WEST

ARNO

CITY CENTRE EAST

OLTRARNO

CITY CENTRE WEST
Pages 100–113

CITY CENTRE NORTH
Pages 84–99

CITY CENTRE EAST
Pages 60–83

OLTRARNO
Pages 114–127

EASTERN TUSCANY

Arezzo

UMBRIA

CENTRAL TUSCANY

EASTERN TUSCANY
Pages 186–201

CENTRAL TUSCANY
Pages 202–225

gna

EYEWITNESS TRAVEL GUIDES

FLORENCE
& TUSCANY

EYEWITNESS TRAVEL GUIDES

FLORENCE & TUSCANY

Main contributor: CHRISTOPHER CATLING

DK PUBLISHING

LONDON • NEW YORK • MUNICH
MELBOURNE • DELHI

PROJECT EDITOR Shirin Patel
ART EDITOR Pippa Hurst
EDITORS Maggie Crowley,
Tom Fraser, Sasha Heseltine
US EDITORS Laaren Brown, Mary Ann Lynch
DESIGNERS Claire Edwards,
Emma Hutton, Marisa Renzullo
MAP CO-ORDINATORS Simon Farbrother, David Pugh

CONTRIBUTORS Anthony Brierley, Kerry Fisher,
Tim Jepson, Carolyn Pyrah

MAPS Jan Clark, James Mills-Hicks
(Dorling Kindersley Cartography)

PHOTOGRAPHERS Philip Enticknap, John Heseltine, Kim Sayer

ILLUSTRATORS Stephen Conlin, Donati Giudici Associati srl,
Richard Draper, Robbie Polley

Reproduced by Colourscan (Singapore)
Printed and bound by L. Rex Printing Company Limited, China

First American Edition, 1994
03 04 05 10 9 8

Published in the United States by
DK Publishing, Inc., 375 Hudson Street,
New York, New York 10014

**Reprinted with revisions 1994, 1996, 1997 (twice),
1999, 2000, 2001, 2002, 2003**

Library of Congress Cataloging-in-Publication Data
Catling, Christopher.
Florence & Tuscany / main contributor, Chris Catling. -- Rev. ed.
p.   cm. -- (DK eyewitness travel guides)
Includes index.
ISBN 0–7894-9428-0 (alk. paper)
1. Tuscany (Italy) –– Guidebooks.   2. Florence (Italy) –– Guidebooks.
I. Title: Florence and Tuscany. II. Title. III. Eyewitness travel guides.
DG732.C37 2003
914.5'50493––dc21   2002031328

FLOORS ARE REFERRED TO THROUGHOUT IN ACCORDANCE WITH EUROPEAN USAGE;
IE THE "FIRST FLOOR" IS THE FLOOR ABOVE GROUND LEVEL.

See our complete product line at
www.dk.com

**The information in this
Dorling Kindersley Travel Guide is updated annually.**
Every effort has been made to ensure that this book is as up-to-date
as possible at the time of going to press. Some details, however,
such as telephone numbers, opening hours, prices, gallery hanging
arrangements and travel information are liable to change. The
publishers cannot accept responsibility for any consequences arising
from the use of this book, nor for any material on third party
websites, and cannot guarantee that any website address in this
book will be a suitable source of travel information. We value the
views and suggestions of our readers very highly. Please write to:
Publisher, DK Eyewitness Travel Guides, Dorling Kindersley,
80 Strand, London WC2R 0RL, Great Britain.

CONTENTS

Putto in Palazzo Vecchio

INTRODUCING
FLORENCE AND
TUSCANY

Flag from Siena's Palio

A Tuscan country scene in the Crete

Cheese seller in Siena

Panzanella salad

Fresco in Santa Maria Novella

The Duomo in Florence

HOW TO USE THIS GUIDE

THIS GUIDE helps you get the most from your stay in Florence and Tuscany. It provides both expert recommendations and detailed practical information. *Introducing Florence and Tuscany* maps the region and sets it in its historical and cultural context. *Florence Area by Area* and *Tuscany*

Area by Area describe the important sights, with maps, pictures and detailed illustrations. Suggestions for food, drink, accommodation and shopping are in *Travellers' Needs*, and the *Survival Guide* has tips on everything from the Italian telephone system to getting to Tuscany and travelling around the region.

FLORENCE AREA BY AREA

The historic centre of the city has been divided into four sightseeing areas. Each has its own chapter, which opens with a list of the sights described. All the sights are numbered and plotted on an *Area Map*. The detailed information for each sight is presented in numerical order, making it easy to locate within the chapter.

Sights at a Glance lists the chapter's sights by category: Churches; Museums and Galleries; Historic Buildings; Streets and Piazzas.

All pages relating to Florence have red thumb tabs.

A locator map shows where you are in relation to other areas of the city centre.

1 Area Map
For easy reference, the sights are numbered and located on a map. The sights are also shown on the *Florence Street Finder* on pages 136–41.

2 Street-by-Street Map
This gives a bird's eye view of the heart of each sightseeing area.

A suggested route for a walk covers the more interesting streets in the area.

Stars indicate the sights that no visitor should miss.

3 Detailed information on each sight
All the sights in Florence are described individually. Addresses, telephone numbers, opening hours and information on admission charges and wheelchair access are also provided.

Introduction
The landscape, history and character of each region is described here, showing how the area has developed over the centuries and what it offers to the visitor today.

TUSCANY AREA BY AREA

In this book, Tuscany has been divided into five regions, each of which has a separate chapter. The most interesting sights to visit have been numbered on a *Pictorial Map*.

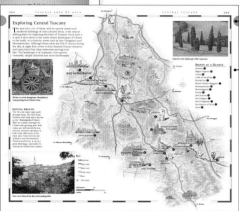

Each area of Tuscany can be quickly identified by its colour coding.

Pictorial Map
This shows the road network and gives an illustrated overview of the whole region. All the sights are numbered and there are also useful tips on getting around the region by car, bus and train.

Detailed information on each sight
All the important towns and other places to visit are described individually. They are listed in order, following the numbering on the Pictorial Map. Within each town or city, there is detailed information on important buildings and other sights.

Stars indicate the best features and works of art.

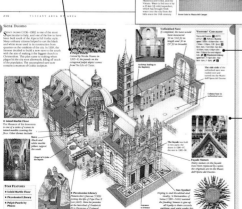

For all the top sights, a Visitor's Checklist provides the practical information you will need to plan your visit.

The top sights
These are given two or more full pages. Historic buildings are dissected to reveal their interiors; museums and galleries have colour-coded floorplans to help you locate the most interesting exhibits.

INTRODUCING FLORENCE AND TUSCANY

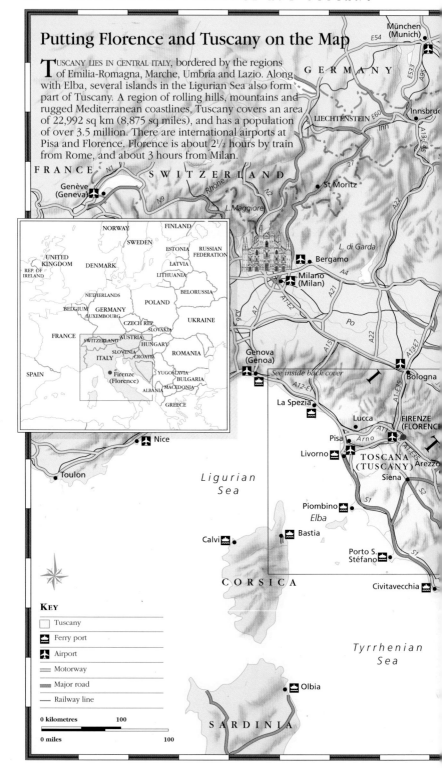

Putting Florence and Tuscany on the Map

Tuscany lies in central Italy, bordered by the regions of Emilia-Romagna, Marche, Umbria and Lazio. Along with Elba, several islands in the Ligurian Sea also form part of Tuscany. A region of rolling hills, mountains and rugged Mediterranean coastlines, Tuscany covers an area of 22,992 sq km (8,875 sq miles), and has a population of over 3.5 million. There are international airports at Pisa and Florence. Florence is about 2½ hours by train from Rome, and about 3 hours from Milan.

See inside back cover

KEY

☐	Tuscany
⚓	Ferry port
✈	Airport
═══	Motorway
▬▬▬	Major road
───	Railway line

0 kilometres   100

0 miles   100

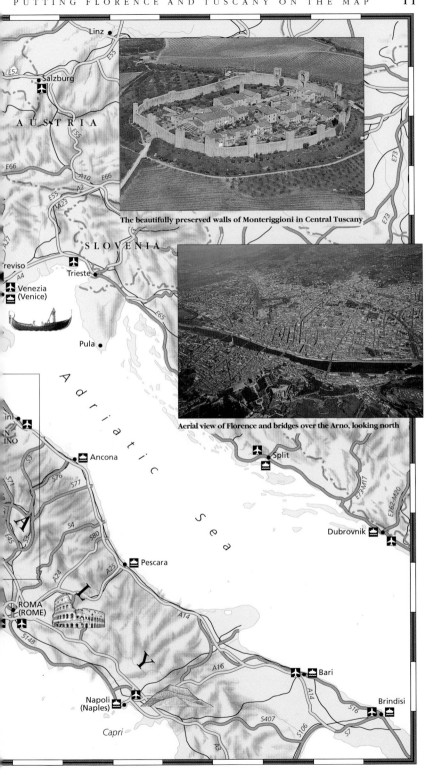

The beautifully preserved walls of Monteriggioni in Central Tuscany

Aerial view of Florence and bridges over the Arno, looking north

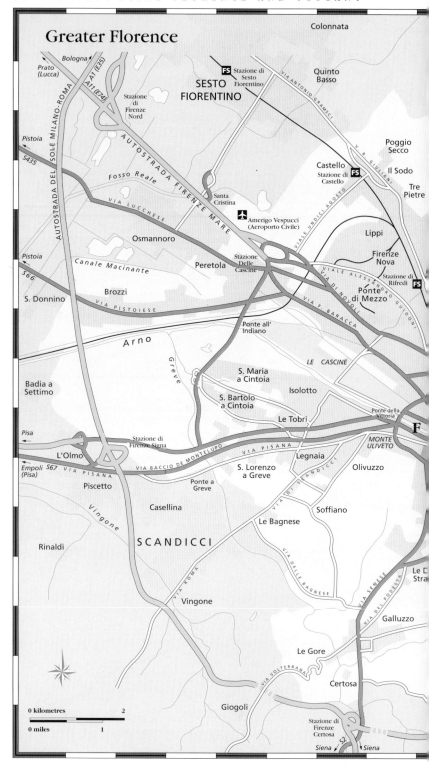

Greater Florence

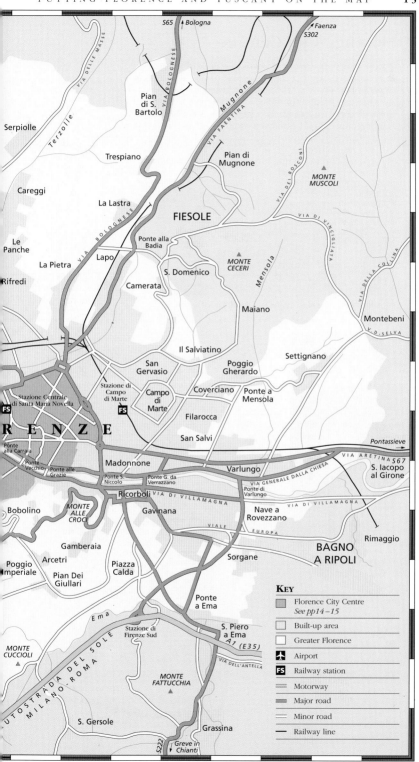

S65 ↑ Bologna

↑ Faenza
S302

Serpiolle

VIA DELLE MASSE

VIA BOLOGNESE

Pian
di S.
Bartolo

Terzolle

Mugnone

VIA FAENTINA

Trespiano

Pian di
Mugnone

VIA DEL BOSCONI

MONTE
MUSCOLI

Careggi

La Lastra

FIESOLE

VIA DI VINCIGLIATA

VIA BOLOGNESE

Le
Panche

Ponte alla
Badia

MONTE
CECERI

Mensola

VIA DELLA COLLINA

La Pietra

Lapo

S. Domenico

Rifredi

Camerata

Maiano

Montebeni

V. D. SELVA

Il Salviatino

Settignano

San
Gervasio

Poggio
Gherardo

Stazione di
Campo
di Marte

Campo
di
Marte

Coverciano

Ponte a
Mensola

Stazione Centrale
di Santa Maria Novella

FS

Filarocca

RENZE

San Salvi

Pontassieve →

Ponte
alla Carraia

Madonnone

Varlungo

VIA ARETINA S67

Ponte
Vecchio

Ponte alle
Grazie

Ponte S.
Niccolo

Ponte G. da
Verrazzano

VIA GENERALE DALLA CHIESA

S. Iacopo
al Girone

Ricorboli

VIA DI VILLAMAGNA

Ponte di
Varlungo

VIA DI VILLAMAGNA

Bobolino

MONTE
ALLE
CROCI

Gavinana

Nave a
Rovezzano

Rimaggio

VIALE   EUROPA

BAGNO
A RIPOLI

Gamberaia

Poggio
Imperiale

Arcetri

Piazza
Calda

Sorgane

Pian Dei
Giullari

Ema

Ponte
a Ema

MONTE
CUCCIOLI

Stazione di
Firenze Sud

S. Piero
a Ema

A1 (E35)

AUTOSTRADA DEL SOLE
MILANO-ROMA

VIA DELL'ANTELLA

MONTE
FATTUCCHIA

S. Gersole

Grassina

S222 ↓ Greve in
Chianti

KEY

▨	Florence City Centre *See pp14–15*
▢	Built-up area
□	Greater Florence
✈	Airport
FS	Railway station
═	Motorway
▬	Major road
═	Minor road
─	Railway line

Florence City Centre

FLORENCE'S BEST SIGHTS are encompassed within such a compact area that the city seems to reveal its treasures at every step. The sights described in this book are grouped within four areas, each of which can be easily explored on foot. In the centre is the massive Duomo, providing a historical as well as geographical focus to the city. Santa Croce to the east and San Marco to the north, with Santa Maria Novella to the west and the Palazzo Pitti in Oltrarno, mark the outlying areas.

City Centre West: Ponte Santa Trinità, with Ponte Vecchio behind

Oltrarno: taking a break in Piazza di Santo Spirito

KEY

	Major sight
FS	Railway station
	Bus terminus
	Coach terminus
P	Parking
	Tourist information
	Hospital with casualty unit
	Police station
	Church
	Synagogue

City Centre North: fountain in Piazza della Santissima Annunziata

City Centre East: main entrance to Palazzo Vecchio

0 metres 500

0 yards 500

A PORTRAIT OF TUSCANY

USCANY IS RENOWNED *throughout the world for its art, history and beautiful landscape. Here the past merges with the present to a remarkable degree, for its people pride themselves on their heritage. Independent and combative, for centuries they have preserved their surroundings and traditions, in which must lie much of Tuscany's eternal fascination for the outsider.*

The people of Tuscany are fiercely proud of their ancestry, which they trace back to the Etruscans. Geneticists have even discovered gene segments that are uniquely Tuscan: there are strong similarities between the faces carved on Etruscan cremation urns *(see pp40–41)* and those of the people on the streets of modern Tuscany.

A classic Tuscan face captured by Botticelli

This legacy also has a political significance. Tuscany still enjoys a kind of grass-roots democracy through referendums on such issues as whether to ban traffic from the centre of Florence. Florentines will, however, take the law into their own hands, as they did when they fought the police in 1990 to prevent the closure of San Lorenzo market. Tuscans also scorn the government in Rome and its bureaucracy. Many people want the autonomy they enjoyed before Italy was united in 1870. This has been sharpened by the revelations of institutionalized corruption in Italy.

The Tuscan love of home has resulted in a strong *campanilismo*: parochialism defined by the sound of the local church bell (in the campanile or belltower). Social anthropologists see in it a survival of medieval inter-city conflicts. It can be observed at many a Tuscan festival when, beneath the pageantry, there is a serious rivalry between a city's different quarters.

A timeless view and way of life: peaceful old age in Casole d'Elsa

◁ **Brilliant, medieval-style pageantry before Siena's Palio** *(see p218)*

A rare sight today – farming with oxen near Pienza

Even the working day of many Tuscans echoes that of their ancestors centuries ago. For people who work out in the fields, the day begins at sunrise, as early as 4:30am in summer. Farm and vineyard labourers will have completed a day's work by noon, when they retire indoors to eat and rest.

Until the 1950s, most Tuscans were familiar with this pattern of life: the region still relied on a feudal system, *mezzadria*, whereby peasants working on the land without payment took a share of the crops as their reward. Today, agricultural produce remains an important ingredient in the Tuscan economy, but only 20 per cent of Tuscans now work in agriculture. Many farming families left the land in favour of a stable income and a shorter working day as factory hands. Town dwellers have a much easier way of life, but the old rhythms prevail: the *siesta* period is still observed, so that almost everything closes for a few hours in the afternoon. Wise travellers soon learn that it pays to follow the same pattern, rising early to join the café throng, before heading out to study ancient frescoes in peace. In the middle of Florence there are several lively early morning markets where you can buy fresh, local produce *(see p267)*. Bargain hunters and food-loving Tuscans frequent them, but by mid-afternoon the stallholders will have packed up.

A cheese stall in Florence

Churches open at 8am, and, except on Sunday when mass is held, there will be few other people to disturb your thoughts if you stray into one. Today, very few Tuscans go regularly to church and Sunday is spent visiting friends, watching sport or enjoying

Clerics in conversation, Colle di Val d'Elsa

family lunch. After the burst of activity that marks the beginning of the day, Tuscan towns adopt a more sedate pace. New building is prohibited inside their walls, so that very many people of school or working age travel out, by bus or car, to schools, offices or factories in the suburbs, leaving the old centres to visitors.

The grape harvest in Chianti

Some of the larger towns, particularly Pisa, Lucca, Florence and Siena, have resisted this tide, determined not to become museum cities given over entirely to tourism. They are thriving

The hour for relaxing in Cortona

service sectors, testimony to the same Tuscan flair for banking, insurance and accountancy that made the Medici family and the "Merchant of Prato" (see p184) some of the richest people in their time. It is, however, the lucky few who work in such beautiful towns. They practise as lawyers, architects, conservationists or designers and are often graduates of the renowned local universities: Pisa, Siena and Florence. For the great majority of Tuscans, however, the working day is spent in purpose-built suburbs, such as the one linking Prato to the Firenze Nuova (New Florence) suburbs west of the city. The Tuscan economy, however, still remains firmly rooted in craft traditions. Top designers from Milan use the textile factories of Prato and Florence for the execution of their designs. Gold-working is not confined to the Ponte Vecchio workshops in Florence – Arezzo produces jewellery which is sold throughout Europe.

THRIVING EXPORTS

Glass, marble and motorcycles are among Tuscany's most important industrial products, while its olive oil and wine are exported worldwide. This explains why Livorno, Tuscany's port, is the second busiest in Italy, while Pisa's Galileo Galilei airport is rapidly becoming a major air-freight distribution centre.

Individual Tuscan artistry can best be admired in the heart of any Tuscan town during the evening promenade – the *passeggiata*. One moment the streets are empty, the next they are filled with elegant people strolling and chatting. The skill of *fare bella figura* ("looking good") is so prized that visitors will be judged by the same standard. It is an opportunity for you to join in the inherently Tuscan aspiration to create a civilized world.

Italian chic, or
bella figura

A Tuscan Town Square

Town bell in the campanile

T HE MAIN SQUARE OR PIAZZA of nearly every Tuscan town is the focus for much of the town's activities. It is here that the townsfolk gather around 6–7pm for the daily *passeggiata*, the traditional evening stroll, or to participate in local festivals and rallies. In most towns there are certain religious and civic buildings that are usually grouped around the piazza. Many of these buildings, you will notice, have standard features, such as the campanile, the *cortile* or the loggia, each of which fulfils a specific function. And often you will find that many of these buildings are still in use today, performing the same function for which they were originally built during the 13th–16th centuries.

Wellhead
Water was a valuable resource that was protected by strict laws to prevent pollution.

Cortile
The arcaded court-yard, or cortile, of a palazzo served as an entrance hall shielded from the outside; it also provided a cool retreat.

Marble or hard sandstone paving

A palazzo is any town house of stature. It is usually named after its owner.

There are three floors in most palazzi. Public reception rooms were on the middle floor, the *piano nobile*.

The ground floor was used for storage and workshops. Today many ground floors are let to businesses, while the owners live above.

Baptismal font

Stemmae
Stone-carved coats-of-arms, belonging to citizens who served as councillors and magistrates, are often seen on public buildings.

The Baptistry, usually octagonal, was a separate building to the west of the church. After baptism, the infant was carried ceremoniously into the church for the first time.

Festival in the Piazza
The prestigious buildings of the main piazza often form an appropriate backdrop to costumed tournaments involving jousting, archery and horsemanship, recalling the medieval arts of war.

Fishtail battlements

Loggia
Many loggias, built to provide shelter from the sun or rain, now harbour colourful street markets.

The Palazzo del Comune (town hall) often houses the Museo Civico (town museum) and the Pinacoteca (art gallery).

Wide central nave, with narrower side aisles

Loggia or colonnade

The campanile rose high so that the town bells could be heard far and wide. The bells were rung to announce public meetings or mass, to sound the curfew, or, when rung furiously *(a stormo)*, to warn of impending danger.

The Duomo (from Latin *Domus Dei* or House of God) is the cathedral, the focal point of the piazza. A smaller parish church is called a *pieve*.

Side Chapel
Wealthy patrons paid for ornate tombs, paintings and frescoes in their own private chapels to commemorate their dead.

Understanding Architecture in Tuscany

Romanesque capital

THE SURVIVAL OF SO MANY fine Gothic and Renaissance buildings is part of Tuscany's immense appeal. Whole streets and squares, such as the Piazza dei Priori in Volterra *(see p163)* and the streets around the Mercato Nuovo in Florence, and even towns such as San Gimignano, have scarcely changed since the 16th century. Simple clues, such as the shape of arches, windows and doorways, reveal the style of the building and when it was built.

Gothic palazzi in Cortona

ROMANESQUE (5TH TO MID-13TH CENTURIES)

The Tuscan Romanesque style developed from late Roman architecture. Early Tuscan churches, such as Sant'Antimo *(see pp42–3)*, have round arches, Roman-style columns and arcades. Profuse surface decoration was introduced in the 12th century, resulting in the jewel-like church façades of Pisa and Lucca.

Interlace and knots are typical motifs.

Capitals are carved with animal and human heads.

Gables often have three tiers of arcading.

A twisted knot

The central portal is flanked by smaller side doors.

Pisa's San Paolo a Ripa d'Arno (see p157), begun in 1210, has restrained geometric patterns on the lower façade and exuberant arcades above.

Marble patterning on stonework

GOTHIC (13TH TO MID-15TH CENTURIES)

Pointed arches are the key feature of Gothic architecture. The style was introduced to Tuscany by French Cistercian monks who built the abbey of San Galgano in 1218 *(see p220)*. Siena then made this style her own, using it for the city's Duomo, palazzi and civic buildings such as Palazzo Pubblico *(see pp214–19)*.

Pinnacles, like miniature spires, bristle from the roofline.

Pointed gables

Gabled niches, sheltering statues of saints or Apostles, are a Gothic innovation.

The crockets are shaped like leaves and flowers.

Santa Maria della Spina (1230–1323), with its pointed gables and spikey pinnacles (see p157), is a typical example of Pisan Gothic architecture.

St Luke, from Orsanmichele

RENAISSANCE (15TH AND 16TH CENTURIES)

Brunelleschi, the father of Renaissance architecture, was inspired by the purity and simplicity of Classical Roman buildings. This style is reflected in his first true Renaissance work, the loggia of the Spedale degli Innocenti in Florence (1419–24) *(see p95)*, with its elegant lines and simple arched bays. The style he created was adopted with enthusiasm by his fellow Florentines, who saw their city as the "new" Rome.

Arch with tear-drop keystone

Courtyard, Spedale degli Innocenti

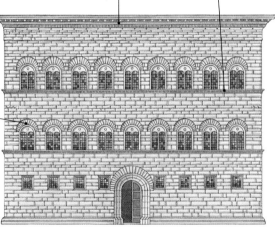

Classical cornices are moulded in Roman style.

String courses define each floor.

Wedge-shaped masonry around semi-circular window arches is characteristic of Renaissance buildings.

Palazzo Strozzi (see p105) *is typical of many Tuscan Renaissance buildings. The rusticated stonework gives an impression of strength and stability.*

BAROQUE (LATE-16TH AND 17TH CENTURIES)

The theatrical Baroque style, much favoured by the popes in Rome, largely passed Tuscany by. Although a few churches in Florence were given new façades in the 17th century, the Florentine version of the Baroque style is very Classical in spirit and not as bold or as exuberant as elsewhere in Italy.

Curved pediments are typical of the Baroque style.

Baroque architects liked to use intricate mouldings.

Scroll

Swag

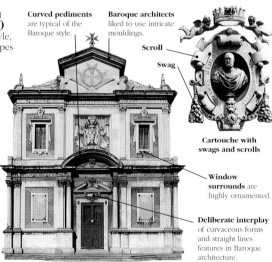

Cartouche with swags and scrolls

Window surrounds are highly ornamented.

Santo Stefano dei Cavalieri (see p153) *has columns and pilasters on its Baroque façade, which give the illusion of depth.*

Deliberate interplay of curvaceous forms and straight lines features in Baroque architecture.

Understanding Art in Tuscany

TUSCANY WAS THE SCENE of one of the most influential and sustained artistic revolutions in history. Its masterpieces record the transition from the stylized charm of medieval art to the Classical beauty and richness of the High Renaissance.

No detailed setting or background

Idealized figures

MEDIEVAL ART

Medieval art served as an aid to prayer and contemplation. The Virgin, patron saint of many Tuscan cities, including Siena, was often depicted as the Queen of Heaven, surrounded by adoring angels and saints.

Gold, symbolizing purity, was used lavishly.

Lack of spatial depth

Unifying flow of drapery

Maestà (1308–11)
The stylized figures in this detail from Duccio's huge altarpiece for Siena cathedral are painted with great delicacy.

The figures form a triangle, symbolizing the Holy Trinity. The viewer's eye is drawn upwards to the figures of Christ and God the Father at the apex.

The Virgin and St John are depicted as real people, rather than idealized figures.

Lorenzo Lenzi, Masaccio's patron, kneels opposite his wife.

RENAISSANCE ART

The artistic revolution known as the Renaissance, which spread throughout Europe from the 15th century onwards, had its roots in Tuscany. Inspired by ancient Roman art, sculptors and painters brought about a "rebirth" of Classical ideals.

They were supported by wealthy and cultured patrons, themselves fascinated by the works of such Classical authors as Plato and Cicero. Nudes, landscapes, portraits, and scenes from mythology

The Trinity (c.1427)
Masaccio pioneered perspective in painting, using architectural illusion to create a three-dimensional effect (see p110).

TIMELINE OF GREAT TUSCAN ARTISTS

	1260–1319 Duccio di Buoninsegna	**1267–1337** Giotto di Bondone		
				1377–1455 Filippo Brunelleschi
1245–1315 Giovanni Pisano				
		1270–1348 Andrea Pisano	**1374–1438** Jacopo della Quercia	
1200	**1250**	**1300**		**1350**
	1245–1302 Arnolfo di Cambio		**1319–47** Ambrogio Lorenzetti	**1378–1455** Lorenzo Ghiberti
	1240–1302 Cimabue	**1283–1344** Simone Martini		**1386–1460** Donatello
1223–84 Nicola Pisano				

☐ **Medieval Artists**

MANNERIST ART

Mannerist artists used "hot" colours, elongated forms and deliberately contorted poses, often within complicated, large-scale compositions.

The twisted pose and vivid colours of Michelangelo's *Holy Family (see p81)* established the key features of the style. Few artists could match the monumental scale of his work, but Bronzino, Pontormo and Rosso Fiorentino brought new life to traditional biblical subjects by their skilful and dramatic composition.

The Martyrdom of St Lawrence (1569)
With Mannerist bravura, Bronzino shows the human body in numerous poses (see p90).

Statues of Roman gods reflect a direct debt to Classical art.

Writhing figures create a sense of dramatic tension.

Flesh and musculature are painted in subtle gradations of light and shade.

---

and everyday life became legitimate subjects for art.

Rejecting the stylized art of the medieval era, Renaissance artists studied anatomy in order to portray the human body more realistically, and strove to develop innovations to please their patrons. They learned how to apply the mathematics of linear perspective to their art, to create the illusion of spatial depth. Painters set figures against recognizable landscapes or city backgrounds, and flattered their patrons by including them as onlookers or protagonists of the scene.

La Maddalena (1438), by Donatello

The greatest Renaissance artists also added another dimension, that of psychological realism. It is evident in Donatello's sculpture *La Maddalena*, which vividly conveys the former prostitute's grief and penitence. Even when painting traditional subjects, they often tried to express the complexities of human character and emotion. The religious elements of the Virgin and Child theme gave way, for example, to an exploration of the mother-child relationship, as in the *Madonna and Child* (c.1455) by Fra Filippo Lippi *(see p82)*.

Pallas, symbolizing wisdom, tames the centaur, representing brute animal impulse.

Pallas and the Centaur
Botticelli's allegory (1485) typifies the Renaissance interest in pagan myth.

1400–82 Luca della Robbia	**1449–94** Ghirlandaio	**1483–1520** Raphael	
1401–28 Masaccio	**1452–1519** Leonardo		**1511–92** Bartolomeo Ammannati
1406–69 Fra Filippo Lippi	**1457–1504** Filippino Lippi	**1486–1531** Andrea del Sarto	
1410–92 Piero della Francesca			**1524–1608** Giambologna
1400	**1450**	**1500**	**1550**
1397–1475 Paolo Uccello	**1445–1510** Botticelli	**1477–1549** Sodoma	**1511–74** Giorgio Vasari
1396–1472 Michelozzo	**1435–88** Verrocchio	**1475–1564** Michelangelo	**1503–72** Agnolo Bronzino
c.1395–1455 Fra Angelico	**1421–97** Benozzo Gozzoli	**1494–1556** Jacopo Pontormo	**1500–71** Benvenuto Cellini
			1495–1540 Rosso Fiorentino

☐ **Renaissance Artists**   ☐ **Mannerist Artists**

Renaissance Frescoes

F RESCOES DECORATE the walls of churches, public
buildings and private palaces throughout Tuscany.
Renaissance artists, in particular, favoured the medium
of fresco painting for decorating new buildings. The
word *fresco*, meaning "fresh", refers to the technique of
painting on to a thin layer of damp, freshly laid plaster.
Pigments are drawn into the plaster by surface tension
and the colour becomes fixed as the plaster dries. The
pigments react with the lime in the plaster to produce
very strong, vivid colours. As the colours do not lie on
the surface, restorers are able to remove the superficial
soot and grime that have accumulated over the years
to reveal the original, embedded colours *(see pp54 – 5)*.

Chiaroscuro
*This is a subtle method of
contrasting light and dark
for dramatic effect.*

Jewel-like Colours
*Artists used rare, costly minerals to
create bright, striking pigments. The blue
of Mary's robe in Piero della Francesca's
Madonna del Parto (c.1460)* (see p193) *
is made from lapis lazuli.*

Earth colours such as reds and
browns came from clay-based
paints containing iron.

White pigment was
used for important
highlights because it
reflects light.

Use of Sinopia
*The outlines of the fresco
were drawn on to the plaster
undercoat using a red pigment called* sinopia. *This
layer was visible through the
final plaster coat, guiding
the artist as he painted in
the details* (see p152).

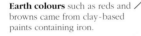

The Giornato
Once the final plaster coat was applied, artists had to work quickly before it dried. This meant painting a small area of plaster each day (the giornato, *or daily portion). Joins between the sections were often concealed in borders, columns and frames.*

Masons left the bare wall surface uneven.

The bare wall was covered with coarse plaster, called *arriccio*, made of clay, hair, sand and lime.

The artist either sketched his design on to the *arriccio* using the pigment *sinopia*, and then painted directly on to the plaster, or he prepared a charcoal drawing on paper which was copied onto the wall.

The final fresco was painted on to a top coat of fine, lime-based plaster called *intonaco*.

Workshops
The master artist worked in tandem with apprentices employed in his workshop. The master concentrated on important features, such as faces and expressive gestures.

Apprentices
While learning their trade, apprentices painted drapery, backgrounds and architectural details in the style of their master.

What to Buy in Tuscany

As a centre for high fashion and quality antiques, Florence is expensive but hard to beat. Bargains also abound, especially in leather goods and shoes. For food lovers there is a wide variety of wines, olive oils and preserves. Away from Florence, small farm estates in Tuscany sell their produce, such as honeys, liqueurs and wines, direct to the public, while many Tuscan towns have their own craft and food specialities. (*See also pp266–9.*)

Desk tidy made of traditional hand-marbled paper

Marbled-paper notebook and box of pencils

Colourful Stationery
Marbled paper is a Florentine speciality. You can buy it in sheets and notebooks, or shaped into carnival masks and even birds and flowers.

Flower-scented air freshener

Soap made to an ancient recipe

Greetings Cards
Beautifully illustrated cards are sold at bookshops and museums.

Hand-made Perfumes and Toiletries
The products in Florentine pharmacies have often been made to ancient formulas by monks and nuns.

Hand-painted majolica

Terracotta and ceramic bowl

Alabaster figurine from Volterra

Ceramics and Reproductions
*Tuscan potters produce highly decorative pieces, from modern originals (*artistiche*) and Renaissance copies (*reproduzioni*) to attractive kitchenware. You can also buy copies of your favourite sculptures.*

Reproductions of Renaissance ceramics

Woven leatherwork
handbag

Elegant document case

Small coin purse

Quality Leather Goods
*Fine leather handbags, wallets and jackets are all
remarkably good value, but fake designer brands
are also sold by street traders and market stalls.*

Hand-crafted men's footwear

Belt with distinctive Gucci buckle

Beautifully
made lady's shoe

Luxury charm bracelet

Designer
silk scarf

Fashionable Footwear
*Even Hollywood filmstars come to
Florence to buy shoes from
boutiques such as Ferragamos.*

Fashion Accessories
*Florence has all the top names in
fashion, including homegrown
couturiers like Gucci.*

Sunflower honey
from Montalcino

Chocolate and biscuit cake

Red wine vinegar
and fine olive oil

Tuscan Delicacies
*Lovers of good food will
want to visit an* alimentari
*(grocer's) to choose from the
fascinating range of stock
available. Tuscan products
to sample and take back
home include bottled
antipasti, fruity olive oils
and a wide variety of
confectionery.*

Artichoke hearts with
peppers and olives

Sun-dried tomatoes
in sunflower oil

Peppers preserved
in olive oil

The Landscape of Tuscany

Tuscany is rich in wildlife, especially flowers and the insects that feed on them, including bees, crickets, cicadas and grasshoppers, whose song is heard during the summer months. For years Tuscan farmers were too poor to afford modern intensive agricultural methods, so the region was, until recently, still farmed by traditional methods. As a result, rural areas have remained relatively unspoiled, a safe haven for many species of flora and fauna – with the exception of the songbird, which has fallen victim to the Tuscan passion for hunting.

Cypress Trees
The flame-shaped cypress is often planted as a windbreak in fields and along roadsides.

Building on hilltops ensures a cooling wind in summer.

The Crete
The clay landscape south of Siena is one of bare hillocks and ravines, denuded of topsoil by heavy rain.

Terracing
The steep hillsides are farmed by cutting terraces and holding the soil in place with stone walls.

Tuscan Farmland
A typical Tuscan farm will combine olive groves and vineyards with fields of maize and barley to feed the cattle and chickens.

Garfagnana Landscape
Much of this region is an unspoilt national park where deer, boar, martens and eagles are protected.

Viticulture
Many families make their own wine and every spare plot is planted with vines.

Olives
The olive tree with its silver-backed leaves is widely cultivated. Many farms sell home-produced olive oil.

TUSCAN WILDLIFE

The best time to see the Tuscan countryside is in May and June when all the flowers are in bloom. Autumn rains bring a second burst of flowering later in the year, and then cyclamen carpet the woodland floors. Even winter has its flowers, such as hellebores and snowdrops.

Animals, Birds and Insects

Hummingbird *hawk moths hover in front of brightly coloured flowers, feeding with their long tongues.*

Swifts perform *aerial acrobatics at dusk, flying high above the city rooftops and towers.*

The green lizard *feeds on grasshoppers and basks on walls in the sunlight.*

Wild boars *are abundant but very shy as they are hunted for their tasty meat.*

Wayside Flowers

The blue chicory *plant flowers all summer and is used as animal fodder.*

Pink, white and red *flowering mallows are a valuable food plant for bees.*

The blood-red poppy *often grows alongside bright white oxeye daisies.*

The almond-scented *bindweed attracts a variety of different insects.*

FLORENCE AND TUSCANY
THROUGH THE YEAR

USCANY IS MOST BEAUTIFUL in May when meadows and waysides are carpeted with the same bright flowers that Botticelli's Flora blithely scatters in *Primavera*, his celebration of spring *(see p82)*. Autumn is equally colourful, when the beech and chestnut woods turn a glorious blaze of seasonal red and gold.

A July harvest, medieval-style

The best months for escaping the heat and the crowds are May, September and October. Easter should

be avoided, as also July and August, because of the long queues outside major museums. During August, when Tuscans head for the sea, you will find shops, bars and restaurants closed. To see traditional festivities like the Palio in Siena or Arezzo's Joust of the Saracen, you will need to book accommodation a year ahead, but there are many other local festivals to enjoy. For information, enquire at main tourist offices *(see p273)*.

SPRING

USCANY BEGINS to wake from winter as Easter approaches. The hillsides are vibrant with the soft green of new leaves and the scent of fresh growth. Even in the cities there is a sense of renewal as hanging baskets and window boxes are displayed outside from April onwards, and wisteria and iris bloom in the public gardens.

Instead of winter's heavy game dishes, asparagus, a speciality of the Lucca area, begins to feature on restaurant menus, along with tender young beans, usually served in lemon juice and oil.

Except at Easter time, the streets and main sights are rarely overcrowded, but the weather can be unpredictable and unseasonably wet.

A window box in bloom: the first sign of spring in Cortona

"Explosion of the Carriage" festival

MARCH

Carnevale *(Shrove Tuesday)*, Viareggio *(see p36)*.
Scoppio del Carro, or the Explosion of the Carriage *(Easter Sunday)*, Piazza del Duomo, Florence. An 18th-century gilded cart is pulled to the cathedral doors by white oxen, and a dove-shaped rocket swoops down a wire from above the High Altar inside to ignite fireworks hidden in the cart. Ostensibly a celebration of the Resurrection, the ceremony has roots in pagan fertility rites. Many Tuscans still believe that a successful firework display means a good harvest.
Festa degli Aquiloni, or Kite Festival *(first Sunday after Easter)*, San Miniato *(see p159)*. Kite lovers perform aerial acrobatics on the Prato della Rocca, the grassy common above San Miniato.

APRIL

Sagra Musicale Lucchese, *(April–early July)* Lucca *(see pp174–5)*. This extensive festival of sacred music is held in the city's numerous Romanesque churches.
Mostra Mercato Internazionale dell'Artigianato, or Exhibition of Crafts *(last week)*, Fortezza da Basso, Florence. An important European exhibition of the work of artists and artisans.

MAY

Maggio Musicale, Florence. This is the city's major arts festival and it now lasts until early June, with concerts by the Orchestra Regionale Toscana, directed by Zubin Mehta, and other international performers. The festival has been extended to include dance (from classical ballet to experimental work) and fringe events.
Festa del Grillo, or the Cricket Festival *(first Sunday after Ascension Thursday)*, Le Cascine, Florence. The huge park to the west of Florence, where Shelley wrote *Ode to the West Wind*, is the setting for this event, a celebration of the joys of spring. Stallholders used to sell live crickets, which were then released to bring good luck. These days the festival is celebrated with handmade crickets.
Balestro del Girifalco, or Falcon Contest *(first Sunday after 22 May)*, Massa Marittima *(see p37)*.

AVERAGE DAILY HOURS OF SUNSHINE

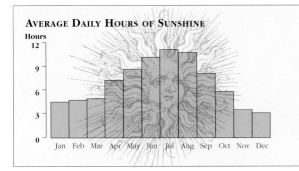

Sunshine Chart
Tuscany has been praised for its light, which has a clear golden quality most noticeable when the intensely sunny days of high summer begin to shorten. Spring and autumn days are still warm, with plenty of hours of sunshine to enjoy.

SUMMER

FROM JUNE onwards, Tuscany's festive calendar becomes increasingly crowded with scores of small town festivals, many of them taking place around Midsummer Day, the feast of John the Baptist, on 24 June. These provide an opportunity to sample local food and wine and join in the atmosphere, or to seek out some of the bigger set-piece festivals.

JUNE

Calcio in Costume, or Football in Costume *(24 June and two other days in June)*, Florence *(see p36)*.
Estate Fiesolana, or Fiesole Summer *(mid-June to end August)*, Fiesole *(see p132)*. Festival of music, arts, drama, dance and film. Many events are staged in the amphitheatre.
Regata di San Ranieri *(17 June)*, Pisa *(see p152)*. Boat

A glorious crop of sunflowers in high summer

races in costume and processions of colourfully decorated boats on the river Arno. After dark, its bankside buildings are illuminated by tens of thousands of flaming torches.
Gioco del Ponte or Game of the Bridge *(last Sunday in June)*, Pisa. A ritual battle played out on a bridge *(see p36)*.

Italian ice cream, a feast for all ages

JULY

Corsa del Palio *(2 July and 16 August)*, Siena. Tuscany's most famous event *(see p218)*.
Pistoia Blues *(early July)*, Piazza del Duomo, Pistoia *(see pp182–3)*. Famous international festival of blues music, lasting for a week.
Settimana Musicale Senese *(last week)*, Siena *(see pp214–15)*. Throughout this "Musical Week", chamber music is performed by the renowned Accademia Musicale Chigiana in splendid settings, such as the Palazzo Chigi-Saraceni.

AUGUST

Festival Pucciniano *(all month)*, Torre del Lago Puccini *(see p171)*. Performances of the composer's operas in an open-air theatre by the lake where he lived.
Rodeo *(all month)*, Alberese. Cowboys of the Maremma *(see pp232–3)* demonstrate horse training and cattle herding.
Cantiere Internazionale d'Arte *(late July–early August)*, Montepulciano *(see p223)*. Directed by the composer Hans Werner Henze, this is an important festival of new work by leading composers, dramatists and choreographers.
Festa della Bistecca *(15 August)*, Cortona *(see pp200–1)*. The Festival of the Beefsteak – a local speciality.
Il Baccanale *(penultimate Saturday)*, Montepulciano *(see p223)*. Feast of wine, food and song to celebrate the local Vino Nobile *(see p256)*.

Celebrating a local saint's day on the streets of Siena

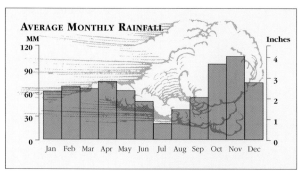

Average Monthly Rainfall

Rainfall Chart
Autumn is the wettest time in Tuscany, with heavy downpours which can last for days, especially late in the season. Late summer storms often bring relief from the intense heat. Winter and spring usually have fairly low rainfall.

Autumn

Autumn is the season of the *vendemmia*, the grape harvest. Visitors should watch for public notices of the many *sagre*, or festivals, that take place throughout the region. These are family-oriented events which typically feature a single local speciality which is in season, such as *funghi porcini* (porcini mushrooms). The first frosts will occur any time from the end of October, and at this point the great tracts of woodland all over Tuscany begin to turn brilliant shades of red and gold.

Autumn in the Val d'Orcia, in southern Tuscany

Grape-picking by hand in a Chianti vineyard

September

Giostra del Saraceno or the Joust of the Saracen *(first Sunday)*, Arezzo *(see p37)*.
Festa della Rificolona *(7 September)*, Piazza della Santissima Annunziata,

Florence. Children from all over the city converge on the square carrying candle-lit paper lanterns to honour the eve of the birth of the Virgin.
Palio della Balestra or Crossbow Festival *(second Sunday)*, Sansepolcro *(see pp192–3)*. Costume parades and flag throwing accompany a crossbow competition between Sansepolcro and the Umbrian town of Gubbio.
Luminara di Santa Croce *(13 September)*, Lucca *(see pp174–5)*. The city's famous relic, the *Volto Santo*, a wooden statue of Christ, is paraded around by torchlight.
Rassegna del Chianti Classico *(second week)*, Greve in Chianti. The biggest Tuscan celebration of local wines.
Mostra Mercato Internazionale dell'Antiquariato *(Sep–Oct)*, Florence. A major biennial antiques fair.

October

Amici della Musica *(Oct–Apr)*, Florence. The "Friends of Music" concert season begins.
Sagra del Tordo or Festival of the Thrush *(last Sunday)*, Montalcino *(see p37)*.

Participant in the Joust of the Saracen festival in Arezzo

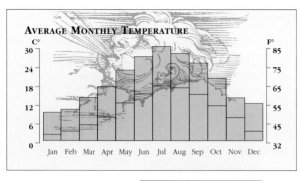

Temperature Chart
July is the hottest, driest month, with June and August only marginally less so. These are the least comfortable months for sight-seeing. Choose late spring or early autumn for this, when you can also sit outside until late.

NOVEMBER

Festival dei Popoli *(Nov–Dec)*, in venues throughout Florence. Tuscany's most important film festival. Open to everyone, it shows films in their original language with Italian subtitles.

WINTER

THIS CAN BE a good time to visit Florence and enjoy the city's museums and churches in tranquillity. It can be bitterly cold, but the skies are blue and the city is often bathed in golden sunlight, making this many photographers' favourite season. All over Tuscany, town squares are filled with the aroma of roasting chestnuts, and in December, the last of the olive crop is being harvested in the southernmost parts.

DECEMBER

Fiaccole di Natale, or Festival of Christmas Torches *(Christmas Eve)*, Abbadia di San Salvatore, near Montalcino *(see p220)*. Carols and torchlight processions in memory of the shepherds from the first Christmas Eve.

JANUARY

Capodanno. New Year's Day is celebrated with gusto all over Tuscany. There are firework displays, and volleys from hunters firing into the air, and from exploding firecrackers: all are part of a ritual to frighten away the ghosts and spirits of the old year and welcome in the new.

Roasting chestnuts, Montalcino

Pitti Immagine Uomo, Pitti Immagine Donna, Pitti Immagine Bimbo *(throughout January)*, Fortezza da Basso, Florence. At these prestigious fashion shows, leading Italian designers and international couturiers present their spring and summer collections for men, women and children.

FEBRUARY

Carnevale *(Sundays before Lent, Shrove Tuesday)*, Viareggio *(see p171)*. A festive event renowned for its parades, competitions and amusing floats, often inspired by topical themes *(see p36)*.

There are many other opportunities to enjoy pre-Lent celebrations, such as the equally splendid carnival festivities that take place in San Gimignano and Arezzo.

PUBLIC HOLIDAYS

New Year's Day (1 Jan)
Epiphany (6 Jan)
Easter Monday
Liberation Day (25 Apr)
Labour Day (1 May)
Ferragosto (15 Aug)
All Saints' Day (1 Nov)
Immaculate Conception (8 Dec)
Christmas Day (25 Dec)
Santo Stefano (26 Dec)

Florence's Piazza di Santo Spirito in winter – serene and free of crowds

Festivals in Tuscany

MANY TUSCAN FESTIVALS celebrate battles and historical events that took place centuries ago; others have their origins in medieval tournaments. Yet they are not merely a pastiche of history, put on for the benefit of tourists. They are living festivals, mounted with an amazing degree of skill and commitment to authenticity and perfection. This can be seen in such details as the embroidery on the costumes worn by the participants and in the exhilarating displays of horsemanship, jousting or archery. Here is a selection of Tuscany's best.

Football in Costume at fever pitch

FLORENCE

CALCIO IN COSTUME, or Football in Costume (a festival held over three days in June, one of which is always 24 June), is a colourful combination of football and rugby. This ancient game involves four teams of 27 men. Each team represents a medieval *rione* (district) of the city. The game is usually held in a main *piazza* of one of the participating quarters, and always attracts a lively crowd. It is often violent and, in recent years, the fierce rivalry has also been acted out off the playing field.

The final prize is a live cow. The game on 24 June coincides with Midsummer and the feast of John the Baptist, the patron saint of Florence. These events are all celebrated by a firework display at 10pm, best seen from the north bank of the Arno, between Ponte Vecchio and Ponte alle Grazie.

WESTERN TUSCANY

THE LAST SUNDAY in June is the occasion for the Gioco del Ponte, or Game of the Bridge, in Pisa *(see pp152–3)*. This battle, in Renaissance costume, takes place between the Pisans who live north of the river Arno and those who live south. Arranged into teams, they attempt to push a seven-tonne carriage over the historic Ponte di Mezzo (literally, the Middle Bridge), which divides the city. On the actual day, the river's banks are crowded with thousands of onlookers. This event probably has its roots in pre-Renaissance times, when there was no regular army and all citizens had to be trained and ready for war.

Some of the participants wear suits of antique armour which date from the 15th and 16th centuries, and their shields bear the colours of the city's different districts. This regalia is kept in the Museo Nazionale di San Matteo *(see p153)* when it is not in use.

Pisa's Game of the Bridge

NORTHERN TUSCANY

CARNEVALE (Carnival) in Viareggio *(see p171)* on Shrove Tuesday is nationally renowned for its imaginative floats. These carry elaborate satirical models of politicians and other public figures. After courting controversy in recent years, however, this celebration is now more of a family event, but there is still an abundance of pointed visual jokes that can be appreciated by those in the know. The designers of the floats enjoy much flattery and prestige, and their creations remain on view all year. As elsewhere, the occasion is one of concentrated merrymaking, and it combines both ancient pagan rituals and Christian values.

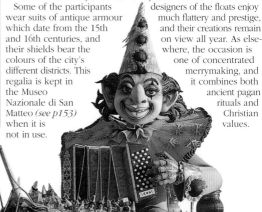

One of the spectacular floats from the Viareggio Carnival

Knights waiting to charge at the Joust of the Saracen in Arezzo

The festival is essentially an excuse for gastronomic over-indulgence, and a celebration of its thriving local economy, which is based on olive oil and wine production. Brunello is widely regarded as one of the finest of Italian wines.

Visitors are welcome to participate, and more conventional specialities, such as *porchetta* (roast suckling pig), are available for those who prefer not to eat songbirds. Archery competitions are also held in Montalcino during August to mark the beginning of the hunting season.

EASTERN TUSCANY

THE PIAZZA GRANDE in Arezzo *(see pp194–5)* is the scene of the Giostra del Saracino, or Joust of the Saracen. Held on the first Sunday in September, this tournament dates back to the Crusades in the Middle Ages, when all Christendom dedicated itself to driving the North African Arabs (the Moors) out of Europe.

There are lively and colourful processions to precede the event, in which eight costumed knights charge towards a wooden effigy of the Saracen. The aim is to try to hit the Saracen's shield with lances and then avoid a cat-of-three-tails swinging back and unseating them. Each pair of knights represents one of Arezzo's four rival *contrade* (districts), and their supporters occupy a side each of Piazza Grande. They are quiet when

their own *contrada* knights are jousting, but make as much noise as is possible to distract the opposition. The winner receives a gold lance.

CENTRAL TUSCANY

THE MOST IMPORTANT festival in this region is Siena's Palio *(see p218)*, but the Sagra del Tordo, or Festival of the Thrush, is also a great attraction. It takes place in Montalcino *(see pp220–21)* on the last Sunday in October. The 14th-century Fortezza (castle) is the setting for an archery contest which is fought in traditional costume by members of the town's four *contrade*. This is accompanied by considerable consumption of the local red Brunello wine and, much to the horror of many bird-lovers, of charcoal-grilled thrush.

Archery at the Festival of the Thrush in Montalcino

SOUTHERN TUSCANY

BALESTRO DEL GIRIFALCO, or the Falcon Contest, takes place in Massa Marittima *(see p230)* on the first Sunday after the feast of San Bernardino (22 May) and again on the first Sunday in August. It is preceded by a long procession through the town of people in dazzling Renaissance costume, accompanied by flag-waving and music. The contest itself is a test of ancient battle skills and the teams represent the town's three traditional historic divisions, which are known as *terzieri* or thirds. Marksmen come forward and try to shoot down a mechanical falcon, tethered on a wire, with their crossbows. Great precision is required to hit the target and the whole contest is imbued with intense *terzieri* rivalry.

Renaissance finery at the Falcon Contest in Massa Marittima

THE HISTORY OF FLORENCE AND TUSCANY

TUSCANY IS RICH in historical monuments. Etruscan walls encircle many of the region's hilltop towns and the streets within are lined with medieval and Renaissance palazzi, town halls testifying to the ideals of democracy and self-government, and churches built on the ruins of ancient pagan temples. The countryside, too, is dotted with castles and fortified villages, symbols of the violence and intercommunal strife that tore Tuscany apart for so many years during the medieval period. Typical of these is the hilltop town of San Gimignano *(see pp208–11)*, with its defensive towers.

Some of the most imposing castles, such as the Fortezza Medicea in Arezzo *(see p194),* bear the name of the Medici family. Their coat of arms, found all over Tuscany, is a reminder

The Marzocco lion, emblem of Florence

of the role they played in the region's history. They presided over the simultaneous birth of Humanism and the Renaissance and, later, when they were Grand Dukes of Tuscany, patronized eminent scientists and engineers such as Galileo. Tuscany has also played a part in wider events: Napoleon was exiled to Elba, and Florence served briefly as capital of the newly united Italy (1865–71).

Much damage was done to Tuscany's art and monuments by World War II bombing and the floods of 1966. However, major restoration projects undertaken as a result have stimulated research into up-to-date scientific methods. In this way, Tuscany's artistic heritage continues to inspire contemporary life – something it has always done for the many creative people who live and work here and for its endless trail of admiring visitors.

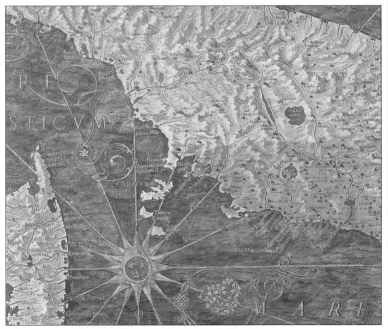

16th-century map of Italy, showing Pisa and the river Arno leading to Florence

◁ San Gimignano, held by its patron saint, and little changed since Taddeo di Bartolo (1362–1422) painted it

Etruscan and Roman Tuscany

THE ETRUSCANS MIGRATED to Italy from Asia Minor around 900 BC, attracted to the area they called Etruria (now in Tuscany, Lazio and Umbria) by its mineral wealth. This they exploited to produce weapons, armour, tools and jewellery to trade with Greece. After a fierce war with Rome in 395 BC, the Etruscan civiliza-

Etruscan earrings worked in gold

tion was eclipsed by Roman rule. Many aspects of Roman religion can be attributed to the Etruscans, including animal sacrifice and divination – reading the will of the gods in animal entrails or cloud patterns. Everyday Etruscan life and the preoccupation with the afterlife are reflected in detailed carved cremation urns and tombs like those at Volterra *(see pp162–3)*.

Wax writing tablets were used to keep household accounts.

A covered wagon carved on the urn shows the Etruscans were skilled at carpentry.

Bronze Chimera *(4th-century BC)*
The wounded chimera (part goat, lion and serpent) is a dramatic example of Etruscan bronze casting.

Athletic Games
Tomb paintings depicting chariot races, dancing and athletics suggest that the Etruscans had festivals similar to the Olympic Games of the ancient Greeks.

ETRUSCAN CREMATION URN

Much of what is known about the Etruscans comes from studying the contents of their tombs. This 1st-century BC terracotta cremation urn from Volterra is carved with scenes from Etruscan domestic life.

The relief depicts the last journey of the deceased into the underworld.

TIMELINE

9th century BC Earliest evidence of Etruscans on Elba

508 BC Lars Porsena, Etruscan ruler of Chiusi, leads an unsuccessful attack on Rome

474 BC Etruscans defeated in Asia Minor by their commercial rivals; trade with Greece suffers and Etruscan ports such as Populonia begin to decline

900 BC	800	700	600	500	400	300

7th century BC Beginning of extensive maritime trade with Greece and the Near East

6th century BC Founding of the Dodecapolis, a confederation of the 12 most powerful Etruscan cities

Coin from Populonia

395 BC Rome captures Veii in Lazio, signalling the end of Etruscan independence

Circular Chandelier
Sixteen oil lamps decorate the rim of this bronze chandelier, made around 300 BC.

The family of the deceased watches the funeral cortège.

Statue of Venus
Under Roman rule, the Etruscans adopted new deities like Venus, goddess of beauty.

Lead Tablet
Etruscan priests recorded details of their prayers and religious rites on lead tablets. However, their language has not yet been fully deciphered, and many of their beliefs and traditions are not yet understood.

WHERE TO SEE ANCIENT TUSCANY

The famous bronzes of the *Chimera* and the *Orator* are in Florence's Museo Archeologico (*p99*). Good museum collections are in Fiesole (*pp132–3*), Volterra (*p162*), Chiusi (*p224*), Cortona (*p200*) and Grosseto (*p234*). There are tombs at Vetulonia (*p234*) and Sovana (*p234*), and the ruins of an Etruscan town have been excavated near Roselle (*p234*).

Etruscan Rock-cut Tomb
The tombs in Sovana date from the 3rd century BC (p234).

Roman Theatre
The bath and theatre complex excavated in Volterra was built after Rome conquered the city in the 4th century BC (p163).

---

205 BC All Tuscany now under Roman control; the Etruscans forced to pay tribute in bronze, grain and iron

90 BC Etruscans granted Roman citizenship, marking the end of their existence as a distinct culture

AD 250 Christianity brought to Florence by Eastern merchants; St Minias martyred in the city

AD 313 Constantine grants official status to Christianity

| 200 | 100 | AD 1 | 100 | 200 | 300 | 400 |

Bronze of a Roman Orator c. 300 BC

20 BC Military colony of Saena (Siena) founded

59 BC Florentia (Florence) founded as a town for retired Roman army veterans

AD 405 Flavius Stilicho defeats the Ostrogoths besieging Florence

Early Medieval Tuscany

Medieval carved stone lion

THE CHURCH kept the flame of learning alive during the dark years when Tuscany was under attack from Teutonic tribes such as the Goths and Lombards. Charlemagne, responding to the pope's request for help, drove the Lombards out of Tuscany in the 8th century. He was crowned Holy Roman Emperor as his reward, but this was soon to spark off a long conflict between church and emperor about who should rule Italy.

Early churches have simple wooden joists.

Mosaic Madonna
A 12th-century mosaic of the Virgin from Cortona (see p200) is typical of the Byzantine-influenced art of the early medieval period.

The capitals are carved with biblical scenes.

Knight on Horseback
This 11th-century carving from Sovana's cathedral symbolizes the conflict between pope and emperor over control of the church.

Priests' quarters

Chapel of Sant'Agata
Like most early churches in Tuscany, the 12th-century octagonal brick chapel in Pisa, with its pyramid-shaped roof, was built on the grave of a Christian saint martyred by the Romans (see p152).

Semi-circular chapels with limpet-shell roofs are a typical feature of the period.

TIMELINE

552 Totila the Goth attacks Florence

570 Lombards conquer northern Italy

Carts used by Charlemagne's army in battle

500	600	700	800

774 Charlemagne, King of the Franks, begins a campaign to subjugate the Lombards

7th-century Lombardic gold crown in Museo Archeologico, Florence (see p99)

800 Charlemagne crowned Holy Roman Emperor

The bells in the campanile were rung to call the village to church and prayer.

The ambulatory ran behind the altar and was used for processions.

Countess Matilda
Matilda, the last of the Margraves, ruled Tuscany in the 11th century and built many churches in the area.

Baptismal Font
Scenes taken from the lives of Moses and Christ adorn the 12th-century font at San Frediano, Lucca (see pp174–5).

SANT'ANTIMO (see p224)
Founded, according to legend, by Charlemagne in 781, the shape of the church demonstrates the influence of the Roman *basilica* (law court) on the design of early churches; the altar occupies the position of the magistrate's chair.

WHERE TO SEE EARLY MEDIEVAL TUSCANY

Well-preserved early medieval churches are found throughout Tuscany: in San Piero a Grado (see p157); Barga (p170); Lucca (pp174–5); San Quirico d'Orcia (p221); Massa Marittima (p230); Sovana (p232); San Miniato al Monte in Florence (p130); and in Fiesole (p132).

Castello di Romena
The 11th-century tower near Bibbiena was built by the Guidi family, who dominated the area.

Santi Apostoli in Florence
Founded in 786, the church includes columns from ancient Roman baths (p109).

1062 Pisa captures Sicily and becomes the foremost Mediterranean port

1152 Frederick Barbarossa is crowned Holy Roman Emperor and invades Italy

1186 Siena cathedral begun

900　　　1000　　　1100　　　1200

c.1025–30 Guido d'Arezzo invents a form of musical notation

1063 Pisa cathedral begun

1115 Countess Matilda dies

1125 Florence captures and destroys Fiesole

12th-century Tuscan School Crucifixion

Late Medieval Tuscany

DURING THE 13TH CENTURY Tuscany grew rich on textile manufacturing and trade. Commercial contact with the Arab world led the Pisan mathematician Fibonacci to introduce Arabic numerals to the West; a new understanding of geometry followed and Tuscan architects began to build ambitious new buildings. At the same time, Tuscan bankers developed the book-keeping principles that still underlie modern accountancy and banking practice. It was also an age of conflict. Cities and factions fought ruthlessly and incessantly to secure wealth and power.

Defensive towers protected the city.

Contented citizens had time for leisure.

Condottieri (mercenaries) were hired to settle conflicts.

Dante's Inferno
Dante (in blue) was caught in the Guelph-Ghibelline conflict and was exiled from Florence in 1302. He took revenge in his poetry, describing his enemies' torments in Hell.

Petrarch and Boccaccio
Petrarch and Boccaccio (top and bottom left), like Dante, wrote in the Tuscan dialect, not Latin. Petrarch's sonnets and Boccaccio's tales were very popular.

GOOD GOVERNMENT

Ambrogio Lorenzetti's early 14th-century allegorical fresco in Siena's Palazzo Pubblico *(see pp214–15)* shows thriving shops, fine buildings and dancing citizens, symbolizing the benefits of good government. Another fresco, *Bad Government*, shows rape, murder, robbery and ruin.

TIMELINE

1215 Start of conflict between Guelph supporters of the pope and Ghibelline supporters of the Holy Roman Emperor

1252 First gold florin minted

1260 Siena defeats Florence at Montaperti

1278 Campo Santo begun in Pisa

1200	1220	1240	1260	1280

1220 Frederick II of Germany is crowned Holy Roman Emperor and lays claim to Italy

1224 St Francis receives the "stigmata" (the wounds of Christ) at La Verna

1284 Pisan navy defeated by Genoa; the beginning of Pisa's decline as a port

Florin stamped with the lily of Florence

Wool Traders' Emblem
Luca della Robbia's roundel depicts the Lamb of God, symbol of the Calimala (wool importers), whose trade guild was the most powerful in Florence.

A building boom resulted from increased prosperity.

St Francis (1181–1226)
From monasteries founded in Tuscany by St Francis, the Franciscans brought about a major religious revival in reaction to the excesses of the church.

Bankers in Siena
Tuscan banks provided loans to popes, monarchs and merchants. Many bankers were ruined when Edward III of England defaulted on his debts in 1342.

WHERE TO SEE LATE MEDIEVAL TUSCANY

San Gimignano's spectacular towers *(see pp208–11)* show what most Tuscan cities must have looked like during the Middle Ages. Siena has the best surviving late medieval town hall *(pp214–15)*, and Pisa's Leaning Tower, Duomo and Baptistry *(pp154–6)* reflect the willingness of architects of this period to experiment with new styles.

Medieval building techniques
Circular putlock holes show where medieval builders placed their scaffolding timbers.

Lucignano
Some of Tuscany's best-preserved medieval architecture, including several defensive towers, can be seen in Lucignano (p199).

1294 Work begins on Florence's cathedral

1300 Giovanni Pisano carves pulpit for Pisa's cathedral

1350 Pisa's Leaning Tower completed; Boccaccio begins writing *The Decameron*

1377 Sir John Hawkwood appointed Captain General of Florence

| 1300 | 1320 | 1340 | | 1380 |

1302 Dante begins writing *The Divine Comedy*

1299 Work begins on Palazzo Vecchio in Florence

1345 Work begins on Florence's Ponte Vecchio

1348–93 Black Death carries off half the Tuscan population

Sir John Hawkwood, English mercenary

1374 Death of Petrarch

The Renaissance

Della Robbia roundel from the Cappella de' Pazzi (1430)

UNDER ASTUTE Medici leadership, Florence enjoyed a period of peace and prosperity. Rich bankers and merchants invested in fine palaces to replace their cramped tower houses, and paid for the adornment of churches. The result was an outpouring of art and architecture, remarkable for its break with the Gothic past and its conscious attempt to give "rebirth" to Classical values. The rediscovery of works by ancient philosophers like Cicero and Plato profoundly influenced the intellectual preoccupations of the day. Their ideas inspired the Humanists, who emphasized the role of knowledge and reason in human affairs.

Textile Market
The thriving Florentine textiles industry allowed the textile guilds and merchants like the dye importer Rucellai (see p104) to become patrons of the arts.

Terracotta roundels of babies in swaddling bands, added by Andrea della Robbia in 1487, reflect the building's function as an orphanage.

Battle of San Romano *(1456)*
Florence hired condottieri *(mercenaries) to fight its battles. Its citizens were therefore free to concentrate on making the city wealthy. Uccello's striking depiction of the Florentine victory over Siena in 1432 is an early attempt to master perspective.*

Classical arches illustrate the Florentine passion for ancient Roman architecture.

SPEDALE DEGLI INNOCENTI

The archetypal Renaissance building, Brunelleschi's colonnade (1419–26) for the Spedale degli Innocenti *(see p95)* is a masterpiece of restrained Classical design. Europe's first orphanage, the Spedale is also a major social monument.

TIMELINE

1402 Florence Baptistry doors competition *(see p66)*

1416 Donatello completes his *St George (see p67)*

1425–7 Masaccio paints *The Life of St Peter* frescoes in Santa Maria del Carmine *(see pp126–7)*

1436 Brunelleschi completes dome for Florence cathedral *(see pp64–5)*. Work starts on San Marco *(see pp96–7)*

1400	1410	1420		1440

1406 Pisa falls to Florence

1419 Work begins on the Spedale degli Innocenti

Cosimo il Vecchio

1434 Cosimo il Vecchio returns from exile

Grey sand-stone and white plaster contrasts radically with the rich surface ornamentation of late medieval architecture.

Classical Corinthian capital

Humanist Scholars
By studying a broad range of subjects, from art to politics, the Humanists fostered the idea of Renaissance man, equally skilled in many activities.

David *(1475)*
A favourite Florentine subject (see p77), Verrocchio's bronze emphasizes David's youth and vulnerability.

Pazzi Family Emblem
The wealthy Pazzi were disgraced after trying to assassinate Lorenzo the Magnificent and seize control of Florence in 1478.

WHERE TO SEE RENAISSANCE TUSCANY

Most of Florence was rebuilt during the Renaissance. Highlights include San Lorenzo *(see pp90–91)*, Masaccio's frescoes in the Brancacci Chapel *(pp126–7)*, many paintings in the Uffizi *(pp80–83)* and the sculptures at the Bargello *(pp68–9)*.

Pienza Duomo *(1459)*
Pope Pius II's plans for a model Renaissance city at Pienza (p222) were never fully realized.

San Marco Cloister *(1437)*
Cosimo il Vecchio paid for Michelozzo's cloister (pp96–7) and used it as a retreat.

1454–66 Piero della Francesca's *The Legend of the True Cross (see pp196–7)*

1480 Botticelli's *Primavera*. The villa at Poggio a Caiano begun *(see p161)*

Lorenzo the Magnificent

1450	1460	1470	1480	1490

1464 Death of Cosimo il Vecchio

1469 Lorenzo the Magnificent comes to power

1478 Pazzi conspiracy

1485 Botticelli's *The Birth of Venus*

1492 Death of Lorenzo the Magnificent

The Medici of Florence

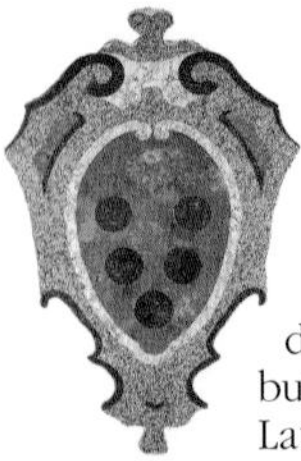

THE MEDICI FAMILY held power in Florence almost continuously from 1434 until 1743. Their rule began discreetly enough with Cosimo il Vecchio, son of a self-made man, Giovanni di Bicci. For years, Cosimo and his descendants directed policy with popular support, but without ever being voted into office. Later generations gained titles and power but ruled by force. Two were elected pope and, after the Republic *(see pp50–51)*, the decadent Alessandro took the title Duke of Florence. From him control passed to Cosimo I, who was crowned Grand Duke of Tuscany.

Medici coat of arms, San Lorenzo

Giovanni di Bicci
An astute merchant banker, he founded the Medici fortune.

Giovanni di Bicci
(1360–1429)

① Cosimo il Vecchio
(1389–1464)

② Piero the Gouty
(1416–69)

③ Lorenzo the Magnificent
(1449–92)

Giuliano
(1453–78)

Giulio, Pope Clement VII
(1478–1534)

④ Piero
(1472–1503)

⑤ Giovanni, Pope Leo X
(1475–1521)

⑦ Giuliano, Duke of Nemours
(1479–1516)

⑧ Alessandro, Duke of Florence
(1511–37: parentage uncertain)

⑥ Lorenzo, Duke of Urbino
(1492–1519)

Catherine, Duchess of Urbino *m* Henry II of France (1519–89)

Lorenzo the Magnificent
A poet and statesman, Lorenzo was the model Renaissance man. One of his greatest achievements was to negotiate peace among the cities of northern Italy.

Catherine of France
Catherine married Henri II of France in 1533. She is shown with two of her sons, who both became French kings: Charles IX and Henri III. Yet another son became Francis II of France.

Pope Leo X
Elected pope when only 38, Leo's corrupt plans to fund the rebuilding of St Peter's in Rome triggered a furious reaction that led to the birth of the Protestant movement.

MEDICI PATRONAGE

As one of the most powerful families in Florence, the Medici were responsible for commissioning some of the greatest works of the Renaissance. Many artists flattered their patrons by placing them prominently in the foreground of their paintings. In Botticelli's *Adoration of the Magi* (1475), the grey-haired king who is pictured kneeling at the feet of the Virgin is Cosimo il Vecchio. The kneeling figure in the white robe is his grandson, Giuliano. The young man holding a sword, on the far left of the painting, is thought to be a rather idealized portrait of Lorenzo the Magnificent, Cosimo's other grandson.

Adoration of the Magi (1475) by Botticelli

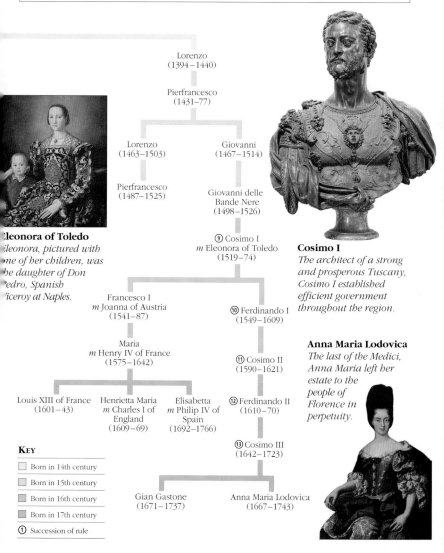

Eleonora of Toledo
Eleonora, pictured with one of her children, was the daughter of Don Pedro, Spanish Viceroy at Naples.

Lorenzo
(1394–1440)

Pierfrancesco
(1431–77)

Lorenzo
(1463–1503)

Pierfrancesco
(1487–1525)

Giovanni
(1467–1514)

Giovanni delle
Bande Nere
(1498–1526)

⑨ Cosimo I
m Eleonora of Toledo
(1519–74)

Francesco I
m Joanna of Austria
(1541–87)

Maria
m Henry IV of France
(1575–1642)

Louis XIII of France
(1601–43)

Henrietta Maria
m Charles I of
England
(1609–69)

Elisabetta
m Philip IV of
Spain
(1692–1766)

⑩ Ferdinando I
(1549–1609)

⑪ Cosimo II
(1590–1621)

⑫ Ferdinando II
(1610–70)

⑬ Cosimo III
(1642–1723)

Gian Gastone
(1671–1737)

Anna Maria Lodovica
(1667–1743)

Cosimo I
The architect of a strong and prosperous Tuscany, Cosimo I established efficient government throughout the region.

Anna Maria Lodovica
The last of the Medici, Anna Maria left her estate to the people of Florence in perpetuity.

KEY

☐ Born in 14th century

☐ Born in 15th century

☐ Born in 16th century

☐ Born in 17th century

① Succession of rule

The Florentine Republic

Savonarola (1452–98)

In 1494, when Piero de' Medici abandoned Florence to the invading troops of Charles VIII of France, the city was declared a Republic. Under the leadership of the religious fundamentalist, Girolamo Savonarola, the people were encouraged to believe that God was their only ruler. After his execution in 1498, the Republic survived 32 years of constant attack. Finally, in 1530, the Medici Pope, Clement VII, and the Holy Roman Emperor, Charles V of Spain, combined forces and returned the city to Medici rule.

Palazzo Vecchio Frieze
The inscription, "Christ is King", on this Republican frieze implies that no mortal ruler has absolute power.

Present-day Boboli Gardens

Charles VIII Enters Siena
When the French invaded Tuscan cities in 1494, Savonarola claimed it was God's punishment for the Tuscan obsession with profane books and art. He ordered such objects burned in bonfires of "vanity".

Judith and Holofernes
Donatello's statue of the virtuous Judith slaying the tyrant Holofernes was placed in front of the Palazzo Vecchio in 1494 to symbolize the end of Medici rule.

THE SIEGE OF FLORENCE (1529–30)
Besieged by 40,000 papal and imperial troops, the citizens of Florence held out for ten months before starvation and disease led to their surrender. Vasari's fresco in the Palazzo Vecchio shows the full extent of the city's defences and the scale of the enemy assault.

TIMELINE

Chancellor Soderini

1498 Savonarola burnt at the stake

1504 Michelangelo completes *David* (see p77)

1512 Florence besieged by Cardinal Giovanni de' Medici

1495

1505

1510

1494 Charles VIII attacks Florence. Savonarola seizes power from Medici family

1502 Soderini elected first chancellor of the Republic

1509 Pope Julius II begins driving the French from Italian soil

1513 Giovanni de' Medici crowned Pope Leo X

Execution of Savonarola

Savonarola was an inspirational orator who commanded great popular support. His political enemies had him executed for heresy in 1498.

All roads out of Florence were blocked.

Artillery platform

Troops camped to the south.

Niccolò Machiavelli

The author of The Prince, *a treatise on the ruthless skills required to be a successful politician, was the last Republican chancellor.*

WHERE TO SEE REPUBLICAN TUSCANY

A plaque in Piazza della Signoria *(see pp76–7)* marks the spot where Savonarola was executed; his cell can be seen in San Marco *(pp96–7)*. Michelangelo's *David (p94)* symbolizes the victory of the youthful Republic over tyranny. The Republican council met in the Salone dei Cinquecento *(p76).*

Tower of San Miniato
This was reinforced in 1530 as a gun platform (pp130–31).

Michelangelo's Sketches
During the siege of 1530, Michelangelo worked in the safety of the Cappelle Medicee (pp90–91).

Crystal casket belonging to Pope Clement VII

| | **1525** | **1530** | |

1520 Michelangelo begins work on Medici tombs *(see p91)*

1521 Giulio de' Medici crowned Pope Clement VII and Medici rule restored in Florence

1527 Florentine Republic reconstituted when Rome is sacked by imperial troops

1530 Siege of Florence by combined forces of pope and emperor

1531 Alessandro de' Medici becomes first Duke of Florence

1532 Posthumous publication of Machiavelli's *The Prince*

The Grand Duchy

COSIMO I WAS CREATED GRAND DUKE of Tuscany in 1570, having forced Tuscany into a state of political unity for the first time. A period of prosperity followed, in spite of the corrupt and debauched nature of Cosimo's heirs. When the Medici line ended in 1737, the Grand Duchy was inherited by the Austrian Dukes of Lorraine. They were removed from power in 1860 during the Risorgimento, when the Italian people joined forces to overthrow their foreign rulers. From 1865–70, Florence was the nation's capital. With the final unification of Italy in 1870, however, the centre of power returned to Rome.

Leopoldo and Family
Leopoldo I, later Emperor Leopold II of Austria, introduced many reforms, including abolition of the death penalty.

The Church rejected Galileo's discoveries.

Galileo explains his theory of gravity.

Livorno Harbour
Livorno became a free port in 1608: ships from every nation were granted equal docking rights, and the resulting influx of Jewish and Moorish refugees contributed to the city's prosperity.

The Old Market
Florence's Old Market was knocked down in 1865, when the city was briefly the Italian capital. In its place is the triumphal arch of the Piazza della Repubblica (see p112).

THE AGE OF SCIENCE

Galileo was one of several brilliant scientists who benefited from Medici patronage during the 17th century, making Tuscany a centre of scientific innovation. His experiments and astronomical observations laid the foundations for modern empirical science, but led to his persecution for contradicting the teachings of the Roman Catholic Church.

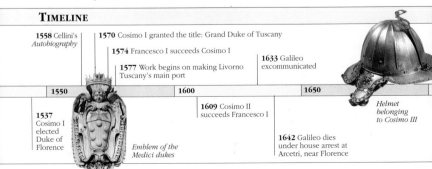

TIMELINE

1558 Cellini's *Autobiography*

1570 Cosimo I granted the title: Grand Duke of Tuscany

1574 Francesco I succeeds Cosimo I

1577 Work begins on making Livorno Tuscany's main port

1633 Galileo excommunicated

1550	1600	1650	1

1537 Cosimo I elected Duke of Florence

1609 Cosimo II succeeds Francesco I

1642 Galileo dies under house arrest at Arcetri, near Florence

Emblem of the Medici dukes

Helmet belonging to Cosimo III

The Grand Tour

It became fashionable for wealthy 18th-century European aristocrats to visit Tuscany. This detail from Zoffani's Tribuna *(1770) shows a tour of the Uffizi.*

Galileo conducted his experiments using specially designed equipment *(see p74).*

Cosimo II gave refuge to Galileo after the Church accused him of heresy.

WHERE TO SEE GRAND DUCHY TUSCANY

The Uffizi art collection *(see pp80–83)* was assembled by the Medici at this time, along with the collections in the Palazzo Pitti *(pp120–23)*, the building from which the Grand Dukes ruled Tuscany for over 300 years. The story of Galileo and his contemporaries is told in the Museo di Storia della Scienza in Florence *(p74)*. The frescoes of the Sala del Risorgimento, in the Palazzo Pubblico, Siena *(p214)*, depict the events that preceded the final unification of Italy.

Palazzo dei Cavalieri
Francavilla's statue of Cosimo I (1596) marks the entrance to Vasari's ornate Palazzo (p152).

Napoleon's Bathroom
Napoleon never used this bathroom (1790–99), built for him at the Palazzo Pitti (pp120–23).

National Rule
Florence ran up huge debts while serving as the Italian capital. This cartoon shows a protest against the seat of power (the Palazzo Vecchio) being transferred to Rome.

1765 Grand Duke Leopoldo I introduces many social reforms

1796 Napoleon's first Italian campaign

1799 France defeats Austria: Tuscany ruled by Louis de Bourbon, then by Napoleon's sister, Elisa Baciocchi

1815 Napoleon defeated at Waterloo

1822 Shelley drowns near Livorno

1840 Ruskin visits Florence

1750	1800	1850

1743 Death of Anna Maria Lodovica, last of the Medici

1737 End of Medici dynasty; rule passes to Austrian House of Lorraine

1814 Napoleon exiled to Elba

John Ruskin (1819–1900), who revived critical interest in the Renaissance

1865 Florence chosen as capital of new Italian state

1871 Italian capital returns to Rome

The Modern Era

THE 20TH CENTURY has seen many threats to Florence's fragile artistic heritage. The city's historic bridges, except for the Ponte Vecchio, were destroyed during World War II, and worse was to come in 1966 from devastating floods. Traffic and pollution have also taken their toll, leading to tough environmental controls aimed at preserving the historic city centre. Fortunately, the city has energetically risen to these challenges. It continues to thrive both on its proud heritage as a tourist destination and as a living, working city with a robust commercial and industrial base.

ATTENZIONE
a mt. 150
ZONA
PEDONALE

Traffic Control
In 1988 Florence banned cars from the city centre.

La Bohème *(1896)*
This popular opera by Puccini, Tuscany's greatest composer, often features in the region's music festivals (see p33).

Firenze Nuova
Florentine commerce and industry are moving to the suburb of "New Florence", leaving the city centre free for cultural and creative enterprises.

ART RESTORATION

Great pride is taken in Tuscany's artistic heritage, and modern scientific methods are used to analyse frescoes before restoration, such as *The Procession of the Magi (see p89)*. These methods include computer-aided mapping of the pigments and plotting any structural damage.

TIMELINE

Domenico Tiburzi, folk hero and notorious Maremman bandit		**1922** Mussolini heads Italy's first Fascist government		**1943** Fall of the Fascists	
	1896 First performance of Puccini's *La Bohème*		**1940** Italy enters World War II		
1890	**1900**	**1910**	**1920**		**1940**
	1915 Italy enters World War I on the side of the Allies (France, Britain and Russia)				
	1896 Domenico Tiburzi is caught and shot after 24 years on the run		**1944** Many historic structures in Tuscany are damaged by Allied bombing or retreating Nazis		

The 1966 Floods
On 4 November, floodwater from the Arno rose to 6 m (19.5 ft) above street level. Many art treasures were ruined; some are still in restoration.

A scanned image lets restorers trace existing outlines and reconstruct damaged areas.

Fashion
Many Florentine designers have become household names. These include Pucci, who invented the "Palazzo Pyjamas", Gucci, Ferragamo (see p266) and, more recently, rising stars like Daelli and Coveri.

Commands for operating the computer program

Railway station *(1935)*
The Functionalist station is one of the city centre's few notable modern buildings (see p113).

San Giovanni Battista *(1964)*
Giovanni Michelucci's modern church stands near Amerigo Vespucci airport.

Tourism
Florence and Tuscany have long been popular destinations for tourists (see p53). Florence now receives some 5 million visitors each year.

1966 Floods in Florence

1957–65 Italian industrial boom

1987 The Sorpasso: Italian economy outstrips that of France and the UK

1950	1960	1970		1990	2000

'46 Italy becomes a ...ublic

Bomb damage at the Uffizi

1993 The Uffizi damaged in a terrorist explosion

1999 Italy joins the single European currency

FLORENCE AREA BY AREA

Florence at a Glance

H ISTORIC FLORENCE is fairly compact and the sights
described on the following pages are easily reached
on foot or by bus. The sights are grouped within the four
areas shown on the map below, each of which has its
own section within this book. Most visitors head first
for City Centre East, with the
magnificent Duomo, the heart
of the city. City Centre North
is associated with the Medici,
while City Centre West has
smart shops. Across the Ponte
Vecchio is Oltrarno, with the
treasures of the Palazzo Pitti.

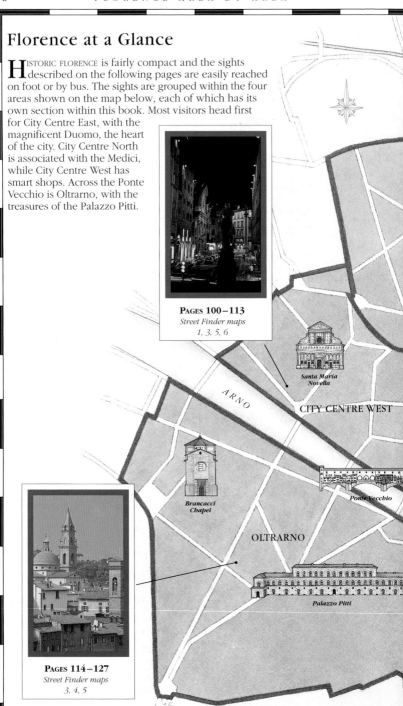

PAGES 100–113
*Street Finder maps
1, 3, 5, 6*

Santa Maria
Novella

CITY CENTRE WEST

Ponte Vecchio

Brancacci
Chapel

OLTRARNO

Palazzo Pitti

ARNO

PAGES 114–127
*Street Finder maps
3, 4, 5*

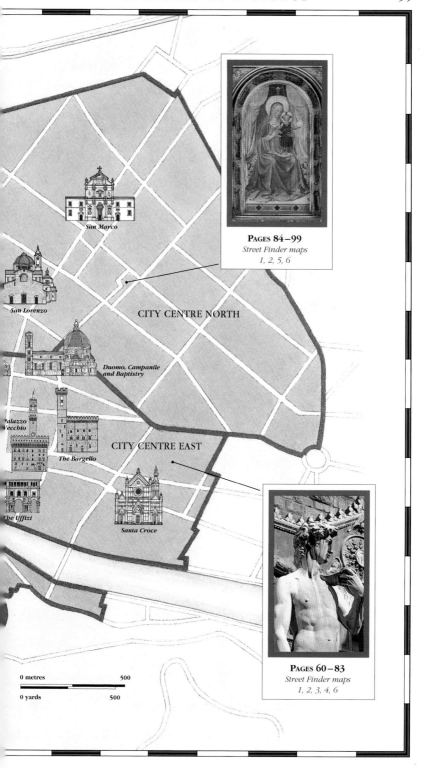

San Marco

PAGES 84–99
Street Finder maps
1, 2, 5, 6

San Lorenzo

CITY CENTRE NORTH

Duomo, Campanile
and Baptistry

Palazzo
Vecchio

The Bargello

CITY CENTRE EAST

The Uffizi

Santa Croce

PAGES 60–83
Street Finder maps
1, 2, 3, 4, 6

0 metres   500

0 yards   500

CITY CENTRE EAST

THE DOMINANT building in this part of Florence is the magnificent Duomo, the first place most people will visit when they arrive in the city. Traffic is now banned in the Piazza del Duomo, which makes it easier to appreciate the immensity

Duomo clock, decorated in 1443 by Paolo Uccello

of this great building. It is, in fact, so large that a comprehensive view is impossible from such close quarters. As you wander the streets to the south you will continually catch glimpses of its multi-coloured marble cladding.

The area's other major church, Santa Croce, containing the tombs and monuments of many great Florentines, sits at the centre of the traditional artisans' quarter. These streets have few prestigious palaces, but there is a lively and attractive sense of community. It is here that you will find characterful neighbourhood shops and restoration workshops where specialists continue to repair the many books and works of art damaged in the 1966 floods *(see pp54–5)*.

SIGHTS AT A GLANCE

Museums and Galleries
The Bargello pp68–9 **6**
Casa Buonarroti **10**
Casa di Dante **4**
Museo di Firenze com'era **8**
Museo Horne **12**
Museo dell'Opera del Duomo **2**
Museo di Storia della Scienza **13**
Palazzo Nonfinito **7**
Palazzo Vecchio pp78–9 **17**
The Uffizi pp80–83 **18**

Churches
Badia Fiorentina **5**
Duomo, Campanile and Baptistry pp64–5 **1**
Orsanmichele **3**
Santa Croce pp72–3 **11**
Santo Stefano al Ponte **14**

Historic Streets and Piazzas
Piazza della Signoria pp76–7 **16**

Shops
Erboristeria **15**

Ice-Cream Parlours
Bar Vivoli Gelateria **9**

KEY

	Street-by-Street map *See pp62–3*
i	Tourist information
P	Parking

0 metres 400
0 yards 400

◁ **Michelangelo's *David* in Piazza della Signoria**

Street-by-Street: Around the Duomo

Statue on Orsanmichele façade

MUCH OF FLORENCE WAS REBUILT during the Renaissance, but the eastern part of the city retains a distinctly medieval feel. With its confusing maze of tiny alleyways and hidden lanes, it would still be recognizable to Dante. His house, the Casa di Dante, still stands near the parish church where he first glimpsed his beloved, Beatrice Portinari *(see p70)*. He would also recognize the Bargello and, of course, the Baptistry. One of the oldest streets is the Borgo degli Albizi. Now lined with Renaissance palaces, it follows the line of the ancient Roman road to Rome.

The dome, completed in 1436, was designed by Brunelleschi to dwarf even the great buildings of ancient Greece and Rome.

★ **Duomo, Campanile and Baptistry**
The vast Duomo holds up to 20,000 people. It is elegantly partnered by Giotto's campanile and the Baptistry, whose doors demonstrate the artistic ideas that led to the Renaissance ❶

The Loggia del Bigallo was built for the Misericordia by Alberto Arnoldi in 1358. During the 15th century, abandoned children were displayed here for three days. If, after this time, their parents had not claimed them, they were sent to foster homes.

★ **Orsanmichele**
The carvings on the walls of this Gothic church depict the activities and patron saints of the city's trade guilds, such as the Masons and Carpenters ❸

Via dei Calzaiuoli, lined with smart shops, is the focus of the *passeggiata*, the traditional evening stroll.

★ **Museo dell'Opera del Duomo**
Works removed from the Duomo, Campanile and Baptistry, like this panel by Verrocchio, are displayed here ❷

LOCATOR MAP
See Florence Street Finder map 6

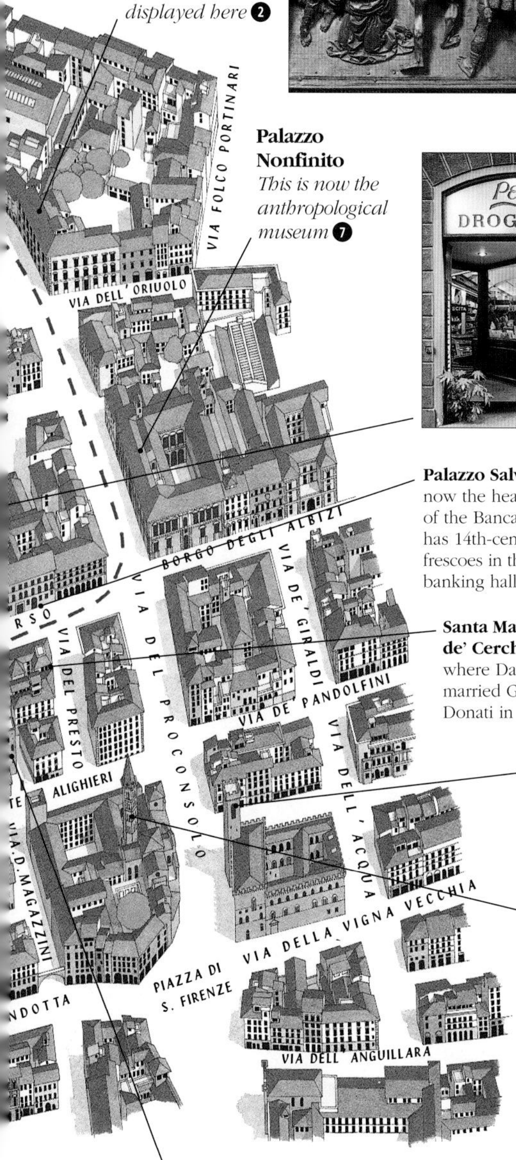

Palazzo Nonfinito
This is now the anthropological museum ❼

Pegna, a mini-super-market tucked away in the Via della Studio, sells a range of gourmet treats including chocolate, honey, wine, balsamic vinegar and olive oil *(see p267).*

Palazzo Salviati, now the head office of the Banca Toscana, has 14th-century frescoes in the main banking hall.

Santa Margherita de' Cerchi is where Dante married Gemma Donati in 1285.

★ **The Bargello**
The city's old prison is home to a rich collection of applied arts and sculpture, like this figure by Cellini (1500–71) ❻

Badia Fiorentina
The Badia's bell regulated daily life in medieval Florence ❺

STAR SIGHTS

★ **Duomo, Campanile and Baptistry**

★ **The Bargello**

★ **Museo dell'Opera del Duomo**

★ **Orsanmichele**

Casa di Dante
This medieval house is a museum devoted to Dante's life and work ❹

KEY

– – – Suggested route

0 metres   100

0 yards   100

Duomo, Campanile and Baptistry ❶

Sᴇᴛ ɪɴ ᴛʜᴇ ʜᴇᴀʀᴛ of Florence, Santa Maria del Fiore – the Duomo, or cathedral, of Florence – dominates the city with its enormous dome. Its sheer size was typical of Florentine determination to lead in all things, and to this day, no other building stands taller in the city. The Baptistry with its celebrated doors *(see p66)* is one of Florence's oldest buildings, dating perhaps to the 4th century. In his capacity as city architect, Giotto designed the Campanile in 1334; it was completed in 1359, 22 years after his death.

The Campanile
At 85 m (276 ft), the Campanile is 6 m (20 ft) shorter than the dome. It is clad in white, green and pink Tuscan marble.

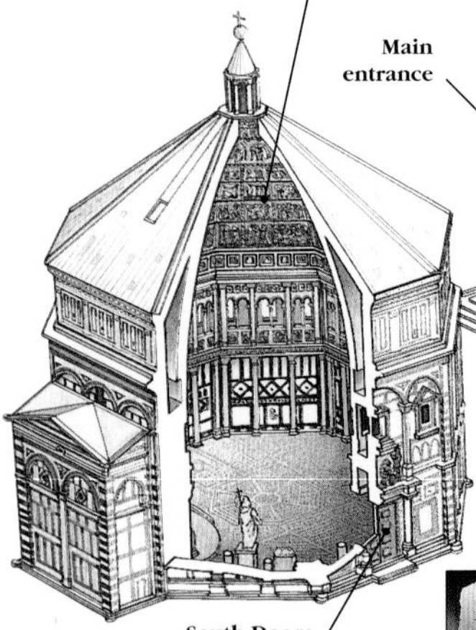

Gothic windows

The Neo-Gothic marble façade echoes the style of Giotto's Campanile, but was only added in 1871–87.

★ Baptistry Ceiling
Colourful 13th-century mosaics illustrating the Last Judgment are set above the large octagonal font where many famous Florentines, including Dante, were baptized.

Main entrance

The terracotta panels with bas-reliefs are by Andrea Pisano.

South Doors

Steps to Santa Reparata
The crypt contains the remains of the 4th-century church of Santa Reparata, demolished in 1296 to make way for the cathedral.

STAR FEATURES

★ Brunelleschi's Dome

★ Baptistry Ceiling

The top of the dome offers spectacular views over the city.

★ Brunelleschi's Dome

Brunelleschi's revolutionary achievement was to build the largest dome of its time without scaffolding. As you climb the 463 steps to the top, you can see how an inner shell provides a platform for the timbers that support the outer shell.

Bricks of varying size were set in a self-supporting herringbone pattern – a technique Brunelleschi copied from the Pantheon in Rome.

Last Judgment frescoes by Vasari

VISITORS' CHECKLIST

Piazza del Duomo. **Map** 2 D5 (6 D2). 1, 6, 14, 17, 23. **Duomo** 055 230 28 85. **Open** 10am–5pm Mon–Sat (to 3:30 Thu, to 4:45 Sat); 1:30–4:45pm Sun. 7:30am, 8:30am, 9am, 9:30am, 6:30pm Mon–Sat; 5pm (English) Sat; 7:30am, 9am, 10:30am, noon, 6pm Sun. **Dome Open** 8:30am–7pm Mon–Sat (to 5:40 Sat). **Crypt Open** 10am–5:30pm daily (to 5:15 Sat, from 1:30 Sun; to 4pm Thu Oct–Jun). **Campanile Open** 8:30am–7:30pm daily. **Baptistry Open** noon–7pm Mon–Sat, 8:30am–2pm Sun. **All closed** 1 Jan & relig hols. **Adm charge.** www.operaduomo.firenze.it

Chapels at the East End
The three apses house five chapels each and are crowned by a miniature copy of the dome. The 15th-century stained glass is by Lorenzo Ghiberti and other artists.

Entrance to steps to the dome

The octagonal marble sanctuary around the High Altar was decorated by Baccio Bandinelli.

Marble Pavement
As you climb up to the dome, you can see that the 16th-century marble pavement is laid out as a maze.

TIMELINE

4th–5th centuries The Baptistry and Santa Reparata church built

1403–24 Ghiberti's North Doors added

1338 Andrea Pisano's South Doors added
Panel from South Doors

1425–52 Ghiberti's East Doors, the "Gate of Paradise", added

1887 Long-delayed completion of the cathedral façade

400	600	800	1000	1200	1400	1600	1800

897 First documented record of the Baptistry

1209 Zodiac pavement laid in Baptistry

1271 *The Last Judgment* completed on Baptistry ceiling

11th–13th centuries Baptistry re-clad in green and white marble

1436 Dome completed

1359 Giotto's Campanile completed

1296 Arnolfo di Cambio begins the new cathedral on the site of Santa Reparata

The East Doors of the Baptistry

L ORENZO GHIBERTI'S celebrated doors were commissioned in 1401 to mark Florence's deliverance from the plague. Ghiberti was chosen after a competition involving seven leading artists, including Donatello and Brunelleschi. Ghiberti's and Brunelleschi's trial panels *(see p69)* are so different

Lorenzo Ghiberti

from Florentine Gothic art of the time that they are often regarded as the first products of the Renaissance.

Ghiberti's winning panel

The "Gate of Paradise"
Having spent 21 years on the North Doors, Ghiberti worked on the East Doors from 1424 to 1452. Michelangelo enthusiastically dubbed them the "Gate of Paradise". The original panels are in the Museo dell'Opera del Duomo; those on the Baptistry are copies.

The jagged rocks, symbolizing Abraham's pain, are carefully arranged to emphasize the sacrificial act.

Abraham and the Sacrifice of Isaac

Architecture is used to create the illusion of spatial depth. Ghiberti was a master of perspective.

Joseph Sold into Slavery and Recognized by his Brothers

KEY TO THE EAST DOORS

1	2
3	4
5	6
7	8
9	10

1 Adam and Eve are Expelled from Eden
2 Cain Murders his Brother, Abel
3 The Drunkenness of Noah and his Sacrifice
4 Abraham and the Sacrifice of Isaac
5 Esau and Jacob
6 Joseph Sold into Slavery
7 Moses Receives the Ten Commandments
8 The Fall of Jericho
9 The Battle with the Philistines
10 Solomon and the Queen of Sheba

Duomo, Campanile and Baptistry ❶

See pp64–5.

Museo dell'Opera del Duomo ❷

Piazza del Duomo 9. **Map** 2 D5 (6 E2). **☎** *055 230 28 85.* **Open** *9am–7:30pm Mon–Sat; 9am–1:30pm Sun & public hols.* **Closed** *1 Jan, Easter Sun, 25 Dec.* **Adm charge.** 🔲 🎦 🅿 🚻 ♿

THE MUSEUM has recently opened after extensive remodelling. Parts of the museum have been replanned, and there are now a series of rooms dedicated to the history of the Duomo. Information about the renovation is available in English and Italian.

From the ticket booth, the main room is reached through open spaces containing Etruscan and Roman reliefs, carvings and sarcophagi. The main ground floor room contains statues from the workshop of Arnolfo di Cambio, which were once placed in the cathedral's niches. Some are by Arnolfo himself, including the Gothic *Madonna of the Glass Eyes*.

Pulley used to build Brunelleschi's dome

Nearby are found Nanni di Banco's *St Luke*, Bernardo Ciuffagni's *St Matthew* and, most striking of all, Donatello's *St John*. The three were carved between 1408 and 1415. A newly-added side room contains 14th–15th century religious paintings and a number of reliquaries, one of which contains the finger of San Giovanni.

Michelangelo's *Pietà* has pride of place on the staircase. The hooded figure of Nicodemus is widely believed to be a self-portrait. That Mary Magdalene is the inferior work of a pupil is strikingly obvious.

The first room on the upper floor is dominated by two choir lofts, dating to the 1430s, by Donatello and Luca della Robbia. Carved in crisp white

Carving from della Robbia's choir loft in the Museo dell'Opera del Duomo

marble and decorated with coloured glass and mosaic, both depict children playing musical instruments and dancing. But while della Robbia's figures seem innocent, Donatello's look like frenzied participants in some primitive ritual.

Among a number of works by Donatello in this room are his statue of *La Maddalena* (1455) *(see p25)* and several Old Testament figures, including the prophet Abakuk (1423–5), affectionately known by Florentines as *lo zuccone* (marrow-head).

The room to the left contains an exhibition of the tablets which used to decorate the bell tower, some by Andrea Pisano and della Robbia.

Leaving this room, visitors descend to a lower level housing examples of the tools used by Brunelleschi's workmen, and a copy of di Cambio's original cathedral façade. Visitors then ascend to a courtyard, where one finds some of the original panels of doors of the baptistry, as well as the exit.

Orsanmichele ❸

Via dell'Arte della Lana. **Map** 3 C1 (6 D3). **☎** *055 28 49 44.* **Open** *9am–noon (to 1pm Sat & Sun) & 4–6pm daily.* **Closed** *1st & last Mon of each month; 1 Jan, 1 May, 25 Dec.* ⓿

THE NAME is a corruption of *Orto di San Michele*, a former monastic garden. Orsanmichele was built in 1337 as a grain market, but was converted into a church almost immediately after its completion. The open arcades became windows, and though these are now bricked in, the original Gothic tracery can still be seen. The exterior walls have 14 niches, each containing a statue of the patron saint of one of Florence's major *Arti* (guilds).

The interior has two parallel naves. To the right stands an extraordinary 1350s altar by Andrea Orcagna. It is covered in cherubs and carved reliefs and encrusted with coloured marble and glass. Close by is Bernardo Daddi's *Virgin and Child* (1348), its frame beautifully carved with angels.

St George on the façade of Orsanmichele

The Bargello ❻

BUILT IN 1255 as the city's town hall, the Bargello is the oldest seat of government surviving in Florence. In the 16th century it was the residence of the chief of police and a prison: executions took place here until 1786. After extensive renovation, it became one of Italy's first national museums in 1865. The Bargello houses a superb collection of Florentine Renaissance sculpture, with rooms dedicated to the work of Michelangelo, Donatello, Giambologna and Cellini, as well as a collection of Mannerist bronzes and examples from the decorative arts.

Arms and Armour Collection

Ivory Collection

Mercury by Giambologna
Giambologna's famous 1564 bronze shows an athletic youth poised for flight.

Magdalen Chapel

GALLERY GUIDE
To the right of the entrance hall, the Michelangelo Room is presided over by his Bacchus *(1497). The courtyard staircase leads up to the Upper Loggia, filled with statues of birds by Giambologna. To the right is the Donatello Room, which contains the panels for the Baptistry doors competition of 1401. The Magdalen Chapel and Islamic Collection are also on the first floor. The Verrocchio Room, the Andrea and Giovanni della Robbia rooms, the Arms and Armour Collection and the Room of the Small Bronzes are on the second floor.*

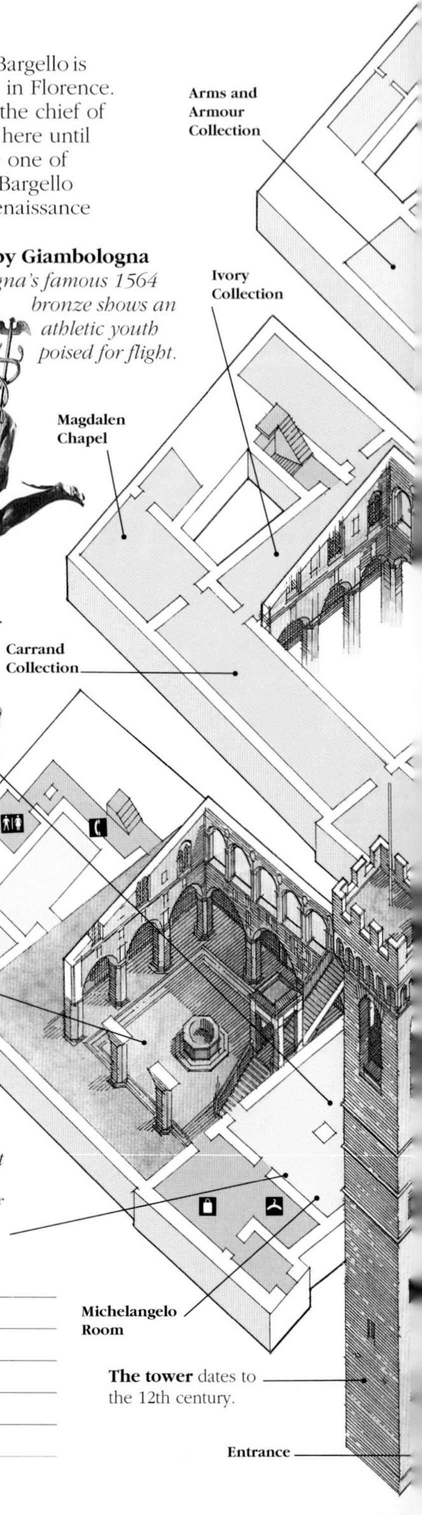

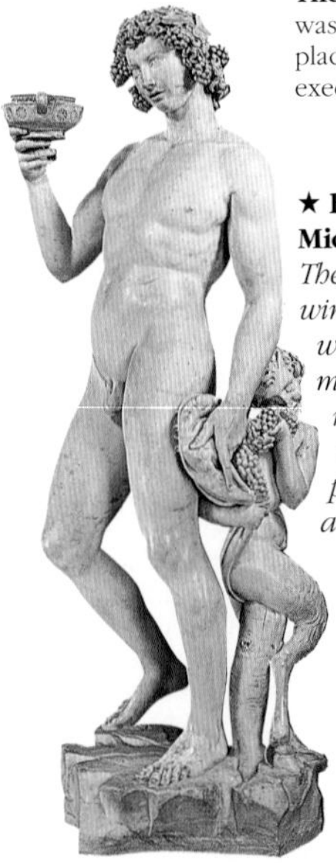

Carrand Collection

The courtyard was once the place of execution.

★ Bacchus by Michelangelo
The Roman god of wine with a small satyr was Michelangelo's first major work (1497). The modelling is Classical, but the unsteady, drunken posture mocks the poise of ancient works.

KEY

☐ Ground floor

☐ First floor

☐ Second floor

☐ Temporary exhibitions

☐ Non-exhibition space

Michelangelo Room

The tower dates to the 12th century.

Entrance

Lady with a Posy
This bust, attributed to Andrea Verrocchio (1435–88), may have been done in collaboration with his pupil, Leonardo da Vinci.

Room of the Small Bronzes

VISITORS' CHECKLIST

Via del Proconsolo 4. **Map** 4 D1 (6 E3). ☎ 055 238 86 06; bookings: 055 294 883. ▦ 14, A. **Open** 8:30am–1:50pm daily. **Closed** 1 Jan, 1 May, 25 Dec, 2nd & 4th Mon & 1st, 3rd & 5th Sun of each month. **Adm charge.** ⌀ ♿

Ivory Saddle
Made for the Medici, this saddle inlaid with ivory was used during jousts in 15th-century Florence.

Upper Loggia

★ David by Donatello
Cast during the 1430s, Donatello's famous bronze was the first nude statue by a Western artist since Classical times (see pp46–7).

Donatello Room

Islamic Collection

★ Baptistry Doors Competition Panel
Brunelleschi's bronze panel depicting Abraham about to slay Isaac was made in 1401 for the Baptistry doors competition (see p66).

The Bargello has a daunting and heavily fortified façade.

STAR EXHIBITS

- ★ **Baptistry Doors Competition Panel**

- ★ **David by Donatello**

- ★ **Bacchus by Michelangelo**

BARGELLO PRISON

Among the notorious figures executed here was Bernardo Baroncelli. He went to the gallows in 1478 for his part in the failed attempt to assassinate Lorenzo the Magnificent in the Pazzi conspiracy *(see p47)*. Baroncelli's body, hanging from a window in the Bargello as a warning to other anti-Medici conspirators, was sketched by Leonardo da Vinci.

Casa di Dante ❹

Via Santa Margherita 1. **Map** 4 D1
(6 E3). ☎ 055 21 94 16. **Open**
Mar–Oct: 10am–6pm Wed–Mon,
10am–2pm Sun; Nov–Feb: 10am–4pm
Wed–Mon, 10am–2pm Sun. **Closed**
1 Jan, 25 Dec. **Adm charge.** 📷

IT IS UNCERTAIN whether
the poet Dante (1265–
1321) was actually born
here, but at least the
house looks the part. In
1911, the remains of a
13th-century
tower house
were restored to
give the building
its rambling
appearance.
   Inside, there is
a small museum
dedicated to Dante's life and
work. The downstairs rooms
are used for exhibitions of
modern art and sculpture.
   Just a short stroll north of
the house is the parish church
of Santa Margherita de' Cerchi,
built during the 11th century.
It is here that Dante is said to
have first caught sight of
Beatrice Portinari, whom he
idolized in his poetry. The
church, which is often used
for Baroque chamber
music and organ recitals,
contains a fine altarpiece by
Neri di Bicci (1418–91).

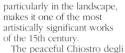

Bust of Dante on the
façade of Casa di Dante

Badia Fiorentina ❺

Via del Proconsolo. **Map** 4 D1 (6 E3).
☎ 055 23 44 545. **Open** *4:30–*
6:30pm Mon–Fri; 10:30–11:30am
Sun & public hols. 🚫

THE ABBEY, one of Florence's
oldest churches, was
founded in 978 by Willa, the
widow of Count Uberto of
Tuscany. Their son, Count Ugo,
was buried inside the church
in 1001. His splendid tomb was
carved by Mino da Fiesole and
dates from 1469–81. Mino
also carved the altarpiece
and, in the right transept, the
tomb of Bernardo Giugni, the
Florentine statesman, with
its fine effigy of Justice.
   Filippino Lippi's *The Virgin*
Appearing to St Bernard
(1485) also enlivens an
otherwise drab and solemn
interior. Its remarkable detail,

particularly in the landscape,
makes it one of the most
artistically significant works
of the 15th century.
   The peaceful Chiostro degli
Aranci is hard to find. Look
for a door to the right of the
altar. Sadly, the orange trees
that the monks once cultivated
are no longer here. The
two-tier cloister, built by
Rossellino in 1435–40, has
a well-preserved fresco
cycle showing scenes from
the life of St Benedict.
   Dating from the
15th century, it
was restored as
recently as 1973.
An early fresco
by Bronzino
(1503–72) can
also be seen in
the north walkway. Excellent
views of the hexagonal
campanile, mentioned in
Dante's *Paradiso*, are available from the cloister.
   In the 14th century, a series
of readings and lectures
devoted to Dante's work were
given at the Badia by the poet
Boccaccio. In keeping with
the spirit of these meetings,
the abbey is today often used
for talks and concerts.

The Bargello ❻

See pp68–9.

Palazzo Nonfinito ❼

Via del Proconsolo 12. **Map** 2 D5
(6 E2). ☎ 055 239 64 49.
Open *9am–1pm Wed–Mon.*
Closed *1 Jan, 25 Apr, Easter Sun,*
1 May, 24 Jun, 15 Aug, 8 Dec,
25–26 Dec, 31 Dec. 🚫

THE PALAZZO NONFINITO
(Unfinished Palace) was
begun by Buontalenti in 1593
and was still incomplete
when it became Italy's first
museum of anthropology and
ethnology in 1869. The most
striking architectural feature is
an imposing inner courtyard
usually attributed to Cigoli
(1559–1613).
   The museum's opening
hours are severely restricted.
However, it's worth setting
aside some time to see the
collection of art from Italy's
former African colonies, and
material carried away by
Captain Cook, the 18th-
century British explorer, on
the last of his Pacific voyages.

The Virgin Appearing to St Bernard (1485) by Filippino Lippi

19th-century copy of the *Pianta della Catena*, showing Florence's cityscape

Museo di Firenze com'era ❽

Via dell'Oriuolo 24. **Map** 2 D5 (6 F2). 📞 055 261 65 45. **Open** 9am–2pm Fri–Wed (last adm: 30 mins before closing). **Closed** 1 Jan, Easter Sun, 1 May, 15 Aug, 25 Dec. **Adm charge**.

THE MUSEUM traces the development of the city through drawings, plans and paintings. One of the most fascinating exhibits is the *Pianta della Catena*, a 19th-century copy of a woodcut made around 1470. The title refers to the chain-like border that surrounds the whole image, which shows Florence at the height of the Renaissance. Some buildings, for instance the Palazzo Pitti, can be seen.

The Palazzo Pitti features again in the delightful sequence of lunettes made by the Flemish artist Giusto Utens in 1599. They show all the Medici villas and gardens, with fascinating vignettes of rural life *(see pp121 and 161)*.

One room is devoted to a scheme devised by Giuseppe Poggi, the city architect involved in remodelling much of central Florence during its brief stint as the capital of Italy in 1865–71. If the scheme had been implemented, large parts of the centre would have been destroyed. The scheme was halted after an international outcry, but not before buildings had been cleared for the new Piazza della Repubblica *(see p112)* and the 14th-century walls had been torn down.

Bar Vivoli Gelateria ❾

Via Isola delle Stinche 7r. **Map** 4 D1 (6 F3). 📞 055 29 23 34. **Open** Mar–Oct: 7:30am–1am Tue–Sat, 9:30am–1am Sun; Nov–Feb: 7:30am–midnight Tue–Sat, 9:30am–midnight Sun. **Closed** 1st 20 days of Jan & last 20 days of Aug.

Bar Vivoli Gelateria

THIS TINY ice-cream parlour attracts large crowds and long queues for its rich iced concoctions. Vivoli claims to make the "best ice cream in the world", and the walls of the bar are covered in press clippings from ice-cream connoisseurs that strongly support this view.

The bar stands at the heart of the colourful Santa Croce district, with its narrow alleys and tiny squares. Here, you will find small shops that serve the local community, rather than cater for tourists, and scores of little workshops where craftsmen make picture frames or mend furniture. Via Torta is typical of the area.

Casa Buonarroti ❿

Via Ghibellina 70. **Map** 4 E1. 📞 055 24 17 52. **Open** 9:30am–2pm Wed–Mon. **Closed** 1 Jan, Easter Sun, 25 Apr, 1 May, 15 Aug, 25 Dec. **Adm charge**. 🚫 ♿

MICHELANGELO (whose surname was Buonarroti) lived briefly in this group of three houses which he bought as an investment in 1508. Subsequent generations of his descendants added what they could to a significant collection of his works.

Among these is his earliest known work, the *Madonna della Scala*, a marble *tavoletta*, or rectangular relief, carved in 1490–92. There is also a relief from 1492, showing *The Battle of the Centaurs*, and the design, never used, for the façade of San Lorenzo, shown in a wooden model.

Santa Croce ⓫

THE MAGNIFICENT GOTHIC CHURCH of Santa Croce (1294) contains the tombs of many famous Florentines, including Michelangelo and Galileo. The spacious, airy interior is enhanced by the radiant frescoes of Giotto and his gifted pupil, Taddeo Gaddi, painted early in the 14th century. Incorporated into the cloister beside the church is Brunelleschi's Classical Cappella de' Pazzi (Pazzi Chapel), a masterpiece of Renaissance architecture. The rest of the monastic buildings ranged around the cloister form a museum of religious painting and sculpture.

The façade was reclad with coloured marble in 1863 paid for by an English benefactor, Francis Sloane.

Galileo's Tomb
Condemned by the church in 1616, Galileo was denied a Christian burial until 1737, when this tomb by Giulio Foggini was erected.

Dante died in exile in 1321 and is buried in Ravenna. His admirers erected a memorial to the great poet in 1829.

Machiavelli *(see p51)* was buried here in 1527. His monument, by Innocenzo Spinazzi, was erected in 1787.

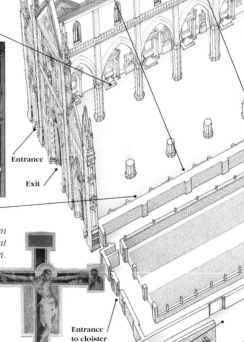

Entrance

Exit

Michelangelo's Tomb
Michelangelo never completed the Pietà *he planned for his own tomb (see p67). This monument was designed in 1570 by Vasari. The figures are Painting, Architecture and Sculpture.*

Entrance to cloister

Cimabue's Crucifixion
This ruined 13th-century masterpiece is a reminder of the destructive 1966 floods.

Entrance to museum

STAR FEATURES

★ Cappella de' Pazzi

★ Tomb of Leonardo Bruni

★ Fresco by Gaddi in Baroncelli Chapel

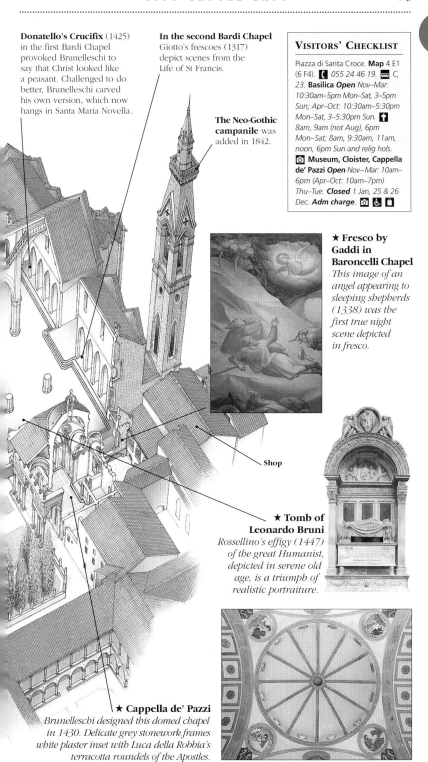

Donatello's Crucifix (1425) in the first Bardi Chapel provoked Brunelleschi to say that Christ looked like a peasant. Challenged to do better, Brunelleschi carved his own version, which now hangs in Santa Maria Novella.

In the second Bardi Chapel Giotto's frescoes (1317) depict scenes from the Life of St Francis.

The Neo-Gothic campanile was added in 1842.

★ **Fresco by Gaddi in Baroncelli Chapel**
This image of an angel appearing to sleeping shepherds (1338) was the first true night scene depicted in fresco.

Shop

★ **Tomb of Leonardo Bruni**
Rossellino's effigy (1447) of the great Humanist, depicted in serene old age, is a triumph of realistic portraiture.

★ **Cappella de' Pazzi**
Brunelleschi designed this domed chapel in 1430. Delicate grey stonework frames white plaster inset with Luca della Robbia's terracotta roundels of the Apostles.

The kitchen, which was built on the top floor to stop fumes passing through the entire house, now contains Horne's collection of Renaissance pots and cooking utensils.

Museo di Storia della Scienza ⑬

Piazza de' Giudici 1. **Map** 4 D1 (6 E4). 055 265 311. B, 23. **Open** winter: 9:30am–5pm Mon–Sat (to 1pm Tue), 10am–1pm second Sun of the month; summer: 9:30am–5pm Mon–Sat (to 1pm Tue & Sat). **Closed** 1 Jan, 25 Apr, 1 May, 24 Jun, 15 Aug, 8, 25 & 26 Dec. **Adm charge**.

Museo Horne

Santa Croce ⑪

See pp72–3.

Museo Horne ⑫

Via de' Benci 6. **Map** 4 D1 (6 F4). 055 24 46 61. **Open** 9am–1pm Mon–Sat. **Closed** 1 Jan, Easter Sun, Easter Mon, 25 Apr, 1 May, 15 Aug, 1 Nov, 25–26 Dec. **Adm charge**.

THE MUSEUM'S small collection of paintings, sculpture and decorative arts was left to the city by Herbert Percy Horne (1844–1916), the English art historian. It is housed in a splendid example of a Renaissance *palazzino* (small town house), built in 1489 for the wealthy Alberti family.

The arrangement of rooms, with a working and storage area at ground level and grander apartments above, is typical of many Renaissance houses. The Alberti family, who grew wealthy from the city's thriving cloth trade, had wool-dyeing vats in the basement and drying racks in the courtyard.

Most of the museum's major artifacts, for instance a number of important 17th- and 18th-century drawings, are now housed in the Uffizi. However, the collection still boasts at least one major exhibit: Giotto's 13th-century *St Stephen* polyptych (an altarpiece with more than three panels). There is also a *Madonna and Child* attributed to Simone Martini (1283–1344) and *Madonna* by Bernardo Daddi (c.1312–48).

THIS SMALL MUSEUM is something of a shrine to the Pisa-born scientist Galileo Galilei (1564–1642). Exhibits include his telescopes and the lens he used to discover the largest moons of Jupiter.

The museum also features large-scale reconstructions of his experiments into motion, weight, velocity and acceleration. These are sometimes demonstrated by the attendants.

In memory of Galileo, in 1657 Florence founded the world's first-ever scientific institution, the Accademia del Cimento (Academy for Experimentation). Some of the academy's inventions, such as early thermometers, hygrometers and barometers

are on show here. Of equal interest are the huge globes made during the 16th and 17th centuries to illustrate the motion of the planets and stars.

Also look out for Lopo Homem's map of the world, dating to 1554, and the nautical instruments invented by Sir Robert Dudley, the Elizabethan marine engineer. He was employed by the Medici dukes to build the harbour at Livorno from 1607–21 *(see p158)*.

Galileo Galilei (1564–1642), court mathematician to the Medici

Santo Stefano al Ponte ⑭

Piazza Santo Stefano al Ponte. **Map** 3 C1 (6 D4). 055 22 58 43. Phone to check opening times.

ST STEPHEN "by the bridge", dating to 969, is so called because of its close proximity to the Ponte Vecchio.

Armillary sphere of 1564, used to map the stars and planets

MAPPING THE WORLD

The same preoccupation with space that made Florentine artists such masters of perspective also made them excellent navigators and mapmakers. Florentine cartographers based their maps on the observations and navigational records of early explorers. That is how America came to be named after the Florentine Amerigo Vespucci rather than Christopher Columbus. When Columbus returned from his transatlantic voyage, King Ferdinand of Spain hired Vespucci, an expert navigator, to check whether Columbus really had discovered a new route to the Indies. Vespucci was the first to realize that Columbus had discovered a new continent and he described his own voyage in a series of letters to Piero de' Medici. As soon as the letters were made public, Florentine cartographers rushed out revised maps of the world based on Vespucci's account. Out of loyalty to a fellow Florentine, they named the New World Amerigo, which was later corrupted to America.

Tip of South America still unmapped

Argentina mapped for the first time

Africa and Arabia well-mapped thanks to centuries of trading

The Antipodes were yet to be "discovered"

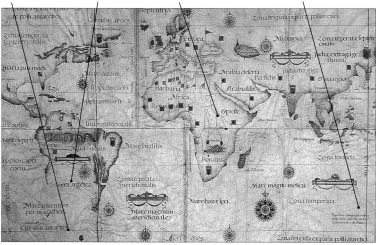

16th-century map by the Portuguese cartographer Lopo Homem, in the Museo di Storia della Scienza

The Romanesque façade, dating to 1233, is its most important architectural feature. Florentines, however, know the church better as a venue for some top-quality orchestral concerts.

Erboristeria **⑮**

Spezieria–Erboristeria Palazzo Vecchio. Via Vacchereccia 9r.
Map 3 C1 (6 D3). 📞 055 239 60 55.
Open 9am–7pm Mon–Sat, first & last Sun of month. **Closed** 25 Dec.

THIS ANCIENT HERBALIST'S shop, known as the Palazzo Vecchio, is hidden among the pavement cafés that line the Via Vacchereccia, off Piazza della Signoria. It has a lovely frescoed interior. Several such shops in Florence sell a range of herbal soaps, pot pourri, cosmetics and fragrances made to ancient recipes by monks and nuns in various parts of Tuscany. Another *erboristeria* is situated just around the corner at Calimala 4r. Called the Erboristeria della Antica Farmacia del Cinghiale (Herbalist at the Old Boar Pharmacy), it takes its name from the famous bronze boar statue in the Mercato Nuovo opposite *(see p112)*.

Piazza della Signoria **⑯**

See pp76–7.

Palazzo Vecchio **⑰**

See pp78–9.

The Uffizi **⑱**

See pp80–83.

Arno façade of the Uffizi with the Vasari Corridor *(pp106–7)* above

Piazza della Signoria ⑯

T HE PIAZZA IS A UNIQUE outdoor sculpture gallery and, with the Palazzo Vecchio *(see pp78–9)*, has been at the heart of Florentine politics since the 14th century. Citizens gathered here when called to a *parlamento* (a public meeting) by the Palazzo's great bell. The statues, some copies, commemorate major events in the city's history. Many are linked to the rise and fall of the Florentine Republic *(pp50–51)*, during which the religious leader Girolamo Savonarola was burned at the stake here.

Campanile

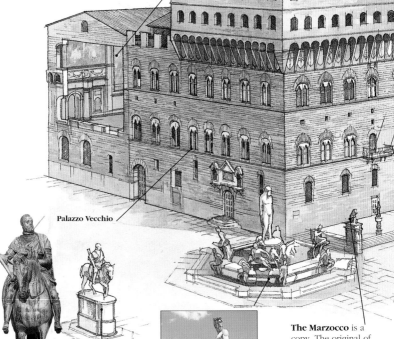

Salone dei Cinquecento
This vast council chamber, built in 1495, is decorated with Vasari's frescoes on the history of Florence.

Palazzo Vecchio

Grand Duke Cosimo I
Giambologna's equestrian statue (1595) celebrates the man who subjugated all Tuscany under his military rule (see pp52–3).

The Marzocco is a copy. The original of Donatello's heraldic lion is in the Bargello.

★ Neptune Fountain
Ammannati's Mannerist fountain (1575) of the Roman sea god surrounded by water nymphs commemorates Tuscan naval victories.

Pageantry
For centuries the piazza has been the city's venue for public rallies and festivities, as shown in this 18th-century engraving.

VISITORS' CHECKLIST

Map 4 D1 (6 D3). 🚌 A, B. Pedestrian area.

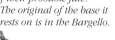
★ **Perseus**
Cellini's bronze statue (1554) of Perseus holding Medusa's head was meant to warn Cosimo I's enemies of their probable fate. The original of the base it rests on is in the Bargello.

The Uffizi café, on the roof of the Loggia dei Lanzi, offers fine views over the piazza.

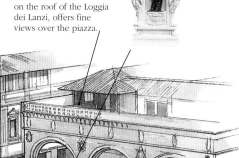

Hercules and Cacus (1534) by Bandinelli

★ **The Rape of the Sabine Women** (1583) *The writhing figures in Giambologna's famous statue were carved from a single block of flawed marble.*

The Loggia dei Lanzi (1382), by Orcagna, is named after Cosimo I's bodyguards, the Lancers. The back wall is lined with ancient Roman statues of priestesses.

★ **David**
The original of Michelangelo's celebrated statue of David was moved from its initial location in the Piazza della Signoria into the Accademia in 1873 (see p94).

STAR FEATURES

★ **David by Michelangelo**

★ **Neptune Fountain by Ammannati**

★ **The Rape of the Sabine Women by Giambologna**

★ **Perseus by Cellini**

Palazzo Vecchio ⑰

THE PALAZZO VECCHIO ("Old Palace") still fulfils its original role as Florence's town hall. It was completed in 1322 when a huge bell, used to call citizens to meetings or warn of fire, flood or enemy attack, was hauled to the top of the imposing belltower. The palazzo has retained its medieval appearance, but much of the interior was remodelled for Duke Cosimo I when he moved into the palace in 1540. Leonardo and Michelangelo were asked to redecorate the interior, but it was Vasari who finally undertook the work. His many frescoes (1563–5) glorify Cosimo and his creation of the Grand Duchy of Tuscany.

★ Sala dei Gigli (Room of the Lilies)
Gold fleurs-de-lis, emblems of Florence, cover the walls in between Ghirlandaio's frescoes (1485) of Roman statesmen.

PALACE GUIDE

A monumental staircase leads to the first-floor Salone dei Cinquecento, with its frescoed walls and marble statues. Above this is a suite of decorated rooms once used by the rulers of Florence. Parts of the Salone dei Cinquecento, the Studiolo of Francesco I, the Treasury of Cosimo I and the staircase of the Duke of Athens are only accessible by tour. The tours follow the "secret routes" made for the rulers.

Heraldic Frieze
Shields on the façade symbolize episodes in Florentine history. The crossed keys represent Medici papal rule.

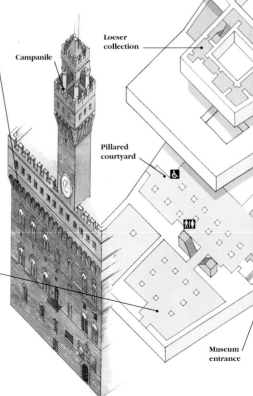

Loeser collection

Campanile

Pillared courtyard

Museum entrance

★ Cortile and Putto Fountain
Michelozzi's courtyard, with its copy of Verrocchio's Putto Fountain, dates to 1565.

KEY TO FLOORPLAN

- ☐ Ground floor
- ☐ First floor
- ☐ Mezzanine floor
- ☐ Second floor
- ☐ Temporary exhibition space
- ☐ Non-exhibition space

Eleonora di Toledo's Rooms

Cosimo I's wife had a suite of rooms decorated with scenes of virtuous women. Penelope, wife of the Greek hero Odysseus, is shown waiting faithfully for her husband to return.

The Map Room

VISITORS' CHECKLIST

Piazza della Signoria.
Map 4 D1 (6 D3). ☎ *055 276 84 65.* 🚌 *A, B.*
Open *9am–7pm Mon–Wed, Fri & Sat, 9am–2pm Thur, Sun & public hols (last adm: 45 mins before closing). Some extended hours in summer.* **The Secret Routes**; *open daily, plus Mon & Fri pm in summer.*
Closed *1 Jan, Easter, 1 May, 15 Aug, 25 Dec.* **Adm charge**.
🚫 ♿

The Quartiere degli Elementi contains Vasari's allegories of Earth, Fire, Air and Water.

Putto with Dolphin

Verrocchio's bronze fountain head (1470) is displayed in the Terrazzo di Giunone. The small room next door has fine views of San Miniato al Monte.

Pope Leo X's rooms

The Salone dei Cinquecento was a meeting place for the leaders of the Florentine Republic *(see pp50–51).*

Cappella di Eleonora

Egyptian soldiers in pursuit of Moses drown in the Red Sea, in the biblical frescoes (1540–45) by Bronzino in Eleonora di Toledo's chapel.

Treasury osimo I

★ Victory by Michelangelo

Michelangelo's nephew presented this statue (1533–4), intended for the tomb of Pope Julius II, to Cosimo I in 1565, following the Duke's military triumph over Siena.

STAR FEATURES

★ **Cortile and Putto Fountain**

★ **Victory by Michelangelo**

★ **Sala dei Gigli**

The Uffizi ⓭

THE UFFIZI WAS BUILT in 1560–80 as a suite of offices (*uffici*) for Duke Cosimo I's new Tuscan administration (*see p48*). The architect, Vasari, used iron reinforcement to create an almost continuous wall of glass on the upper storey. From 1581 Cosimo's heirs, beginning with Francesco I, used this well-lit space to display the Medici family art treasures, creating what is now the oldest gallery in the world.

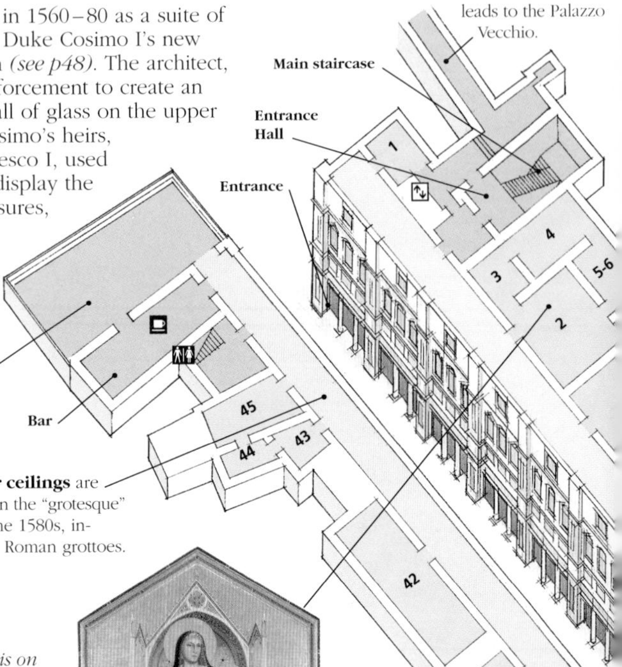

The Vasari Corridor leads to the Palazzo Vecchio.

Main staircase

Entrance Hall

Entrance

The café terrace merits a visit for its unusual views of the Piazza della Signoria (*see pp76–7*).

Bar

Corridor ceilings are frescoed in the "grotesque" style of the 1580s, inspired by Roman grottoes.

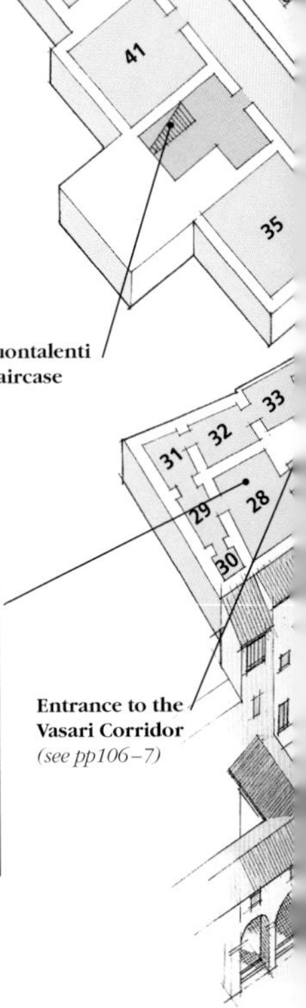

Buontalenti staircase

Entrance to the Vasari Corridor (*see pp106–7*)

GALLERY GUIDE

The Uffizi art collection is on the top floor of the building. Ancient Greek and Roman sculptures are in the broad corridor running round the inner side of the horseshoe-shaped building. The paintings are hung in a series of rooms off the main corridor, in chronological order, to reveal the development of Florentine art from Gothic to High Renaissance and beyond. Most of the best-known paintings are in rooms 7–18. To avoid the long queues, book your ticket and visiting time in advance.

The Ognissanti Madonna
Giotto's grasp of spatial depth in this altarpiece (1310) was a milestone in the mastery of perspective.

★ The Venus of Urbino (*1538*)
Titian's sensuous nude was condemned for portraying the goddess in such an immodest pose.

STAR PAINTINGS

★ **The Duke and Duchess of Urbino by Piero della Francesca**

★ **The Birth of Venus by Botticelli**

★ **The Holy Family by Michelangelo**

★ **The Venus of Urbino by Titian**

★ **The Duke and Duchess of Urbino** *(1460)*
Piero della Francesca's panels are among the first true Renaissance portraits. He even recorded the Duke's booked nose – broken by a sword blow.

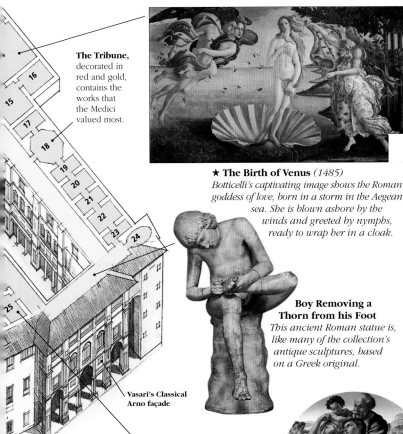

The Tribune, decorated in red and gold, contains the works that the Medici valued most.

★ **The Birth of Venus** *(1485)*
Botticelli's captivating image shows the Roman goddess of love, born in a storm in the Aegean sea. She is blown ashore by the winds and greeted by nymphs, ready to wrap her in a cloak.

Boy Removing a Thorn from his Foot
This ancient Roman statue is, like many of the collection's antique sculptures, based on a Greek original.

Vasari's Classical Arno façade

KEY

- ☐ East Corridor
- ☐ West Corridor
- ☐ Arno Corridor
- ☐ Gallery Rooms 1–45
- ▨ Non-exhibition space

★ **The Holy Family** *(1507)*
Michelangelo's painting, the first to break with the convention of showing Christ on the Virgin's lap, inspired Mannerist artists through its expressive handling of colour and posture (see p25).

Exploring the Uffizi's Collection

THE UFFIZI OFFERS an unrivalled opportunity to see some of the greatest works of the Renaissance. The collection was born from the immense wealth of the Medici family *(see pp48–9)*, who commissioned work from many great Florentine masters. Francesco I housed the family collection at the Uffizi in 1581. His descendants added to it until 1737, when Anna Maria Lodovica, last of the Medici, bequeathed it to the people of Florence.

GOTHIC ART

FOLLOWING THE COLLECTION of antiquities in room 1, the gallery's next six rooms are devoted to Tuscan Gothic art from the 12th to 14th centuries.

Giotto (1266–1337) introduced a degree of naturalism that was new in Tuscan art. The angels and saints in his *Ognissanti Madonna* (1310), in room 2, express a range of human emotions, from awe and reverence to puzzlement. The throne in this painting, and the temple in Lorenzetti's *Presentation in the Temple* (1342) in room 3, show a concern for three-dimensional depth quite at odds with the flatness of much Gothic art.

Giotto's naturalism extends throughout the works in room 4, devoted to the 14th-century Florentine School. One of the most obvious examples is the *Pietà* (1360–65), attributed to Giottino. Look at the difference between the characters' expressions, their medieval, rather than Biblical, style of dress and the blood, still fresh on the cross.

EARLY RENAISSANCE

A BETTER UNDERSTANDING of geometry and perspective allowed Renaissance artists to create an illusion of space and depth in their works. Paolo Uccello (1397–1475) was obsessed with perspective; witness his nightmarish *The Battle of San Romano* (1456) *(see p46)* in room 7.

Also in this room are two panels by Piero della Francesca (1410–92), depicting the Duke and Duchess of Urbino on one side and representations of their virtues on the other. Painted between 1465 and 1470, these are two of the first Renaissance portraits.

If these works seem coldly experimental, Fra Filippo

Lippi's *Madonna and Child with Angels* (1455–66), in room 8, is a masterpiece of warmth and humanity. Like so many Renaissance artists, Lippi uses a religious subject to celebrate earthly delights, such as feminine beauty and the Tuscan landscape.

Madonna and Child with Angels (1455–66) by Fra Filippo Lippi

BOTTICELLI

THE BOTTICELLI paintings in rooms 10–14 are the highlight of the Uffizi's collection. The brilliant colours and crisp draughtsmanship of, for instance, *The Birth of Venus* (about 1485) *(see p81)*, are a reminder that Renaissance artists often experimented with

***Primavera* (1480) by Botticelli**

new pigments to achieve striking colour effects. The subject of this painting, the Roman goddess Venus, is also significant. By painting Venus instead of the Christian Virgin, Botticelli expressed the fascination with Classical mythology common to many Renaissance artists.

The same is true of his other famous work, *Primavera* (about 1480). It breaks with the tradition of Christian religious painting by illustrating a pagan rite of spring. Other works to see here include the *Adoration of the Magi* (about 1475), a thinly disguised Medici family portrait *(see p49)*.

LEONARDO DA VINCI

Detail from *The Annunciation* (1472–5) by Leonardo da Vinci

ROOM 15 contains works attributed to the young Leonardo. Still under the influence of his teachers, he was already developing his own masterly style, as in *The Annunciation* (1472–5) and the unfinished *Adoration of the Magi* (1481).

THE TRIBUNE

THE OCTAGONAL tribune, with its mother-of-pearl ceiling, was designed in 1584 by Buontalenti so that Francesco I could display all his favourite works from the Medici collection in one room.

Notable paintings include Bronzino's portrait (1545) of Eleonora di Toledo with her son, Giovanni *(see p49)*, and the same artist's portrait of Bia, Cosimo I's illegitimate daughter. It was painted just before her

Portrait of *Bia* (1542) by Bronzino

early death in 1542. *The Medici Venus*, probably dating to the 1st century BC, is a Roman copy of the Greek original by Praxiteles. A small room off the Tribune contains a copy of the Hellenistic sculpture, *The Hermaphrodite*.

NON-FLORENTINE ART

THE WORKS in rooms 19 to 23 show how rapidly the artistic ideas and techniques of the Renaissance spread beyond Florence. Umbrian artists like Perugino (1446–1523) and Northern European painters such as Dürer (1471–1528) are well represented.

THE ARNO CORRIDOR

THE CORRIDOR overlooking the Arno, which links the east and west wings of the Uffizi, offers fine views of the hills to the south of Florence.

The ancient Roman statues displayed here were mainly collected by the Medici during the 15th century. Their anatomical precision and faithful portraiture were much admired and copied by Renaissance artists, who saw themselves as giving rebirth to Classical perfection in art.

The Roman statues were equally popular during the 17th and 18th centuries with visitors on their way to Rome on the Grand Tour *(see p53)*. The Renaissance works, which attract visitors today, were largely ignored until John Ruskin, the art historian, wrote about them in the 1840s.

HIGH RENAISSANCE AND MANNERISM

MICHELANGELO'S *The Holy Family* (1506–8), in room 25, is striking for its vibrant colours and the unusually twisted pose of the Virgin *(see p81)*. This painting proved to be enormously influential with the next generation of Tuscan artists, notably Bronzino (1503–72), Pontormo (1494–1556) and Parmigianino (1503–40). The latter's *Madonna of the Long Neck* (about 1534) in room 29, with its contorted anatomy and bright, unnatural colours, is a remarkable example of what came to be known as the Mannerist style.

Two other masterpieces of the High Renaissance are located nearby. Raphael's tender *Madonna of the Goldfinch* (1506), in room 26, still shows signs of earthquake damage dating to 1547. Titian's *The Venus of Urbino* (1538), said to be one of the most beautiful nudes ever painted, is in room 28.

Madonna of the Goldfinch (1506) by Raphael

LATER PAINTINGS

ROOMS 41–45 of the Uffizi hold paintings acquired by the Medici in the 17th and 18th centuries. These include works by Rubens (1577–1640) and Van Dyck (1599–1641) in room 41 (sometimes closed); Caravaggio (1573–1610) in room 43; and Rembrandt (1606–69) in room 44.

CITY CENTRE NORTH

THIS AREA of Florence is stamped with the character of Cosimo il Vecchio. The man who founded the great Medici dynasty maintained his position of power by astute management of the city's financial affairs, as opposed to resorting to threats and violence. Cosimo was a highly educated and sophisticated man with a passion for building, and he wanted the churches, palazzi and libraries that he built to last a thousand years, like the buildings of ancient Rome. To this end, he commissioned some of the greatest architects and artists of the time

Roundel on Spedale degli Innocenti

to build the churches of San Lorenzo and San Marco as well as the Medici's first home, the Palazzo Medici Riccardi. He is regarded as one of the great innovators of the Renaissance in Florence. Even after the Medici family had moved across the river Arno to the Palazzo Pitti in 1550, the Grand Dukes made their final journey back to the north of the city to be buried in the extravagant Cappelle Medicee in San Lorenzo. For the tombs in the New Sacristy, Michelangelo contributed his magnificent allegorical sculptures, *Day and Night*, and *Dawn and Dusk*.

SIGHTS AT A GLANCE

Churches and Synagogues
San Lorenzo pp90–91 **2**
San Marco pp96–7 **7**
Santa Maria Maddalena dei Pazzi **16**
Santissima Annunziata **14**
Tempio Israelitico **17**

Historic Buildings
Palazzo Medici Riccardi **5**
Palazzo Pucci **4**
Spedale degli Innocenti **12**

Museums and Galleries
Cenacolo di Sant'Apollonia **6**
Conservatorio **10**
Galleria dell'Accademia **9**
Museo Archeologico **15**
Opificio delle Pietre Dure **11**

Gardens
Giardino dei Semplici **8**

Streets, Piazzas and Markets
Mercato Centrale **1**
Piazza di San Lorenzo **3**
Piazza della Santissima Annunziata **13**

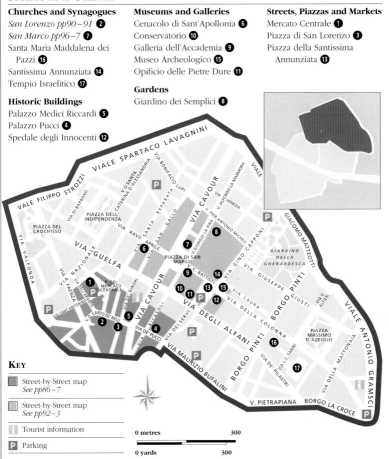

KEY

- Street-by-Street map See pp86–7
- Street-by-Street map See pp92–3
- Tourist information
- **P** Parking

0 metres 300
0 yards 300

◁ **Virgin and Child** by Fra Angelico (c.1440) in San Marco

Street-by-Street: Around San Lorenzo

Bust, Palazzo Medici Riccardi

THIS AREA is stamped with the character of Cosimo il Vecchio, founder of the Medici dynasty, who commissioned San Lorenzo and the Palazzo Medici Riccardi. Around San Lorenzo, a huge general market fills the streets, its colourful awnings almost obscuring the various monuments. The market is a reminder that Florence has always been a city of merchants. Many of the products on sale – leather goods and silk, wool and cashmere garments – are very good value especially if, like the Florentines, you are prepared to bargain.

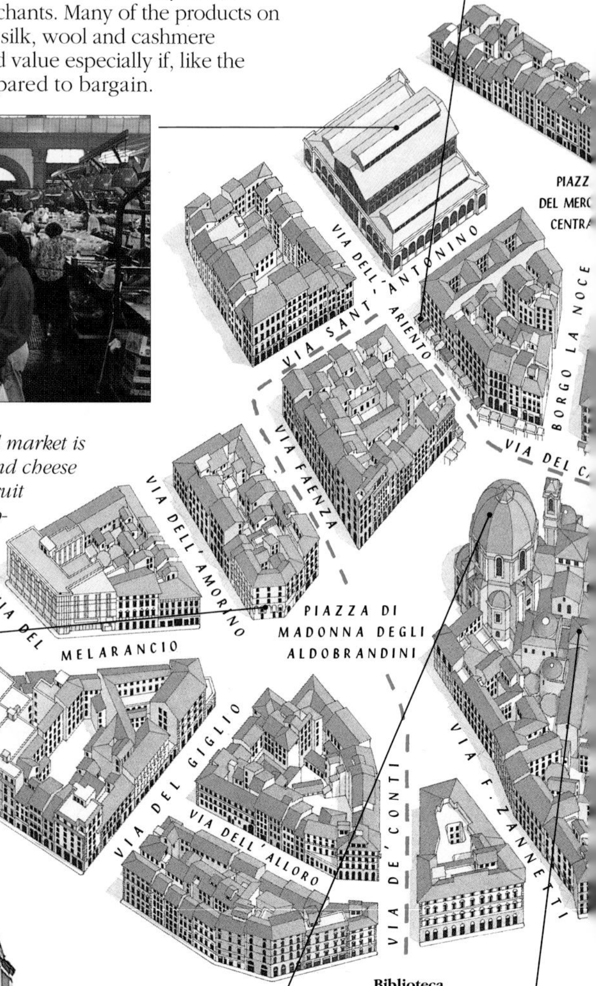

Cheap cafés and cooked meat stalls abound in the vicinity of the market. They sell traditional Italian take-away foods, such as tripe and roast suckling pig, chicken and rabbit.

Mercato Centrale
Built in 1874, the central market is packed with fish, meat and cheese stalls downstairs, while fruit and vegetables are sold upstairs beneath the glass and cast-iron roof ❶

Palazzo Riccardi-Manelli, begun in 1557, stands on the site of the house where Giotto was born in 1266.

The Cappelle Medicee are situated in San Lorenzo, but are reached from a separate entrance in Piazza di Madonna degli Aldobrandini. Michelangelo designed the New Sacristy and two Medici tombs. Some of his pencil sketches survive on the walls inside.

Biblioteca Mediceo-Laurenziana

STAR SIGHTS

★ **San Lorenzo**

★ **Palazzo Medici Riccardi**

The Biblioteca Riccardiana, founded in the 16th century, was opened to the public in 1715. It comprises a series of frescoed reading rooms which house a collection of precious manuscripts, including Dante's *Divine Comedy*.

LOCATOR MAP
See Florence Street Finder maps 5, 6

Via de' Ginori is lined with fine 16th-century palazzi.

San Giovannino degli Scolopi church was begun by Ammannati in 1579.

★ Palazzo Medici Riccardi
The palazzo, built between 1444–64, served as the Medici family home and the headquarters of their banking empire ❺

Palazzo Pucci
This is the home of designer Emilio Pucci ❹

★ San Lorenzo
The unfinished façade belies the noble interior, which was designed for the Medici by Brunelleschi in 1425–46 ❷

KEY

— — — Suggested route

| 0 metres | 100 |
| 0 yards | 100 |

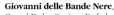

Giovanni delle Bande Nere, Grand Duke Cosimo I's father *(see p49)*, is depicted in battle dress in this statue by Baccio Bandinelli (1540).

Mercato Centrale

Mercato Centrale ❶

Via dell'Ariento 10–14. **Map** 1 C4
(5 C1). **Open** *7am–2pm Mon–Sat.*
Underground car park *open
7am–8:30pm Mon–Sat.*

RIGHT IN THE HEART of the
San Lorenzo street market
is Florence's busiest food
market, the bustling Mercato
Centrale. It is housed in a vast
two-storey building made of
cast-iron and glass, which was
built in 1874 by Giuseppe
Mengoni. During restoration in
1980, a mezzanine floor was
constructed and a car park was
added in the basement. For
reduced rate parking, have
a market vendor stamp your
receipt. On the ground floor
there are dozens of stalls
selling meat, fish, cheese
and typical Tuscan takeaway
foods, such as *porchetta* (roast
suckling pig). Fruit, vegetables
and flowers are sold on
the top floor.

San Lorenzo ❷

See pp90–91.

Piazza di San Lorenzo ❸

Map 1 C5 (6 D1). 🏛 *summer: 7am–
8pm; winter: 8am–8pm Tue–Sat.*

AT THE WESTERN END of the
piazza, near the entrance
to San Lorenzo church, there
is a statue of Giovanni delle
Bande Nere, mercenary and
father of Cosimo I, first Medici
Grand Duke *(see p49)*. It was
carved by Baccio Bandinelli
in 1540, and is almost hidden
from view among the market
stalls stretching all the way up
the side of San Lorenzo
church and into the streets
leading off the piazza. The
stalls closest to the church
cater mostly for tourists,
selling leather goods, T-shirts
and souvenirs. In the streets
around the market, everything
from lentils to bargain-priced
clothes is sold. The neighbouring shops have become
an integral part of the market,
selling cheeses, hams, home-
baked bread, pastries,
fabrics and table linen.

**Statue of Giovanni delle Bande Nere
in Piazza di San Lorenzo**

Palazzo Pucci ❹

Via de' Pucci 6. **Map** 2 D5 (6 E1).
📞 *055 28 30 61.* **Closed** *to
the public.*

THE PALAZZO PUCCI is the
ancestral home of clothes
designer Emilio Pucci,
Marchese di Barsento. The
Pucci family, traditionally
friends and allies of the
Medici, feature prominently
in Florence's history, and this
large palace was built in the
16th century to designs by
Bartolomeo Ammannati.
   Emilio Pucci's boutique is at
Via della Vigna Nuova
97–99r. *Haute couture* clients
are fitted out in the palatial
rooms which are above the
showroom. Pucci is most
famous for smart but casual
clothes, and designed the
stylish blue uniforms worn by
Florentine traffic police, the
vigili urbani (see p276).

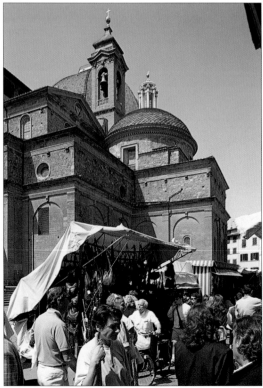

San Lorenzo street market

Palazzo Medici Riccardi ❺

Via Cavour 1. **Map** 2 D5 (6 D1).
📞 *055 276 03 40*. **Cappella dei
Magi Open** *9am–7pm Thu–Tue.*
Closed *1 May, 25 Dec.* **Adm charge**.
*Reservation is advisable in busy
periods.* 🚫 ♿

HOME OF THE MEDICI for
100 years from 1444, the
palazzo was later acquired
by the Riccardi family and
now houses government
offices. It was built to an
austere design by Michelozzo
for Cosimo il Vecchio,
who rejected Brunelleschi's
original plans for the palazzo
as being too flamboyant –
Cosimo did not want to be
seen flaunting his wealth to
his rivals. The windows on
either side of the entrance
were added in 1517 and
designed by Michelangelo.

Through the main door, the
courtyard walls are covered
in ancient Roman masonry
fragments. The roundels
above the arcade show
scenes copied from antique
intaglios now on display in
the Museo degli Argenti *(see
p123)*. Donatello's statue of
David (now in the Bargello,
see pp68–9), was originally
here, but today the place of
honour is given to Bandinelli's
marble statue of *Orpheus*.

Only two rooms in the
palazzo are open to the
public. In the Cappella dei
Magi is a colourful fresco of
The Procession of the Magi
painted by Benozzo Gozzoli
in 1459–60, which depicts
several members of

**Statuary in the garden of the
Palazzo Medici Riccardi**

***The Last Supper* (1445–50) by Andrea del Castagno in Sant'Apollonia**

the Medici dynasty *(see
pp48–9)*. The Sala di Luca
Giordano is named after the
Neapolitan artist who painted
its walls with *The Apotheosis
of the Medici* in High Baroque
style in 1683. The palazzo
often plays host to temporary
art exhibitions, for which
there is an additional
admission charge.

Cenacolo di Sant'Apollonia ❻

Via XXVII Aprile 1. **Map** 2 D4.
📞 *055 238 86 07.* **Open** *8:15am–
1:50pm Tue–Sun.* **Closed** *certain days
(phone to check).* 📷 ♿

THE CLOISTER and refectory of
what was originally a convent for the Camaldolite order
of nuns are now used by the
students of Florence University.
On the main wall of the refectory is a fresco of *The Last
Supper* painted in 1445–50,
one of the few surviving
works by Andrea del Castagno,
pupil of Masaccio and among
the first Renaissance artists to
begin to experiment with
perspective. Here Judas sits
isolated in the foreground of
the picture, disrupting its
balance and breaking up the
long white strip of tablecloth.
He is shown in profile with the
face of a satyr: a mythological
creature, half-man, half-goat,
often used in Renaissance
paintings to represent evil.

San Marco ❼

See pp96–7.

Giardino dei Semplici ❽

Via Micheli 3. **Map** 2 E4. 📞 *055 275
74 02.* **Open** *9am–1pm Mon–Fri,
Sun in spring; call for info.***Closed**
*1 Jan, 6 Jan, 25 Apr, Easter Sun &
Mon, 1 May, 13–17 Aug, 1 Nov,
24–26 Dec, 31 Dec.* 📷 ♿

Giardino dei Semplici

THE WORD "SEMPLICI" refers
to the raw ingredients,
"simples", used by medieval
apothecaries in preparing
medicine – thus the Giardino
dei Semplici was where medic-
inal herbs were grown and
studied. It was set up in 1545
by Niccolò Tribolo for Cosimo
I in the area between Via
Micheli, Via Giorgio la Pira and
Via Gino Capponi. The garden
retains its original layout but
now the collection includes
tropical plants as well as flora
native to Tuscany.

Around the garden are small
specialist museums: a geology
collection includes fossils; the
mineralogy section shows the
geological structure of Elba,
whose ores attracted bronze
traders in the 10th century
BC. The botanical museum
has specimens of rare plants.

San Lorenzo ❷

SAN LORENZO was the parish church of the Medici family, and they lavished their wealth on its adornment. Brunelleschi rebuilt the church in Renaissance Classical style in 1419, although the façade was never completed. In 1520 Michelangelo began work on the Medici tombs and designed the Biblioteca Mediceo-Laurenziana in 1524 to house the manuscripts collected by the Medici. In both the New Sacristy and the Cappella dei Principi, extensive scaffolding has been erected (for an indefinite period) to protect visitors from falling marble.

The huge dome by Buontalenti echoes that of Brunelleschi's Duomo *(see pp64–5).*

★ **Cappella dei Principi**
The marble decoration of the Medici mausoleum, begun in 1604 by Matteo Nigetti, was not completed until 1962.

The Old Sacristy was designed by Brunelleschi (1420–29) and painted by Donatello.

★ **Michelangelo's Staircase**
The Mannerist pietra serena sandstone staircase to the Biblioteca is one of Michelangelo's most innovative designs. It was built by Ammannati in 1559.

Michelangelo designed the desks and ceiling of the Biblioteca, which is entered from Manetti's graceful, tiered cloister, built in 1462.

The Martyrdom of St Lawrence
Bronzino's huge Mannerist fresco of 1659 is a masterly study of the human form in various contorted poses (see p25).

The formal cloister garden is planted with clipped box hedges, pomegranate and orange trees.

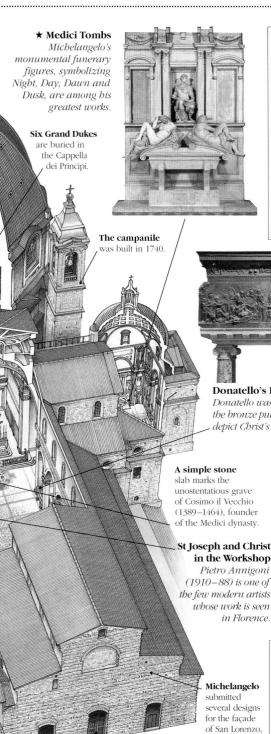

★ Medici Tombs
Michelangelo's monumental funerary figures, symbolizing Night, Day, Dawn and Dusk, are among his greatest works.

Six Grand Dukes
are buried in the Cappella dei Principi.

The campanile
was built in 1740.

A simple stone
slab marks the unostentatious grave of Cosimo il Vecchio (1389–1464), founder of the Medici dynasty.

St Joseph and Christ in the Workshop
Pietro Annigoni (1910–88) is one of the few modern artists whose work is seen in Florence.

Michelangelo
submitted several designs for the façade of San Lorenzo, but it remains unfinished.

Entrance to church

Donatello's Pulpits
Donatello was 74 when he began work on the bronze pulpits in the nave in 1460; they depict Christ's Passion and Resurrection.

VISITORS' CHECKLIST

Piazza di San Lorenzo (Basilica and Biblioteca), Piazza di Madonna degli Aldobrandini (Cappelle Medicee). **Map** 1 C5 (6 D1). 🚌 many routes. **Basilica** 📞 055 21 66 34. **Open** 10am–5pm Mon–Sat. ✝ 8am, 9:30am, 6pm daily (also at 11am Sun & relig hols). 📷 **Adm charge**. **Biblioteca** 📞 055 21 44 43. **Open** 9am–1pm Mon–Sat. **Closed** public hols. **Cappelle Medicee** 📞 055 238 86 02 (055 29 48 83 to book). **Open** 8:30am–5pm daily (to 1:50pm public hols; last adm: 30 mins before closing). **Closed** 1st, 3rd & 5th Mon of every month. **Adm charge**. 📷

STAR FEATURES

★ **Cappella dei Principi**

★ **Michelangelo's Staircase**

★ **Medici Tombs by Michelangelo**

Street-by-Street: Around San Marco

THE BUILDINGS IN THIS PART of Florence once stood on the fringes of the city, serving as stables and barracks. The Medici menagerie, including lions, elephants and giraffes, was housed here. Today it is the student quarter, and in term-time Piazza di San Marco is filled with young people waiting for lectures at the university or at the Accademia di Belle Arti. This is the world's oldest art school, set up in 1563, with Michelangelo as a founder *(see p94)*.

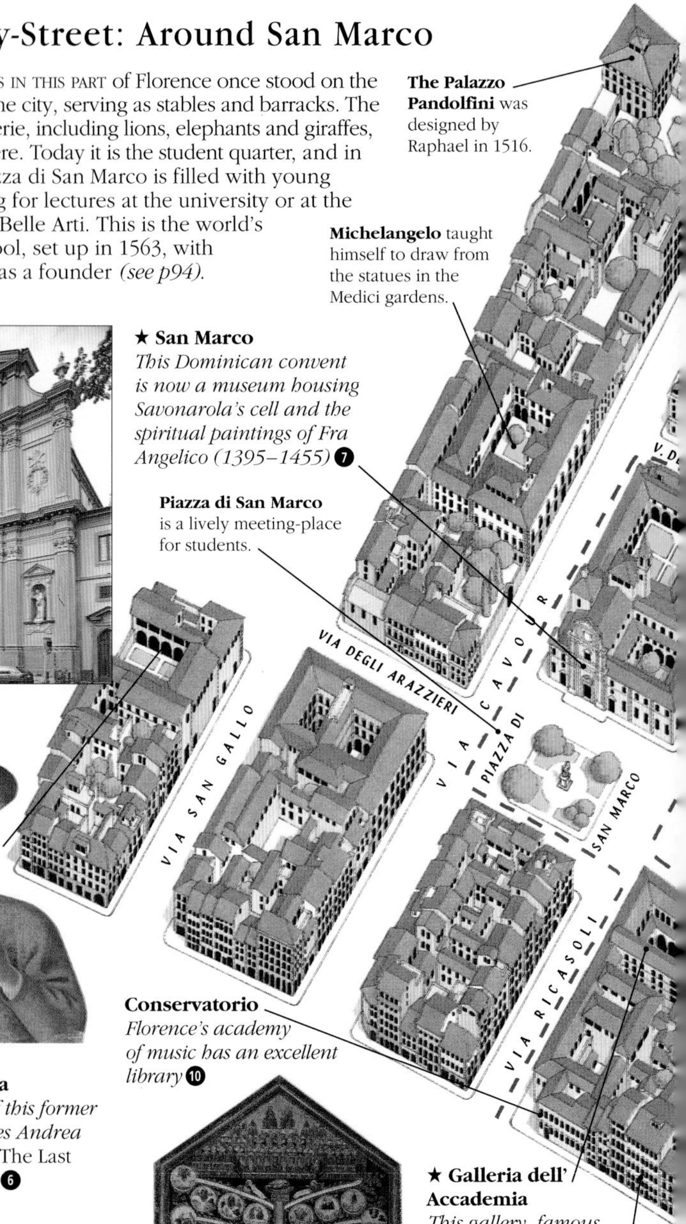

The Palazzo Pandolfini was designed by Raphael in 1516.

Michelangelo taught himself to draw from the statues in the Medici gardens.

★ **San Marco**
This Dominican convent is now a museum housing Savonarola's cell and the spiritual paintings of Fra Angelico (1395–1455) ❼

Piazza di San Marco
is a lively meeting-place for students.

VIA DEGLI ARAZZIERI

VIA SAN GALLO

VIA CAVOUR

PIAZZA DI SAN MARCO

VIA RICASOLI

V. D...

Cenacolo di Sant'Apollonia
The refectory of this former convent features Andrea del Castagno's The Last Supper *(1450)* ❻

Conservatorio
Florence's academy of music has an excellent library ❿

★ **Galleria dell' Accademia**
This gallery, famous for Michelangelo's David, *also contains Bonaguida's* Tree of the Cross *(1330)* ❾

Opificio delle Pietre Dure
Precious mosaics are restored here ⓫

STAR SIGHTS

★ **Galleria dell' Accademia**

★ **San Marco**

★ **Spedale degli Innocenti**

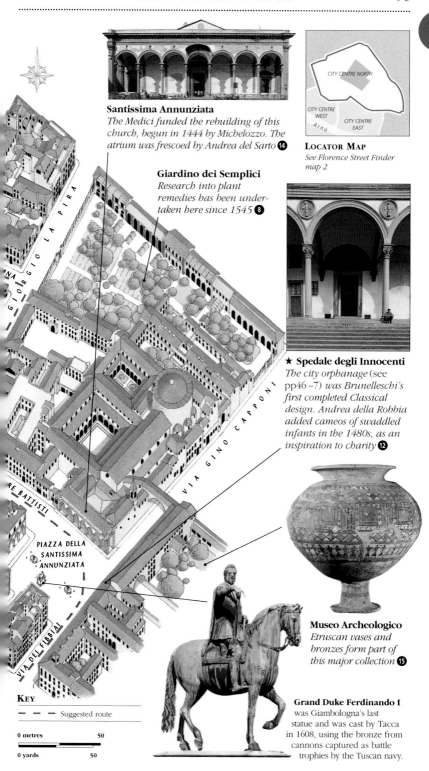

Santissima Annunziata
The Medici funded the rebuilding of this church, begun in 1444 by Michelozzo. The atrium was frescoed by Andrea del Sarto ⓮

LOCATOR MAP
See Florence Street Finder map 2

Giardino dei Semplici
Research into plant remedies has been undertaken here since 1545 ⓼

★ **Spedale degli Innocenti**
The city orphanage (see pp46–7) was Brunelleschi's first completed Classical design. Andrea della Robbia added cameos of swaddled infants in the 1480s, as an inspiration to charity ⓬

Museo Archeologico
Etruscan vases and bronzes form part of this major collection ⓯

Grand Duke Ferdinando I
was Giambologna's last statue and was cast by Tacca in 1608, using the bronze from cannons captured as battle trophies by the Tuscan navy.

KEY

– – – Suggested route

0 metres   50
0 yards   50

The central section of the 15th-century *Cassone Adimari* by Scheggia

Galleria dell'Accademia ⑨

Via Ricasoli 60. **Map** 2 D4 (6 E1).
☎ *055 238 86 09 (information);*
055 29 48 83 (reservations). **Open**
8:15am–6:50pm Tue–Sun (extended
hours in summer). **Closed** *1 Jan,*
1 May, 25 Dec. **Adm charge**. 🚫 ♿

THE ACADEMY of Fine Arts in Florence was founded in 1563 and was the first school in Europe set up to teach the techniques of drawing, painting and sculpture. The art collection displayed in the gallery was formed in 1784 with the aim of providing the students of the academy with material to study and copy.

Since 1873, many of Michelangelo's most important works have been in the Accademia. Perhaps

Madonna del Mare (c.1470)
by Sandro Botticelli

the most famous of all dominates the collection: Michelangelo's *David* (1504). This colossal Classical statue (5.2 m/17 ft) depicts the biblical hero who killed the giant Goliath. It was commissioned by the city of Florence and positioned in front of the Palazzo Vecchio. This established Michelangelo, then aged 29, as the foremost sculptor of his time. In 1873 it was moved to the Accademia, to protect it from the weather and pollution. One copy of *David* is now to be found in its original position in Piazza della Signoria *(see pp76–7)* and a second stands in the middle of Piazzale Michelangelo *(see p131)*.

Michelangelo's other masterpieces include a statue of St Matthew finished in 1508, and the *Quattro Prigioni* (the four prisoners) which were sculpted between 1521 and 1523 and intended to adorn the tomb of Pope Julius II. Presented to the Medici in 1564 by Michelangelo's cousin, the muscular figures struggling to free themselves from the stone are among the most dramatic of his works. The statues were moved to the

David by Michelangelo

Grotta Grande in the Boboli Gardens in 1585, where casts of the originals can now be seen *(see pp124–5)*.

The gallery contains an important collection of paintings by 15th- and 16th-century local artists: contemporaries of Michelangelo such as Fra Bartolomeo, Filippino Lippi, Bronzino and Ridolfo del Ghirlandaio. There are many major works including the *Madonna del Mare* (Madonna of the Sea), attributed to Botticelli (1445–1510), and *Venus and Cupid* by Jacopo Pontormo (1494–1556), based upon a preparatory drawing by Michelangelo. Also on display is an elaborately painted wooden chest, the *Cassone Adimari*, by Scheggia, Masaccio's step-brother. Dating from around 1440, it was originally used as part of a bride's trousseau, and is covered with details of Florentine daily life, clothing and architecture. The bridal party are pictured standing in front of the Baptistry.

Pacino di Bonaguida's *Tree of Life* (1310) is a prominent painting among the collections of Byzantine and late 13th- and 14th-century religious art, much of which is stylized and heavily embossed with gold.

The Salone della Toscana (Tuscany Room) is full of 19th-century sculpture and paintings by members of the Accademia, and a series of original plaster models by the sculptor Lorenzo Bartolini. Born in 1777, he became professor at the Accademia in 1839, a post he held until his death in 1850. His work includes busts of major figures such as the poet Lord Byron and the composer Franz Liszt.

Detail from 14th-century *Madonna and Saints* in the Accademia

Conservatorio Musicale Luigi Cherubini ❿

Piazza delle Belle Arti 2. **Map** 2 D4 (6 E1). 🄲 *055 29 21 80.* **Library closed** to the public.

Some of Italy's finest musicians trained at this musical academy, named after the Florentine composer Luigi Cherubini (1760–1842). The conservatory owns a range of ancient musical instruments, now on display in the Palazzo Vecchio *(see pp78–9)*. The collection was acquired by Ferdinando, the last of the Medici Grand Dukes, and includes violins, violas and cellos made by Stradivari, Amati and Ruggeri. There is also a harpsichord by Bartolomeo Cristofori, who invented the piano in the early 18th century. He was responsible for many of the most important acquisitions.

The conservatory has one of the best music libraries in Italy, holding many original manuscripts by composers like Monteverdi and Rossini.

***Pietre dure* table (1849) by Zocchi**

Opificio delle Pietre Dure ⓫

Via degli Alfani 78. **Map** 2 D4 (6 F1). 🄲 *055 265 11.* **Open** *8:15am–2pm Mon–Sat (to 7pm Tue). Last adm: 30 mins before closing.* **Closed** *public hols.* **Adm charge.**

Situated in the former monastery of San Niccolò, the *opificio* (factory) is a national institute specializing in teaching the Florentine craft of producing inlaid pictures using marble and semi-precious stones. This tradition has flourished since the end of the 16th century, when it was funded through the patronage of the Medici Grand Dukes, who decorated their mausoleum with *pietre dure*.

There is a museum in the same building displaying 19th-century workbenches, tools, vases and portraits showing *pietre dure* work. Several table tops decorated with *pietre dure* are on display: one inlaid with a harp and garlands by Zocchi, made in 1849, another with flowers and birds, designed by Niccolò Betti in 1855. A stockpile of exquisite marbles and other semi-precious stones dates back to Medici times.

Spedale degli Innocenti ⓬

Piazza della Santissima Annunziata 12. **Map** 2 D4 (6 F1). 🄲 *055 249 17 08.* **Open** *8:30am–2pm Thu–Tue (last adm: 30 mins before closing).* **Closed** *1 Jan, Easter, 25 Dec.* **Adm charge.** 🚫

This "hospital" is named after Herod's biblical Massacre of the Innocents following the birth of Jesus. It opened in 1444 as the first orphanage in Europe, and part of the building is still used for this purpose. UNICEF, the United Nations Children's Fund, also has offices here. Brunelleschi's arcaded loggia *(see pp46–7)* is decorated with glazed terracotta roundels, added by Andrea della Robbia around 1498, showing babies wrapped in swaddling bands. At the left-hand end of the portico is the *rota*, a rotating stone cylinder on which mothers could place their unwanted children anonymously and ring the orphanage bell. The stone was then turned around and the child was taken in.

Within the building there are two elegant cloisters built to Brunelleschi's designs. The larger Chiostro degli Uomini (Men's Cloister), built between 1422 and 1445, is decorated with *sgraffito* designs of cherubs and roosters scratched into the wet plaster. The smaller Women's Cloister (1438) leads to a gallery which has several paintings donated by children from the orphanage who went on to be successful in later life. Outstanding among these is the *Adoration of the Magi* (1488) painted by Domenico del Ghirlandaio, showing the massacre in the background.

Andrea della Robbia's roundels (c.1490) on the Spedale degli Innocenti

San Marco ❼

Dominican friar in grey habit

THE CONVENT of San Marco was founded in the 13th century and enlarged in 1437 when Dominican monks from nearby Fiesole moved here at the invitation of Cosimo il Vecchio. He paid a considerable sum to have the convent rebuilt by his favourite architect, Michelozzo, whose simple cloisters and cells are the setting for a remarkable series of devotional frescoes (c.1438–45) by Fra Angelico.

Cells 38 and 39 were reserved for Cosimo il Vecchio when he retreated to the convent to find spiritual sustenance and peace.

The Mocking of Christ
Fra Angelico's beautiful allegorical fresco (c.1440) shows Jesus blindfolded and being struck by a Roman guard.

Cells 12 to 15 contain relics of the religious fanatic Savonarola, made prior of San Marco in 1491 *(see pp50–51)*.

An ancient cedar stands in Michelozzo's Sant'Antonino cloister.

Entrance to San Marco

Entrance to Museo di San Marco

The Deposition (1435–40)
This poignant scene of the dead Christ, and other works by Fra Angelico and his School, are displayed in the former Pilgrims' Hospice.

KEY TO FLOORPLAN

☐ Ground floor

☐ First floor

▨ Non-exhibition space

Sant'Antonino cloister

The dormitory cells contain scenes from *The Life of Christ*, intended to inspire prayer and contemplation.

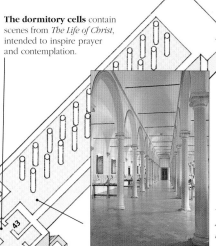

★ Library
Michelozzo designed Europe's first public library, in a light and airy colonnaded hall, for Cosimo il Vecchio in 1441.

Visitors' Checklist

Piazza di San Marco. **Map** 2 D4. *many routes.* **Church** *055 28 76 28.* ***Open*** *7am–noon, 4–8pm.* *7:30am, 6:30pm Mon–Sat; 10:30am, 11:30am, 12:30pm, 6:30pm Sun & relig hols.* **Museum** *055 238 86 08 (reservations: 055 29 48 83).* ***Open*** *8:30am–1:50pm daily (to 6:50pm Sat, to 7pm Sun; last adm: 30 mins before closing).* ***Closed*** *2nd & 4th Mon & 1st, 3rd & 5th Sun of month, 1 Jan, 1 May, 25 Dec.* ***Adm charge.***

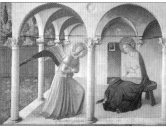

★ The Annunciation *(c.1445)*
Fra Angelico shows his mastery of perspective by placing Gabriel and the Virgin in an elaborate loggia, inspired by Michelozzo.

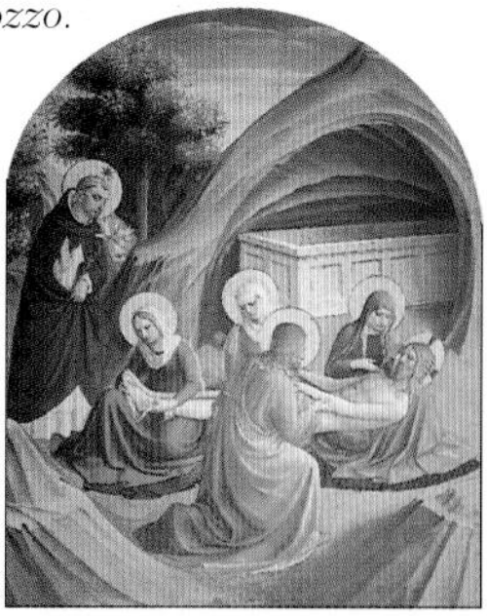

The Entombment
Fra Angelico's tender fresco (c.1442) in Cell 2 shows Mary Magdalene and St. John mourning Christ.

Staircase to first floor

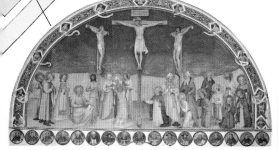

★ The Crucifixion *(1441–42)*
Fra Angelico was moved to tears as he painted this image of the Crucifixion of Christ in the Chapter House.

Star Features

★ The Annunciation by Fra Angelico

★ The Crucifixion by Fra Angelico

★ Library by Michelozzo

Mannerist fountain by Pietro Tacca in Piazza della Santissima Annunziata

Piazza della Santissima Annunziata ⑬

Map 2 D4.

THE DELICATE nine-bay arcade on the eastern side of this elegant square was designed by Brunelleschi in 1419 and forms the façade to the Spedale degli Innocenti *(see p46)*. Brunelleschi's round arches gave rise to the Classical style widely copied by Renaissance architects. In the centre of the square is an equestrian statue of Duke Ferdinando I, started by Giambologna towards the end of his career. It was finished in 1608 by his assistant, Pietro Tacca, who also designed the two stylized Mannerist bronze fountains in the square.

A fair is held annually in the piazza on the feast of the Annunciation, 25 March, when homemade sweet biscuits called *brigidini* are sold from the stalls.

Santissima Annunziata ⑭

Piazza della Santissima Annunziata.
Map 2 E4. **(055 239 80 34.
Open 7:30am–12:30pm, 4–6:30pm daily.

THE CHURCH of the Holy Annunciation was founded by the Servite order in 1250 and later rebuilt by Michelozzo between 1444 and 1481. There is a series of early 16th-century frescoes in the atrium by Mannerist artists Rosso Fiorentino, Andrea del Sarto and Jacopo Pontormo, but many of these frescoes have suffered from damp and are fading. The most celebrated are *The Journey of the Magi* (1511) and *The Birth of the Virgin* (1514) by del Sarto.

The interior is dark and heavily decorated, with a frescoed ceiling completed by Pietro Giambelli in 1669.

The church also boasts one of the most revered shrines in Florence, a painting of the Virgin Mary begun in 1252 by a monk. Devout Florentines believe it was finished by an angel, and many newly wed couples traditionally come here after their wedding ceremony to present a bouquet of flowers to the Virgin and pray for a long and fruitful marriage. Nine chapels radiate from the sanctuary. The central one was reconstructed by Giambologna to use as his tomb, and contains bronze reliefs and a crucifix sculpted by him.

Through the door in the north transept of the church is the Chiostro dei Morti (Cloister of the Dead), so called because it was originally used as a burial ground and is packed with memorial stones. The fresco above the entrance porch is by Andrea del Sarto. Painted in 1525, it shows the Holy Family resting on their flight to Egypt and is usually known as *La Madonna del Sacco*, since Joseph is depicted leaning on a sack.

The Cappella di San Luca off the cloister has been owned by the Accademia delle Arte del Disegno since 1565 and a special service dedicated to artists is held here every year on St Luke's day (which falls on 18 October). Benvenuto Cellini is among the artists buried in the vault below.

***The Birth of the Virgin* (1514) by Andrea del Sarto**

The François Vase, covered in figures from Greek mythology

Museo Archeologico ^⑮

Via della Colonna 36. **Map** 2 E4.
[055 235 75. **Open** 2–7pm
Mon, 8:30am–7pm Tue, Thu,
8:30am–2pm Wed, Fri–Sun (phone to
check). **Closed** 1 Jan, 1 May, 25 Dec.
Adm charge. 📷 ♿

THE ARCHAEOLOGICAL Museum is in a palazzo built by Giulio Parigi for the Princess Maria Maddalena de' Medici in 1620. It now exhibits outstanding collections of Etruscan, Greek, Roman and ancient Egyptian artifacts.

A section on the second floor is dedicated to Greek vases, with a room given over to the François Vase, found in an Etruscan tomb at Fonte Rotella near Chiusi (see p224). Painted and signed in 570 BC, it is decorated with six rows of black and red figures depicting scenes from Greek mythology. The Etruscan collection was very badly damaged by the 1966 flood and only a fraction is now on display, although restoration work is being continued.

In addition to the splendid series of bronze Etruscan statues, on the first floor of the museum there are two famous bronzes. The *Chimera (see p40)*, sculpted in the 4th century BC, is a mythical lion with a goat's head imposed on its body and a serpent for a tail, shown here cowering in terror. It was

Bronze Etruscan warrior

ploughed up in a field near Arezzo in 1553 and presented to Cosimo I de' Medici by Giorgio Vasari, the artist, author and critic. The *Arringatore* (Orator) was found c.1566 near Lake Trasimeno in central Italy and is inscribed with the name of an Etruscan aristocrat, Aulus Metullus. The sculpture dates from the 1st century BC, and the figure, splendidly dressed in a Roman toga, appears to be addressing his audience.

Part of the Egyptian collection was acquired during a joint French and Tuscan expedition in 1829. It is rich in wooden, cloth and bone artifacts, preserved in the dry atmosphere of the desert tombs in which they were found. They include a near-complete chariot of bone and wood found in a tomb near Thebes (dating to c.15th century BC), along with textiles, hats, ropes, furniture, purses and baskets.

Santa Maria Maddalena dei Pazzi ^⑯

Borgo Pinti 58. **Map** 2 E5. [055
247 84 20. **Church and chapter
house open** 9am–noon, 3–7pm
daily. **Closed** for mass 5:30–6pm. 📷

THIS FORMER CONVENT has been restored following the floods of 1966. Originally run by the Cistercian order, it was taken over by Carmelites in 1628, and Augustinian monks have lived here since 1926. The chapterhouse, which is entered from the crypt, contains the famous *Crucifixion and Saints* fresco painted in 1493–6 by Perugino (his real name was Pietro Vannucci), who was one of the founders of the Umbrian School of artists. This beautiful and well-preserved fresco is regarded as a masterpiece, bearing all Perugino's trademarks, most notably the background, which is a detailed landscape of wooded hills and winding streams painted in soft blues

and greens. The main chapel, decorated with coloured marble by Ciro Ferri (1675), is one of the best examples of the High Baroque style in a Florentine church. In 1492 Giuliano da Sangallo designed the church's unusual and striking portico, with its square-topped, Ionic-style arcades.

Tempio Israelitico ^⑰

Via Farini 4. **Map** 2 F5. [055
24 52 52. **Synagogue and Museum
open** Oct–Mar: 10am–1pm, 2–4pm
Sun–Thu, 10am–1pm Fri; Apr–Oct:
10am–1pm, 2–5pm Sun–Thu,
10am–1pm Fri. 🚫 **Closed** Jewish hols.

Interior of the Tempio Israelitico

THE GREEN copper-covered dome of Florence's main synagogue stands out on the horizon as you look down on the city from the surrounding hills. As elsewhere in Europe, Jews in Florence were alternately welcomed and persecuted over the years. In the early 17th century they flocked to Livorno and then to Florence when it was freed from its strong political ties with Spain by Grand Duke Ferdinando I (1549–1609).

In the Inquisition, Grand Duke Cosimo III (1642–1723) passed laws forbidding Christians to work for Jewish families and businesses. In the 1860s the Jewish ghetto was cleared to make way for the Piazza della Repubblica (see p112). The synagogue was built by Marco Treves in 1874–82 in Spanish-Moorish style. It has a museum of ritual objects dating from the 17th century.

CITY CENTRE WEST

AT ONE END of this part of Florence is the main railway station – a rare example of modern architecture in the city centre. At the other end, a magnet for visitors and Florentines alike, is the Ponte Vecchio, the city's oldest bridge. It is lined with jewellers' shops, here since 1593, and presents a scene little changed since.

Between these two focal points there is something to interest most people, from the frescoes of Santa Maria Novella and Santa Trinità to the awesome Palazzo Strozzi. Nearby is Piazza della Repubblica,

Detail from Strozzi Chapel in Santa Maria Novella

originally laid out as part of the grandiose plans to remodel Florence when it was briefly the nation's capital. Most locals may consider it an eyesore, but the cafés here have always been very popular. This is also the part of Florence in which to shop, from the leather goods, silks and woollens of the Mercato Nuovo to the elegant showrooms of the top couturiers in Via della Vigna Nuova and Via de' Tornabuoni. In the smaller streets off these, local artisans still continue Florence's proud tradition of craftsmanship, from stonecutting to restoration work.

SIGHTS AT A GLANCE

Museums and Galleries
Museo Marino Marini (San Pancrazio) **1**
Palazzo Davanzati **10**
Palazzo Rucellai **2**

Churches
Ognissanti **16**
Santa Maria Novella pp110–11 **17**
Santa Trinità **7**
Santi Apostoli **8**

Bridges
Ponte Vecchio pp106–7 **9**

Markets
Mercato Nuovo **12**

Historic Buildings
Palazzo Antinori **14**
Palazzo di Parte Guelfa **11**
Palazzo Strozzi **5**
Stazione di Santa Maria Novella **18**

Historic Streets and Piazzas
Piazza della Repubblica **13**
Piazza di Santa Trinità **6**
Via dei Fossi **15**
Via de' Tornabuoni **4**
Via della Vigna Nuova **3**

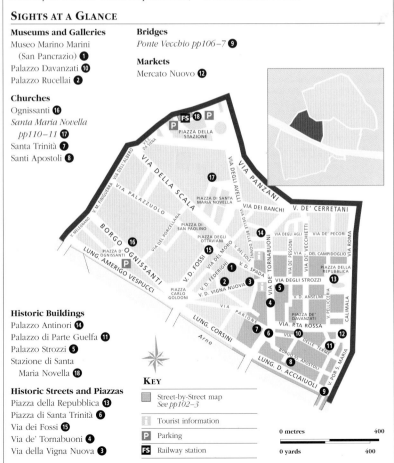

KEY

	Street-by-Street map See pp102–3
	Tourist information
P	Parking
FS	Railway station

0 metres 400
0 yards 400

◁ **View from Ponte Santa Trinità towards Piazza di Santa Trinità**

Street-by-Street: Around Piazza della Repubblica

U NDERLYING THE STREET PLAN of modern Florence is the far older pattern of the ancient Roman city founded on the banks of the Arno. Nowhere is this more evident than in the rectilinear grid of narrow streets in the western half of the city centre. Here the streets lead north from the river Arno to the Piazza della Repubblica, once the site of the forum, the main square of the ancient Roman city. It later became the city's main food market *(see p52)* until the city authorities decided to tidy it up in the 1860s, building the triumphal arch that now stands in today's café-filled square.

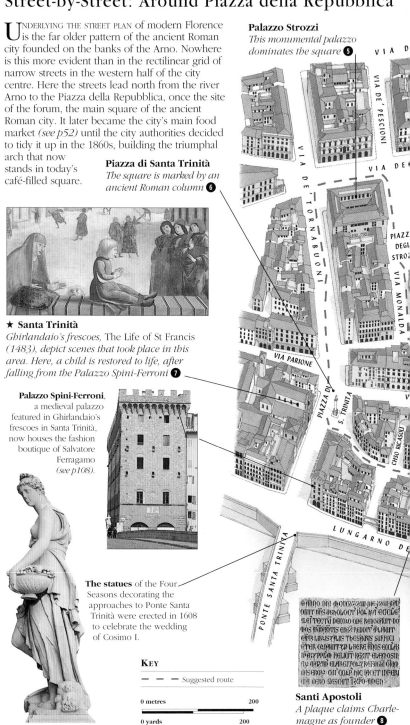

Palazzo Strozzi
This monumental palazzo dominates the square ❺

Piazza di Santa Trinità
The square is marked by an ancient Roman column ❻

★ Santa Trinità
Ghirlandaio's frescoes, The Life of St Francis *(1483), depict scenes that took place in this area. Here, a child is restored to life, after falling from the Palazzo Spini-Ferroni* ❼

Palazzo Spini-Ferroni, a medieval palazzo featured in Ghirlandaio's frescoes in Santa Trinità, now houses the fashion boutique of Salvatore Ferragamo *(see p108).*

The statues of the Four Seasons decorating the approaches to Ponte Santa Trinità were erected in 1608 to celebrate the wedding of Cosimo I.

Santi Apostoli
A plaque claims Charlemagne as founder ❽

KEY

‒ ‒ ‒ Suggested route

0 metres   200
0 yards   200

LOCATOR MAP
*See Florence Street Finder
maps 5, 6*

★ **Piazza della Repubblica**
*The Roman-style triumphal
arch celebrates Florence's
stint as Italy's capital
(1865–71)* ⑬

Mercato Nuovo
*Designed as a
covered general
market in 1547,
Mercato Nuovo is
full of expensive
souvenir stalls* ⑫

Palazzo Davanzati
*Frescoes with exotic birds
decorate the Sala dei
Papagalli, which was once
the dining room of this
14th-century palazzo* ⑩

★ **Ponte Vecchio**
*Giotto's pupil, Taddeo Gaddi, designed this
medieval bridge in 1345. It is the oldest –
and most popular – of Florence's bridges
and retains many of its original features* ⑨

**Palazzo di
Parte Guelfa**
*This was the head-
quarters of the Guelphs,
the dominant political
party of medieval
Florence* ⑪

STAR SIGHTS

★ **Piazza d. Repubblica**

★ **Ponte Vecchio**

★ **Santa Trinità**

Museo Marino Marini (San Pancrazio) ❶

Piazza San Pancrazio. **Map** 1 B5 (5 B2). **[** 055 21 94 32. **Open** *10am–5pm Mon, Wed–Sat (Jun–Sep: 10am–11pm Thu), 10am–1pm Sun.* **Closed** *1 May, Aug, 25 Dec.* **Adm charge.** 🖼 🅰 📷

THE FORMER CHURCH of San Pancrazio has been turned into a museum devoted to the work of Italy's best known abstract artist, Marino Marini (1901–80). Marini was born in Pistoia, where more of his work can be seen in the Palazzo del Comune and in the newly opened Centro Marino Marini (*see p182*). Marini studied art in Florence before moving on to teaching in Monza and at the prestigious Brera Academy in Milan. He is noted for rugged and elemental bronzes, many of them on the theme of horse and rider, which express a range of moods and experiences, from sombre weariness to joyous eroticism.

San Pancrazio itself is one of the oldest churches in Florence. It was founded in

Bronze statue, *Cavaliere* (1949), by Marini in the Museo Marino Marini

the 9th century, though its most attractive features are from the Renaissance period, including a graceful Classical façade and porch (1461–7) by Leon Battista Alberti.

San Pancrazio was the parish church of the wealthy merchant Giovanni Rucellai. Inside, in the Cappella di San Sepolcro, built by Alberti in 1467, is Rucellai's tomb, which is modelled on the Holy Sepulchre in Jerusalem (the tomb of Christ).

Palazzo Rucellai ❷

Via della Vigna Nuova 16. **Map** 1 C5 (5 B2). **Archivio Alinari** *open 9am–6pm Mon–Fri.*

BUILT IN 1446–57, this is one of the most ornate Renaissance palaces in the city. It was commissioned by Giovanni Rucellai, whose wealth derived from the family business, the import of a rare and costly red dye made from a lichen found only on Majorca. The dye was called *oricello*, from which the name Rucellai is derived.

Giovanni commissioned several buildings from the architect Leon Battista Alberti, who went on to write the influential treatise on architecture called *De Re Aedificatoria* (Concerning Architecture) in 1452. He designed this palace almost as a textbook illustration of the major Classical orders. In ascending order of complexity, the pilaster strips on the ground floor are Doric, those above are Ionic and those on the top floor are Corinthian.

Two symbols are carved into the entablature: the Rucellai's billowing sails of Fortune and the ring symbol of the Medici family. The ring is a reminder that Bernardo Rucellai formed an alliance with the Medici in the 1460s by marrying Lorenzo de' Medici's sister, Lucrezia. The Loggia del Rucellai, opposite the palace, was built to commemorate the marriage.

The palazzo used to house the Museo Alinari, but the collection has been moved to Largo Fratelli Alinari 15 and is now known as the Archivio Alinari. The Alinari brothers began taking pictures of Florence in the 1840s, not long after the invention of photography. The firm they set up in 1852 specialized in supplying top-quality prints, postcards and art books to foreigners on the Grand Tour who flocked to the city during the 19th century. Today, this archive of their photographs provides a fascinating insight into the social history of Florence over the last 150 years.

19th-century view of Lungarno degli Acciaiuoli, from Palazzo Rucellai

Via della Vigna Nuova ❸

Map 3 B1 (5 B3).

REFLECTING ITS ASSOCIATIONS with wealthy Renaissance Florentines, such as the Rucellai, Via della Vigna Nuova, like nearby Via de' Tornabuoni, has a number of fashionable clothes shops. All the major Italian designers can be found, as well as smaller shops selling quality silks, cashmeres and lingerie. Among the top names doing business are Enrico Coveri (No. 27–29r), Gucci (No. 11r), Dolce & Gabbana (No. 25r), Valentino (No. 47r) and Versus-Versace (No. 38r).

Armani shop, Via della Vigna Nuova

Via de' Tornabuoni ❹

Map 1 C5 (5 C2).

VIA DE' TORNABUONI is the most elegant shopping street in Florence. Leading jewellers and couturiers have boutiques here, including Salvatore Ferragamo (No. 14r), Max Mara (No. 19r), Enrico Coveri (No. 81r), Gucci (No. 73r), Prada for men (No. 67r), Prada for women (No. 53r), Armani (No. 48/50r), Bulgari (No. 61r), Cartier (No. 40r) and Damiani (No. 30r). Further up the road is the excellent Seeber bookshop (No. 68r), founded in 1865 for the expatriate community and still selling publications in English and many other languages.

THE BIGGEST PALAZZO IN FLORENCE

The Strozzi family were exiled from Florence in 1434 for their opposition to the Medici, but in 1466 the banker Filippo Strozzi, having built up a fortune in Naples, returned to the city, determined to outdo his great rivals. He became a man obsessed. For years he bought up and demolished other palaces around his home. At last, he acquired enough land to achieve his ambition: to build the biggest palace ever seen in

**Filippo Strozzi
(1428–91)**

Florence. Having spent so much money to get this far, nothing was left to chance. Astrologers were brought in to choose the most favourable day on which to lay the foundation stone, and the walls of the monumental palace began to rise in 1489. Two years later Filippo Strozzi was dead, and, though his heirs struggled on with the building, the cost of pursuing Filippo's grandiose vision finally left them penniless and bankrupt.

Palazzo Strozzi ❺

Piazza degli Strozzi. **Map** 3 C1 (5 C3). **Piccolo Museo di Palazzo Strozzi** *closed* for restoration.

THE STROZZI PALACE is awesome because of its sheer size: 15 buildings were demolished to make way for it, and although it is only three storeys high, each floor is as tall as a normal palazzo. The palace was commissioned by the wealthy banker Filippo Strozzi, but he died in 1491, only two years after the foundation stone was laid.

The building was not completed until 1536, and three major architects had a hand in its design – Giuliano da Sangallo, Benedetto da Maiano and Simone del Pollaiuolo (also known as Cronaca). The exterior, built of huge rusticated masonry blocks, remains unspoiled. Look out for the original Renaissance torch-holders, lamps and rings for tethering horses, which adorn the corners and façades.

To the left of the courtyard entrance, the Piccolo Museo di Palazzo Strozzi explains the building's history through models and drawings. The elegance of the courtyard itself has been destroyed by a huge iron fire escape, constructed when the building was converted to a major exhibition venue. The Biennale dell'Antiquariato, one of Italy's biggest antique fairs, is held here every alternate year in September–October (*see p34*).

The palace also houses various learned institutes and an excellent library, the Gabinetto Vieusseux, named after the 19th-century Swiss scholar Gian Pietro Vieusseux. He founded a scientific and literary association in 1818, which was attended by, among others, the French author Stendhal.

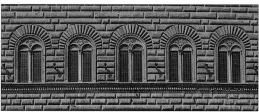

Exterior of Palazzo Strozzi, with masonry block rustication

Ponte Vecchio 🟘

T HE PONTE VECCHIO, or Old Bridge –
indeed, the oldest bridge in
Florence – was built in 1345. It was
the only bridge in the city to escape
being blown up during World War II.
There have always been workshops
on the bridge, but the butchers,
tanners and blacksmiths who were
here originally (and who used the river
as a convenient rubbish tip) were
evicted by Duke Ferdinando I in 1593
because of the noise and stench they
created. The workshops were
rebuilt and let to the more
decorous goldsmiths, and
the shops lining and overhanging the bridge continue
to specialize in new and
antique jewellery to this day.

Private Corridor
*The aerial corridor
built by Vasari along
the eastern side of the
bridge is hung with
the self-portraits of
many great artists,
including Rembrandt,
Rubens and Hogarth.*

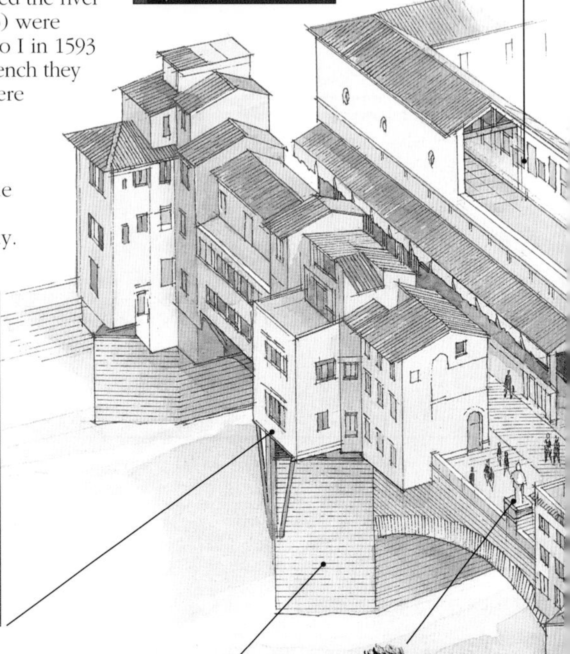

Medieval Workshops
*Some of the oldest work-
shops have rear extensions
overhanging the river,
supported by timber
brackets called* sporti.

**The three-arched
medieval bridge** rests
on two stout piers with
boat-shaped cutwaters.

VASARI'S CORRIDOR

The Corridoio Vasariano
was built in 1565 by Giorgio
Vasari, court architect to the
Medici dukes. The elevated
corridor links the Palazzo
Vecchio to the Palazzo Pitti,
via the Uffizi. This private
walkway allowed members of
the Medici family to move
about between their various
residences, admiring the
paintings on the corridor's
walls, without having to
step into the street below and
mix with the crowds.

Palazzo Vecchio

The Uffizi

Ponte
Vecchio

Arno

Palazzo Pitti

Bust of Cellini
*A bust of Benvenuto Cellini
(1500–71), the most famous
of all Florentine goldsmiths,
was placed in the middle of
the bridge in 1900.*

★ Bridge at Sunset
*The Ponte Vecchio is especially attractive when viewed
in the setting sun from Ponte Santa Trinità, or from
one of the river embankments.*

VISITORS' CHECKLIST

Map 3 C1 (5 C4). 🚌 *B,D.
Pedestrian area.*

★ Jewellers' Shops
*The shops sell everything
from affordable modern
earrings to precious
antique rings.*

Mannelli Tower
*This medieval tower was built
to defend the bridge. The
Mannelli family stubbornly
refused to demolish it to make
way for the Vasari Corridor.*

**The Vasari
Corridor**, supported
on brackets, circumvents
the Mannelli tower.

**Circular
windows** called
oculi (eyes) light
the corridor.

Viewpoint
*There are few better places
for enjoying the river views;
buskers, portrait painters
and street traders congregate
on the bridge, adding to the
colour and bustle.*

STAR FEATURES

★ Jewellers' Shops

★ Bridge at Sunset

Piazza di Santa Trinità

Piazza di Santa Trinità ❻

Map 3C1 (5C3).

Noble palazzi line this busy square. To the south is the Palazzo Spini-Ferroni, originally built in 1290 but much rebuilt in the 19th century; today the ground floor houses the famous boutique of Salvatore Ferragamo *(see p266)*, specializing in shoes and leather goods. To the north, on the corner with Via delle Terme, is the Palazzo Bartolini-Salimbeni. Built during 1520–29, it is one of the city's best examples of High Renaissance architecture. In between the two palazzi is a column of oriental granite originally from the Baths of Caracalla in Rome and given to Cosimo I by Pope Pius IV in 1560. The figure of Justice on top was made in 1581.

Just south of the square is the Ponte Santa Trinità, considered the most beautiful bridge in Florence. It affords fine views of the surrounding hills and especially the Ponte Vecchio *(see pp106–7)*. It was originally built in wood in 1252, and then rebuilt by Ammannati in 1567 as a monument to Cosimo I's defeat of Siena. Michelangelo is credited with the elegant design, based on an intriguing elliptical curve echoing those on the famous Medici tombs *(see p91)*. The statues of the Four Seasons at each end were added in 1608 for Cosimo II's marriage to Maria of Austria. The bridge was restored after it was blown up by the Germans in 1944, and the statues were dredged up from the river bed.

Look west from here to the golden-yellow Palazzo Corsini (1648–56), with statues on the roof balustrade. It is one of the best examples of Baroque architecture in Florence.

Santa Trinità ❼

Piazza di Santa Trinità. **Map** 3 C1 (5 C3). ☎ 055 21 69 12. **Open** 8am–noon, 4–6pm Mon–Sat, 4–6pm Sun. 📷 ♿

The nave of Santa Trinità

The original church, built in the second half of the 11th century by the Vallombrosan monastic order, was very plain – a reflection of the austerity of the order, which was founded in Florence in 1092 to restore the simplicity of monastic rule. Gradually, the building became more ornate, with a Baroque façade added in 1593. Inside, the east wall shows traces of its Romanesque predecessor.

Ghirlandaio's frescoes in the Sassetti Chapel (right of the High Altar) show what the church looked like in 1483–6. In one scene St Francis of Assisi performs a miracle in the Piazza di Santa Trinità, with the church and the Palazzo Spini-Ferroni in the background. The donors of the chapel, Francesco Sassetti and his wife Nera Corsi, are portrayed on either side of the altar. In another scene, St Francis is receiving the Rule of the Franciscan order from Pope

Ponte Santa Trinità

Honorius III in the Piazza della Signoria. Sassetti, who was general manager of the Medici bank, is shown with his son, Teodoro, and with Lorenzo de' Medici to his right, along with Antonio Pucci. Lorenzo's sons are climbing up steps with their tutors, led by the Humanist scholar Agnolo Poliziano, or Politian. The altar painting, *The Adoration of the Shepherds* (1485), is also by Ghirlandaio; he is the first, dark-haired shepherd. The black sarcophagi of Sassetti and his wife are by Giuliano da Sangallo.

Santi Apostoli 🕽

Piazza del Limbo. **Map** 3 C1 (5 C4). 📞 055 29 06 42. **Open** 10am–noon, 4–7pm daily. ⌀

T HE LITTLE CHURCH of the Holy Apostles is, along with the Baptistry, among the oldest surviving churches in Florence. Florentines like to think that the church was founded in 800 AD by the first Holy Roman Emperor, Charlemagne, but it more likely dates to 1059–1100. The church has a simple Romanesque façade and the basilican plan typical of early Christian churches, but with 16th-century side aisles.

Santi Apostoli fronts Piazza del Limbo, so called because there was a cemetery here for infants who died before they were baptized. Hence, according to medieval theology, their souls dwelt in limbo – halfway between heaven and hell.

Della Robbia glazed terracotta tabernacle in Santi Apostoli

Ponte Vecchio 🕘

See pp106–7.

Fresco in a bedroom in the Palazzo Davanzati

Palazzo Davanzati 🕙

Via Porta Rossa 13. **Map** 3 C1 (5 C3). 📞 055 238 86 10. **Open** partially; 8:30am–1:50pm daily. **Closed** 1 Jan, 1 May, 25 Dec, 1st, 3rd & 5th Mon and 2nd & 4th Sun of the month.

A LSO KNOWN as the Museo dell'Antica Casa Fiorentina, the Palazzo Davanzati is preserved as a typical house of wealthy Florentines of the 14th century. Unfortunately, due to structural problems, the main museum is currently closed to the public. However, a small exhibition, including photographs and a few items from the museum, has been organized in the entrance of the building. The entrance courtyard was designed to trap unwanted visitors; pelting holes in the vaulted ceiling were used for dropping missiles. In the more peaceful inner courtyard, a staircase links all the floors. In one corner is a well and a pulley system so buckets of water could be raised to each floor – this ingenious mechanism was quite a luxury since most households had to fetch all their water from a public fountain.

The main living room on the first floor looks plain, but hooks beneath the ceiling show that the walls would have been hung with tapestries. Many rooms have bathrooms attached, and are decorated with frescoes of scenes from a French romance.

Palazzo di Parte Guelfa 🕚

Piazza di Parte Guelfa. **Map** 3 C1 (6 D3). **Closed** to the public.

T HIS CHARACTERFUL building served as the headquarters of the Guelph party and the residence of its captains from around 1266, after the Guelphs began to emerge as the stronger of the two medieval factions struggling for control over Florence. In the complex politics of the period, the Guelphs supported the Pope and the Ghibellines took the side of the Holy Roman Emperor in the dispute over who should rule northern Italy *(see p44).*

The lower part of the building dates to the 13th century, but the upper part was added by Brunelleschi in 1431. There are *stemmae* (coats-of-arms) under the crenellations. The elegant open staircase, added in 1589, is by Vasari.

Emblem of the Guelphs

Santa Maria Novella ⓱

THE GOTHIC CHURCH of Santa Maria Novella contains some of the most important works of art in Florence. The church was built by the Dominicans from 1279 to 1357. Beside the church is a cemetery walled in with *avelli* (grave niches), which continue along the façade and the wall beyond. The cloisters form a museum. Here, the frescoes in the Spanish Chapel show the Dominicans as whippets – *domini canes* or hounds of God – rounding up the "stray sheep".

Green Cloister
The name comes from the green tinge to Uccello's Noah and the Flood frescoes, unfortunately damaged by the 1966 floods.

Monastic buildings

★ Spanish Chapel
The chapel used by the Spanish courtiers of Eleonora of Toledo, the wife of Cosimo I (see p49), has dramatic frescoes on the theme of salvation and damnation.

★ The Trinity
Masaccio's pioneering work is a masterpiece of perspective and portraiture (see p24).

Entrance to museum

Entrance

The billowing sail emblem of the Rucellai *(see p104)* appears on the façade because they paid for its completion in 1470.

Alberti added the volutes in 1458–70 to hide the roofs over the side chapels.

Strozzi Chapel

The 14th-century frescoes by Nardo di Cione and his brother, Andrea Orcagna, were inspired by Dante's epic poem, The Divine Comedy. *Dante himself is portrayed in the* Paradise *fresco on the left, along with members of the Strozzi family.*

VISITORS' CHECKLIST

Piazza di Santa Maria Novella.
Map 1 B5 (5 B1). ☎ *055 21 59 18 (church), 055 28 21 87 (museum).* 🚌 *A, 6, 11, 12, 36, 37.* **Church Open** *9:30am–5:30pm Mon–Thu; 1–5:30pm Fri–Sun.* ✝ *7:30am, 8:30am, 6pm Mon–Sat; 8:30am, 10:30am, noon, 6pm Sun & religious hols.* **Adm charge**.
📷 ♿ **Museum Open** *9am–2pm Sat–Thu (last adm: 30 mins before closing).* **Closed** *1 Jan, Easter Sun, 1 May, 25 Dec.* **Adm charge**. 🚫 ♿

The arcade arches are emphasized by grey and white banding.

★ Tornabuoni Chapel

Ghirlandaio's famous fresco cycle, The Life of John the Baptist *(1485), portrays Florentine aristocrats and contemporary costumes and furnishings. Opposite is his other masterpiece,* The Life of the Virgin.

★ Filippo Strozzi Chapel

Filippino Lippi's dramatic frescoes show St John raising Drusiana from the dead and St Philip slaying a dragon. Boccaccio set the beginning of The Decameron *in this chapel.*

The walls of the old cemetery are decorated with the emblems and badges of wealthy Florentines.

Interior

The nave piers are spaced closer at the east end to create the illusion of an exceptionally long church.

STAR FEATURES

★ **The Trinity by Masaccio**

★ **Filippo Strozzi Chapel**

★ **Tornabuoni Chapel**

★ **Spanish Chapel**

Mercato Nuovo ⑫

Map 3 C1 (6 D3). **Open** Apr–Oct:
9am–7pm daily; Nov–Mar: 9am–7pm
Tue–Sat.

THE MERCATO NUOVO (New Market) is sometimes called the "Straw Market" because goods woven out of straw, such as hats and baskets, were sold here from the end of the 19th century until the 1960s. In fact, it was originally built in 1547–51 as a central market for silk and other luxury goods. Today's stallholders sell leather goods and souvenirs, and on summer evenings buskers gather to entertain visitors.

To the south of the market is a little fountain called Il Porcellino. This is a 17th-century copy in bronze of a Roman marble statue of a wild boar that can be seen in the Uffizi. Its snout gleams like gold, thanks to the superstition that any visitor who rubs it will return to Florence some day. Coins dropped in the water basin below are collected and distributed to the city's charities.

Bronze boar in Mercato Nuovo

Piazza della Repubblica ⑬

Map 1 C5 (6 D3).

UNTIL 1890, when the present square was laid out, this had been the site of the Mercato Vecchio (Old Market) and before that of the ancient Roman forum. A single column from the old market still stands on the square, topped by an 18th-century statue of Abundance. Dominating the western side of the square is a triumphal arch built in 1895 to celebrate

One of the many pavement cafés in Piazza della Repubblica

the fact that Florence was then the capital of Italy. The demolition of the Old Market was intended as the first step in a wholesale remodelling of Florence, but leading members of the English community led an international campaign opposing this grand scheme, which would have led to the destruction of almost every historic building in the city centre. Fortunately, the campaign was successful and the demolition halted.

The square, popular with both tourists and locals, is lined with pavement cafés, such as the very smart Gilli (No. 39r) or the Giubbe Rosse (No. 13–14r), so called because of the red jackets of the waiters. In the early part of this century, the Giubbe Rosse was the haunt of writers and artists, including those of Italy's avant-garde Futurist movement. Rinascente, one of Florence's department stores *(see p269)*, is on the eastern side of the square.

Palazzo Antinori ⑭

Piazza Antinori 3. **Map** 1 C5 (5 C2).
Closed to the public. **Cantinetta
Antinori** [055 29 22 34.
Open 12:30–2:30pm, 7–10:30pm
Mon–Fri. 🍴 ♿

THE PALAZZO ANTINORI, originally the Palazzo Boni e Martelli, was built in 1461–6 and with its elegant courtyard is considered one of the finest small Renaissance *palazzi* of Florence. It was

acquired by the Antinori family in 1506 and has remained with them since.

The family owns large and productive estates all over Tuscany and in the neighbouring region of Umbria, producing a range of well-regarded wines, olive oils and liqueurs. You can sample these in the frescoed wine bar to the right of the courtyard, the Cantinetta Antinori.

The wine bar also specializes in typical Tuscan cuisine, with dishes such as *crostini alla toscana,* together with traditional cheeses and a range of other produce from the Antinori estates.

Via dei Fossi ⑮

Map 1 B5 (5 B3).

Shop in Via dei Fossi selling reproduction statuary

VIA DEI FOSSI and the nearby streets contain some of the most absorbing shops in Florence, many of them specializing in antiques and works of art and statuary, and in classic Florentine products. Bottega Artigiana del Libro (Lungarno Corsini 40r) stocks handmade marbled papers, albums, notebooks and carnival masks. Fallani Best (Borgo Ognissanti 15r) has Art Nouveau and Art Deco furnishings and sculpture, and Antonio Frilli (Via dei Fossi 26r) specializes in marble sculpture – original Art Nouveau works and copies of famous Renaissance pieces. Neri (Via dei Fossi 57r) also sells top-quality antiques and G Lisio (Via dei Fossi 41r), makes handwoven tapestries and rich Renaissance-style fabrics. Attached to the convent of the same name, the frescoed Farmacia di Santa Maria Novella (Via della Scala 16r) dates to the 16th century and sells toiletries and liqueurs made by Dominican monks.

Ognissanti

Borgo Ognissanti 42. **Map** 1 B5 (5 A2). (055 239 87 00. **Open** 8:30am–12:30pm, 3:30–5:30pm Mon–Fri; 9:30–10:30am, 3:30–5pm Sat; 9:30–10:30am, 3:30–6pm Sun. **Closed** first and last Mon of month. 🚫 ♿ **Cenacolo del Ghirlandaio open** 9am–noon Mon, Tue & Sat (348 645 03 90).

THE CHURCH of All Saints, or Ognissanti, was the parish church of the merchant family of the Vespucci, one of whose members, the 15th-century navigator Amerigo, gave his name to the New World. Amerigo is depicted in Ghirlandaio's fresco of the *Madonna della Misericordia* (1472) in the second chapel on the right.

Amerigo Vespucci was the first to realize that the land discovered by Columbus was a new continent, not the eastern shore of the Indies. He made two voyages following

The cloister of Ognissanti with 17th-century frescoes

Columbus's route and, because his letters enabled cartographers to draw the first maps *(see p75)* of the new land, it was given his name.

Ognissanti is also the burial place of Sandro Botticelli. His fresco of *St Augustine* (1480) can be seen on the south wall. It is complemented by Ghirlandaio's *St Jerome* (1480) on the opposite wall.

Alongside the church is a cloister and refectory, containing Ghirlandaio's fresco *The Last Supper* (1480), with its background of birds and trees.

Santa Maria Novella 🛈

See pp110–11.

Stazione di Santa Maria Novella 🛈

Map 1 B4 (5 B1). **Closed** 1:30–4:15am daily. **Train information open** 7am–9pm daily. **Market open** 9:30am–8pm daily. 🛈 **open** 8:30am–5:30pm Mon–Sat. (055 21 22 45. **Bank open** 8:20am–1:20pm, 2:45–3:45 Mon–Fri. **Chemist open** 24 hours. 🚻

THE CENTRAL RAILWAY STATION is considered one of the finest examples of modern architecture in Italy *(see p55)*. It was designed in 1935 by a group of young Tuscan artists, including Giovanni Michelucci and Piero Berardi, who subscribed to the "Functionalist" view that the form of a building should reflect the purpose for which it was built.

Ghirlandaio's *Madonna della Misericordia* (1472) in Ognissanti, with the boy Amerigo Vespucci

OLTRARNO

Oltrarno means "over the Arno", and living on the south bank of the river was once considered inferior. Here lived people who did not have sufficient wealth to build a palazzo within the city centre. That stigma did not change until the household of the Medici Grand Dukes moved to Oltrarno in 1550.

MEDICI POWER BASE

The Palazzo Pitti became the base from which Tuscany was ruled for the next 300 years. Eleonora di Toledo, the Spanish wife of Cosimo I, purchased the Palazzo Pitti in 1549. Suffering from a wasting disease, perhaps malaria or tuberculosis, Eleonora persuaded Cosimo that her health might well improve if they lived in the relatively rural setting of Oltrarno. Over the years the Palazzo Pitti

Statue, Museo Bardini

increased almost threefold in size in comparison with the original plans, and the Boboli Gardens were laid out on the land around it. A few Florentine aristocrats followed the Medici lead and moved across the river to make their homes here. In the late 16th and 17th centuries, many palazzi were built in the area surrounding Via Maggio and Piazza di Santo Spirito. Today, this is primarily a quiet area full of artisan workshops and antique shops, contrasting with the elegant palazzi and the unfinished austere façade of Santo Spirito. The local merchants' association organizes guided tours, events and fairs to expose visitors to the artisan treasures on the south bank. It is a fascinating area to wander around and discover the true character of Florence.

SIGHTS AT A GLANCE

Churches
Brancacci Chapel pp126–7 ⑩
Santa Felicità ⑤
San Frediano in Cestello ⑪
Santo Spirito ①

Museums and Galleries
Cenacolo di Santo Spirito ②
Museo Bardini ⑧
Museo "La Specola" ⑨
Palazzo Pitti pp120–21 ⑥

Streets and Piazzas
Piazza di Santo Spirito ③
Via Maggio ④

Gardens
Boboli Gardens pp124–5 ⑦

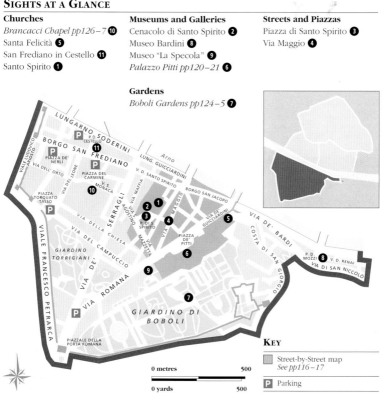

KEY

| | Street-by-Street map |
| --- | See pp116–17 |

P Parking

0 metres 500
0 yards 500

◁ **Rooftops of the Oltrarno and the spire and dome of Santo Spirito**

Street-by-Street: Oltrarno

Medici coat of arms

Fᴏʀ ᴛʜᴇ ᴍᴏsᴛ ᴘᴀʀᴛ, the Oltrarno area consists of relatively small houses and shops selling antiques, bric-à-brac and foodstuffs. The Via Maggio breaks this pattern, with its numerous imposing 16th-century palazzi close to the Medici's Palazzo Pitti. As it is one of the main routes into the city, the road is busy and there is constant traffic noise. Step into the side streets, however, and you escape the noise and bustle to discover traditional Florence; restaurants are authentic and reasonably priced, and the area is full of workshops restoring antique furniture.

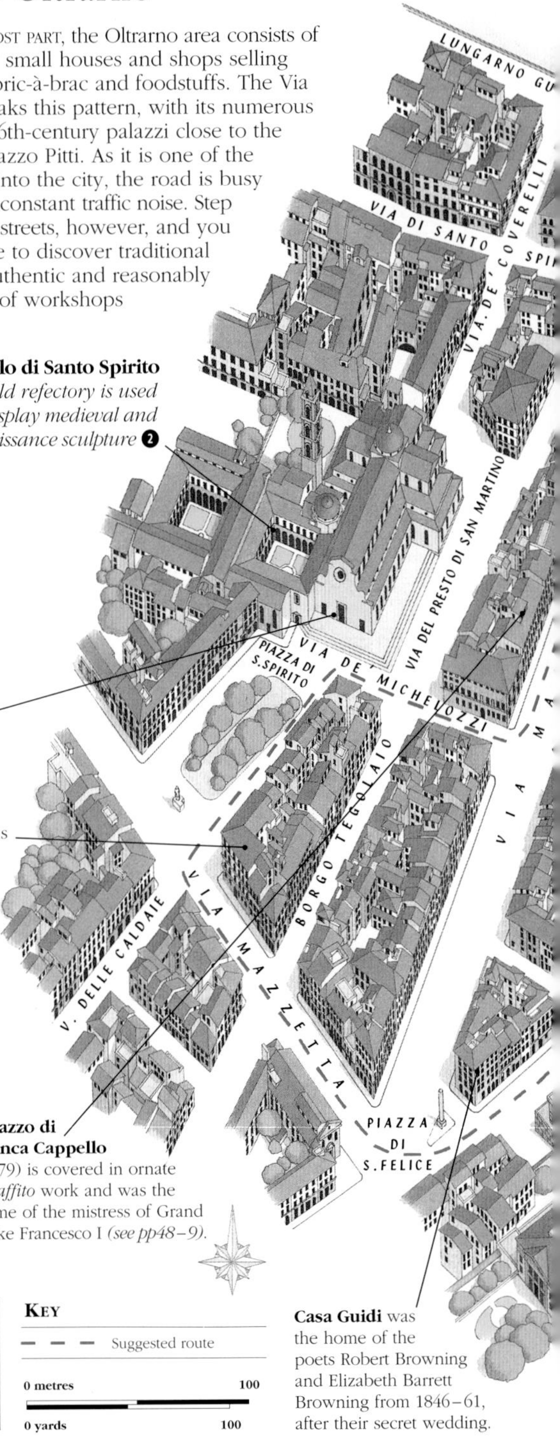

Cenacolo di Santo Spirito
The old refectory is used to display medieval and Renaissance sculpture ❷

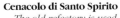

Santo Spirito
Simplicity is the keynote of Brunelleschi's last church. It was completed after his death in 1446 ❶

Palazzo Guadagni (1500) was the first in the city to be built with a rooftop loggia, setting a trend among the aristocracy.

Palazzo di Bianca Cappello (1579) is covered in ornate *sgraffito* work and was the home of the mistress of Grand Duke Francesco I *(see pp48–9).*

Casa Guidi was the home of the poets Robert Browning and Elizabeth Barrett Browning from 1846–61, after their secret wedding.

Sᴛᴀʀ Sɪɢʜᴛs
★ **Palazzo Pitti**
★ **Boboli Gardens**

Kᴇʏ

– – – Suggested route

0 metres   100

0 yards   100

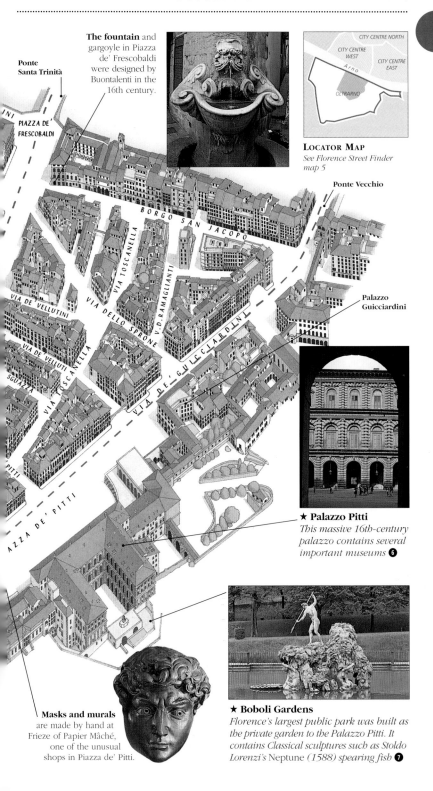

The fountain and gargoyle in Piazza de' Frescobaldi were designed by Buontalenti in the 16th century.

LOCATOR MAP
See Florence Street Finder map 5

Ponte Santa Trinità

PIAZZA DE' FRESCOBALDI

Ponte Vecchio

BORGO SAN JACOPO

VIA TOSCANELLA

VIA DELLO SPRONE

V. D. RAMAGLIANTI

VIA DE' VELLUTINI

VIA DE' VELLUTI

VIA TOSCANELLA

SGUAZZA

PITTI

AZZA DE' PITTI

VIA DE' GUICCIARDINI

Palazzo Guicciardini

★ **Palazzo Pitti**
This massive 16th-century palazzo contains several important museums **6**

Masks and murals are made by hand at Frieze of Papier Mâché, one of the unusual shops in Piazza de' Pitti.

★ **Boboli Gardens**
Florence's largest public park was built as the private garden to the Palazzo Pitti. It contains Classical sculptures such as Stoldo Lorenzi's Neptune *(1588) spearing fish* **7**

Santo Spirito ❶

Piazza di Santo Spirito. **Map** 3 B2 (5 A4).
🚻 D. 📞 055 21 00 30. **Open** 8am–
noon, 4–6pm Mon, Tue, Thu, Fri;
8:30am–noon Wed; 4–6pm Sat &
Sun. 🚫

T HE AUGUSTINIAN foundation
of this church dates from
1250. The present building has
an unfinished 18th-century
façade, which dominates the
northern end of Piazza di Santo
Spirito. Brunelleschi designed
the church in 1435, but it was
not completed until the late
1400s, well after his death.

Inside, the harmony of the
proportions has been somewhat spoiled by the elaborate
Baroque baldacchino and the
High Altar, which was finished
in 1607 by Giovanni Caccini.
The church has 38 side altars,
decorated with 15th- and 16th-
century Renaissance paintings
and sculpture, among them
works by Cosimo Rosselli,
Domenico Ghirlandaio and
Filippino Lippi. The latter
painted a *Madonna and
Child* (1466) for the Nerli
Chapel in the south transept.

In the north aisle, a door
beneath the organ leads to
a vestibule with an ornate
coffered ceiling. It was
designed by Simone del
Pollaiuolo, more commonly
known as Cronaca, in 1491.
The sacristy adjoining the
vestibule was designed by
Giuliano da Sangallo in 1489.

Cenacolo di Santo Spirito ❷

Piazza di Santo Spirito 29. **Map** 3 B1
(5 B4). 📞 055 28 70 43. **Open**
10:30am–1:30pm Tue–Sat (last adm:
30 mins before closing). **Closed** Mon;
1 Jan, Easter Sun, 1 May, 15 Aug, 25
Dec. **Adm charge**. 🚫 📷

A LL THAT SURVIVES of the
monastery that stood
next to Santo Spirito is the
refectory (*cenacolo*), now a
small museum. Inside is a
fresco, *The Crucifixion*
(1360–65), attributed to the
followers of Andrea Orcagna
and his brother Nardo di
Cione. In a city that has a
wealth of Renaissance art,
this is a rare and beautiful
example of High Gothic
religious work.

The Fondazione Salvatore
Romano, a collection of 11th-
century Romanesque sculpture,
is displayed in the refectory.

The façade of Palazzo Guadagni

Piazza di Santo Spirito ❸

Map 3 B2 (5 A4). 🚻 D. 🛗 2nd
(Antiques) & 3rd (Health) Sun of month.

T HIS PART OF FLORENCE is best
appreciated by wandering
around the square and its
market, looking at the many
furniture restorers' workshops
and medieval palazzi. The
biggest house in the square is
the Palazzo Guadagni at No.
10, on the corner with Via
Mazzetta. It was built around
1505, probably to the designs
of Cronaca. The windows
have distinctive stone
surrounds with tear-drop
shaped keystones. The top
floor forms an open loggia,
the first of its kind to be built
in the city. The loggia set a
fashion among 16th-century
Florentine aristocrats, who
incorporated the design into
their own palazzi.

Via Maggio ❹

Map 3 B2 (5 B5).

O PENED IN THE mid-13th
century, this road became
a fashionable residential area
after the Medici Grand Dukes
moved to the Palazzo Pitti in
1550 (*see pp120–21*). It is
lined with 15th- and 16th-
century palazzi, such as the
Palazzo Ricasoli at No. 7, and
antique shops. Via Maggio
runs into Piazza di San Felice,
where a plaque marks the
Casa Guidi. The English poets
Elizabeth and Robert Browning
rented an apartment here
after eloping in 1847. Inspired
by Tuscan art and landscape,
this is where they wrote
much of their best poetry.

Colonnaded aisle in Santo Spirito

The Virgin from *The Annunciation* (1528) by Pontormo

Santa Felicità ❺

Piazza di Santa Felicità. **Map** 3 C2 (5 C5). 📞 055 21 30 18. **Open** 9am–noon, 3–6pm Mon–Sat, 4:30–6pm Sun. 🚫 ♿

A CHURCH HAS STOOD on this site since the 4th century AD, but the current building dates from the 11th century. It was extensively remodelled by Ferdinando Ruggieri in 1736–9, but some original Gothic features and the porch added by Vasari in 1564 were retained.

The Capponi family chapel to the right of the entrance houses two masterpieces by Mannerist artist Jacopo da Pontormo: *The Annunciation* and *The Deposition*. Painted in 1525–8, the frescoes make use of vivid colours such as light green, salmon pink, apricot and gold. The roundels around the base of the ceiling vault depict the Four Evangelists, also painted by Pontormo, with help from his pupil Agnolo Bronzino.

Palazzo Pitti ❻

See pp120–23.

Boboli Gardens ❼

See pp124–5.

Museo Bardini ❽

Piazza de' Mozzi 1. **Map** 4 D2 (6 E5). 📞 055 234 24 27. **Open** at irregular hours due to restoration (call for information). **Closed** 1 Jan, Easter Sun, 1 May, 15 Aug, 25 Dec. **Adm charge.** 🚫

S TEFANO BARDINI WAS a 19th-century antiquarian and avid collector of architectural materials – mostly salvaged from the churches and palazzi demolished when the Piazza della Repubblica was built in the 1860s *(see p112)*. In 1883 he built his palazzo in Piazza de' Mozzi almost entirely from recycled medieval and Renaissance masonry, including carved doorways, chimney pieces and staircases as well as painted and coffered ceilings. The rooms are full of sculpture, statues, paintings, armour, musical instruments, ceramics and antique furnishings. In 1922 this collection of antiquities was bequeathed to the people of Florence.

Museo Bardini, Piazza de' Mozzi

Museo "La Specola" ❾

Via Romana 17. **Map** 3 B2 (5 B5). 📞 055 22 88 251. **Open** 9am–1pm Thu–Tue. **Closed** public hols. 📷 📹 *in English, on request.* **Adm charge.**

T HIS UNUSUAL museum is in the Palazzo Rottigiani, built in 1775 and now used by the natural science faculty of Florence University. The name "la Specola" refers to the observatory built on the roof of the building by Grand Duke Pietro Leopoldo in the late 18th century. It now contains the museum, which has a zoological section exhibiting vast numbers of preserved animals, insects and fish, and an anatomical section with some extremely realistic 18th-century wax models showing various grotesque aspects of human physiology and disease.

Brancacci Chapel ❿

See pp126–7.

San Frediano in Cestello ⓫

Piazza di Cestello. **Map** 3 B1 (5 A3). 🚌 D, 6. 📞 055 21 58 16. **Open** 9–11:30am, 4:30–6pm Mon–Sat, 5–6:30pm Sun. 📷

T HE SAN FREDIANO area, with its small, low houses, has long been associated with the wool and leather industries. The parish church of San Frediano in Cestello stands beside the Arno looking across the river. It has a bare stone exterior with a large dome that is a local landmark. It was rebuilt on the site of an older church in 1680–89 by Antonio Maria Ferri: the fresco and stuccowork inside are typical of the late 17th and early 18th centuries. Nearby is a well-preserved stretch of the 14th-century city walls. The Porta San Frediano, built in 1324, has a tower overlooking the road to Pisa. Its wooden doors have retained their original 14th-century locks and detailed ironwork.

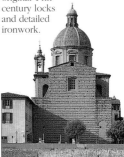

The dome and plain façade of San Frediano in Cestello

Palazzo Pitti ❻

T HE PALAZZO PITTI, begun in 1457, was
originally built for the banker Luca Pitti.
Its huge scale showed Pitti's determination
to outrival the Medici family. Ironically, they
later bought the palazzo when building costs
bankrupted Pitti's heirs. In 1550 it became
the main Medici residence and subsequently
all Florentine rulers lived here. Today the
richly decorated rooms exhibit treasures
from the Medici collections (see pp122–3)
and the Habsburg-Lorraine court.

Inner Courtyard
*Ammannati designed the courtyard in
1560–70. The Artichoke Fountain by
Francesco Susini (1641) was topped by
a bronze artichoke, since lost.*

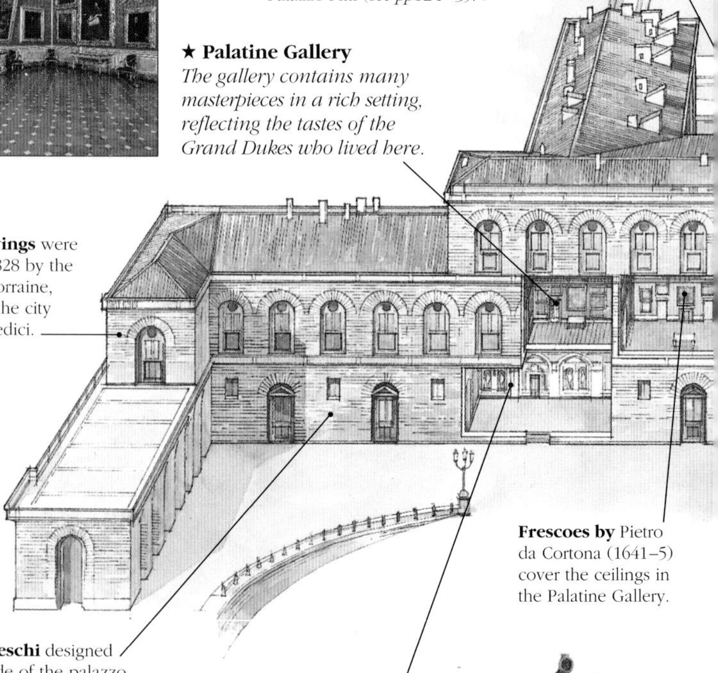

The Boboli Gardens were
laid out where stone had
been quarried to build the
Palazzo Pitti (see pp124–5).

★ Palatine Gallery
*The gallery contains many
masterpieces in a rich setting,
reflecting the tastes of the
Grand Dukes who lived here.*

The side wings were
added in 1828 by the
Dukes of Lorraine,
who ruled the city
after the Medici.

Frescoes by Pietro
da Cortona (1641–5)
cover the ceilings in
the Palatine Gallery.

Brunelleschi designed
the façade of the palazzo,
but it was later extended
to 200 m (650 ft), three
times its original length.

★ Museo degli Argenti
*As well as silverware,
the museum displays
gold, stone and glass-
ware. This view of
Piazza della Signoria (see
pp76–7) is made
of precious stones.*

STAR SIGHTS

★ Palatine Gallery

★ Museo degli Argenti

Galleria d'Arte Moderna
The gallery, on the second floor of the palazzo, spans the years from 1784 to 1924. The Tuscan Maremma (c.1850), by Giovanni Fattori, is a highlight of the collection.

The Carriage Museum offers another glimpse of the sumptuous, opulent life of the dukes.

Galleria del Costume
The clothes reflect changing fashion at the court of the Grand Dukes during the 18th and 19th centuries.

Entrance to museums and galleries

Massive Windows
The windows of the Palazzo Pitti were built to be larger than the main door of the Palazzo Medici Riccardi.

Royal Apartments
The south wing was used for ceremonial occasions and receiving ambassadors.

VISITORS' CHECKLIST

Piazza Pitti. **Map** 3 C2 (5 B5). D, 11, 36, 37. **Palatine Gallery & Royal Apartments** 055 238 86 14. **Open** 8:15am–6:50pm Tue–Sun. **Closed** 25 Dec. **Galleria d'Arte Moderna** 055 238 86 01. **Galleria del Costume** 055 238 87 13. **Museo degli Argenti** 055 238 87 09. **Open** 8:15am–1:50pm daily. **Closed** 2nd & 4th Sun and 1st, 3rd & 5th Mon of the month. **Museo delle Porcellane** (enter via Boboli Gardens, see p125). 055 238 86 05. **Open** 9am–1:30pm daily. **Closed** 1st, 3rd & 5th Mon & 2nd & 4th Sun of every month. **All museums closed** public hols. **Ticket offices close 45 mins before the closing time of the museums. Adm charge** for each museum. **Palatine Gallery** ticket admits to **Royal Apartments**. **Galleria d'Arte Moderna** ticket admits to **Galleria del Costume**.

Exploring the Palazzo Pitti

THE PALATINE GALLERY was realized by the Medici family and the Habsburg-Lorraine duchies in the 1600s and 1700s. The frescoed halls were hung with works from their private collection and the gallery was opened to the public in 1833. Other attractions include the royal apartments, the Medici collection of jewellery and treasures, the gallery of modern art and an exhibition of Italian clothing from the 18th, 19th and 20th centuries.

THE PALATINE GALLERY

THE GALLERY CONTAINS a superb collection of works dating from the Renaissance and Baroque. They are hung as the 17th- and 18th-century Grand Dukes wished, placed purely for their effect, regardless of subject or chronology. The decoration of the rooms in the gallery reflects the tastes and preoccupations of the time. Rooms 4 to 8 are painted with Baroque ceiling frescoes begun by Pietro da Cortona between 1641–7, and finished by his pupil Ciro Ferri in 1666. They allegorize the education of a prince by the gods. In Room 1, the prince is torn from the love of Venus by Minerva (knowledge) and in the following rooms he is taught science from Apollo, war from Mars and leadership from Jupiter. Finally Saturn welcomes him to Mount Olympus, home of the gods in Roman mythology.

The other rooms in the gallery were private apartments and range from the opulence of the formal drawing rooms to the severity of Napoleon's bathroom (Room 27) (*see p53*), in a suite of rooms designed by Giuseppe Cacialli for the emperor in 1813 following his conquest of northern Italy.

***Mary Magdalene* by Titian (c.1535)**

Although some of the Medici collection has been transferred to the Uffizi over the years, the Palatine Gallery is still packed with masterpieces by artists such as Botticelli, Perugino, Titian, Andrea del Sarto, Pontormo, Tintoretto, Veronese, Caravaggio, Rubens and Van Dyck, among others. There are approximately 1,000 paintings here, providing a vast survey of 16th- and 17th-century European painting.

The Sala di Venere (Venus) is dominated by the statue of *Venus Italica* by Antonio Canova, commissioned by Napoleon in 1810 as a replacement for *The Medici Venus* in the Uffizi Gallery, which was to be taken to Paris. Napoleon was not normally so generous, as his agents were renowned for stealing a large number of fine works of art from Italy during the Napoleonic Wars.

Several of Titian's works in the following rooms were commissioned by the Duke of Urbino. *La Bella* (1536) is a portrait of a lovely but unknown woman, whom he also used as a model in other paintings. His portrait, *Mary Magdalene*, in the Sala di Apollo, was painted between 1530–35 in an overtly sensual manner, bathed in soft light.

Some of Raphael's best High Renaissance work is in the Palatine, including *Portrait of a Woman* (c.1516) and

THE PALATINE GALLERY
The gallery is on the first floor of the Palazzo Pitti.

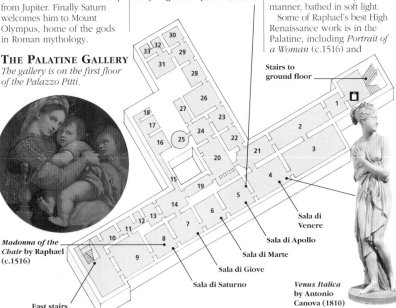

Stairs to ground floor

30
33 32 29
31
28
26
27
18   23
17   24
16 25 22
20
21
15   19
5
14
13
12 11   7   6
10   8
9

Madonna of the Chair by Raphael (c.1516)

Sala di Venere

Sala di Apollo

Sala di Marte

Sala di Giove

Sala di Saturno

East stairs

***Venus Italica* by Antonio Canova (1810)**

Madonna of the Chair (c.1510) in the *tondo* (roundel) form which became very popular during the Renaissance.

The Consequences of War by Peter Paul Rubens (1638) is an allegorical painting of the Thirty Years' War (1618–48), showing Venus preventing Mars from unleashing his fury on the cowering, beleaguered figure of Europe, completely robed in black mourning.

ROYAL APARTMENTS

The Throne Room

T HE ROYAL APARTMENTS on the first floor of the south wing of the palazzo were built in the 17th century. They are decorated with frescoes by various Florentine artists and a series of portraits of the Medici by the Flemish painter Justus Sustermans, who worked at the court between 1619–81. In the late 18th and early 19th centuries, the apartments were completely revamped in Neo-Classical style by the Dukes of Lorraine when they succeeded the Medici dynasty as the rulers of Florence *(see pp52–3)*.

The apartments are lavishly appointed with ornate gold and white stuccowork ceilings and rich decoration, as on the walls of the Parrot Room, which are covered with an opulent crimson fabric detailed with a bird design. The apartments' varied ownership is revealed in their design, which embraces three distinct artistic periods.

MUSEO DEGLI ARGENTI

T HIS MUSEUM is on the ground and mezzanine floors, below the Palatine Gallery, in the rooms used by the Medici as their summer apartments. It displays the massive private wealth of the Medici dynasty: the collection encompasses rare and beautiful examples of ancient Roman glassware, ivory, carpets, crystal and amber and fine works by Florentine and German goldsmiths. The pride of the collection are 16 *pietre dure* vases displayed in the Sala Buia. These belonged to Lorenzo the Magnificent and are from the ancient Roman and Byzantine periods.

14th-century gold and jasper vase

The family's lavish tastes are reflected in the museum's polished ebony furniture inlaid with semi-precious marbles and stones. Portraits of the Medici hang throughout the rooms, including a series of the Grand Duchesses, and Cosimo I and his family carved in an onyx cameo.

GALLERIA D'ARTE MODERNA

H ERE THE PAINTINGS span the period from 1784 to 1924; many of them were collected by the Dukes of Lorraine to decorate the Palazzo Pitti.

The present museum has combined this collection with pictures donated by the state and various private collectors. The museum contains Neo-Classical, Romantic and religious works, but probably the most important collection is of the group of late 19th-century artists known as the *Macchiaioli* (spot-makers), similar to French Impressionists. The *Macchiaioli* used bright splashes of colour to represent the sun-dappled Tuscan landscape. This collection was given to the city of Florence in 1897 by the art critic Diego Martelli, and includes paintings by Giovanni Fattori *(see p121)* and Giovanni Boldini. Two works by Camille Pissarro hang in the same room.

GALLERIA DEL COSTUME

O PENED IN 1983, the gallery is on the ground floor of the Palazzo Meridiana. This was designed in 1776 by Gaspare Maria Paoletti for the Royal Family; they lived until the abolition of the monarchy *(see p50)*. The exhibits reflect the changing tastes in the courtly fashion of the late 18th century up to the 1920s. Some of the rooms have been restored to correspond to a 1911 inventory. The gallery has recently been renovated.

The Italian Camp after the Battle of Magenta (c.1855) by Giovanni Fattori

Boboli Gardens ❼

THE BOBOLI GARDENS were laid out for the Medici after they bought the Palazzo Pitti in 1549. An excellent example of stylized Renaissance gardening, they were opened to the public in 1766. The more formal parts of the garden, nearest the palazzo, consist of box hedges clipped into symmetrical geometric patterns. These lead to wilder groves of ilex and cypress trees, planted to create a contrast between artifice and nature. Statues of varying styles and periods are dotted around, and the vistas were planned to give views over Florence.

★ Amphitheatre
Stone for the Palazzo Pitti was quarried here and the hollow was turned into a stage for the first-ever opera performances.

Kaffeehaus
The Rococo-style pavilion, built in 1776, now houses a coffee house. It is open during the summer and offers beautiful views over the city.

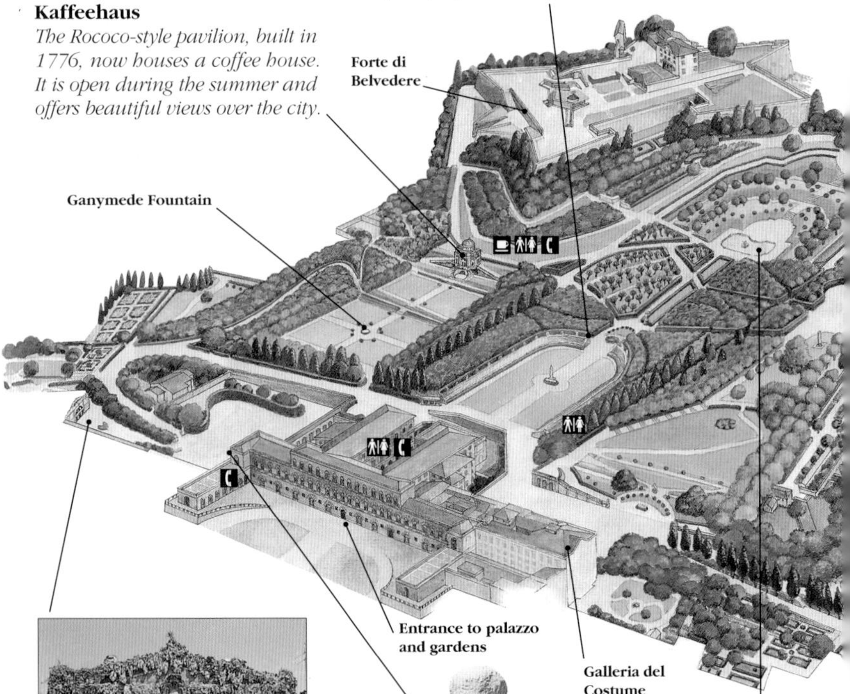

Forte di Belvedere

Ganymede Fountain

Entrance to palazzo and gardens

Galleria del Costume

The Neptune Fountain was built between 1565–8 by Stoldo Lorenzi.

★ La Grotta Grande
The casts of Michelangelo's Quattro Prigioni *(see p94) are built into the walls of this Mannerist folly (1583–8), which also houses Vincenzo de' Rossi's* Paris *with* Helen of Troy *(1560) and* Venus Bathing *(1565) by Giambologna.*

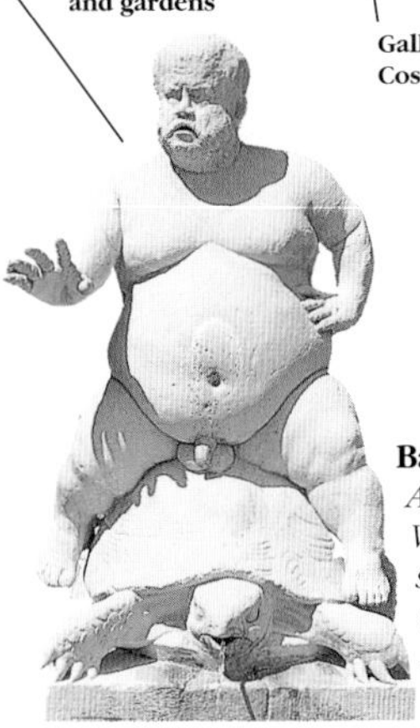

Bacchus Fountain *(1560)*
A copy of the original by Valerio Cioli, the statue shows Pietro Barbino, Cosimo I's court dwarf, as Bacchus, the Roman god of wine, astride a turtle.

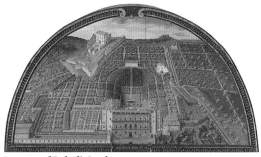

Lunette of Boboli Gardens
The Flemish artist Giusto Utens painted this picture of the Palazzo Pitti and Boboli Gardens in 1599.

VISITORS' CHECKLIST

Piazza de' Pitti. **Map** 3 B2 (5 B5). **Boboli Gardens** 055 265 18 16. D, 11, 36, 37. **Open** Jun–Aug: 8:15am–7:30pm daily; Apr, May, Sep & Oct: 8:15am–6:30pm daily; Nov–Feb: 8:15am–4:30pm daily; Mar: 8:15am–5:30pm daily. **Closed** 1st & 4th Mon of month, 25 Dec, 1 Jan. **Adm charge**. **Galleria del Costume** 055 238 87 13. **Open** 8:30am–2pm Tue–Sun. **Closed** Mon & 2nd Sun of each month. **Adm charge**.

The Porcelain Museum is accessed via the Rose Garden.

Viottolone
The avenue of cypress trees, planted in 1637, is lined with Classical statues.

★ L'Isolotto (Little Island)
Statues of dancing peasants surround the moated garden, with a copy of Giambologna's Oceanus Fountain (1576) as the centrepiece. The original is now in the Bargello (see pp68–9).

Hemicycle (semicircular lawn)

Entrance

Orangery
Zanobi del Rosso's Orangery (1785) was built to protect rare, tender plants from frost.

STAR FEATURES

★ **Amphitheatre**

★ **La Grotta Grande**

★ **L'Isolotto (Little Island)**

Brancacci Chapel ⑩

THE CHURCH of Santa Maria del Carmine is famous for *The Life of St Peter* frescoes in the Brancacci Chapel, commissioned by the Florentine merchant Felice Brancacci around 1424. Masolino began the work in 1425 but many of the scenes are by his pupil, Masaccio, who died before completing the cycle. Filippino Lippi finished the work 50 years later, in 1480. Masaccio's use of perspective in *The Tribute Money* and the tragic realism of his figures in *The Expulsion of Adam and Eve* placed him at the vanguard of Renaissance painting. Many great artists, including Leonardo and Michelangelo, later visited the chapel to study his pioneering work.

In every scene, St Peter is distinguished from the crowds as the figure in the orange cloak.

St Peter Heals the Sick
Masaccio's realistic portrayal of cripples and beggars was revolutionary in his time.

The grouping of stylized figures in Masaccio's frescoes reflects his interest in the sculpture of his contemporary Donatello *(see p69).*

Masaccio's simple style allows us to focus on the figures central to the frescoes without distracting detail.

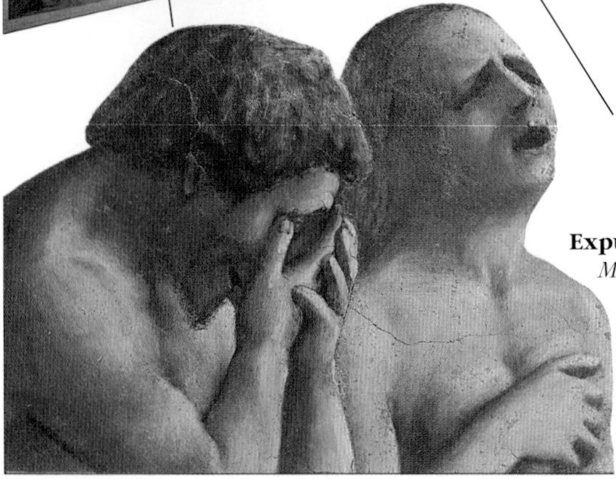

Expulsion of Adam and Eve
Masaccio's ability to express emotion is well illustrated by his harrowing portrait of Adam and Eve being driven out of the Garden of Eden, their faces wracked by misery, shame and the burden of self-knowledge.

KEY TO THE FRESCOES: ARTISTS AND SUBJECTS

☐ Masolino

☐ Masaccio

☐ Lippi

VISITORS' CHECKLIST

Piazza del Carmine. **Map** 3 A1 (5 A4). [055 238 21 95. 🚌 D.
Open 10am–5pm Mon, Wed– Sat; 1–5pm Sun (arrive early). **Closed** public hols. **Adm charge.** Ⓟ

1 Expulsion of Adam and Eve
2 The Tribute Money
3 St Peter Preaching
4 St Peter Visited by St Paul
5 Raising the Emperor's Son; St Peter Enthroned
6 St Peter Healing the Sick
7 St Peter Baptizing the Converts
8 St Peter Healing the Cripple; Raising Tabitha
9 Temptation of Adam and Eve
10 St Peter and St John Giving Alms
11 Crucifixion; Before the Proconsul
12 The Release of St Peter

Masolino's *Temptation of Adam and Eve* is gentle and decorous, in contrast with the emotional force of Masaccio's painting on the opposite wall.

Woman in a Turban
The freshness of Masaccio's original colours is seen in this rediscovered roundel, hidden behind the altar for 500 years.

St Peter is depicted against a background of Florentine buildings.

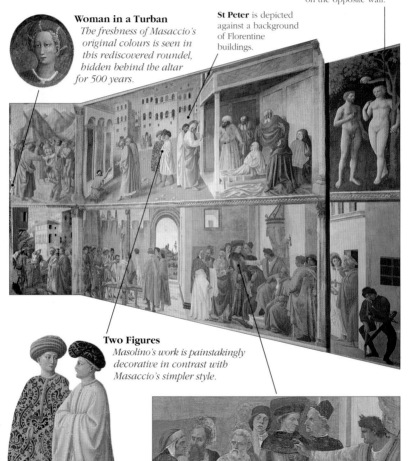

Two Figures
Masolino's work is painstakingly decorative in contrast with Masaccio's simpler style.

Before the Proconsul
Filippino Lippi was called in to complete the unfinished cycle of frescoes in 1480. He added this emotional scene showing the Proconsul sentencing St Peter to death.

TWO GUIDED WALKS

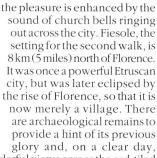

Bust, Museo Faesulanum

I N FLORENCE the countryside is never very far away, and you can be walking down the quiet, rural lanes within just a few minutes of leaving the Ponte Vecchio *(see pp106–7)*, in the bustling heart of the city. The first walk is popular with the Florentines, who like to stroll on a Sunday beneath the city walls and take in the panoramic views that can be enjoyed from San Miniato al Monte and the Piazzale Michelangelo. Depending on time of day, the pleasure is enhanced by the sound of church bells ringing out across the city. Fiesole, the setting for the second walk, is 8 km (5 miles) north of Florence. It was once a powerful Etruscan city, but was later eclipsed by the rise of Florence, so that it is now merely a village. There are archaeological remains to provide a hint of its previous glory and, on a clear day, wonderful views across the red-tiled roof-tops of Florence and of the cypress-dotted hills of the Mugello.

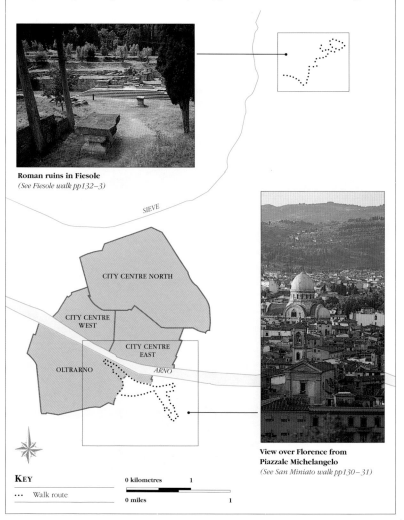

Roman ruins in Fiesole
(See Fiesole walk pp132–3)

SIEVE

CITY CENTRE NORTH

CITY CENTRE WEST

CITY CENTRE EAST

OLTRARNO

ARNO

View over Florence from Piazzale Michelangelo
(See San Miniato walk pp130–31)

KEY

··· Walk route

0 kilometres 1

0 miles 1

◁ **Looking up the steps to the church of San Miniato al Monte**

A Two-Hour Walk to San Miniato al Monte

THIS WALK TAKES YOU from the centre of Florence to the exquisitely decorated church of San Miniato al Monte high on a hill in the south of the city. The route follows quiet lanes along the city walls, and then takes in the bustling Piazzale Michelangelo, packed with souvenir stalls, before returning to the town centre.

No. 19 Costa di San Giorgio ③

From the Ponte Vecchio ① walk south down Via de' Guicciardini and take the second turning left into the square fronting Santa Felicità ②. On the left of the church, take the steep road to the right, Costa di San Giorgio. No. 19 ③ was once the home of Galileo. The Porta San Giorgio (St George's Gate) ④ is straight ahead at the end of the lane.

Built in 1260, this is the oldest city gate to survive in Florence. The weathered fresco within the arch is *The Virgin with St George and St Leonard* by Bicci di Lorenzo (1460). On the outer face of the arch is a carving of St George fighting the dragon, a copy of the original 1284 work, which has been removed and is currently being restored.

The Forte di Belvedere ⑤ is to the right through the gate, and was designed by Bernardo Buontalenti in 1590. Originally the fortress was built to guard the city against attack from its political rivals, but it soon became a private refuge for the Medici Grand Dukes. From here there are extensive views over the Boboli Gardens ⑥ below, and across to the olive groves and cypress trees in the countryside south of the city. Head downhill along Via di Belvedere, which runs along

a stretch of city walls (to the left) dating from 1258. Porta San Miniato ⑦, a small arch in the wall, is situated at the bottom of the hill.

San Miniato al Monte

Turn right into Via del Monte alle Croci and walk uphill for 500 m (550 yds) to the Viale Galileo Galilei. Bear right and cross the road to the vast stone steps leading to the terrace in front of San Miniato al Monte ⑧. Catch your breath and admire the view of the Forte di Belvedere.

San Miniato al Monte is one of the most unspoiled of all the Romanesque churches in Tuscany. It was built in 1018 over the shrine of the early Christian martyr, San Miniato (St Minias). He was a rich Armenian merchant beheaded for his beliefs by Emperor Decius in the 3rd century. The façade was begun around 1090 and has geometric patterning in green-grey and white marble, typical of the Romanesque style. The statue on the gable shows an eagle carrying a bale of cloth, the symbol of the powerful Arte di Calimala (guild of wool

The façade of San Miniato al Monte ⑧

View across to San Miniato al Monte from Forte di Belvedere ⑤

importers) who financed the church in the Middle Ages. The restored 13th-century mosaic below the gable shows Christ, the Virgin and St Minias. Inside the church, the High Altar is raised above the nave and there is a Byzantine-style mosaic in the apse, again of St Minias with Christ and the Virgin. Below this is the crypt, built using columns salvaged from ancient Roman buildings. The floor of the nave is covered with seven marble mosaic panels of lions, doves and the signs of the Zodiac (1207); similar intarsia work panels can be seen on the raised marble choir and

13th-century mosaic on San Miniato façade

pulpit. In the north wall is the funeral chapel of the 25-year-old Cardinal of Portugal, Iacopo di Lusitania, who died in Florence in 1439. Antonio Rossellino carved the figure of the cardinal guarded by angels on the elaborate marble tomb (1466). The terracotta roundels on the ceiling, showing the Holy Spirit and Virtues, were painted by Luca della Robbia (1461). Outside, the massive belltower was begun in 1523 by Baccio

d'Agnolo, but was never finished. Cannons were installed here to shoot at the Medici troops during the Siege of Florence *(see pp50–51)*. The cemetery ⑨ surrounding the church opened in 1854 and this contains tombs the size of miniature houses, built to show off family wealth.

Leave San Miniato by an arch in the buildings to the west and follow the path that

San Salvatore al Monte ⑩

threads down to the church of San Salvatore al Monte ⑩. Here steps lead down to the Viale Galileo Galilei; take a right turn to reach Piazzale Michelangelo ⑪. The piazzale was laid out in the 1860s by Giuseppe Poggi, and is dotted with copies of Michelangelo's famous statues. It is lined with souvenir stalls and has far-reaching views over the roof-tops of central Florence.

Either take the No. 13 bus back to the city centre, or the stone steps on the west side of the piazza down to Porta San Niccolò ⑫, a 14th-century gateway in the city wall. Go left along Via di San Niccolò and Via de' Bardi, lined with medieval buildings. This includes the 13th-century Palazzo de' Mozzi ⑬ on Via de' Bardi; the Museo Bardini ⑭ *(see p119)* is opposite. From here you can return along the Arno to the Ponte Vecchio ①.

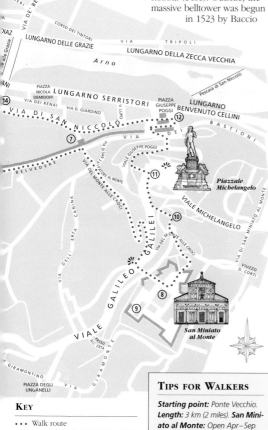

Piazzale Michelangelo

San Miniato al Monte

KEY

• • • Walk route

✷ View point

| 0 metres | 500 |
| 0 yards | 500 |

TIPS FOR WALKERS

Starting point: *Ponte Vecchio.*
Length: *3 km (2 miles).* **San Miniato al Monte:** *Open Apr–Sep 8am–noon, 2–7pm daily; Oct–Mar 8am–noon, 2:30–6pm daily.*
Stopping-off points: *There are several cafés along the route.*

David in Piazzale Michelangelo ⑪

A Two-Hour Walk through Fiesole

THE VILLAGE OF FIESOLE stands in the foothills of the Mugello region, 8 km (5 miles) north of Florence, and has substantial Roman and Etruscan remains. The area has been a popular summer retreat since the 15th century, thanks to its fresh breezes and hilltop position.

The belltower of the Duomo ②

Piazza Mino da Fiesole

The No. 7 bus arrives in Fiesole's main square ① after a 30-minute journey from Florence through countryside dotted with villas. Settled in the 7th century BC, Fiesole was a powerful force in central Italy by the 5th century BC. It began to decline after the Romans founded Florence in the 1st century BC, but kept its independence until 1125, when Florentine troops razed most of the city. The Duomo of San Romolo ② in the piazza was begun in 1028 and has a massive belltower. The bare Romanesque interior has columns which are topped with reused Roman capitals.

From here, walk up the square to the front of the 14th-century Palazzo Comunale ③. Here there is a bronze statue of King Vittorio Emanuele II and Garibaldi, called *Incontro di Teano* (Meeting at Teano) ④. Returning to the church, take the first turning right, down Via Dupre, to the Roman theatre ⑤ and into the archaeological park.

After its defeat by Florence in 1125, Fiesole went into a decline, and many Etruscan and Roman remains went

The bronze statue
Incontro di Teano ④

undisturbed until excavation in the 1870s. The Teatro, built in the 1st century BC, is used for the annual Estate Fiesolana festival *(see pp36–7)*. Its tiers of stone seats can hold 3,000 spectators. Next to the theatre is the Museo Faesulanum ⑥, built in 1912–14. Inside are finds from the Bronze Age onwards: coins, jewellery and ceramics, bronzes and marble sculpture. The building is a copy of the 1st-century Roman temple whose remains are in the northern part of the complex. It is built on Etruscan foundations, and part of the Roman frieze dating from the 1st century BC is still intact. There are some partly restored Roman baths close by ⑦, and, at

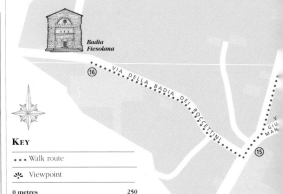

Roman theatre complex ⑤

TIPS FOR WALKERS

Starting point: *Piazza Mino da Fiesole.*

Length: *1.5 km (1 mile). Allow at least 2 hours for the walk to include time to visit the various museums. Note that Via di San Francesco is steep.*

Badia Fiesolana: *Open Sunday morning for services.*

Getting there: *No. 7 bus from Santa Maria Novella bus station, or Piazza di San Marco in Florence.*

Stopping-off points: *There are several cafés around Piazza Mino da Fiesole.*

Badia Fiesolana

⑯ VIA DELLA BADIA DEI ROSCETTINI

⑮

KEY

• • • Walk route

☼ Viewpoint

0 metres	250
0 yards	250

the northern edge of the park, 4th-century BC Etruscan walls ⑧. From the theatre turn into Via Dupre to Museo Bandini ⑨ to the right, with a collection of medieval religious paintings built up by local aristocrat Angelo Bandini in the 19th century.

Back in Piazza Mino da Fiesole, turn right down Via di San Francesco to the left of the Palazzo Vescovile ⑩. There are views over Florence and back to Fiesole ⑪ on the road up to Sant'Alessandro church ⑫, which has a Neo-Classical façade combined with a 9th-century

Fiesole from Via di San Francesco

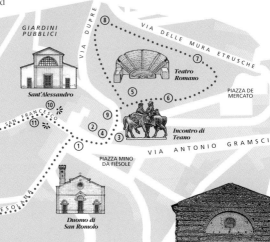

Façade of Badia Fiesolana ⑯

Romanesque interior. Original Roman columns used in the nave are made out of *cipollino* (onion ring) marble. From here carry on up to San Francesco ⑬, a Franciscan friary founded in 1399 and restored in 1907. It has a pretty cloister and a museum of artifacts collected by the monks.

From Fiesole to San Domenico

Retrace your steps or walk through the park back to the town centre. Continue down Via Vecchia Fiesolana. On the left is the Villa Medici ⑭, built in 1461 by Michelozzo for Cosimo de' Medici. Walk down Via Bandini and Via Vecchia Fiesolana to San Domenico. In this little hamlet is the 15th-century

church of San Domenico ⑮, with two good works by Fra Angelico, Dominican prior of the monastery here until 1437. The *Madonna with Angels* and *The Crucifixion* are in the chapter house and were both painted around 1430.

Opposite, Via della Badia dei Roccettini leads to the Badia Fiesolana ⑯, a pretty church with a Romanesque façade of inlaid marble. The interior is decorated with local grey sandstone, *pietra serena*. The No. 7 bus back to Florence can be caught from the village square in San Domenico.

The 15th-century church of San Francesco ⑬

FLORENCE STREET FINDER

Mfor sights, restaurants, hotels and shops in Florence refer to the maps in the *Florence Street Finder* (*see* How the Map References Work *opposite*).

Where two map references are provided, the second (in brackets) relates to the large-scale maps, 5 and 6.

A complete index of street names is on pages 142–3. The key map below shows the area of Florence covered by each of the six maps in the *Florence Street Finder*. The maps encompass the four city-centre areas (colour-coded pink), which include all the sights. (*See also* Florence City Centre, *pp14–15.*)

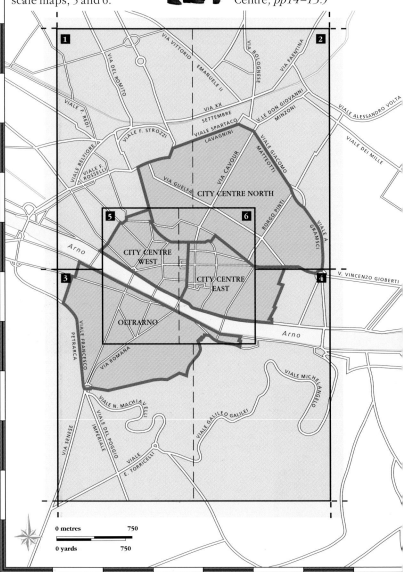

0 metres 750

0 yards 750

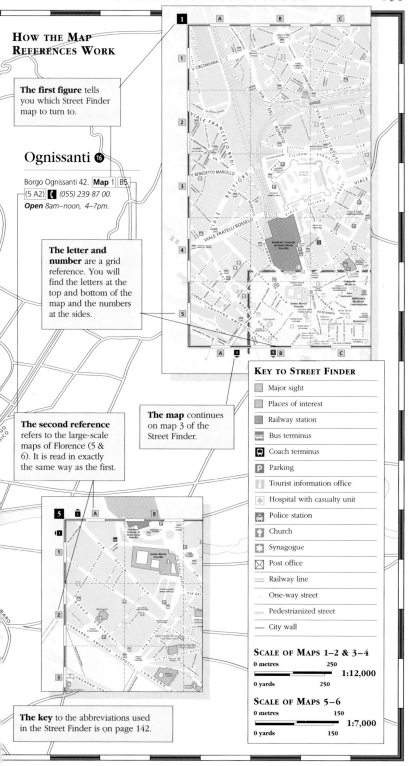

HOW THE MAP REFERENCES WORK

The first figure tells you which Street Finder map to turn to.

Ognissanti ⑯

Borgo Ognissanti 42. **Map** 1 B5
(5 A2) ☎ (055) 239 87 00.
Open 8am–noon, 4–7pm.

The letter and number are a grid reference. You will find the letters at the top and bottom of the map and the numbers at the sides.

The second reference refers to the large-scale maps of Florence (5 & 6). It is read in exactly the same way as the first.

The map continues on map 3 of the Street Finder.

The key to the abbreviations used in the Street Finder is on page 142.

KEY TO STREET FINDER

- Major sight
- Places of interest
- Railway station
- Bus terminus
- Coach terminus
- **P** Parking
- **i** Tourist information office
- Hospital with casualty unit
- Police station
- Church
- Synagogue
- ⊠ Post office
- Railway line
- One-way street
- Pedestrianized street
- City wall

SCALE OF MAPS 1–2 & 3–4

0 metres	250
0 yards	250

1:12,000

SCALE OF MAPS 5–6

0 metres	150
0 yards	150

1:7,000

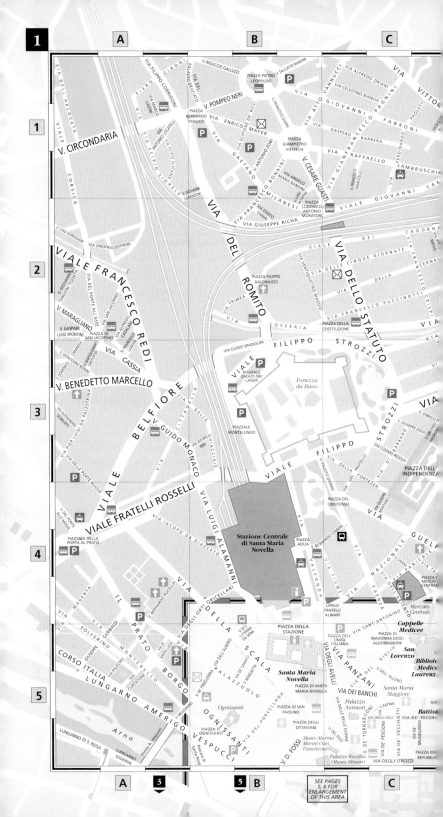

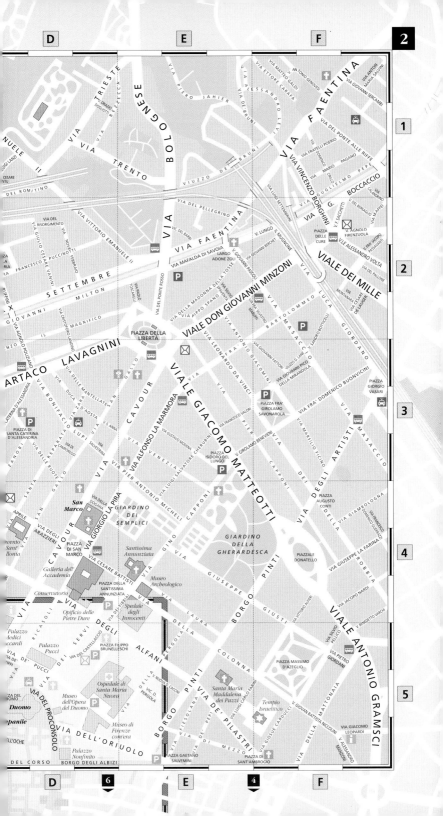

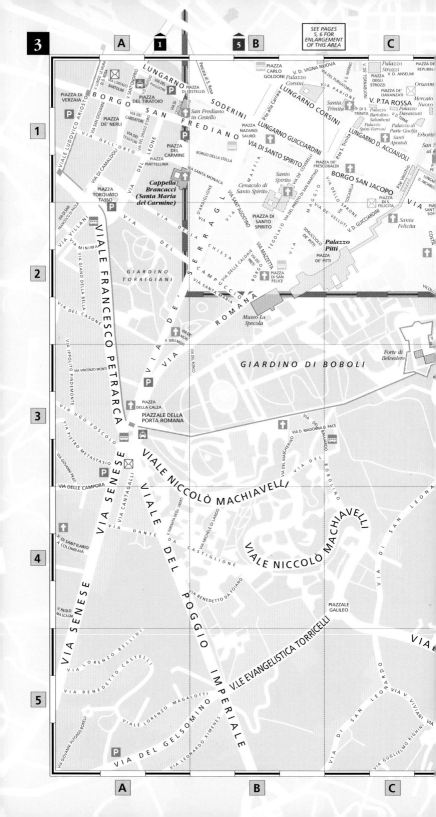

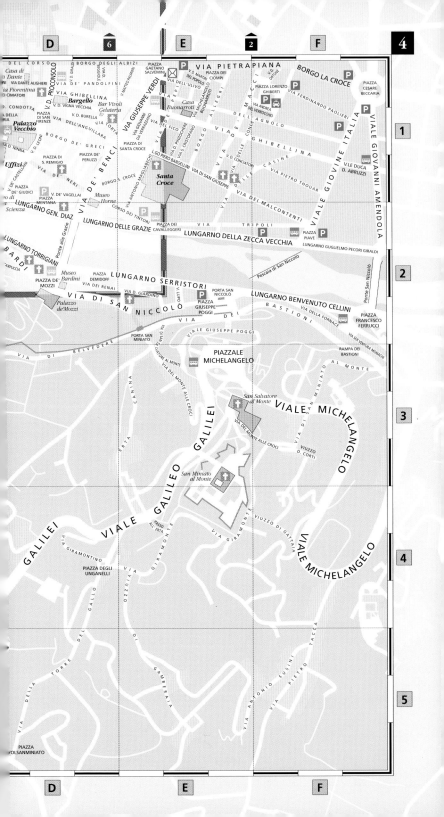

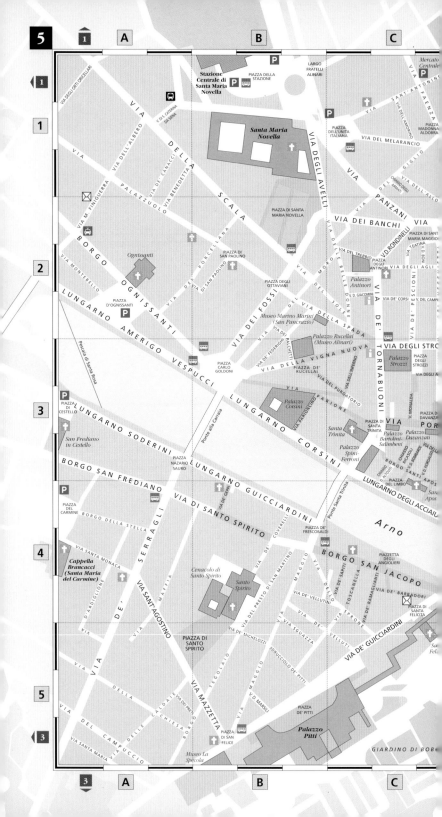

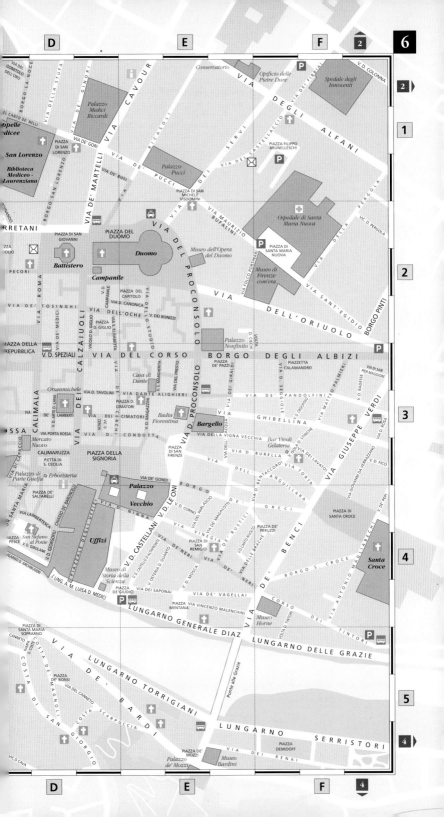

Street Finder Index

KEY TO ABBREVIATIONS USED IN THE STREET FINDER

d.	di, del, dell', dello, della, dei, de', delle, degli	**Lung.** **P.** **P.ta**	Lungarno Piazza Porta	**P.te** **S.** **SS.**	Ponte San, Sant', Santa, Santo Santi, Santissima	**V.** **Vic.** **V.le**	Via Vicolo Viale

Map references in parentheses refer to the larger scale map.

TUSCANY AREA
BY AREA

Tuscany at a Glance

Tuscany is rich in culture and land-scape. Out of Florence, most visitors' first port of call is Pisa, in Western Tuscany, with its Leaning Tower. Northern Tuscany has mountains and beaches, and Eastern Tuscany the lush forests of the Mugello. Siena and San Gimignano in Central Tuscany draw their own visitors, while Southern Tuscany with its sparse vegetation and unspoiled beaches is more off the beaten track.

Sights in Tuscany are grouped within their own sections in this book, corres-ponding with the colour-coded map below.

NORTHERN TUSCANY

Lucca

Pisa

NORTHERN TUSCANY
Pages 164–185

WESTERN TUSCANY
Pages 148–163

SOUTHERN TUSCANY
Pages 226–237

0 kilometres   20

0 miles   20

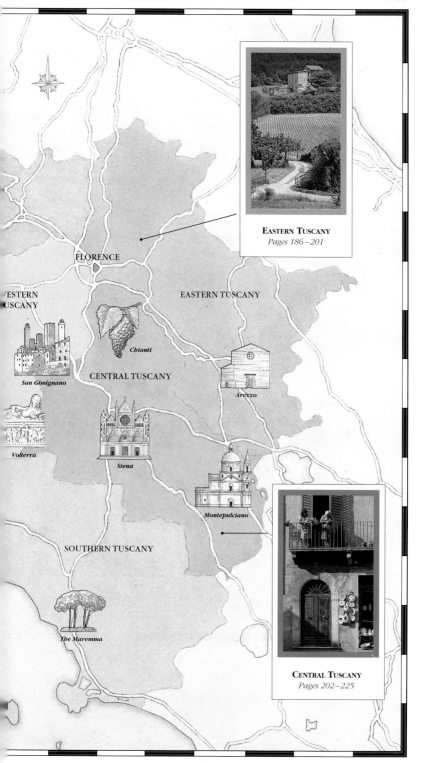

EASTERN TUSCANY
Pages 186–201

FLORENCE

WESTERN
TUSCANY

EASTERN TUSCANY

Chianti

San Gimignano

CENTRAL TUSCANY

Arezzo

Volterra

Siena

Montepulciano

SOUTHERN TUSCANY

The Maremma

CENTRAL TUSCANY
Pages 202–225

WESTERN TUSCANY

USCANY'S HARD-WORKING ECONOMIC ENGINE, *this area is charac-terized by its factories and ports, particularly Livorno. There are also some extraordinary sights, most famously the Leaning Tower of Pisa. To the south, the windswept ancient Etruscan town of Volterra, standing high on a barren plateau, has some of the finest museums and medieval architecture in Italy.*

From the 11th to the 13th centuries, when at the height of its powers, Pisa dominated the Western Mediterranean. Its strong navy opened up extensive trading links with North Africa, and brought to Italy the benefits of Arabic scientific and artistic achievement.

These new ideas had a profound effect on 12th- and 13th-century architects working in western Tuscany. Many of the era's splendid buildings, for instance Pisa's Duomo, Baptistry and Campanile, are decorated with complex geometric patterns made from beautiful inlaid marble, alternating with bizarre arabesques.

During the 16th century the Arno estuary began to silt up, ending Pisan supremacy. In 1571, work began to establish Livorno as the region's main port. This proved so successful that it remains Italy's second busiest port. Pisa, meanwhile, has become the gateway to Tuscany following the extensive development of Galileo Galilei airport. The Arno valley is mainly an industrial area, with huge factories producing glass, furniture, motorcycles, leather and textiles. Even so, there are some rewarding sights lurking within the urban sprawl, like the Romanesque church of San Piero a Grado or the entertaining museum in Vinci, which contains models of many of Leonardo da Vinci's brilliant inventions.

South of the Arno valley, the land-scape is pleasant but unremarkable, consisting of rolling hills and expanses of agricultural land. But the imposing ancient town of Volterra, with its unmatched collection of Etruscan artifacts, demands a visit.

Landscape of rolling hills near Volterra

◁ **The Leaning Tower, rising above the terracotta roofs of Pisa**

Exploring Western Tuscany

Pisa, WITH ITS WORLD-FAMOUS LEANING TOWER, and Volterra,
with a wealth of ancient Etruscan remains, are the
highlights of the region. There is, however, much more to
see, especially in the gentle hilly countryside that rises on
either side of the Arno
valley. It was here that
Renaissance architects
pioneered new styles
of villa building; their
work can be admired
at Poggio a Caiano and
Artimino. San Miniato is
gloriously sited on a
hilltop commanding
extensive views;
the museum
in Vinci, on the
other side of the
valley, celebrates
the inventive genius
of Leonardo da Vinci.

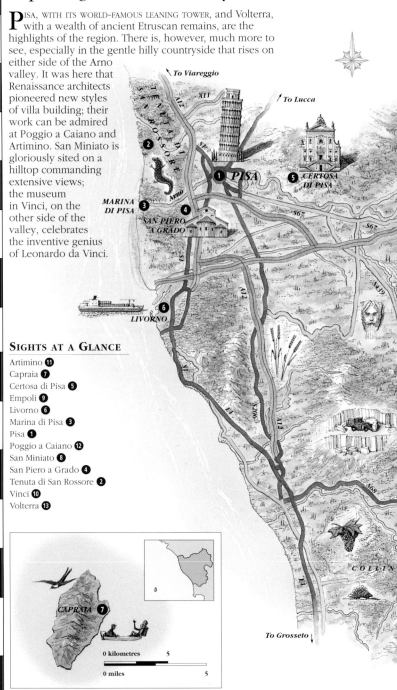

Sights at a Glance

0 kilometres   5

0 miles   5

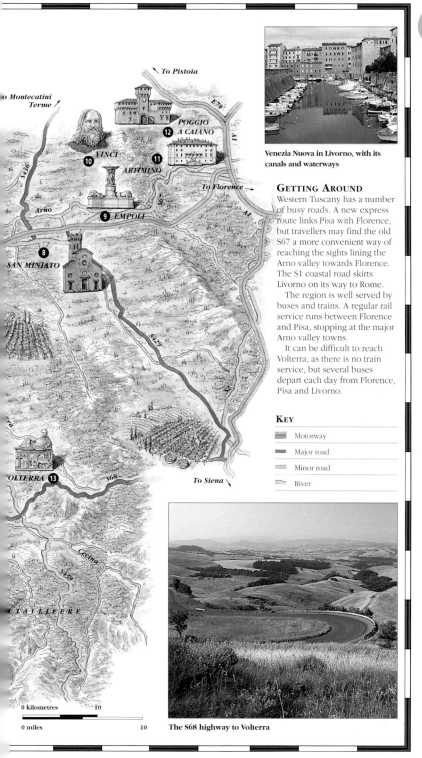

Venezia Nuova in Livorno, with its canals and waterways

GETTING AROUND

Western Tuscany has a number of busy roads. A new express route links Pisa with Florence, but travellers may find the old S67 a more convenient way of reaching the sights lining the Arno valley towards Florence. The S1 coastal road skirts Livorno on its way to Rome.

The region is well served by buses and trains. A regular rail service runs between Florence and Pisa, stopping at the major Arno valley towns.

It can be difficult to reach Volterra, as there is no train service, but several buses depart each day from Florence, Pisa and Livorno.

KEY

▦	Motorway
▦	Major road
▦	Minor road
〰	River

The S68 highway to Volterra

Pisa ❶

Inlaid marble, Duomo façade

FROM THE 11TH TO THE 13TH centuries, Pisa's powerful navy ensured the city's dominance in the Western Mediterranean. Trading links with Spain and North Africa led to a scientific and cultural revolution *(see p44)* reflected in the splendid buildings of the era: the Duomo, Baptistry and Campanile. Pisa's decline was assured when the Arno began to silt up. Salt marsh, partly a nature reserve, now divides the city from the sea.

Campo dei Miracoli

🔒 Campo dei Miracoli
See pp154–5.

🏛 Museo delle Sinopie
Piazza del Duomo. **Open** Apr–Sep: 8am–7:40pm daily; Mar & Oct: 9am–5:40pm daily; Nov–Feb: 9am–4:40pm daily. **Adm charge**.

This fascinating museum displays sketches from the fresco cycle that once covered the walls of Campo Santo cemetery *(see pp154–5)*. The frescoes disintegrated when the cemetery was bombed in 1944, but the underlying sketches survived. They were removed from the walls for conservation before being rehoused in the museum. There are also displays showing how fresco artists went about their work.

🏛 Museo dell'Opera del Duomo
Piazza Duomo. **[** 050 56 05 47. **Open** Apr–Sep: 8am–7:40pm daily; Mar & Oct: 9am–5:40pm daily; Nov–Feb: 9am–4:40pm daily. **Adm charge**. ♿

Housed in the cathedral's 13th-century former Chapter House, the museum was opened in 1986. All the exhibits were formerly in the Duomo and Baptistry. Modern display methods ensure that they are excellently presented. Exhibits such as the intricately inlaid marble arabesque panels and fine Corinthian capitals reveal the twin influences of Rome and Islam on Pisan architects in the 12th and 13th centuries. Be sure to see the imposing 10th-century hippogriff (half horse, half gryphon); this statue, cast in bronze by Islamic craftsmen, was looted by Pisan adventurers during the wars against the Saracens.

The museum also contains 13th-century statues and sculptures by Nicola and Giovanni Pisano, including Giovanni's ivory *Virgin and Child* (1300) carved for the Duomo's High Altar. There are paintings from the 15th to 18th centuries, a fine Roman and Etruscan archaeological collection, and ecclesiastical treasures and vestments dating from the 12th century.

The museum cloister offers a wonderful view of the Leaning Tower *(see p156).*

🚌 Piazza dei Cavalieri
The Piazza dei Cavalieri stands at the heart of Pisa's student quarter. The huge building on the north side of the square, covered in exuberant black and white *sgraffito* decoration (designs scratched into wet plaster), is the Palazzo dei Cavalieri and houses one of Pisa University's most prestigious colleges: the Scuola Normale Superiore. The site was originally occupied by Pisa's medieval town hall, but Cosimo I ordered its destruction when the city fell under Florentine rule. The council chamber, however, was spared and is now a lecture hall. The present flamboyant building was designed in 1562 by Vasari, as the headquarters of the Cavalieri di San Stefano, an order of knights created by Cosimo in 1561. An equestrian statue of Cosimo by Pietro Francavilla (1596) stands outside. Santo Stefano dei Cavalieri

10th-century bronze hippogriff

Virgin and Child **polyptych (1321) by Simone Martini**

(1565–9), the knights' church, stands next to the Palazzo dei Cavalieri. Also designed by Vasari, it has a splendid gilded and coffered ceiling. The walls are hung with figureheads and battle standards. There is also a splendid organ (look out for notices of recitals).

On the other side of the Palazzo dei Cavalieri is the Palazzo dell'Orologio, incorporating the medieval town jail. The building, which is now housing a library, was the scene of a most shameful and gruesome historical episode. In 1288 Count Ugolino, mayor of Pisa, was accused of treachery and walled up with his sons and grandsons. The entire male side of the Ugolino family was wiped out.

🏛 Museo Nazionale di San Matteo

Piazzetta San Matteo in Soarta.
☎ *050 54 18 65.* **Open**
9am–7pm Tue–Sun.
Adm charge.
The medieval convent of San Matteo, with its elegant Gothic façade, is located alongside the Arno. For many years, the museum inside has been partially closed. Many exhibits are poorly labelled and the rooms leading off the cloister are unnumbered. Nevertheless, the museum presents a unique opportunity to examine the complete sweep of Pisan and

**Grand Duke
Cosimo I**

Florentine art from the 12th to the 17th centuries.

Most of the earliest works portray the Virgin and Child. These include Simone Martini's fine polyptych (1321) and a 14th-century statue, the *Madonna del Latte,* attributed to Nino Pisano, another member of the talented family of sculptors. The half-length statue, in gilded marble, shows Christ feeding at his mother's breast. A number of early Renaissance pieces deserve to be sought out, particularly Masaccio's *St Paul* (1426), Gentile da Fabriano's radiant 15th-century *Madonna and Child,* and Donatello's reliquary bust of *San Rossore* (1424–7).

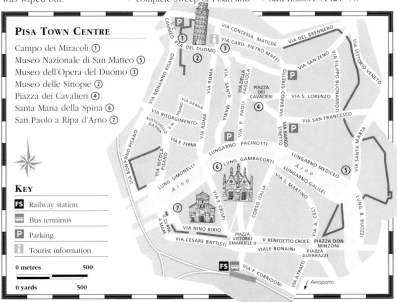

PISA TOWN CENTRE

Campo dei Miracoli ①
Museo Nazionale di San Matteo ⑤
Museo dell'Opera del Duomo ③
Museo delle Sinopie ②
Piazza dei Cavalieri ④
Santa Maria della Spina ⑥
San Paolo a Ripa d'Arno ⑦

KEY

FS Railway station

🚌 Bus terminus

P Parking

ℹ Tourist information

0 metres	500
0 yards	500

Campo dei Miracoli

Cemetery memorial

PɪsA's WORLD FAMOUS Leaning Tower is just one of the splendid religious buildings that rise from the emerald-green lawns of the "Field of Miracles". Lying to the northwest of the city centre, it is partnered by the Duomo, begun in 1063, the Baptistry of 1152–1284 and the Campo Santo cemetery begun in 1278. These buildings combine definite Moorish elements, such as inlaid marble in geometric patterns (arabesques), with delicate Romanesque colonnading and spiky Gothic niches and pinnacles.

Campo Santo
The cemetery contains earth from the Holy Land and carved Roman sarcophagi.

The domed Cappella del Pozzo was added in 159

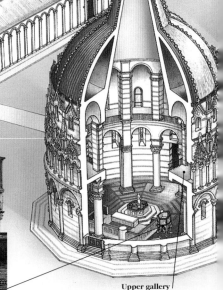

The Triumph of Death
These late 14th-century frescoes depict various allegorical scenes such as this of a knight and lady overwhelmed by the stench of an open grave.

★ Baptistry Pulpit
Nicola Pisano's great marble pulpit, completed in 1260, is carved with lively scenes from The Life of Christ.

Upper gallery

★ Portale di San Ranieri
Bonanno Pisano's bronze panels for the south transept doors depict The Life of Christ. *Palm trees and Moorish buildings show Arabic influence.*

Frescoes were added to the dome's interior after a fire in 1595.

The Leaning Tower *(see p156)* was completed in 1350, when its seven bells were hung.

Fragments of the 11th-century marble floor survive beneath the dome.

A frieze shows that work began in 1173.

Gleaming white Carrara marble decorates the walls.

Cathedral Pulpit *The carved supports for Giovanni Pisano's pulpit (1302–11) symbolize the Arts and Virtues.*

This 12th-century wall tomb is for Buschetto, the Duomo's original architect.

★ Duomo Façade
Coloured sandstone, glass and majolica plates decorate the lombard-style 12th-century façade. Its patterned surface includes knots, flowers and animals in inlaid marble.

STAR FEATURES

- ★ **Portale di San Ranieri**
- ★ **Baptistry Pulpit by Nicola Pisano**
- ★ **Duomo Façade**

The Leaning Tower of Pisa

A LL THE BUILDINGS of the Campo dei Miracoli lean because of their shallow foundations and sandy silt subsoil, but none tilts so famously as the Torre Pendente – the Leaning Tower. Begun in 1173, the tower began to tip sideways before the third storey was completed. Even so, construction continued until its completion in 1350. Recent engineering interventions have corrected the tilt by 38 cm (14 in), and the tower was reopened in December 2001.

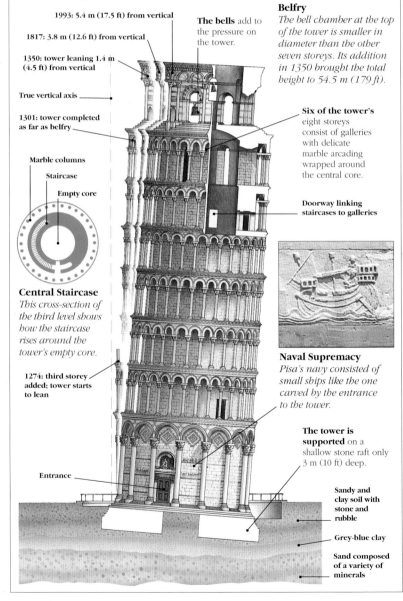

Belfry
The bell chamber at the top of the tower is smaller in diameter than the other seven storeys. Its addition in 1350 brought the total height to 54.5 m (179 ft).

1993: 5.4 m (17.5 ft) from vertical

1817: 3.8 m (12.6 ft) from vertical

1350: tower leaning 1.4 m (4.5 ft) from vertical

The bells add to the pressure on the tower.

True vertical axis

1301: tower completed as far as belfry

Marble columns

Staircase

Empty core

Six of the tower's eight storeys consist of galleries with delicate marble arcading wrapped around the central core.

Doorway linking staircases to galleries

Central Staircase
This cross-section of the third level shows how the staircase rises around the tower's empty core.

1274: third storey added; tower starts to lean

Naval Supremacy
Pisa's navy consisted of small ships like the one carved by the entrance to the tower.

Entrance

The tower is supported on a shallow stone raft only 3 m (10 ft) deep.

Sandy and clay soil with stone and rubble

Grey-blue clay

Sand composed of a variety of minerals

Santa Maria della Spina by the river Arno in Pisa

🏛 **Santa Maria della Spina**

Lungarno Gambacorti.
Open by permission.
The roofline of this tiny church bristles with spiky Gothic pinnacles, miniature spires and niches sheltering statues of apostles and saints. All of this is highly appropriate for a church that was built to house an unusual precious relic: a thorn taken from the Crown of Thorns forced on to Christ's head during the cruel mock coronation that preceded His crucifixion.

🏛 **San Paolo a Ripa d'Arno**

Piazza San Paolo a Ripa d'Arno.
📞 050 415 15. **Open** by appt. ♿
Worth visiting almost solely for its impressive 12th-century façade, this church was built in the same Pisan Romanesque style as the Duomo (see pp154–5).

The Romanesque chapel (see p42) at the east end is dedicated to St Agatha. It is built entirely from brick, with a cone-shaped roof; Islamic influence is said to account for its highly unusual octagonal shape.

Tenuta di San Rossore ❷

Road map B2. 🚂 Pisa. 📞 050 52 55 00 (050 53 01 01 for guided tours). **Open** 8:30am–7:30pm Sat & Sun. 📷 English (by appt).

NORTH OF THE ARNO, the Tenuta di San Rossore is part of a vast nature reserve, the Parco Naturale di San Rossore, stretching to the north of Tuscany. Wild boar and deer are said to roam among the pine forests and salt marsh. Gombo, to the west, is where the drowned body of the poet Shelley was found in 1822.

Marina di Pisa ❸

Road map B2. 🏃 3,000. 🚌
🛥 Sun in summer, Tue in winter.

Moorings at Marina di Pisa, at the mouth of the river Arno

MUCH OF THE salt marsh to the west of Pisa has now been drained and reclaimed, and a large US Air Force base (Camp Darby) now occupies the area south of the Arno. There are extensive sandy beaches on the Arno estuary, and here lies Marina di Pisa, a seaside resort with some pretty Art Nouveau houses, backed by pine woods.

On the drive there you may catch sight of grazing camels – these are the descendants of a large herd established under Duke Ferdinand II in the mid-17th century. The village of Tirrenia, with its sandy beaches, lies 5 km (3 miles) south of Marina di Pisa.

San Piero a Grado ❹

Road map B2. 📞 050 96 00 65.
Open 8am–7pm daily. ♿

SAN PIERO is a handsome 11th-century church built on the spot where St Peter is believed to have first set foot on Italian soil in AD 42. According to the New Testament Book of Acts, he arrived at a set of landing steps by the Arno. Archaeologists have discovered the foundations of Roman port buildings underneath the present church, which stands at the point where the Arno once flowed into the sea. Silt deposits mean that the church now stands some 6 km (3.5 miles) from the shore.

An unusual feature of the church is the lack of any façade. Instead, it has semicircular apses at both the east and west ends. The exterior is decorated with blind arcading and with Moorish-style ceramic plates set into the masonry around the eaves – an unusual feature that it shares with the Duomo in San Miniato (see p159).

The present church was built during the reign of Pope John XVIII (1004–9) and the varied capitals of the nave come from ancient Roman buildings. High up on the nave walls there are frescoes by Deodato Orlandi, painted around 1300, on The Life of St Peter. These are interspersed with portraits of all the popes from St Peter to John XVII.

Interior of San Piero a Grado, with frescoes by Deodati Orlandi

The 18th-century Certosa di Pisa

Certosa di Pisa ❺

Road map C2. 🚌 *from Pisa.*
📞 *050 93 84 30.* **Open** *9am–
6:30pm Tue–Sat, 9am–noon Sun
(adm on the hour in morning, half
past the hour afternoons; last adm:
1 hour before closing).* **Adm charge**.

THIS Carthusian monastery
was founded in 1366 and
rebuilt during the 18th century.
The splendid church is lavishly
decorated, and some buildings
form the University of Pisa's
Museo di Storia Naturale.
Exhibits include 16th-century
anatomical wax models.
  Nearby is the **Pieve di Calci**,
a fine 11th-century Romanesque church. The unfinished
campanile is alongside.

🏛 **Museo di Storia Naturale**
Certosa di Pisa. 📞 *050 93 77 51.*
Open *mid-Sep–mid-Jun: 9am–6pm
Tue–Sat, 10am–7pm Sun; mid-Jun–mid-
Sep: 10am–7pm Tue–Fri, 4pm–midnight
Sat, Sun. Closed public hols, 1–10 Jun.*
Adm charge. ♿ *partial.*
🔒 **Pieve di Calci**
Piazza della Propositura, Calci.
Open *daily.* ♿

Livorno ❻

Road map B3. 🏘 *168,370.*
🚉 🚌 🚢 ℹ *Piazza Cavour 6.*
(0586 20 46 11). 🅿

THE FACT THAT LIVORNO is now
a bustling city, Italy's
second busiest container port,
is thanks to Cosimo I. In 1571
he chose Livorno, then a tiny
fishing village, as the site for
Tuscany's new port after Pisa's
harbour silted up. From
1607–21 the English marine
engineer Sir Robert Dudley
built the great sea wall that
protects the harbour.

In 1608 Livorno was declared
a free port, open to all traders,
regardless of religion or race.
Jews, Protestants, Arabs,
Turks and others who came
here, fleeing wars or religious
persecution, contributed
greatly to the city's success.

🏛 **Piazza Grande**
When the architect Buon-
talenti planned the new city
of Livorno in 1576, he
envisaged the huge Piazza
Grande at the heart of a
network of wide avenues.
  The square's original appearance has, however, been lost.
This is partly due to contro-
versial post-war rebuilding,
which cut the square into two
halves: the present Piazza
Grande, to the south, and the
Largo Municipio, to the north.

🔒 **Duomo**
Piazza Grande. **Open** *daily.*
A prominent victim of
Livorno's wartime bombing
was the late 16th-century
cathedral by Pieroni and
Cantagallina. It was rebuilt
in 1959, retaining the original
entrance portico, with its
Doric arcades.
  The original building
was designed by Inigo
Jones, who served
his apprenticeship
under the architect
Buontalenti. Jones later
used an almost identical
design for
the arcades of his
Covent Garden
piazza in London.

🏛 **Piazza Micheli**
The piazza, with its views of
the 16th-century Fortezza
Vecchia, contains Livorno's
best-known monument: the
Monumento dei Quattro Mori.
  Bandini's bronze figure of
Duke Ferdinand I dates to
1595; but Pietro Tacca's four
Moorish slaves, also cast in
bronze, were not added until
1626. Naked and manacled,
the dejected slaves are a stark
reminder that Livorno once
had a thriving slave market.

Venezia Nuova canals

🏛 **Venezia Nuova**
Originally laid out in the
middle of the 17th century,
this area, which includes
the 18th-century
octagonal church of
Santa Caterina, is
spread between a
handful of canals,
reminiscent of
Venetian waterways.
Although it only
covers a few blocks,
Venezia Nuova is one
of the city's most scenic
areas.

***Monumento dei Quattro Mori* by Bandini and Tacca in Piazza Micheli**

Fortezza Vecchia, Livorno harbour

The Fortezza Nuova, sur-rounded by a moat, dates to 1590. Its interior has been converted to a public park.

🛏 Piazza XX Settembre

Lying south of the Fortezza Nuova, the piazza is renowned for its bustling "American Market". The market's name derives from the large amounts of American army surplus sold here after World War II.

A US army base, Camp Darby, still operates to the north of Livorno.

🏛 English Cemetery

Via Giuseppe Verdi 63. **C** 0586 80 20 92. **Open** by appt. **&**
The 19th-century memorials to British and American emigrés, long untended, are considerably overgrown. Among them is the grave of Tobias Smollett (1721–71), the misanthropic Scottish novelist. He claimed to live in Italy for health reasons, and, predictably, constantly complained about the place.

🏛 Museo Civico

Via San Jacopo Acquaviva.
C 0586 80 80 01. **Open** Tue–Sun 10am–1pm, 4–7pm. **Adm charge**.
The Museo Civico houses tem-porary exhibitions and also contains several paintings by Giovanni Fattori (1825–1908) (see p123). He was an artist of the *Macchiaioli* School, whose work was similar to that of the French Impressionists.

Capraia ❼

🚢 from Livorno. 👥 300.
ℹ Agenzia Viaggi Parco, Via Assunzione 42 (0586 90 50 71).

This tiny mountainous island appeals mainly to bird watchers and divers who go to explore the rocky coastline.

Nearby Gorgona, a penal colony, can also be visited by booking in advance. Contact tourist information in Livorno.

San Miniato ❽

Road map C2. 👥 3,852. 🚌
ℹ Piazza del Popolo 3 (0571 427 45).
🏪 Tue, 1st & 2nd Sun of each month.

San Miniato suffers from its proximity to the vast indus-trial conurbation of the Arno valley. Straddling the crest of one of the region's highest hills, it manages, however, to remain somewhat aloof. There are a number of fine historic buildings, including the 13th-century Rocca (castle) built for Frederick II (1194–1250), the German Holy Roman Emperor.

The town played a major part in Frederick's Italian military campaigns. He dreamed of rebuilding the ancient Roman empire that lay divided between papal and Imperial authority. To this end he conquered large areas of Italy. His battles

fuelled fierce local struggles between the imperial Ghibellines and the papal Guelphs (see p44).

Local people still refer to the town as San Miniato *al Tedesco* (of the German).

Façade of Duomo in San Miniato

🔒 Duomo

Piazza del Duomo. **Open** daily.
Only the red-brick façade survives from the original 12th-century building. The majolica plates set within it show evidence of trade with Spain or North Africa. They seem to represent the North Star and the constellations of Ursus Major and Minor: key reference points for early navigators.

The campanile, the Torre di Matilda, is named in honour of the great Countess Matilda (see p43), who was born in Livorno in 1046.

🚇 Piazza della Repubblica

The Piazza della Repubblica (also known as the Piazza del Seminario) occupies a long, narrow space dominated by the decorated façade of the 17th-century seminary. The frescoes and *sgraffito* (scenes scratched out of plaster) on the façade show allegories of the Virtues painted below quotations from key religious texts, for instance the writings of Pope Gregory (540–604).

To the right of the seminary are several well-restored 15th-century shops. Buildings like these can be seen in many medieval frescoes, such as Lorenzetti's 14th-century *Good Government (see p44)*.

Piazza Farinata degli Uberti in Empoli

Empoli ➒

Road map C2. 🚹 43,500. 🚉
🚌 🅹 *Via Giuseppe del Papa 98
(0571 76 115)*. 🚌 *Thu.*

Aⁿ INDUSTRIAL TOWN, specializing in textiles and glass manufacturing, Empoli is worth visiting for the excellent Museo della Collegiata.

🚇 Piazza Farinata degli Uberti

Empoli's arcaded main square is surrounded by a number of 12th-century buildings, notably the church of Sant'Andrea, with its black and white marble façade. The large fountain dating to 1827, with water nymphs and lions, is by Luigi Pampaloni.

🏛 Museo della Collegiata di Sant'Andrea

Piazza della Propositura 3.
📞 0571 762 84.
Open 9am–noon, 4–7pm Tue–Sun. **Closed** public & relig hols. **Adm charge**.
The museum contains a collection of Renaissance paintings and sculpture. Of particular interest are Masolino's *Pietà* fresco (1425) and a marble font by Rossellino, dating to 1447.

🔒 Santo Stefano

Via dei Neri. **Open** for concerts & exhibitions.
Visitors to Santo Stefano can see fresco fragments by Masolino, dating to 1424, and two 15th-century Annunciation statues by Rossellino. Bicci di Lorenzo's painting, *St Nicholas*

Façade of the seminary in Piazza della Repubblica

🏛 Museo Diocesano d'Arte Sacra

Piazza Duomo. 📞 0571 41 82 71.
Open Apr–Oct: 10am–1pm, 3–7pm Tue–Sun; Nov–Mar: 10am–1pm, 3–6pm Tue–Sun. **Adm charge**.
Located next to the Duomo, the Museo Diocesano d'Arte Sacra contains a number of important 15th-century works gathered from local churches. These include a *Crucifixion* by Filippo Lippi and a terracotta bust of Christ attributed to Verrocchio.

🏰 Rocca

A staircase behind the Museo Diocesano leads towards Frederick II's ruined 13th-century Rocca (castle). While the remains are run-down, the site offers extraordinary views along the entire Arno valley, from Fiesole to Pisa.

Pietà by Masolino in Museo della Collegiata

of Tolentino (1445), in the second chapel on the north side, shows Empoli as it was in the mid-15th century.

Vinci ➓

Road map C2. 🚹 2,000.
🚌 🚌 *Wed.*

Tʜɪs ʜɪʟʟᴛᴏᴘ ᴛᴏᴡɴ is the birthplace of Leonardo da Vinci (1452–1519). To celebrate his extraordinary genius, the 13th-century castle in the centre of the town was restored in 1952 to create the **Museo Leonardiano**. Among the displays are wooden models of Leonardo's machines and inventions, based on the drawings from his notebooks shown alongside. These range from his conception of a car, to an armoured tank and even a machine-gun. A pair of skis, designed for walking on water, show that he could occasionally miss the mark. The museum is best avoided on Sundays, when it can be extremely crowded.

Close to the museum is Santo Stefano church and the font in which Leonardo was baptized. His actual birthplace, the **Casa di Leonardo**, is 2 km (1.25 miles) from the town centre at Anchiano. This simple farmhouse is worth visiting if you feel like a pleasant, undemanding walk through superb poppy fields; but don't expect to be overawed by the exhibits. These mostly consist of a few reproduction drawings.

🏛 Museo Leonardiano

Castello dei Conti Guidi. **📞** *0571 560 55.* **Open** *Mar–Oct: 9:30am– 7pm daily; Nov–Feb: 9:30am–6pm daily.* **Adm charge**.

🏛 Casa di Leonardo

Anchiano. **📞** *0571 560 55.* **Open** *Mar–Oct: 9:30am–7pm daily; Nov–Feb: 9:30am–6pm daily.*

Model bicycle based on drawings by Leonardo, Museo Leonardiano

Artimino ⑪

Road map *C2.* 🚌

ARTIMINO IS A FINE example of a *borgo*, a small fortified hamlet. Despite its proximity to the big industrial conglomerations of Florence and Prato, the stupendous views from this hilltop site are of wooded green hills, with not a factory in sight. The hamlet itself is only remarkable for the unspoiled Romanesque church of San Leonardo. Outside the walls, however, higher up the hill, lies the **Villa di Artimino**, designed by Buontalenti in 1594 for Grand Duke Ferdinando I. It is often referred

to as the "Villa of a Hundred Chimneys", because of the numerous and highly ornate chimney pots crowding the roofline. The building is now used as a conference centre, but the Museo Archeologico Etrusco in the basement, which exhibits Etruscan and Roman artifacts from nearby excavations, is open to the public.

Lovers of the work of Pontormo (1494–1557) should set aside time to visit the church of **San Michele** in Carmignano, only 5 km (3 miles) north of Artimino. It contains his great masterpiece, *The Visitation* (1530).

🏛 Villa di Artimino

📞 *055 879 20 30 (villa), 055 871 80 81 (museum).* **Villa open** *Tue by appt.* **Museo Archeologico Etrusco open** *9am–4pm Mon, Tue, Thu–Sat, 9:30am–12:30pm Sun.* **Adm charge**.

⛪ San Michele

Piazza SS. Francesco e Michele 1, Carmignano. **Open** *daily.*

Poggio a Caiano ⑫

Road map *C2.* **📞** *055 87 70 12.* **Open** *daily (except 2nd and 3rd Mon of each month).* **Adm charge**. ♿

THE VILLA di Poggio a Caiano, built by Giuliano da Sangallo for Lorenzo de' Medici *(see p48)* in 1480, was the first Italian villa to be designed in the Renaissance

Villa di Artimino

style. Its original severity is now softened by the graceful, curved staircase (added in 1802–7) leading up to the villa terrace, with its views of the gardens and parkland beyond.

The villa's principal room is the barrel-vaulted *salone*, with its 16th-century frescoes by Andrea del Sarto and Franciabigio. They were commissioned by the future Leo X, the Medici pope, to portray his family as great statesmen in the manner of ancient Roman figures.

The *salone* also contains Pontormo's colourful *Conette* fresco (1521). Surrounding the circular window of the end wall, it portrays the Roman garden deities, Vertumnus and Pomona – a perfect evocation of a Tuscan summer afternoon.

Among the other rooms is the bedchamber of Bianca Cappello, mistress and later wife of Grand Duke Francesco I. The couple died here within a few hours of each other, apparently poisoned. They may, however, simply have succumbed to a lethal viral infection.

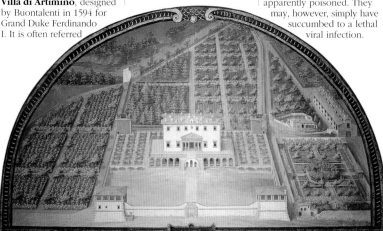

***Villa di Poggio a Caiano** from the set of lunettes by Giusto Utens (see p71)*

Volterra ⑬

Stucco figure in the Duomo

Situated, like many Etruscan cities, on a high plateau, Volterra offers uninterrupted views over the surrounding hills. In many places the ancient Etruscan walls still stand. Volterra's famous Museo Guarnacci contains one of the best collections of Etruscan artifacts in Italy. Many of the exhibits were gathered from the numerous local tombs. After its museums and medieval buildings, the city is famous for its craftsmen who carve beautiful white statues from locally mined alabaster.

🏛 Museo Etrusco Guarnacci

Via Don Minzoni 15. **[** 0588 863 47.
Open Mar–Oct: 9am–6:45pm daily; Nov–Feb: 9am–1:45pm daily.
Closed 1 Jan, 25 Dec.
Adm charge. 🔾 partial.

The pride of the Guarnacci Museum is its collection of 600 Etruscan funerary urns. Adorned with detailed carving, they offer a unique insight into Etruscan customs and beliefs *(see pp40–41)*.

The museum's two main exhibits are on the first floor. Room 20 contains the terracotta "Married Couple" urn. The elderly couple on the lid are portrayed realistically, with haggard, careworn faces.

Room 22 contains an even more unusual exhibit, the elongated bronze known as the *Ombra della Sera* (Shadow of the Evening). This name was bestowed by the poet Gabriele d'Annunzio, who said the bronze reminded him of the shadow thrown by a human figure in the dying light of the evening sun. It is probably a votive figure dating to the 3rd century BC, but it is difficult to speak of it with any certainty; unusually, it was cast with no clothes or jewellery to indicate rank, status or date. It is only by chance that this remarkable figure has survived. It was ploughed up by a farmer in 1879 and used as a fire poker until someone recognized it as a masterpiece of Etruscan art.

Ombra della Sera

Detail from *The Deposition* (1521) by Rosso Fiorentino

🏛 Pinacoteca e Museo Civico

Via dei Sarti 1. **[** 0588 875 80.
Open mid-Mar–Oct: 9am–7pm daily; Nov–mid-Mar: 9am–1:45pm daily.
Closed 1 Jan, 25 Dec. **Adm charge**.

Volterra's excellent art gallery is situated in the 15th-century Palazzo Minucci-Solaini. The best works are by Florentine artists. Ghirlandaio's *Christ in Majesty* (1492) shows Christ hovering above an idealized Tuscan landscape. The San Giusto monastery, for which it was intended, was abandoned after a landslip like the one shown in the middle distance and beyond. Luca Signorelli's *Madonna and Child with Saints* (1491) shows his debt to Roman art through the reliefs on the base of the Virgin's throne. His *Annunciation*, painted in the same year, is a beautiful composition.

The museum's main exhibit is Rosso Fiorentino's Mannerist work *(see p25)*, *The Deposition* (1521). Attention is focused on the grief-stricken figures in the foreground and the pallid, empty shell of Christ's body, its dead weight symbolizing that His spirit is elsewhere.

⛪ Duomo

Piazza San Giovanni. **Open** daily.

Work on Volterra's cathedral began in the 1200s and continued intermittently over the next two centuries.

To the right of the High Altar stands a Romanesque wood-carving of *The Deposition* (1228). The Altar itself is flanked by graceful marble angels carved by Mino da Fiesole in 1471; they face the same artist's elegant tabernacle, carved with figures of Faith, Hope and Charity.

The nave, remodelled in 1581, has an unusual coffered ceiling with stucco figures of bishops and saints painted in rich blue and gold. The pulpit, in the middle of the nave, dates to 1584, but was created using sculptural reliefs from the late 12th and early 13th centuries. The *Last Supper* panel, facing into the nave and thought to be the work of the Pisan artist, Guglielmo

View from Volterra over the surrounding landscape

Detail from one of the panels decorating the Duomo pulpit

Pisano, has a number of humorous details including a monster snapping at the heels of Judas. Nearby, in the north aisle, Fra Bartolomeo's *The Annunciation* (1497) hangs above one of the side chapel altars.

More sculptures are housed in the oratory off the north aisle, near the main entrance. The best is a tableau of the Epiphany, preserved behind glass. The remarkably humane painted terracotta figures of the Virgin and Child in the foreground are believed to be by Zaccaria da Volterra (1473–1544), a local sculptor.

🏛 Museo d'Arte Sacra
Via Roma 13. **☎** *0588 862 90.*
Open *Mar–Nov: 9am–1pm, 3–6pm daily; Nov–Mar: 9am–1pm daily.*
Closed *1 Jan, 1 May, 25 Dec.*
Adm charge.
This museum in the Palazzo Arcivescovile, contains sculpture and architectural fragments from the Duomo and a number of local churches. The most important exhibit is a 15th-century della Robbia terracotta of St Linus, Volterra's patron saint.

The collection also has a range of church bells, from the 11th to 15th centuries, some church silver and several illuminated manuscripts.

🏛 Teatro Romano
Viale Ferrucci. **Open** *mid-Mar– Nov: 11am–5pm daily, except when raining.*
Adm charge.
Situated just outside the city walls, the ancient Roman theatre, dating to the first century BC, is one of the best-preserved in Italy. Enough of the original structure has survived to enable an almost complete reconstruction.

VISITORS' CHECKLIST

Road map C3. **👥** *12,200.* **ℹ** *Via Giusto Turazza 2 (0588 861 50).* **🏪** *Sat.* **🎭** *Astiludio (1st Sun in Sep).* **ⓦ** *www.provolterra.it*

🏛 Piazza dei Priori
This fine square is dominated by the Palazzo dei Priori, dating to 1208. A sober building, it is said to have been the model for the Palazzo Vecchio in Florence (*see pp78–9*).

The 13th-century Porcellino tower, on the other side of the square, is named after the small pig, now almost worn away, carved at its base.

🏛 Arco Etrusco
One of Volterra's more unusual sights, the Etruscan arch is in fact part Roman. Only the columns and the severely weathered basalt heads, representing Etruscan gods, date to the 6th-century BC original. The features of each head are now barely visible.

Plaque outside the Palazzo dei Priori

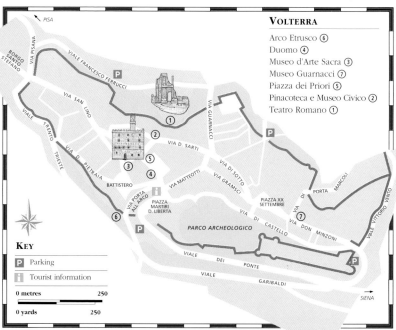

VOLTERRA

KEY

P Parking

ℹ Tourist information

0 metres 250

0 yards 250

NORTHERN TUSCANY

O F ALL THE REGIONS OF TUSCANY, *this one offers something for everyone. The historic towns are rich in art, architecture and music festivals, while many sporting activities can be enjoyed along the coast or in the mountains. The landscape, too, is marked by a vast range of features, from marble quarries to market gardens, and from mountain ranges and nature reserves to beaches.*

The heavily populated Lucchese plain between Florence and Lucca is dominated by industry: the textile factories of Prato produce three out of every four woollen garments exported from Italy. But in spite of their large suburbs, cities such as Prato, Pistoia and, above all, Lucca have rewarding churches, museums and galleries within their historic city centres.

The land between the cities is fertile and is therefore intensively cultivated. Asparagus and cut flowers are two of the most important crops, and the wholesale flower market at Pescia is one of the biggest in Italy. East of Lucca towards Pescia are garden centres and nurseries where huge quantities of young trees and shrubs are grown in long, neat rows.

North of the Lucchese plain the scenery is very different again. A series of foothills is covered in olive groves which produce some of the finest oil in Italy. Then, the land rises to the wild and mountainous areas of the Garfagnana, the Alpi Apuane (Apuan Alps) and the Lunigiana, with its fortified towns and castles built by the Dukes of Malaspina. Here you will find some of Tuscany's highest peaks, rising to 2,000 m (6,550 ft) or more. Vast areas of the mountains are designated as nature parks and the wild scenery attracts ramblers, trekkers and riders as well as hang-gliding enthusiasts.

Finally, the coastal area, known as the Versilia, includes some of Italy's most elegant and popular beach resorts. It stretches from the famous marble-quarrying town of Carrara in the north down to the area's main town, Viareggio, and to Torre del Lago Puccini, the lakeside home of Giacomo Puccini, where he wrote nearly all his operas.

Lucca's Piazza del Mercato, echoing the shape of the original Roman amphitheatre

◁ **The village of Vagli di Sotto on Lago di Vagli in the Parco Naturale delle Alpi Apuane**

Exploring Northern Tuscany

THE BEAUTIFUL TOWN of Lucca is a favourite base for exploring. Northwards, industrial suburbs give way to the olive groves, chestnut woods and bare mountains of the Alpi Apuane and the Garfagnana region, a popular area for outdoor sports, from trekking and canoeing to skiing. Castles dot the rugged Lunigiana, while beaches line the Versilia. Due east are large towns with historic centres: Pistoia and Prato.

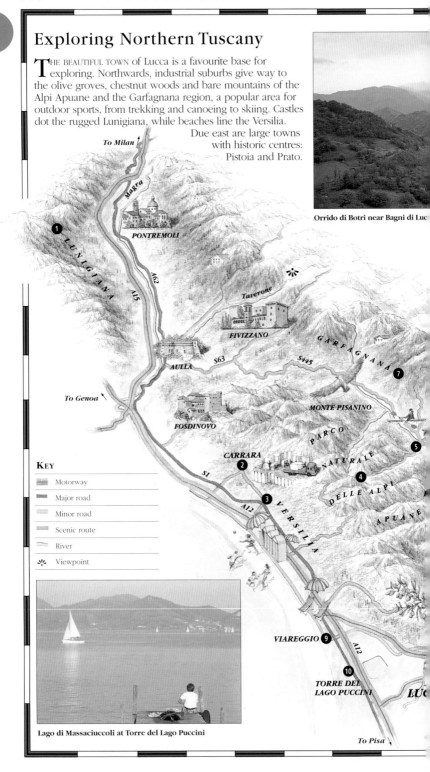

Orrido di Botri near Bagni di Luc[ca]

To Milan

PONTREMOLI

LUNIGIANA

Magra

A62

A15

Taverone

FIVIZZANO

AULLA   S63   S445

GARFAGNANA

To Genoa

FOSDINOVO

MONTE PISANINO

PARCO

CARRARA ②

S1

③   A12

VERSILIA

NATURALE

④

DELLE ALPI

APUANE

⑦

⑤

①

KEY

▦	Motorway
▦	Major road
▦	Minor road
▦	Scenic route
⌇	River
☀	Viewpoint

VIAREGGIO ⑨   A12

⑩

TORRE DEL LAGO PUCCINI   LUC

Lago di Massaciuccoli at Torre del Lago Puccini

To Pisa

GETTING AROUND

Lucca, Montecatini Terme, Prato and Pistoia are all on the A11 autostrada and are easy to reach by car from Pisa, Florence and other major cities outside Tuscany, such as Bologna. There are several trains a day between Pisa and Florence via Lucca, Montecatini Terme, Prato and Pistoia, and along the coast between Pisa and Carrara. From Lucca you can also travel by train up the Serchio valley to Castelnuovo di Garfagnana. But, since this is a mountainous region, much of it is only accessible by car.

SIGHTS AT A GLANCE

The hamlet of Montefegatesi in the Alpi Apuane

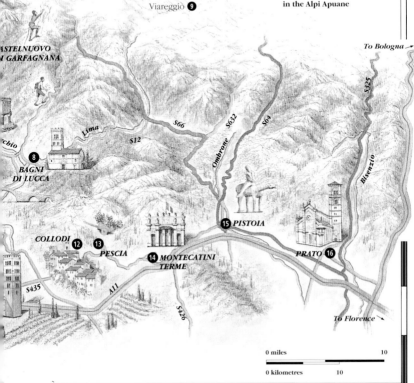

Sun, sand and sea – essential components of a holiday at a beach resort of the Versilia

The Lunigiana ❶

Road map A1. **FS** 🚌 *Aulla.*
ℹ️ *Aulla (0187 42 14 39).*

THE LUNIGIANA (Land of the Moon) region takes its name from the port of Luni – so called because of the moon-like luminescence of the marble shipped from here in Roman times. From the 16th century onwards, the Dukes of Malaspina built castles here and fortified villages against banditry. Malaspina castles can be seen at Massa, Fosdinovo, Aulla, Fivizzano and Verrucola.

At Pontremoli, the 14th-century Castello del Piagnaro houses the **Museo delle Statue-Stele Lunigianesi**, which shows prehistoric carved stone figures from the region.

🏛 **Museo delle Statue-Stele Lunigianesi**
Castello del Piagnaro, Pontremoli.
📞 *0187 83 14 39.* **Open** *9am–noon, 2–5pm Tue–Sun.* **Adm charge**.

Carrara ❷

Road map B1. 👥 *70,000.* **FS**
🚌 ℹ️ *Viale XX Settembre (0585 84 44 03).* 🛒 *Mon.*

CARRARA IS WORLD FAMOUS for its white marble. The 300 or so quarries near the town date to Roman times, making this the oldest industrial site in continuous use in the world. In Carrara itself there are numerous showrooms and workshops where the marble is sawn into sheets or sculpted into statues and ornaments. Many of the workshops welcome visitors. You can also discover more about the techniques of crafting marble at the **Museo Civico del Marmo**.

Carrara's **Duomo** uses the local marble to good effect in its Pisan-Romanesque façade featuring a rose window. In the same square is the house where Michelangelo used to stay on his visits to buy marble for his sculptures. The façade is marked by a plaque and by carvings of the sculptor's tools.

Tour buses from Carrara regularly visit the quarries at Colonnata and at Fantiscritti, where a museum displays various marble quarrying techniques. You can also drive there, following the numerous signs that say "Cave di Marmo".

🏛 **Museo Civico del Marmo**
Viale XX Settembre. 📞 *0585 84 57 46.*
Open *Nov–Apr: 8:30am–1:30pm Mon–Sat; May & Oct: 10am–5pm Mon–Sat; Jun–Sep: 10am–8pm Mon–Sat.*

🔓 **Duomo**
Piazza del Duomo. **Open** *daily.*

The Versilia ❸

Road map B2. **FS** 🚌 *Viareggio.*
ℹ️ *Viareggio (0584 96 22 33).*

THE VERSILIA, sometimes called the Tuscan Riviera because of the many beach resorts that line this 30-km (18-mile) strip, stretches from Marina di Carrara in the north down to Marina di Torre del

A quarry in the marble-bearing hills around Carrara

Lago Puccini. In the 1820s, towns such as Massa, Pietra Santa and Camaiore developed marinas and lidos along the part of the coast they controlled. These inland towns are linked by roads to their coastal twins. Here villas and hotels with fine walled gardens line the streets, with the mountains of the Alpi Apuane as a backdrop.

The beaches are divided into numerous bathing establishments run by hotels or private operators, who charge for use of the beach and its facilities. Forte dei Marmi is perhaps the most beautiful of these resorts, much favoured by wealthy Florentines and Milanese.

Poster for the Versilia

Parco Naturale delle Alpi Apuane **4**

Road map B1. [FS] [train] *Castelnuovo di Garfagnana.* [i] *Castelnuovo di Garfagnana (0583 64 43 54).*

T HE PARCO NATURALE delle Alpi Apuane, northwest of Castelnuovo di Garfagnana, was designated a nature reserve in 1985. Monte Pisanino is the highest peak in the area at 1,945 m (6,320 ft). It towers above Lago di Vagli, an artificial lake covering the drowned village of Fabbrica. Nearby are Vagli di Sotto (*see p164*) and Vagli di Sopra, ancient villages with rugged stone houses.

To the south, in the valley of the Turrite Secca, a spectacular mountain road leads to Seravezza, passing through a white-walled tunnel called the

The Turrite Secca valley in the Parco Naturale delle Alpi Apuane

Galleria del Cipollaio. Northwest, at Arni, are the Marmitte dei Giganti (Giants' Cooking Pots), great hollows left by the glaciers of the Ice Age.

Southeast at Calomini is a 12th-century rock-cut hermitage, home to a Capuchin monk. Further on is the Grotta del Vento (Cave of the Wind), at Fornovolasco. To the east, past Barga, at Coreglia Antelminelli, is the **Museo della Figurina di Gesso**, devoted to the history of locally made

The 13th-century Rocca at Castelnuovo di Garfagnana

plaster figurines, once sold by traders all over Europe.

m Museo della Figurina di Gesso
Via del Mangano 17, Coreglia Antelminelli. [C] *0583 780 82.* **Open** 9am–1pm Mon–Fri, 10am–1pm Sat–Sun, 3pm–5pm daily **Adm charge.**

Castelnuovo di Garfagnana **5**

Road map B1. [icon] *6,300.* [FS] [train] [i] *Loggiato Porta 10 (0583 64 43 54).* [icon] *Thu.*

V ISITORS to the Garfagnana use the town as a base for sporting activities. Information is available from the **Cooperativa Garfagnana Vacanze**. The 13th-century Rocca (castle) is now the town hall. Ludovico Ariosto, author of the epic poem *Orlando Furioso* (1516), lived here as governor between 1522 and 1525.

[icon] Cooperativa Garfagnana Vacanze
Piazza delle Erbe 1. [C] *0583 651 69.* **Open** Jun–Sep: 9am–1pm, 3:30–7:30pm daily; Oct–May: 9am–1pm, 3:30–5:30pm daily.

Barga ❻

Road map C1. 👥 *11,000.* **FS** 🚌
🚢 *Sat.*

BARGA IS the most attractive of the towns that line the Serchio valley leading northwards from Lucca, and it makes an excellent base for touring the Garfagnana region. The little walled town with its steep streets paved with stone is the setting for a highly regarded opera festival held in July in the 18th-century Teatro dell'Accademia dei Differenti. The festival is always well attended.

View over Barga rooftops

🏠 Duomo
Propositura. **Open** *daily.*
Barga's Duomo stands on a grassy terrace at the highest point in the town. There are glorious views from here of the gleaming white marble and limestone peaks of the Alpi Apuane.
The 11th-century Duomo is dedicated to San Cristoforo (St Christopher). The exterior is decorated with interesting Romanesque carvings of interlaced knots, wild beasts and knights in armour. Over the north portal, a frieze thought to be a scene from a folk tale depicts a banquet.
Inside, there is a huge wooden statue of St Christopher, dating to the 12th century, and a gilded tabernacle guarded by two charming terracotta angels by Luca della Robbia.
Most impressive of all is the massive marble pulpit, standing fully 5 m (16.5 ft) tall, supported by pillars which in turn rest on the back of man-eating lions. The pulpit is the work of Guido Bigarelli of Como and dates to the early 13th

century. The lively sculptures on the upper part depict the Evangelists, the Three Magi, the Annunciation, the Nativity and the Baptism of Christ.

The Garfagnana ❼

Road map C1. **FS** 🚌 *Castelnuovo di Garfagnana.* 🛈 *Castelnuovo di Garfagnana (0583 64 43 54).*

THIS MOUNTAINOUS region can be explored from Barga, Seravezza, or Castelnuovo di Garfagnana (*see p169*). Here too is the Parco Naturale delle Alpi Apuane (*see p169*). From Castelnuovo a scenic drive takes you to the Alpe Tre Potenze. You can return via San Pellegrino in Alpe with its **Museo Etnografico**, and also visit the nature park, **Parco dell' Orecchiella** and the **Orto Botanico Pánia di Corfino** with its collection of local Alpine plants.

Romanesque sculpture in Pieve di Brancoli

🏛 Museo Etnografico
Via del Voltone 15, San Pellegrino in Alpe. 📞 *0583 64 90 72.* **Open** *Tue–Sun (phone for times).* **Adm charge**.
🌿 Parco dell'Orecchiella
Centro Visitatori, Orecchiella. 📞 *0583 61 90 98.* **Open** *Jun & Sep: Sat & Sun; Jul–15 Sep: daily; Apr–Nov: Sun.* ♿
🌿 Orto Botanico Pánia di Corfino
Parco dell'Orecchiella. **Open** *Jul–Aug daily; May–Jun & Sep: Sun.*

Bagni di Lucca ❽

Road map C2. 👥 *7,402.* 🚌
🛈 *Via Umberto I (0583 88 88 81).*
🚢 *Wed & Sat.*

VISITORS COME TO Bagni di Lucca for its lime sulphate springs. In the 19th century it was one of Europe's most fashionable spa towns (*see p181*): the Casino, built in 1837, was the first to be licensed in Europe. Also from that time are the Neo-Gothic **English Church**, the elegant **Palazzo del Circolo dei Forestieri** restaurant and the **Cimitero Anglicano** (Protestant Cemetery). Bagni di Lucca makes a good base for exploring the surrounding hills cloaked in chestnut woods. You can walk to Montefegatesi, a hamlet surrounded by the peaks of the Alpi Apuane, and then continue to Orrido di Botri, a dramatic gorge. To the south of Bagni is San Giorgio or **Pieve di Brancoli**, one of many Romanesque churches in the area founded during the reign of Countess Matilda (1046–1115) (*see p43*).
The Ponte della Maddalena is a hump-backed bridge across the River Serchio just north of the village of Borgo a Mozzano. It is called Ponte del Diavolo (Devil's Bridge) because, according to local legend, the Devil offered to build the bridge in return for possession of the first soul to

Ponte della Maddalena or "Devil's Bridge" near Bagni di Lucca

A seaside café in the popular beach resort of Viareggio

cross it; the canny villagers agreed and, when it was finished, sent a dog across.

🏠 **English Church**
Via Crawford. **☎** 0583 80 99 11.
Open by appt.
⛪ **Palazzo del Circolo dei Forestieri**
Piazza Varraud 10. **☎** 0583 860 38. **Open** Tue–Sun. **♿**
⛪ **Cimitero Anglicano**
Via Letizia. **☎** 0583 80 99 11.
Open by appt.
🏠 **Pieve di Brancoli**
Vinchiana. **☎** 0583 96 52 81.
Open by appt.

Viareggio ⑨

Road map B2. 🏛 60,000.
FS 🚌 **ℹ** Viale Carducci 10 (0584 96 22 33). ✉ Thu.

VIAREGGIO IS FAMOUS for its elegant "Liberty" style (Art Nouveau) villas and hotels, built in the 1920s after the original boardwalk and timber chalets of the resort went up in flames in 1917. One example is the Gran Caffè Margherita, designed by Galileo Chini (see p190). The harbour has an interesting mix of boatyards, luxury yachts and fishing boats, and offers fine views of the Versilia coastline. Viareggio's carnival, held on Sundays from February to Lent and on Shrove Tuesday, is famous throughout Italy (see p36).

Torre del Lago Puccini ⑩

Road map B2. 🏛 11,500. **FS** 🚌
ℹ Via Marconi 225 (0584 35 98 93).
✉ Fri (Jul & Aug: also Sun).

THE COMPOSER Giacomo Puccini (1858–1924) (see p175) lived here, beside Lago di Massaciuccoli, to indulge his passion for shooting waterfowl. Puccini and his wife are buried in the house, the **Museo Villa Puccini**, in the mausoleum between the piano room and the gun room where he kept his rifle ("my second favourite instrument"). The operas are performed in the open-air lakeside theatre in summer (see p33). The reed-fringed lake is now a nature reserve for rare birds and migrants.

🏛 **Museo Villa Puccini**
Piazzale Belvedere Puccini 64.
☎ 0584 34 14 45.
Open Apr–Sep: 10am–12:30pm, 3–6pm daily; Oct–Mar: 9am–noon, 3–5pm Tue–Sun. **Adm charge**. **♿**

Near Puccini's lakeside home at Torre del Lago Puccini

Street-by-Street: Lucca ⓫

LUCCA BECAME A COLONY of ancient Rome in 180 BC, and the town's Roman legacy is still evident in the regular grid pattern of its streets. The remarkable elliptical shape of the Piazza del Mercato *(see p165)* is a survival of the amphitheatre. The name of the church of San Michele in Foro indicates that it stands beside the Roman forum, laid out as the city's main square in ancient times and still serving that function to this day. San Michele is just one of Lucca's many churches built in the 12th and 13th centuries in the elaborate Pisan-Romanesque style.

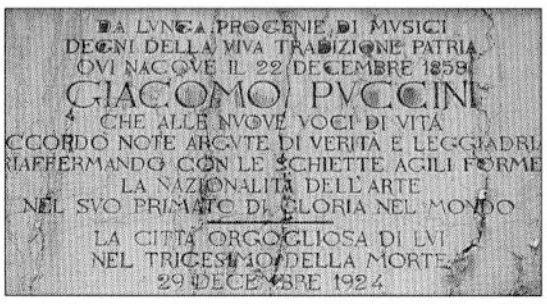

Most of the Renaissance palazzi of Piazza San Michele are now offices.

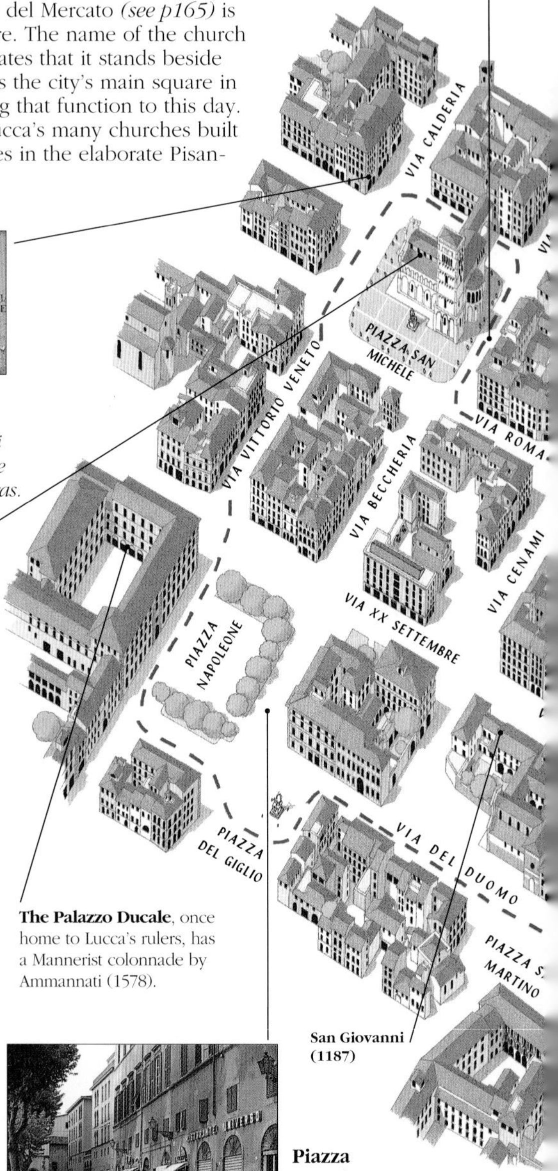

Casa di Puccini
This plaque marks the birthplace of Giacomo Puccini (1858–1924), composer of some of the world's most popular operas.

★ San Michele in Foro
The Madonna on the south-west corner of the church is a copy of the original inside, carved by Matteo Civitali (1436–1501).

The Palazzo Ducale, once home to Lucca's rulers, has a Mannerist colonnade by Ammannati (1578).

San Giovanni (1187)

Piazza Napoleone
The square is named after Napoleon, whose sister, Elisa Baciocchi, was ruler of Lucca (1805–15). The statue is of her successor, Marie Louise de Bourbon.

STAR SIGHTS

★ **San Martino**

★ **San Michele in Foro**

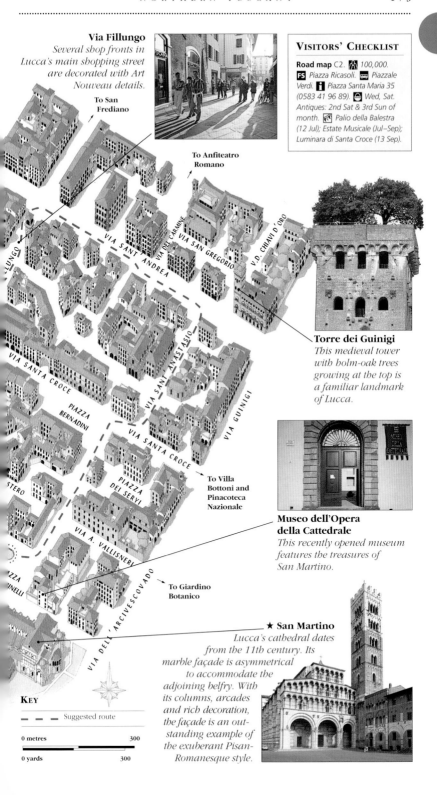

Via Fillungo
Several shop fronts in Lucca's main shopping street are decorated with Art Nouveau details.

To San Frediano

To Anfiteatro Romano

VISITORS' CHECKLIST

Road map C2. 🚲 100,000.
FS *Piazza Ricasoli.* 🚌 *Piazzale Verdi.* 🛈 *Piazza Santa Maria 35 (0583 41 96 89).* 🛒 *Wed, Sat. Antiques: 2nd Sat & 3rd Sun of month.* 🎭 *Palio della Balestra (12 Jul); Estate Musicale (Jul–Sep); Luminara di Santa Croce (13 Sep).*

VIA SANT'ANDREA
VIA DEL CARMINE
VIA SAN GREGORIO
V.D. CHIAVI D'ORO
LUNGO

VIA SANT'ANASTASIO

VIA SANTA CROCE

PIAZZA BERNADINI

VIA SANTA CROCE

VIA GUINIGI

STERO

PIAZZA DEI SERVI

VIA A. VALLISNERI

ZZA INELLI

VIA DELL'ARCIVESCOVADO

To Villa Bottoni and Pinacoteca Nazionale

To Giardino Botanico

Torre dei Guinigi
This medieval tower with holm-oak trees growing at the top is a familiar landmark of Lucca.

Museo dell'Opera della Cattedrale
This recently opened museum features the treasures of San Martino.

★ San Martino
Lucca's cathedral dates from the 11th century. Its marble façade is asymmetrical to accommodate the adjoining belfry. With its columns, arcades and rich decoration, the façade is an outstanding example of the exuberant Pisan-Romanesque style.

KEY

– – – Suggested route

0 metres   300
0 yards   300

Exploring Lucca

Mosaic in San Frediano

LUCCA IS ENCLOSED by massive red brick walls which help to give the city its special character by shutting out traffic and the modern world. Built in 1504–1645, the walls are among the best-preserved Renaissance defences in Europe. Within these walls, Lucca is a peaceful city of narrow lanes, preserving intact its original ancient Roman street plan. Unlike several of Tuscany's hilltop cities, Lucca is flat: many locals use bicycles, which lends the city added charm.

Lucca viewed from the top of the Guinigi Tower

⛪ San Martino
See pp176–7.

✹ Anfiteatro Romano
Piazza del Mercato.

Almost none of the ancient Roman amphitheatre survives: the stone was gradually stolen for use elsewhere, leaving the atmospheric arena-shaped Piazza del Mercato of today *(see p165).* The piazza is enclosed by medieval houses that were built up against the walls of the amphitheatre. Its shape, perfectly preserved, is a striking reminder that Lucca was founded by the Romans around 180 BC. Low archways at north, south, east and west mark the gates through which beasts and gladiators would once have entered the arena.

✹ Palazzo dei Guinigi
Via Sant'Andrea 41. ☎ *336 20 32 21.* **Tower open** *9am–7:30pm daily.* **Closed** *25 Dec.* **Adm charge.**

This house is one of several in Lucca once owned by the powerful Guinigi family, rulers of the city in the 15th century. They kept Florence at bay, so that Lucca, remarkably, was never conquered by the Medici, thus remaining independent until the end of the 18th century. The red brick palazzo, built in the late 14th century, has late-Gothic windows. The striking 41-m (133-ft) defensive tower alongside, the Torre dei Guinigi, has a small roof garden, hence the ilex (holm-oak) trees sprouting incongruously at the top.

✿ Giardino Botanico
Via dell'Orto Botanico 14. ☎ *0583 44 21 60.* **Open** *9:30am–12.30pm daily; 2:30–5:30pm Sat & Sun.* **Adm charge.** ♿

Lucca's delightful botanical garden, tucked into an angle of the city walls, was laid out in 1820. It displays a wide range of Tuscan plants.

🏛 Museo della Cattedrale
Via Arcivescovado. ☎ *0583 49 05 30.* **Open** *summer: 10am–6pm daily; winter: 10am–5pm daily (to 6pm Sat & Sun).* **Adm charge.** ♿

Housed in the 14th-century former Archbishop's Palace, the museum displays the treasures of the Duomo, San Martino. These include the 11th-century carved stone head of a king from the original façade. There is also a rare 12th-century Limoges enamel casket, which possibly held a relic of St Thomas à Becket. The Croce di Pisani made by Vincenzo di Michele in 1411 is a masterpiece showing Christ hanging from the Tree of Redemption, surrounded by angels, the Virgin, St John and the other Evangelists.

🏛 Museo Nazionale Guinigi
Via della Quarquonia. ☎ *0583 555 70.* **Open** *8:30am–7pm Tue–Sat, 8:30am–1pm Sun.* **Adm charge.**

This huge Renaissance villa was built for Paolo Guinigi, who ruled Lucca from 1400 until 1430. The ground floor holds sculpture from Lucca and the surrounding area, including fine Romanesque reliefs from Lucca's churches. The gallery on the floor above displays paintings, furnishings, and choir stalls from Lucca's cathedral, inlaid with marquetry views of the city in 1529.

Romanesque lion at Museo Nazionale Guinigi

The beautiful galleried staircase at Palazzo Pfanner

🏛 Palazzo Pfanner

[0583 49 12 43. **Closed** to the public. **Gardens Open** Mar–Oct: 10am–6pm daily; Nov–Feb: by appt. **Adm charge**.

The Palazzo Pfanner, an imposing house built in 1667, has one of Tuscany's most delightful formal gardens to the rear. (The garden can also be viewed while walking along the ramparts.) Laid out in the 18th century, the garden's central avenue is lined with Baroque statues of ancient Roman gods and goddesses, alternating with lemon trees in huge terracotta pots.

Unfortunately, the house itself, which contains a rich collection of 18th- and 19th-century court costumes, is closed to the public.

🚩 Piazza Napoleone and Piazza del Giglio

These two squares are almost one. The first was laid out in 1806 when Lucca was under the imposed rule of Elisa Baciocchi, Napoleon's sister. The statue in the square is of her successor, Marie Louise de Bourbon. She faces the massive Palazzo Ducale, with its elegant colonnade built by Ammannati in 1578. Behind her is the Piazza del Giglio, with the Teatro del Giglio (1817) on the south side of the square. The theatre saw the first performance in Italy of Rossini's penultimate opera, *William Tell* (1831). Today it is famous for its productions of operas by Puccini, who was born in Lucca.

🏛 Casa di Puccini

Corte San Lorenzo 8 (Via di Poggio). **[** 0583 58 40 28. **Open** Mar–May & Oct–Dec: 10am–1pm, 3–6pm Tue–Sun; Jun–Sep: 10am–6pm daily. **Adm charge**.

The 15th-century house in which Giacomo Puccini (1858–1924) was born contains portraits of the great composer, costume designs for his operas and the piano he used when composing his last opera, *Turandot*. Left unfinished at his death,

The composer Giacomo Puccini

it was completed by Franco Alfano and first performed two years later at La Scala, Milan.

🏛 Pinacoteca Nazionale

Via Galli Tassi 43. **[** 0583 555 70. **Open** 8:30am–7pm Tue–Sat, 8:30am–1pm Sun. **Adm charge**. ☐

Lucca's picture gallery is in the impressive 17th-century Palazzo Mansi, with paintings and furnishings of the same period, typical of the time when Mannerism was being superseded by Baroque and Rococo art. There are also works by Bronzino, Pontormo, Sodoma, Andrea del Sarto, Tintoretto and Salvatore Rosa, including Medici portraits.

🚩 Ramparts

Complete circuit: 4.2 km (2.5 miles).

A promenade runs along the top of the city walls, built in 1504–1645. Marie Louise de Bourbon made the ramparts into a public park in the early 19th century, with a double avenue of trees. It makes a delightful walk with fine views of the town, including glimpses of private gardens. There are occasional guided tours of the chambers and passages inside one of the bastions.

The Porta San Donato along the tree-lined ramparts walk

San Martino

LUCCA'S EXTRAORDINARY CATHEDRAL, with its façade abutting incongruously on to the campanile, is dedicated to St Martin. He is the Roman soldier depicted on the façade dividing his cloak with a sword to share with a needy beggar. This and other scenes from the life of the saint form part of the complex decorations covering the 13th-century façade. There are also reliefs depicting *The Labours of the Months* and intricate panels of inlaid pink, green and white marble showing hunting scenes, peacocks and flowers.

Threshing, the Labour of September

The altar painting in the Sacristy, *The Madonna and Saints* (1449–94), is by Ghirlandaio.

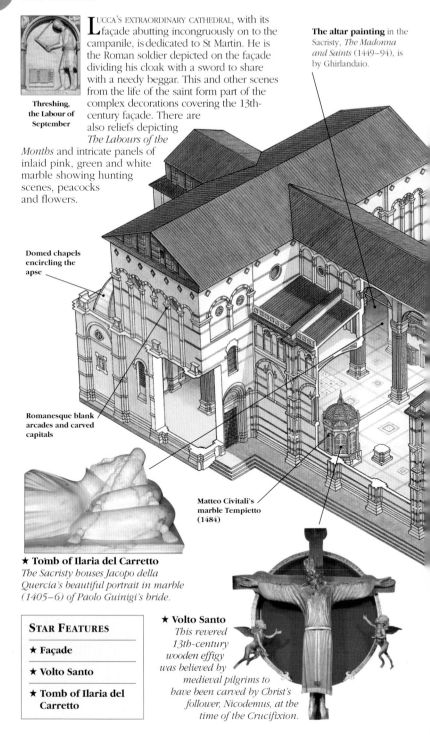

Domed chapels encircling the apse

Romanesque blank arcades and carved capitals

Matteo Civitali's marble Tempietto (1484)

★ **Tomb of Ilaria del Carretto**
The Sacristy houses Jacopo della Quercia's beautiful portrait in marble (1405–6) of Paolo Guinigi's bride.

STAR FEATURES

★ Façade

★ Volto Santo

★ Tomb of Ilaria del Carretto

★ **Volto Santo**
This revered 13th-century wooden effigy was believed by medieval pilgrims to have been carved by Christ's follower, Nicodemus, at the time of the Crucifixion.

★ **Façade**
The gabled façade has three tiers of ornate colonnading (1204). Every one of the carved columns is different, and there are lively hunting scenes above them.

Circular clerestory windows, in the nave and above the aisle roof, light the unusually tall nave of the cross-shaped church.

The campanile was built in 1060 as a defensive tower. The upper two tiers were added in 1261 when the tower was joined to the cathedral.

St Martin
This sculpture of the saint dividing his cloak to share it is a copy. The 13th-century original is now just inside the cathedral entrance.

Inlaid Marble
Scenes from daily life, myths and poems cover the façade. Look out for the maze pattern on the right pier of the porch.

Nicola Pisano (1200–78) carved *The Journey of the Magi* and *The Deposition* round the left doorway.

Doorway Sculptures
This 13th-century relief depicts the beheading of St Regulus. The Labours of the Months round the central door show the tasks appropriate to each season.

Apostles from the mosaic on the façade of San Frediano in Lucca

🔒 San Frediano

Piazza San Frediano. **Open** daily.

The striking façade of Lucca's San Frediano church features a colourful 13th-century mosaic, *The Ascension*, by the School of Berlinghieri. Inside, to the right, is a splendid Romanesque font which could easily be mistaken for a fountain, because it is so big and impressive. The sides are carved with scenes from *The Life of Christ* and the story of Moses. One dramatic scene shows Moses and his followers dressed in 12th-century armour, looking like Crusaders, as they pass through the divided Red Sea with an entourage of camels.

Amico Aspertini's frescoes (1508–9) in the second chapel in the north aisle tell the story of Lucca's precious relic, the Volto Santo *(see p176)*, and give a good idea of what the city looked like in the early 16th century.

Also in the church is a coloured wooden statue of the Virgin, carved by Matteo Civitali, and an altarpiece carved from a single block of marble by Jacopo della Quercia in the Cappella Trenta. It is carved in the shape of a polyptych with five Gothic-spired niches.

Detail from façade of San Michele in Foro

🔒 San Michele in Foro

Piazza San Michele. **Open** daily.

As its name suggests, this church stands on the site of the ancient Roman forum. It has a wonderfully rich Pisan-Romanesque façade that competes in splendour with that of San Martino *(see pp176–7)*. John Ruskin, the English artist and art historian whose work did so much to revive interest in Italian art during the 19th century *(see p53)*, spent many hours sketching the rich mixture of twisted marble columns and Cosmati work (inlaid marble). The façade is almost barbaric in its exuberance, and the inlaid marble scenes depict wild beasts and huntsmen on horseback rather than Christian subjects. Only the huge winged figure of St Michael, standing on the pediment and flanked by two angels, marks this out as a church. The splendour of the façade, built over a long period from the 11th to the 14th centuries, is matched by the arcading of the belltower.

The interior has little of interest except for Filippino Lippi's recently restored *Saints Helena, Jerome, Sebastian and Roch*, among the most beautiful of his paintings.

The square outside is circled by 15th- and 16th-century palazzi, which are now mostly occupied by banks, while the portico of the Palazzo Pretorio to the south shelters a 19th-century statue of Lucca's greatest artist and architect, Matteo Civitali (1436–1501).

🏛 Via Fillungo

Lucca's principal shopping street winds its way through the heart of the city towards the Anfiteatro Romano *(see p174)*. It is a good place to stroll in the cool of the early evening. The upper end, towards San Frediano church, has several shops with Art Nouveau ironwork, while San Cristoforo, the 13th-century church halfway down the street, holds exhibitions of work by local artists.

🏛 Villa Bottini

Via Elisa. 🅒 0583 49 14 49.
Garden open 9am–1pm Mon–Sat.
The pretty walled garden of this late 16th-century building is open to the public. It is also used occasionally in summer for outdoor concerts.

Villa Bottini and garden

A Day Out around Lucca

THIS MOTORING TOUR takes you by a scenic route to the best of the villas around Lucca. After leaving Lucca the first stop is the Romanesque church of San Giorgio at Pieve di Brancoli; then comes the ancient hump-backed Ponte della Maddalena, also known as Devil's Bridge *(see p170)*. In the spa town of Bagni di Lucca the pretty suspension bridge across the Lima dates from 1840. On reaching Collodi, explore the village on foot, as the streets are too steep and narrow for cars. The Villa Garzoni, with its splendid gardens, lies below the town, and the Pinocchio Park is on the other side of the road. Continue to the Villa Torrigiani, which is set in a fine park and contains 13th–18th-century porcelain and furnishings. The tour ends at the 17th-century Villa Mansi, with its Baroque façade and a garden enlivened by statues of Diana and other pagan deities.

Bagni di Lucca ③
Drive on along the S12 for 5 km (3 miles) to the spa town. Then continue along the same road through the town.

Villa Garzoni ④
Turn left at the T-junction on the S12 for Abetone, then right for Collodi and the Villa Garzoni with its terraced gardens.

Ponte della Maddalena ②
Continue for 8 km (5 miles) on the S12 to the bridge.

Borgo a Mozzano

S12

Boveglio

① *Pieve di Brancoli*

Pinocchio Park ⑤
This children's theme park in Collodi is based on the famous puppet's adventures.

San Giorgio ①
Leave Lucca on the S12 to Abetone, staying on the right bank of the Serchio. After 10 km (6 miles) turn right for Pieve di Brancoli and San Giorgio.

LUCCA

Villa Reale
Marlia

Colodi
④⑤

Camigliano
⑦ ⑥
Segromigno in Monte

S435

Villa Mansi ⑦
Heading for Segromino in Monte, turn right at the first junction into Via Piaggiori; then follow signs to Villa Mansi.

Villa Torrigiani ⑥
South of Collodi turn right on the S435 for Lucca. After Borgonuovo, turn right for Camigliano Santa Gemma and left after 1.5 km (1 mile) for the villa.

KEY

▬▬ Tour route

═══ Other roads

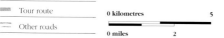

0 kilometres   5

0 miles   2

Terme Tettuccio, Montecatini's oldest and most famous spa, rebuilt in 1925–8

Collodi ⑫

Road map C2. 🏃 3,000. ℹ️ 0583 97 82 05.

THERE ARE two main sights in this town: the **Villa Garzoni** with its theatrical terraced gardens tumbling down the hillside and, for children, the **Pinocchio Park** *(see p179)*.

The author of *The Adventures of Pinocchio* (1881), Carlo Lorenzini, was born in Florence but his uncle was custodian of the Villa Garzoni and Lorenzini frequently stayed here as a child. Fond memories led him to use Collodi as his pen name and in 1956 the town decided to repay the compliment by setting up the theme park.

The park consists of gardens featuring mosaics and sculptural tableaux based on the adventures of the puppet, plus a maze, playground, exhibition centre and children's restaurant.

The Pescia river, running through a fertile, cultivated landscape

---

⚜️ **Villa Garzoni**
📞 0572 42 84 00. **Villa** *closed for restoration.* **Garden open** *daily.* **Adm charge**.

🌱 **Pinocchio Park**
📞 0572 42 96 42. **Open** *8:30am–sunset daily.* **Adm charge**.
♿ partial.
🌐 www. pinocchio.it

Pescia ⑬

Road map C2. 🏃 18,000. 🚌 ℹ️ 0583 97 82 05. 🚃 Sat.

PESCIA'S wholesale flower market is one of Italy's biggest, and there are some interesting sights to visit.

In the church of **San Francesco** are frescoes on *The Life of St Francis* (1235) by Bonaventura Berlinghieri (1215–74). The artist knew St Francis *(see p45)* and it is claimed that the frescoes are an accurate portrait of the saint. The **Duomo**, remodelled in Baroque style by Antonio

---

Ferri in 1693, has a massive campanile that was originally built as a tower within the city walls. It was given its onion-dome "cap" in 1771.

There is a small collection of religious paintings and illuminated manuscripts in the **Museo Civico**, and the **Museo Archeologico della Valdinievole** displays material excavated from nearby Valdinievole, the pretty "Vale of Mist".

🏛️ **San Francesco**
Piazza San Francesco. **Open** *daily.*

🏛️ **Duomo**
Piazza del Duomo. **Open** *daily.*

🏛️ **Museo Civico**
Palazzo Galeotti, Piazza Santo Stefano 1. 📞 0572 47 79 44. **Open** *1–7pm Mon, Wed, Fri, 8am–1pm Tue, Thu, Sat.*

🏛️ **Museo Archeologico della Valdinievole**
Piazza Leonardo da Vinci 1. 📞 0572 47 75 33. **Open** *9am–1pm Mon–Sat, 3–5pm Tue & Thu.*

Montecatini Terme ⑭

Road map C2. 🏃 22,500. 🚌 ℹ️ Viale Verdi 66 (0572 77 22 44). 🚃 Thu.

OF ALL TUSCANY'S many spa towns, Montecatini Terme is the most interesting. It has beautiful formal gardens and the architecture of its spas is particularly distinguished.

Terme Leopoldine (1926), built in the style of a Classical temple, is named after Grand Duke Leopoldo I, who first

Theatre building in Montecatini Alto's main square

encouraged the development of Montecatini Terme in the 18th century.

The most splendid is the Neo-Classical Terme Tettuccio (1925–8) with its circular, marble-lined pools, fountains and Art Nouveau tiles depicting languorous nymphs.

Terme Torretta, named after its mock medieval tower, is noted for its tea-time concerts, while Terme Tamerici has beautifully tended gardens.

Visitors can obtain day tickets to the spas to drink the waters and relax in the reading, writing and music rooms. More information is available from the Direzione delle Terme at Viale Verdi 41.

A popular excursion from Montecatini Terme is to take the funicular railway up to the ancient fortified village of Montecatini Alto. In the quiet main piazza, there are antique shops and well-regarded restaurants with outdoor tables. From the Rocca (castle) you can take in sweeping views over the mountainous countryside, known locally as "Little Switzerland".

Nearby at Ponte Buggianese, in **San Michele** church, you can see modern frescoes by the Florentine artist Pietro Annigoni (1910–88) on the theme of Christ's Passion.

At Monsummano Terme, another of Tuscany's well known spa towns, the **Grotta Giusti** spa prescribes the inhalation of vapours from hot sulphurous springs found in the nearby caves.

Above Monsummano Terme is the fortified hilltop village of Monsummano Alto with its once strategically placed but now ruined castle. Today, few people live in the sleepy village, with its pretty 12th-century church and crumbling houses, but there are some fine views from here.

🔒 **San Michele**
Ponte Buggianese. **Open** by appt.

🏛 **Grotta Giusti**
Monsummano Terme. 📞 0572 511 65. **Open** 9am–7pm Mon–Sat, 9am–1pm Sun. **Adm charge**.

The Terme Tamerici, built in Neo-Gothic style in the early 20th century

TAKING THE WATERS IN TUSCANY

The therapeutic value of bathing was first recognized by the ancient Romans. They were also the first to exploit the hot springs of volcanic origin that they found all over Tuscany. Here they built bath complexes where the army veterans who settled in towns such as Florence and Siena could relax. Some of these spas, as at Saturnia *(see p234)*, are still called by their original Roman names.

Other spas came into prominence during the Middle Ages and Renaissance: St Catherine of Siena (1347–80) *(see p215)*, who suffered from scrofula, a form of tuberculosis, and Lorenzo de' Medici (1449–92), who was arthritic, both bathed in the sulphurous hot springs at Bagno Vignoni *(see p222)* to relieve their ailments. Tuscan spas really came into their own in the early 19th

1920s spa poster

century when Bagni di Lucca was one of the most fashionable spa centres in Europe, frequented by emperors, kings and aristocrats *(see p170)*. However, spa culture in the 19th century had more to do with social life: flirtation and gambling took precedence over health cures.

Today treatments such as inhaling sulphur-laden steam, drinking the mineral-rich waters, hydro massage, bathing and application of mud packs are prescribed for disorders ranging from liver complaints to skin conditions and asthma. Many visitors still continue the tradition of coming to fashionable spas such as Montecatini Terme or Monsummano Terme, not just for the benefits of therapeutic treatment but also for relaxation and in search of companionship.

Pistoia ⑮

The Cappella del Tau symbol

T HE CITIZENS OF PISTOIA acquired a reputation for viciousness and intrigue in the 13th century and the taint has never quite disappeared. The cause was a feud between two of the city's rival factions, the Neri and Bianchi (Blacks and Whites), that spread to involve other cities. Assassination in Pistoia's narrow alleyways was commonplace. The favoured weapon was a tiny but deadly dagger called the *pistole* made by the city's ironworkers, who also specialized in surgical instruments. The city still thrives on metalworking: everything from buses to mattress springs is made here. Its historic centre has several fine buildings.

Baptistry opposite the Cattedrale

🔒 Cattedrale di San Zeno

Piazza del Duomo. **ℂ** 0573 250 95. **Open** daily. **Adm charge**. ⚹ side entrance.
Piazza del Duomo, the city's main square, is dominated by the Cattedrale di San Zeno and its bulky campanile, which was originally built in the 12th century as a defensive watchtower in the city walls.

The interior is rich in funerary monuments. The finest of these, in the south aisle, is the tomb of poet Cino da Pistoia, who is depicted in a relief (1337) lecturing to a class of young boys.

Nearby is the chapel of St James with its extraordinary silver altar decorated with over 600 statues and reliefs. The earliest of these date from 1287 and the altar was not completed until 1456. During that time, nearly every silversmith of note in Tuscany contributed to the extraordinarily rich design. Among them was Brunelleschi, who began his career working in metal before switching to architecture. Also in Piazza del Duomo, facing the Cattedrale, is the octagonal Baptistry, which was finished in 1359.

🏛 Museo di Sanzeno

Palazzo dei Vescovi, Piazza del Duomo. **ℂ** 0573 36 92 72. **Open** 10am–1pm, 3–5pm Tue, Thu & Fri (reservations only). **Adm charge**. ⚹ ⚹ partial.
In the beautifully restored Palazzo dei Vescovi (Bishop's Palace) is the

Museo della Cattedrale. In the basement, you can see the excavated remains of Roman buildings, and upstairs there are some fine reliquaries, crucifixes and chalices made by local goldsmiths during the 13th–15th centuries.

🏛 Museo Civico

Palazzo del Comune, Piazza del Duomo. **ℂ** 0573 37 12 96. **Open** 10am–7pm Tue–Sat, 9am–12:30pm Sun. **Adm charge**. ⚹
On the opposite side of the square is the Palazzo del Comune (Town Hall), which has the Museo Civico upstairs. Exhibits here range from medieval altar paintings to the work of 20th-century Pistoian artists, architects and sculptors.

🏛 Centro Marino Marini

Palazzo del Tau, Corso Silvano Fedi 72. **ℂ** 0573 302 85. **Open** 10am–1pm, 3–4pm Tue–Sat, 10am–1pm Sun. **Adm charge**. ⚹
The work of Marino Marini (1901–80), Pistoia's most famous 20th-century artist, is housed in a museum dedicated to him in the Palazzo del Tau. On display are drawings and casts, which trace the development of his style. Marini specialized in sculpting primitive forms in bronze or clay. His subjects included a horse and rider *(see p104)*, and Pomona, the ancient Roman goddess of fertility.

Pomona by Marino Marini

🔒 Cappella del Tau

Corso Silvano Fedi 70. **ℂ** 0573 322 04. **Open** 8am–2pm Mon–Sat.
This chapel owes its name to the letter T (*tau* in Greek) which appeared on the cloaks of the monks who built it and which symbolized a crutch.

Inside the chapel there are frescoes on *The Creation* and the life of St Anthony Abbot, who founded the order, which is dedicated to tending the sick and crippled.

The Fall, in the Cappella del Tau

🔒 San Giovanni Fuorcivitas

Via Cavour. **Open** daily.
Just north of the Cappella del Tau is the 12th-century church of San Giovanni Fuorcivitas ("St John outside the city", since the church once stood beyond the city walls). Its north flank is strikingly clad in banded marble and there is a Romanesque relief of *The Last Supper* over the portal. Inside is Giovanni Pisano's holy water basin, carved in marble with figures of the Virtues, and an equally masterly pulpit by Guglielmo

Detail of frieze (1514–25) by Giovanni della Robbia, Ospedale del Ceppo

VISITORS' CHECKLIST

Road map C2. ⚏ *93,000.*
FS *Piazza Dante Alighieri.*
▭ *Piazza San Francesco.*
ℹ *Palazzo dei Vescovi, Piazza del Duomo 4 (0573 216 22).*
Information open *daily.*
◉ *Wed & Sat.*
◈ *Giostra dell'Orso (25 Jul).*

da Pisa, carved in 1270 with New Testament scenes. Both works are among the finest of this period, when artists were reviving the art of carving.

⌂ Sant'Andrea
Via Sant'Andrea 21. **Open** *daily.*
The church of Sant'Andrea is reached by walking through Piazza della Sala, the site of Pistoia's lively open-air market. There is a good Romanesque relief of *The Journey of the Magi* over the portal, and inside is Giovanni Pisano's pulpit (completed in 1301). This is considered by some to be his masterpiece, even more accomplished than the pulpit he made in 1302–11 for Pisa cathedral *(see p155).* It is decorated with reliefs depicting scenes from *The Life of Christ.*

⌂ San Bartolomeo in Pantano
Piazza San Bartolomeo 6. **Open** *daily.*
The beautiful Romanesque church of San Bartolomeo in Pantano, dating from 760, houses another celebrated pulpit, carved in 1250 by Guido da Como.

⎵ Ospedale del Ceppo
Piazza Giovanni XXIII.
This hospital and orphanage, founded in 1277, was named after the *ceppo,* or hollowed-out tree trunk, that was used in medieval times to collect donations for its work. The striking façade of the main building features coloured terracotta panels (1514–25) by Giovanni della Robbia illustrating the Seven Works of Corporeal Mercy. The portico is by Michelozzo.

⚥ Zoo
Via Pieve a Celle 160a. **☎** *0573 91 12 19.* **Open** *9am–5pm daily (to 7pm in summer).* **Adm charge.** ♿
There is a small, well-kept zoo just 4 km (2.5 miles) northwest of Pistoia at La Verginina.

Façade of San Bartolomeo

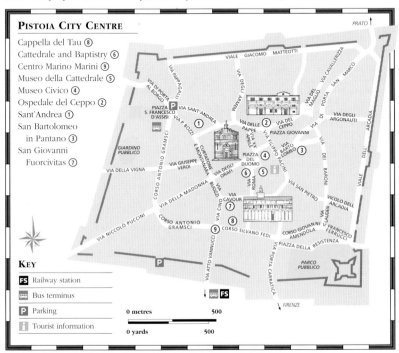

PISTOIA CITY CENTRE

Cappella del Tau ⑧
Cattedrale and Baptistry ⑥
Centro Marino Marini ⑨
Museo della Cattedrale ⑤
Museo Civico ④
Ospedale del Ceppo ②
Sant'Andrea ①
San Bartolomeo in Pantano ③
San Giovanni Fuorcivitas ⑦

KEY
FS Railway station
▭ Bus terminus
P Parking
ℹ Tourist information

0 metres   500
0 yards   500

Prato ⑯

Madonna del Ceppo **by Fra Filippo Lippi in the Museo Civico**

PRATO HAS BEEN ONE OF ITALY'S most important textile-manufacturing cities since the 13th century. One of its most famous citizens was the immensely wealthy Francesco di Marco Datini (1330–1410), who has been immortalized by Iris Origo in *The Merchant of Prato* (1957). Datini left all his money to charity, and the city contains several reminders of him, particularly in his own Palazzo Datini. Prato also attracts pilgrims from all over Italy who come to see the Virgin's Girdle, a prized relic kept in the Duomo and on view five times a year.

Duomo façade and pulpit

🏠 Duomo

Piazza del Duomo. **Open** *daily.*

The Duomo stands on the main square, with the Pulpit of the Holy Girdle to the right of its façade, its frieze of dancing cherubs designed by Donatello (1438). Inside, the first chapel on the left holds the Virgin's Girdle, which is displayed from the pulpit on Easter Sunday, 1 May, 15 August, 8 September and Christmas Day. Frescoes by Agnolo Gaddi (1392–5) relate how the girdle reached Prato. When a local merchant married a Palestinian woman in 1141, she brought it with her. She had inherited it from the Apostle Thomas who was given it by the Virgin before her Assumption. Also in the Duomo is Fra Filippo Lippi's masterpiece, *The Life of John the Baptist* (1452–66); Salome is a portrait of Lippi's mistress, Lucrezia Buti.

🏛 Museo dell'Opera del Duomo

Piazza del Duomo 49. **[** *0574 293 39.* **Open** *9:30am–12:30pm, 3–6:30pm Mon & Wed–Sat; 9:30am–12:30pm Sun.* **Adm charge**.

Donatello's original panels for the Holy Girdle pulpit are currently being restored, but the museum also houses the reliquary (1446) made for the Girdle by Maso di Bartolomeo, and *St Lucy* by Filippino Lippi, the son of Fra Filippo Lippi and Lucrezia Buti.

🚇 Piazza del Comune

The streets around the Duomo contain several important buildings. The city's main street, Via Mazzoni, leads west to the Piazza del Comune with its Bacchus fountain. The original, made in 1659, is in the nearby Palazzo Comunale.

🏛 Museo Civico

Palazzo Pretorio, Piazza del Comune 19. **[** *0574 61 63 02.* **Closed** for restoration. **Adm charge.** **&** partial.

Opposite the Palazzo Comunale is the austere Palazzo Pretorio, housing the Museo Civico (currently closed for restoration). The altar painting *The Story of the Holy Girdle* by Bernardo Daddi (1312–48) and Fra Filippo Lippi's *Madonna del Ceppo*, featuring a portrait of Francesco Datini, a patron of the Ceppo charity (*see p183*) are housed in the museum.

🏛 Palazzo Datini

Via Ser Lapo Mazzei 43. **[** *0574 213 91.* **Open** *9am–12:30pm, 4–7pm Mon–Sat.* **&**

This house where Francesco Datini lived is now a museum. Its archive contains 140,000 business letters and Datini's account books, on which Iris Origo based her biography.

The Story of the Holy Girdle **by Bernardo Daddi in the Museo Civico**

⛪ Santa Maria delle Carceri

*Piazza delle Carceri. **Open** daily.*

Prato's most important church stands on the site of a prison *(carceri)* on whose wall an image of the Virgin miraculously appeared in 1484. The serene domed church (1485–1506), with its harmoniously proportioned interior, is a fine work by the Renaissance architect Giuliano da Sangallo. Inside, the blue and white glazed terracotta roundels of the Evangelists (1490) are by Andrea della Robbia.

♖ Castello dell'Imperatore

*Piazza delle Carceri. **Open** Wed–Sat, Sun morning & Mon.*

This imposing castle was built by the German Holy Roman Emperor, Frederick II, in 1237 during his campaign to conquer Italy.

🏛 Museo del Tessuto

*Piazza del Comune. ☎ 0574 611 503. **Open** 10:30am–6:30pm Mon, Wed–Sat (to 2:30pm Sat). ♿*

The history of Prato's textile industry, the basis of its wealth, is charted in this textile museum.

VISITORS' CHECKLIST

Road map D2. 🚶 170,000. 🚆 Prato Centrale and Porta al Serraglio. 🚌 Piazzas Ciardi, San Francesco & Stazione. ℹ️ Piazza delle Carceri 15 (0574 241 12). **Information open** 9am–6:30pm Mon–Sat. 🚪 Mon.

Located on the city's southern outskirts, it houses historic looms and examples of various types of cloth, such as lush Renaissance embroidery, velvets, lace and damask.

🏛 Centro per l'Arte Contemporanea Luigi Pecci

*Viale della Repubblica 277. ☎ 0574 53 17. **Open** 10am–4pm Wed–Mon (phone to check). **Adm charge**. ♿ 🌐 www.centropecci.it*

Near the Prato Est Autostrada exit, this cultural centre is an interesting modern building in its own right. It is used for changing displays of contemporary art, concerts and films. The permanent collection may be viewed by appointment.

Castello dell'Imperatore (1237), built by Frederick II

PRATO CITY CENTRE

Castello dell'Imperatore ⑦
Duomo ①
Museo Civico ④
Museo dell'Opera del Duomo ②
Palazzo Datini ⑤
Piazza del Comune ③
Santa Maria delle Carceri ⑥

KEY

🚆	Railway station
🚌	Bus terminus
🅿	Parking
ℹ️	Tourist information

0 metres 500
0 yards 500

EASTERN TUSCANY

FROM THE FORESTS *of the Mugello and the Casentino to the heights of La Verna, this is an area of outstanding natural beauty. Hermits and mystics have long favoured its more remote reaches, where ancient monastic orders continue to flourish. Only this part of Tuscany could have produced an enigmatic artist like Piero della Francesca, whose celebrated frescoes decorate San Francesco in Arezzo.*

Eastern Tuscany's main transport route, the A1 Autostrada, channels speeding traffic southwards along the Arno valley towards Arezzo and Rome. Away from this busy artery, Eastern Tuscany is a little-visited region of steep hills cloaked in beech, oak and sweet chestnut trees. It is particularly attractive in autumn, when the huge forests of the Mugello and the Casentino take on fiery shades of red and gold. This is also the season when mushrooms and truffles abound. Driving through the region at this time of year, you'll see them for sale at roadside stalls.

The tiny mountain pastures to the east of the region are grazed both by sheep, whose milk is made into cheese, and by beautiful white cattle, which were once highly prized by the Romans as sacrificial beasts.

This is also a land of saints, hermits and monasteries. The mountain-top sanctuary of La Verna is reputed to be the place where St Francis received the stigmata – marks resembling Christ's wounds. The 11th-century hermitage at Camaldoli was intended as the site for a Benedictine order who wished to live in complete isolation, but proved so popular with religious day-trippers that a visitors' centre soon had to be built nearby. The monastery at Vallombrosa has such glorious woodlands that John Milton was moved to describe them in his epic poem, *Paradise Lost* (1667).

For art-lovers, eastern Tuscany is the region of Piero della Francesca. His frescoes in Arezzo, largely ignored until the late 19th century, form one of the world's greatest fresco cycles.

Pieve di Santi Ippolito e Donato in Bibbiena

◁ **Fertile countryside surrounding Monterchi**

Exploring Eastern Tuscany

The ancient city of Arezzo and the hilltop town of Cortona, with its steep streets, narrow, ladder-like alleys and ancient houses, will amply satisfy visitors in search of culture, art and architecture. The region will also appeal to those who love nature. The woodlands, meadows and streams are ideal for exploring on foot. There are plenty of well-marked paths and picnic areas to encourage you, especially within the beautiful ancient forests surrounding the monasteries at Vallombrosa and Camaldoli.

Key

▨	Motorway
▨	Major road
▨	Minor road
⌐	River
☀	Viewpoint

0 kilometres   10

0 miles   10

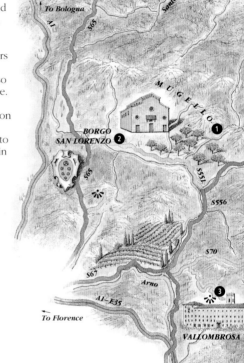

To Bologna

To Florence

VALLOMBROSA

Cortona, with its steep streets and medieval towers

Getting Around

The region's main highways, the A1 Autostrada and the S71, linking Bibbiena, Poppi and the Casentino, offer swift access to most of the region. The remaining roads are delightfully rural, particularly the S70, with its fine views near Vallombrosa, but be prepared for steep gradients and hairpin bends. Some roads in the Casentino are very narrow. There are passing places, but a speed limit of 40 km/h (25 mph) means you should leave plenty of time for your journey.

Bus and rail transport is very limited. An intercity train service links Florence to Arezzo, from where there are irregular bus services to other major towns in the region.

SIGHTS AT A GLANCE

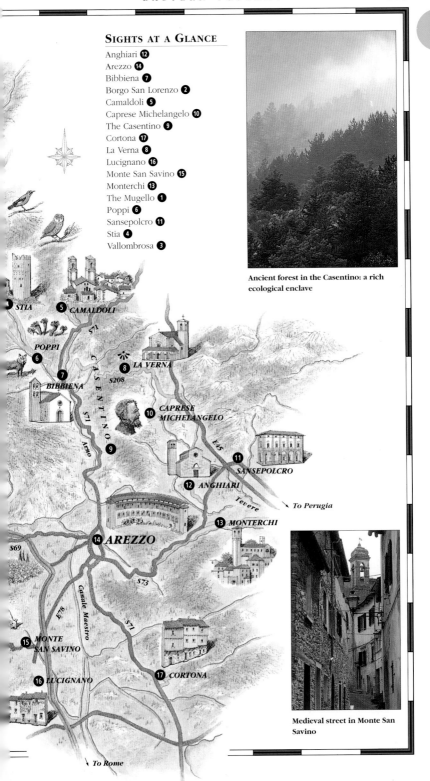

Ancient forest in the Casentino: a rich ecological enclave

STIA ❺ CAMALDOLI

POPPI ❻

❼ BIBBIENA

❽ LA VERNA S208

S71

APNO

CASENTINO

❿ CAPRESE MICHELANGELO

❾

E45

⓫ SANSEPOLCRO

⓬ ANGHIARI

Tevere

To Perugia

⓭ MONTERCHI

S69

⓮ AREZZO

S73

Canale Maestro

E78

S71

⓯ MONTE SAN SAVINO

⓰ LUCIGNANO

⓱ CORTONA

Medieval street in Monte San Savino

To Rome

The Mugello ❶

Road map D2. **FS** 🚌 *Borgo San Lorenzo.* **ℹ** *Via Oreste Bandini 6, Borgo San Lorenzo (055 845 87 93). (Mon, Wed, Fri am).*

THE MUGELLO is the area to the north and east of Florence. The scenic S65 passes the **Parco Demidoff** at Pratolino, to the south of the region. Here you can see a giant statue of the mountain god, Appennino, carved by Giambologna in 1580. Just to the north, the **Convento di Montesenario** offers excellent views. Further east lies the wine town of Rufina, with its **Museo della Vita e del Vino della Val di Sieve**.

🌿 **Parco Demidoff**
Via Fiorentina 6, Pratolino. **(** *055 40 94 27.* **Open** *Apr–Sep: Thu–Sun; Mar & Oct: Sun.* **Adm charge**. 🚻
🏠 **Convento di Montesenario**
Via Montesenario 1, Bivigliano. **(** *055 40 64 41.* **Church Open** *daily.* **Convent Open** *by request.*
🏛 **Museo della Vita e del Vino della Val di Sieve**
Villa di Poggio Reale, Rufina. **(** *055 83 96 51.*

Borgo San Lorenzo ❷

Road map D2. 🏘 *15,500.* **FS** 🚌 **ℹ** *Via Oreste Bandini 6 (055 845 87 93). (Mon, Wed, Fri am).* **ℹ** *Villa Pecori Giraldi, Via Togliatti (055 845 62 63). (Tue am, Fri–Sun pm).* 🛒 *Tue.*

SUBSTANTIALLY REBUILT after an earthquake in 1919, this is the largest town of the Mugello.

Tabernacle of St Francis in Borgo San Lorenzo

The parish church, the **Pieve di San Lorenzo**, has an odd Romanesque campanile, circular in its lower stages and hexagonal above. In the apse, the wall paintings (1906) are by the Art Nouveau artist Galileo Chini. He also worked on the Tabernacle of St Francis (1926), a shrine outside the church, and the Santuario del Santissimo Crocifisso, a church on the edge of town.

To the west are the **Castello del Trebbio**, with its gardens, and the **Villa di Cafaggiolo**, with its bulging clock tower. Among the first Medici villas, both were built for Cosimo il Vecchio by Michelozzo di Bartolommeo (1396–1472).

🏠 **Pieve di San Lorenzo**
Via Cocchi 4. **Open** *daily.*
⚓ **Castello del Trebbio**
San Piero a Sieve. **(** *055 845 87 93 (Mon, Wed, pm Fri).* **Open** *Easter–Oct: Tue–Fri by appt.* **Adm charge**. 🚻
🏛 **Villa di Cafaggiolo**
Cafaggiolo, Barberino di Mugello. **Open** *daily by appt (groups only).* **(** *055 845 87 93 (Mon, Wed, Fri am).* **Adm charge**. 🚻

Woodland landscape at Vallombrosa

Vallombrosa ❸

Road map D2. 🚌 *from Florence.* **(** *055 86 20 03.* **Church open** *from 3:30pm daily.* **Abbey open** *by appt.*

LIKE THE MONASTERIES of the Casentino *(see p192)*, the abbey buildings at Vallombrosa are surrounded by woodland. The routes to this sight are all very scenic.

The Vallombrosan order was founded by Saint Giovanni Gualberto Visdomini in 1038. He aimed to persuade likeminded aristocrats to join him in relinquishing their wealth and adopting a life of great austerity. Contrary to these worthy ideals, the order grew wealthy and powerful during the 16th and 17th centuries. It was then that today's fortresslike abbey was built. Today, the order comprises some 20 monks.

In 1638 the English poet John Milton (1608–74) visited the abbey. The beautiful scenery of this area inspired a passage in his epic poem, *Paradise Lost*.

Façade of Santa Maria Assunta in Stia

Stia ❹

Road map D2. 👥 *3,017.* 🚂 🚌
ℹ️ *Piazza Tanucci 65 (0575 50 41 06) (summer only).* 🍴 *Tue.*

STIA IS A BUSTLING, attractive village on the Arno. In the main piazza is the Roman-esque church of **Santa Maria Assunta**, with a rather plain façade. Inside is a 16th-cen-tury terracotta *Madonna and Child* by Andrea della Robbia.

There are two medieval Guidi family castles close by: **Castello di Palagio**, with an attractive garden, and **Castello di Porciano**, which houses an agricultural museum.

🏰 **Santa Maria Assunta**
Piazza Tanucci. **Open** *daily.* ♿
♣ **Castello di Palagio**
Via Vittorio Veneto. 📞 *0575 58 33 88.* **Open** *Jul–Sep: Sat–Sun, Tue.* **Adm charge.**
♣ **Castello di Porciano**
Porciano. 📞 *055 40 05 17.* **Open** *mid-May – mid-Oct: Sun.* ♿

Camaldoli ❺

Road map E2. 🚌 *from Bibbiena.*
📞 *0575 55 60 12.* **Monastery and hermitage open** *9am–1pm, 3–4pm daily.* **Museo Ornitologico Fores-tale closed** *for renovation.* **Adm charge.** ♿

THE MONASTERY was founded in 1046 and today houses 40 Carthusian monks. Visitors to Camaldoli will want to see not only the monastery but the original *eremo* (hermitage), 2.5 km (1.5 miles) away. A narrow, winding road leads up from the monastic complex to the hermitage through thick forest. This ancient woodland, which is some of the most ecologically rich in Europe, was declared a National Park in 1991.

The hermitage dates back to 1012 when San Romualdo (St Rumbold) came here with a small group of followers, to cut themselves off completely from the outside world.

Today's monks lead a more gregarious life, running a small café in the monastery below. As you descend to the monastery complex you will also pass numerous picnic spots and some of the many local footpaths.

The monks still tend the magnificent beech and chestnut woodland that surrounds the ancient monastery, as their predecessors have for nearly 1,000 years. A pharmacy, dating to 1543, now sells soaps, toiletries and liqueurs made by the monks.

There is a small, privately owned ornithological museum across the road from the monastery, opposite the car park, which illustrates the area's rich bird life.

Poppi ❻

Road map E2. 👥 *6,700.* 🚂 🚌
ℹ️ *Via Nazionale 14, Badia Prataglia (Mar–Dec Tue–Sun) (0575 55 90 54).* 🍴 *Tue.*

THE OLDER PART of Poppi is located high above the town's bus and train termini. Its splendid castle, the imposing **Castello di Poppi**, can be seen from as far away as Bibbiena *(see p192).* Just to the south of the town is the **Zoo Fauna Europa**, which specializes in the conservation of endangered European species like the Apennine wolf and the lynx.

Visible from Poppi, a short drive to the northwest up the Arno valley, is the 11th-century **Castello di Romena** where Dante stayed as a guest of the local rulers in the early 14th century. Romena's *pieve*, dating to 1152, is a typical example of a Romanesque village church.

♣ **Castello di Poppi**
📞 *0575 52 99 64.*
Open *Apr–Oct: daily; Nov–Mar: Tue–Sun.* **Adm charge.**
♿ *partial.*
🐾 **Zoo Fauna Europa**
Poppi. 📞 *0575 52 90 79.*
Open *daily.*
Adm charge. ♿
♣ **Castello di Romena**
Pratovecchio.
📞 *0575 58 13 53.*
Closed *for restoration.*

Castello di Poppi, which towers over Poppi and overlooks the entire Casentino

Casentino landscape

Bibbiena **7**

Road map E2. 🏛 *11,000.* 🚉 🚌
🛈 *Via Berni 25 (0575 59 30 98).*
🛒 *Thu.*

ONE OF THE OLDEST towns in
the region, Bibbiena was
the subject of intense territorial
feuding between Arezzo and
Florence in medieval times. It
is now the commercial centre
of the Casentino region, surrounded by sprawling factories
and industrial buildings.

The town's main attraction is
the **Pieve di Santi Ippolito e
Donato**. Dating from the 12th
century, this church contains
some fine Siena School paintings and an altarpiece by
Bicci di Lorenzo (1373–1452).

Bibbiena's main square, the
Piazza Tarlati, offers excellent
views of Poppi *(see p191).*

🔒 **Pieve di Santi Ippolito
e Donato**
Piazza Tarlati. **Open** *8am–noon,*
3–6pm daily. 🚹

La Verna **8**

Road map E2. 🚌 *from Bibbiena.*
📞 *0575 53 41.* **Open** *6:30am–*
7:30pm daily. 🚹 *partial.*

THE ROCKY OUTCROP on
which La Verna monastery
stands, called La Senna, was
split, according to legend, by
an earthquake when Christ
died on the Cross. The site was
given to St Francis by the
local ruler, Count Orlando
Cattani, in 1213, and it was
here, in 1224, that the saint
was miraculously marked
with the stigmata – the
wounds of Christ.

Today, the monastery is
both a popular tourist sight
and a charismatic
religious centre. Its
modern buildings are
not particularly
attractive, but they
contain numerous
sculptures by the della
Robbia workshops.
There are several
waymarked paths
through the surrounding
woodland, leading to
some excellent viewpoints.

The Casentino **9**

Road map E2. FS 🚌 *from Bibbiena.*
🛈 *Bibbiena.*

THE VAST Casentino region,
an area of tiny villages
dotted among hills covered
with ancient woodland, lies to
the north of Arezzo. The river
Arno has its source here, on

the slopes of Monte Falterona.
Countless streams run down
the region's valleys to join it,
creating stunning waterfalls.

A favourite destination for
walkers, the area is renowned
for its abundant autumn
mushroom crop *(see p198).*

Caprese Michelangelo **10**

Road map E2. 🏛 *1,671.* 🚌 *from*
Arezzo. 🛈 *Via Capoluogo 1 (0575*
79 37 76).

MICHELANGELO BUONARROTI
was born in Caprese on
6 March 1475, while his father
served briefly as the
town's *podestà* – a
combination of mag-
istrate, mayor and
chief of police. His
birthplace is now a
museum, the **Com-
une Casa Natale
Michelangelo**,
housing photos and
copies of the artist's
work. The town
walls feature modern
sculptures and have fine views
over the alpine landscape.
Michelangelo attributed his
keen mind to the mountain air
he breathed here as an infant.

**Michelangelo
Buonarroti
(1475–1564)**

🏛 **Comune Casa Natale
Michelangelo**
Casa del Podestà, Via Capoluogo 1.
📞 *0575 79 37 76.* **Open** *mid-Jun–*
Oct: daily; Nov–mid-Jun: Tue–Sun.

Sansepolcro **11**

Road map E3. 🏛 *15,700.* 🚌
🛈 *Piazza Garibaldi 2 (0575*
74 05 36). 🛒 *Tue, Sat.*

SANSEPOLCRO is a busy industrial town, famous as the
birthplace of the artist Piero
della Francesca (1410–92).
Most visitors come to see the
collection of his work in the
Museo Civico, housed in
the 14th-century Palazzo
Comunale. The museum's
most famous exhibit is Piero's
fresco, *The Resurrection*
(1463), in which a curiously
impassive Christ strides out of
his tomb. The sleeping soldiers
at his feet, in their Renaissance
armour, seem trapped in time,

The monastery at La Verna, founded by St Francis in 1213

while the Son of God takes possession of a primitive, eternal landscape. Other works by Piero are displayed in the same room, notably the *Madonna della Misericordia* (1462).

Sansepolcro is home to a number of other major works. Chief among these are Luca Signorelli's 15th-century *Crucifixion* (also in the Museo Civico) and Rosso Fiorentino's Mannerist *Deposition* in **San Lorenzo** church.

🏛 **Museo Civico**
Via Aggiunti 65. **[** 0575 73 22 18.
Open 9:30am–1pm, 2:30–6pm daily.
Adm charge.

🛐 **San Lorenzo**
Via Santa Croce. **[** 0575 74 05 36.
Open 10am–1pm, 3–6pm daily. 🔼

Anghiari ⑫

Road map E3. 🏠 5,874. 🚌
ℹ️ Via Matteotti 103 (0575 74 92 79). 🗓 Wed.

T HE BATTLE OF ANGHIARI, between Florence and Milan in 1440, was to have been the subject of a fresco by Leonardo in Florence's Palazzo Vecchio. It was never painted – one of the greatest "lost" works of

Anghiari, a typical medieval walled town

the Renaissance. Today, this historic little town sits peacefully amid fields of tobacco, a traditional crop of the upper valley of the river Tevere (Tiber), which rises nearby on the slopes of Monte Fumaiolo.

🏛 **Museo dell'Alta Valle del Tevere**
Piazza Mameli 16. **[** 0575 78 80 01. **Open** 9am–1pm Tue–Sun.
Several major works, such as Jacopo della Quercia's fine wooden *Madonna* (1420), can be seen here. There are also displays of locally made furniture and toys.

🛐 **Santa Maria delle Grazie**
Propositura. **Open** daily. 🔼
The town's main church, dating to the 18th century, contains a High Altar and tabernacle from the della Robbia workshops. There is also a 15th-century *Madonna and Child* painted by Matteo di Giovanni.

🏛 **Museo della Misericordia**
Via Francesco Nenci 13. **[** 0575 78 95 77. **Open** by appt.
The Misericordia, a charitable organization, was founded in the 13th century to look after ailing pilgrims on their way to Rome. Today it operates Tuscany's efficient ambulance service *(see p277)*. This small museum records their work.

Monterchi ⑬

Road map E3. 🏠 1,910. 🚌
ℹ️ Arezzo. 🗓 Sun.

T HE CEMETERY CHAPEL at Monterchi was the site chosen in 1460 by Piero della Francesca for his *Madonna del Parto* (Pregnant Madonna) *(see p26)*, possibly because his mother may be buried here. The recently restored fresco is now in the **Museo Madonna del Parto**. A work of haunting ambiguity, it simultaneously captures the Virgin's pride in the impending birth, the weariness of pregnancy and the sorrow borne of knowing that her child will be no ordinary man.

🏛 **Museo Madonna del Parto**
Via Reglia 1. **[** 0575 707 13.
Open 9am–1pm, 2–7pm Tue–Sun (until 6pm in winter). **Adm charge**.

The Resurrection (1463) by Piero della Francesca in Sansepolcro

Arezzo ⑭

O NE OF THE WEALTHIEST CITIES in Tuscany, Arezzo
produces gold jewellery for shops all over Europe.
It is famous for Piero della Francesca's frescoes and for
its antiques market. Following World War II, there was
much rebuilding – broad avenues have replaced many
of the medieval alleys. The Chimera fountain near the
station is a reminder of the city's past. It is a copy of an
Etruscan bronze *(see p40)* cast here in 380 BC.

Chimera fountain

🏛 San Francesco
See pp196–7.

🏛 Pieve di Santa Maria
Corso Italia 7. **Open** *daily.*
Arezzo's main shopping street,
Corso Italia, leads uphill to
the Pieve di Santa Maria,
which has one of Tuscany's
most ornate Romanesque
façades. Unfortunately, the
complex filigree of interlaced
arches has weathered badly.

The splendid campanile,
the "tower of a hundred
holes", dates to 1330. Its
name derives from the many
arches running through it.

🏛 Piazza Grande
The square is famous for its
regular antiques market *(see
p268)*. On the west side, the
façade of the Palazzo della
Fraternità dei Laici is decorated
with a relief of the Virgin
(1434) by Bernardo
Rossellino. The lower
half of the building
dates from 1377.
The belfry and
clock tower date
from 1552.

The north side
of the square is
occupied by a
handsome arcade
designed by
Vasari in 1573.

♣ Fortezza Medicea e Parco il Prato
📞 0575 37 76 66. **Open** *summer:
8am–8pm; winter: 8am–5pm.* ♿
Antonio da Sangallo the
Younger's imposing fortress
was built for Cosimo I during
the 16th century. It was partly
demolished in the 18th century,
leaving only the ramparts intact.
With its excellent views across
the Arno valley, it remains an
excellent spot for a picnic.

The same can be said of the
city's large public park, the
Parco il Prato, with its
extensive lawns. It contains a
huge statue (1928) of the great
poet Petrarch. The house
where he was born stands at
the entrance to the park.

🏛 Duomo
Piazza del Duomo. **Open** *daily.*
Begun in 1278, the Duomo
remained incomplete until
1510; its façade dates to 1914.
A huge building, its Gothic
interior is lit through windows
containing beautiful 16th-
century stained glass by Guillaume de Marcillat, a French
artist who settled in Arezzo.

High on the wall to the left
of the 15th-century High Altar
can be seen the tomb of Guido
Tarlati, bishop and ruler of
Arezzo from 1312 until
his death in 1327.
Carved reliefs

**Duomo façade, completed as
recently as 1914**

depict scenes from his uncon-
ventional life. Next to the
tomb is a small fresco of Mary
Magdalene by Piero della
Francesca (1410–92).

The Lady Chapel, fronted
by an intricate wrought-iron
screen (1796), contains a terracotta *Assumption* by Andrea
della Robbia (1435–1525).

🏛 Museo del Duomo
Piazzetta behind the Duomo 13.
📞 0575 239 91. **Open** *10am–
12:30pm Thu–Sat.* **Adm charge**.
Among the artifacts removed
from the cathedral are three
wooden crucifixes, dating
from the 12th and 13th
centuries. The oldest of these
was painted by Margaritone di
Arezzo in 1264.

Also of interest are Bernardo
Rossellino's terracotta bas-relief
of *The Annunciation* (1434),
a number of frescoes by Vasari
(1512–74) and an *Annun-
ciation* by Spinello Aretino
(1373–1410).
Vasari and
Aretino were
born locally.

Apse of Pieve di Santa Maria and Palazzo della Fraternità dei Laici in Piazza Grande

🚽 Casa del Vasari

Via XX Settembre 55. **[** 0575 40 90 40.
Open 8:30am–7pm Mon, Wed–Sat,
9am–12:30pm Sun & public hols.

Vasari (1512–74) built this house for himself in 1540 and decorated the ceilings and walls with portraits of fellow artists, friends and mentors. He also painted himself looking out of one of the windows. Vasari was a prolific painter and architect, and is most famous for his book, *Lives of the Most Excellent Painters, Sculptors and Architects* (1530). A contemporary account of many great Renaissance artists, it has, in spite of revealing an often cavalier attitude to the truth, led to Vasari being described as the first art historian.

Detail of fresco from Casa del Vasari

🏛 Museo Statale d'Arte Medioevale e Moderna

Via di San Lorentino 8. **[** 0575 40
90 50. **Open** 9am–7pm Tue–Sat, 9am–
12:30pm Sun & hols. **Adm charge**.

The museum is housed in the graceful 15th-century Palazzo Bruni. Its courtyard contains architectural fragments and sculptures dating from the 10th to the 17th centuries. The varied collection includes one of the best displays of majolica pottery in Italy. There are also several terracottas by Andrea della Robbia and his followers; frescoes by Vasari and Signorelli; and paintings by 19th- and 20th-century artists, including members of the Italian *Macchiaioli* School (*see p123*).

🎵 Anfiteatro Romano e Museo Archeologico

Via Margaritone 10. **[** 0575 208 82.
Open 8:30am–7pm daily.
Adm charge for Museo Archeologico. &

A ruined Roman amphitheatre stands near the Museo Archeologico, to the south of Arezzo. Famous for its extensive collection of Roman Aretine ware, the museum has a

1st-century BC Aretine ware

display showing how this high-quality red-glazed pottery was produced during the 1st century BC and exported throughout the Roman Empire.

🔒 Santa Maria delle Grazie

Via di Santa Maria. **Open** daily.

Completed in 1449 and set in its own walled garden, this jewel of a church, fronted by Benedetto da Maiano's pretty loggia (1482), stands on the southeastern outskirts of the town. The High Altar, by Andrea della Robbia (1435–1525), encloses Parri di Spinello's fresco of the Virgin (1430). A damaged fresco by Lorentino d'Arezzo (1430–1505) is on the right of the altar.

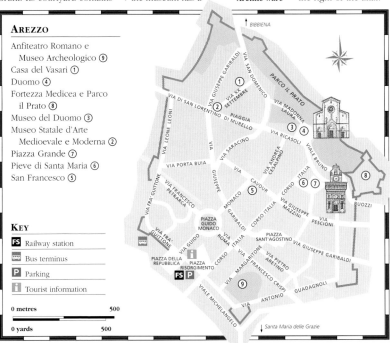

KEY

FS Railway station

🚌 Bus terminus

P Parking

ℹ Tourist information

0 metres   500

0 yards   500

San Francesco

THE 13TH-CENTURY CHURCH of San Francesco contains
Piero della Francesca's *Legend of the True Cross*
(1452–66), one of Italy's greatest fresco cycles. The
frescoes, now visible again after a long restoration, show
how the Cross was found near Jerusalem by the Empress
Helena. Her son, the Emperor Constantine, adopted it as
his battle emblem. In reality, Constantine granted the
Christian faith official recognition through the Edict of
Milan, signed in 313. He is said to have bequeathed the
Empire to the Church in 337, although this was still
hotly disputed when Piero painted the frescoes.
Visitors have a limited time in the chapel and
advance booking is mandatory.

Exaggerated Hats
*Piero often depicted
historical figures in
Renaissance garb.*

Judas reveals
where the Cross
is hidden.

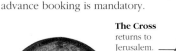

The Cross
returns to
Jerusalem.

Painted Crucifix
*The 13th-century Crucifix
forms the focal point of the
fresco cycle. The figure at the
foot of the Cross represents St
Francis, to whom the church
is dedicated.*

The Empress Helena watches
the Cross being dug up. The
town shown in the background,
symbolizing Jerusalem, is an
accurate representation of 15th-
century Arezzo.

The Annunciation, with
its stately figures and aura
of serenity, is typical of
Piero's enigmatic style.

**The Defeat
of Chosroes**
*The battle scene shows
the chaos of Renaissance
warfare. Piero was influ-
enced by ancient Roman
carving, especially the
battle scenes that often
decorated sarcophagi.*

The Death of Adam
This vivid portrayal of Adam and Eve in old age illustrates Piero's masterly treatment of anatomy. He was one of the first Renaissance artists to paint nude figures.

VISITORS' CHECKLIST

Piazza San Francesco, Arezzo. 📞
0575 90 04 04. **Open** *9am–5pm Mon–Sat.* **Adm charge.** ♿ 🔄
🅦 www.pierodellafrancesca.it

The prophets appear to play no part in the narrative cycle; their presence may be for purely decorative reasons.

The buildings in the fresco reflect the newly fashionable Renaissance style in architecture *(see p23)*.

The wood of the Cross is buried in a pit.

Constantine dreams of the Cross on the eve of battle.

Constantine adopts the Cross as his battle emblem.

The Queen of Sheba recognizes the wood of the Cross.

Solomon's Handshake
The Queen's handshake with Solomon, King of Israel, symbolizes 15th-century hopes for a union between the Orthodox and Western churches.

Mushrooms in Tuscany

Champignon
(Marasmius oreades)

THE PEOPLE OF TUSCANY consider mushrooms a great delicacy. Collecting fungi can be dangerous, unless you are an expert, but you can sample the best varieties in the region's restaurants. The smaller edible varieties are sometimes chopped and combined with mashed garlic to make a pasta sauce. As starters, many menus include *funghi trifolati* (sautéed mushrooms with garlic and parsley), or the region's most popular mushrooms, porcini, served *in gratella* (grilled). The prized truffle is often simply grated over home-made pasta; it has a pronounced flavour and should be used sparingly.

Gathering chanterelles *(right)* and saddle fungus *(left)*

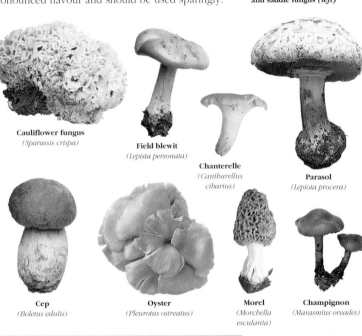

Cauliflower fungus
(Sparassis crispa)

Field blewit
(Lepista personata)

Chanterelle
(Cantharellus cibarius)

Parasol
(Lepiota procera)

Cep
(Boletus edulis)

Oyster
(Pleurotus ostreatus)

Morel
(Morchella esculanta)

Champignon
(Marasmius oreades)

THE BEST TUSCAN MUSHROOMS

Prized species have a rich flavour and a firm texture. They are sold from mid-September to late November at shops and markets throughout the region.

Porcini

This popular mushroom, known in England as the cep, is one of the few wild species available all year, either fresh or dried.

Monte San Savino ⑮

Road map E3. 🏛 *7,794.* **FS** 🚌
ℹ️ *Piazza Gamurrini 25 (0575 84 30 98).* 🛒 *Wed.*

THE TOWN stands on the western edge of the Valdichiana, once a marshy and malaria-ridden plain that was drained by Cosimo I in the 16th century. It is now an area of rich farmland used to rear cattle whose meat is used for *Bistecca alla Fiorentina*, the famous beefsteaks served in Florentine restaurants *(p255)*.

Agriculture has made the town prosperous, and its streets are lined with handsome buildings and churches. Some of these are by the High Renaissance sculptor and architect Andrea Contucci, known as Sansovino (1460–1529), who was born in the town; a number are by Antonio da Sangallo the Elder (1455–1537), his contemporary.

The town's main street, Corso Sangallo, starts at the Porta Fiorentina town gate, built in 1550 to Giorgio Vasari's design. The street leads past the 14th-century Cassero, or Citadel, whose exterior walls are now almost entirely hidden by 17th-century houses. There are good views from the interior, which contains the tourist office and the small

Lucignano, with its circular street plan

Museo di Ceramica with its extensive collection of local work. Further up the street is the handsome Classical Loggia dei Mercanti (1518–20), designed by Sansovino, and the Palazzo Comunale, originally built as the Palazzo di Monte by Sangallo for Cardinal Antonio di Monte in 1515. Sansovino's house can be seen in the Piazza di Monte. He laid out the square, built the fine double loggia with Ionic columns that fronts **Sant'Agostino** church and went on to design the cloister standing alongside it. Inside the church is a series of 15th-century frescoes illustrating scenes from *The Life of Christ*, and Vasari's *Assumption* altarpiece (1539). Sansovino's worn tomb slab lies beneath the pulpit.

Locally made vase, Museo di Ceramica

🏛 **Museo di Ceramica**
Piazza Gamurrini. ☎ *0575 84 30 98.*
***Open** by appt.* **Adm charge**.
⛪ **Sant'Agostino**
Piazza di Monte. ***Open** daily.* ♿

Lucignano ⑯

Road map E3. 🏛 *3,349.* 🚌
ℹ️ *Piazza del Tribunale 1 (0575 838 01).* 🛒 *Thu.*

AN ATTRACTIVE medieval town, Lucignano contains many well-preserved 14th-century houses. The street plan is extremely unusual, consisting of a series of four

concentric rings encircling the hill upon which the town sits, sheltered by its ancient walls. There are four small piazzas at the centre.

The **Collegiata** is fronted by some attractive steps whose circular shape reflects the town's street plan. Completed by Orazio Porta in 1594, the church contains some fine gilded wooden angels added in 1706.

The 14th-century Palazzo Comunale houses the **Museo Comunale**. Its highlight is a massive gold reliquary, 2.5 m (8 ft) high, to which numerous artists contributed over the period 1350–1471. Because of its shape, it is known as the *Tree of Lucignano*.

Also of note are two 14th-century paintings by Luca Signorelli: a lunette showing St Francis of Assisi miraculously receiving the wounds of Christ to his hands and feet, and a *Madonna and Child*. There are several fine 13th- to 15th-century Siena School paintings and a small painting of the Madonna by Lippo Vanni (1341–75).

The vaulted ceiling of the main chamber, the Sala del Tribunale, has frescoes of famous biblical figures and characters from Classical mythology painted from 1438–65 by various Siena School artists.

⛪ **Collegiata**
Costa San Michele.
🏛 **Museo Comunale**
Piazza del Tribunale 22.
☎ *0575 83 80 01.*
***Open** Tue–Sun.*
Adm charge. ♿

Corso Sangallo in Monte San Savino

Cortona **⓱**

CORTONA IS ONE OF THE OLDEST cities in Tuscany. It was founded by the Etruscans *(see p40)*, whose work can still be seen in the foundations of the town's massive stone walls. The city was a major seat of power during the medieval period, able to hold its own against larger towns like Siena and Arezzo; its decline followed defeat by Naples in 1409, after which it was sold to Florence and lost its autonomy. The main street, Via Nazionale, is remarkably flat in comparison with the rest of Cortona. The numerous ladder-like alleys leading off it, for instance the Vicolo del Precipizio (Precipice Alley), are far more typical.

Medieval houses in Via Janelli

Palazzo Comunale

▥ Palazzo Comunale
Closed to the public.
Dating from the 13th century, the building was enlarged at the beginning of the 16th century, to incorporate the distinctive tower. Its ancient steps are the ideal place to linger in the early evening.

▥ Museo dell'Accademia Etrusca
Palazzo Casali, Piazza Signorelli 9.
🕿 0575 63 04 15. **Open** Apr–Sep: 10am–7pm Tue–Sun; Oct–Mar: 10am–5pm Tue–Sun.
Adm charge. 🕭 partial.
This is one of the region's most rewarding museums. It contains a number of major Etruscan artifacts, including a unique bronze chandelier *(see p41)* dating from the 4th century BC. There are also a number of Egyptian objects. These include a wooden model funerary boat dating to the second millennium BC.
  On the west wall of the main hall is a beautiful fresco of Polymnia, the muse of song. It was once believed to be Roman and date from the

1st- or 2nd-century AD, but it is now known to be a brilliant 18th-century fake.

🔒 Duomo
Piazza del Duomo. **Open** daily. 🕭
The present Duomo was designed by Giuliano da Sangallo in the 16th century. Remains of an earlier Romanesque building were incorporated into the west façade. The entrance is through an attractive doorway (1550) by Cristofanello.

▥ Museo Diocesano
Piazza del Duomo 1. 🕿 0575 628 30. **Open** May–Sep: 9:30am–1pm, 3:30–7pm Tue–Sun; Oct–Apr: 10am–1pm, 3–5pm Tue–Sun.
Adm charge. 🕭
Housed in the 16th-century church of Gesù, the museum contains several masterpieces. Chief among these are Fra Angelico's *Annunciation* (1428–30), a *Crucifixion* by

Pietro Lorenzetti (c.1280–1348) and a *Deposition* by Luca Signorelli (1441–1523). There is also a Roman sarcophagus, featuring Lapiths and Centaurs, which was much admired by Donatello and Brunelleschi.

▥ Via Janelli
The medieval houses in this short street are some of the oldest to survive in Italy. A striking feature is their overhanging upper floors, built out on massive timbers.

🔒 San Francesco
Via Maffei. **Closed** to the public.
The church was built in 1245 by Brother Elias, a native of Cortona, who succeeded St Francis as leader of the Franciscan order. He and Luca Signorelli (1441–1523), also born locally, are buried here.

The Annunciation (1428–30) by Fra Angelico in the Museo Diocesano

🚻 Piazza Garibaldi

Located on the eastern edge of town, this square is a favourite haunt of American students who come to Cortona each summer. It offers superb views, notably of the handsome Renaissance church of Santa Maria delle Grazie al Calcinaio.

🏠 Via Crucis and Santa Margherita

The Via Crucis, a long uphill lane with gardens on either side, leading to the 19th-century church of Santa Margherita, was laid out as a war memorial in 1947. It is decorated with Futurist mosaics depicting episodes in Christ's Passion by Gino Severini (1883–1966).

The church, rebuilt from 1856–97 in the Romanesque-Gothic style, has excellent views over the surrounding countryside. Inside, to the right of the altar, lie a number of Turkish battle standards and lanterns captured during 18th-century naval battles. A single rose window remains from the original church.

Santa Maria delle Grazie

🏠 Santa Maria delle Grazie

Calcinaio. **Open** daily.
A pleasant 15-minute stroll from the centre of town, this remarkable Renaissance church (1485) is one of the few surviving works by Francesco di Giorgio Martini (1439–1502). The building is opened on request – ask at the caretaker's house, beyond a garden to the right of the main entrance.

The attractive High Altar (1519), built by Bernardino Covatti, contains a 15th-century image of the Madonna del Calcinaio. The stained glass is by Guillaume de Marcillat *(see p194).*

🏠 Tanella di Pitagora

On the road to Sodo. 📞 0575 61 27 78. **Open** daily.
One of several restored Etruscan tombs on the plain below the town, "Pythagoras's tomb" draws its name from a confusion between Cortona and Crotone, Pythagoras's birthplace. It is known as a "melon" tomb because of the grassy mound built up around it.

Tanella di Pitagora, a typical Etruscan "melon" tomb

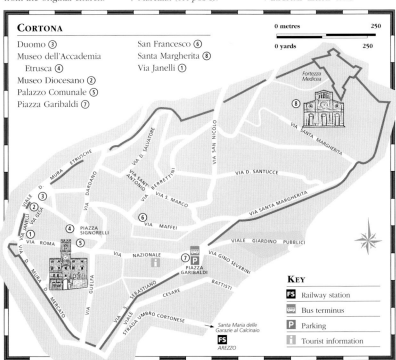

CORTONA

Duomo ③
Museo dell'Accademia Etrusca ④
Museo Diocesano ②
Palazzo Comunale ⑤
Piazza Garibaldi ⑦
San Francesco ⑥
Santa Margherita ⑧
Via Janelli ①

0 metres   250
0 yards   250

KEY

🚆 Railway station
🚌 Bus terminus
🅿 Parking
🛈 Tourist information

CENTRAL TUSCANY

WITH SIENA *at its heart, this is an agricultural area of great scenic beauty, noted for its historic walled towns such as San Gimignano and Pienza. To the north of Siena is the Chianti Classico region, where some of Italy's best wines are produced; to the south is the Crete, with landscapes characterized by round clay hillocks, eroded of topsoil by heavy rain over the centuries.*

The vine-clad hills to the north of Siena are dotted with farmhouses, villas and baronial castles. Many are now turned into luxury hotels or rental apartments, offering various leisure facilities such as tennis courts, swimming pools and riding stables: this is now one of the most popular areas for family holidays in the Tuscan countryside.

To the south of Siena, in the Crete, shepherds tend sheep whose milk is used to produce the *pecorino* cheese popular throughout Tuscany. Cypress trees, planted to provide windbreaks along roads and around isolated farms, are an important sculptural feature in this empty and primeval landscape.

Linking the two regions is the S2 highway, an ancient road along which pilgrims made their way in the Middle Ages, followed by travellers on the Grand Tour *(see p53)* in the 18th and 19th centuries. Romanesque churches line the roads, and the valleys and passes are defended by castles and garrison towns, most of which have hardly changed over the years.

CONSTANT CONFLICT

The history of the region is of a long feud between the two city states of Florence and Siena. Siena's finest hour was its victory in the Battle of Montaperti in 1260, but when Siena finally succumbed to the Black Death, and subsequently to a crushing defeat by Florence in the siege of 1554–5, the city went into decline.

As several other Central Tuscan cities experienced the same fate, this lovely region became a forgotten backwater, frozen in time. But after centuries of neglect, the graceful late-medieval buildings in many of the towns are now being well restored, making this the most architecturally rewarding part of Tuscany to explore.

The beautifully preserved fortified town of Monteriggioni

◁ **A house in San Quirico d'Orcia, bathed in the morning light**

To Florenc

Exploring Central Tuscany

T HE BEAUTIFUL CITY of Siena, with its narrow streets and
medieval buildings of rose-coloured brick, is the natural
starting place for exploring the heart of Tuscany. From here it
is only a short drive to the castle-dotted landscapes of Chianti
to the north, or to historic towns such as San Gimignano and
Montepulciano. Although these towns are full of visitors during
the day, at night they revert to their timeless Tuscan character
and many have first-class restaurants serving local
fare. The landscape is of cypresses, olive groves,
vineyards, simple churches and stone farmhouses.

**Wicker-covered *damigiane* (demijohns)
transporting local Chianti wine**

GETTING AROUND

The S2 is the main road south
through Siena. The S222 links
Florence with Siena and is known
as the *Chiantigiana* (Chianti
Way) as it passes through the
Chianti wine-growing area. Both
routes are well served by bus
services, and tour operators in
both cities offer tours of the
main sites. Train services are
limited to one line between
Florence and Siena. A car is a
great advantage, especially for
visiting the Chianti wine estates.

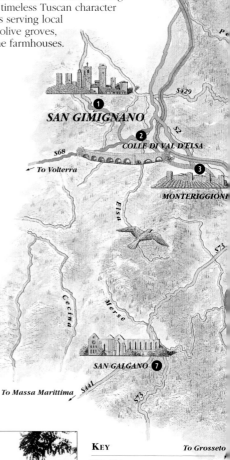

SAN GIMIGNANO ❶

COLLE DI VAL D'ELSA ❷

S429

S2

S68

← *To Volterra*

MONTERIGGIONI ❸

S73

Elsa

Cecina

Merse

Greve

Pe

SAN GALGANO ❼

To Massa Marittima ← S441

S73

View over Siena from the surrounding hills

KEY

To Grosseto

▩▩	Motorway
▩▩	Major road
▩▩	Minor road
▩▩	Scenic route
⬳	River
✢	Viewpoint

0 kilometres   10

0 miles   10

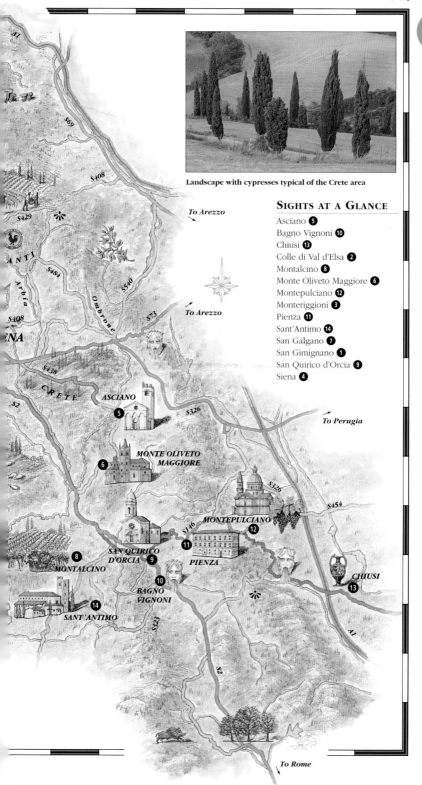

Landscape with cypresses typical of the Crete area

SIGHTS AT A GLANCE

Asciano ⑤
Bagno Vignoni ⑩
Chiusi ⑬
Colle di Val d'Elsa ②
Montalcino ⑧
Monte Oliveto Maggiore ⑥
Montepulciano ⑫
Monteriggioni ③
Pienza ⑪
Sant'Antimo ⑭
San Galgano ⑦
San Gimignano ①
San Quirico d'Orcia ⑨
Siena ④

Palazzo Campana, the gateway to Colle Alta

San Gimignano ①

See pp208–11.

Colle di Val d'Elsa ②

Road map C3. ⛩ *17,200.* 🚆 🚌
ℹ *Via Campana 43 (0577 92 27 91).*
🔄 *Fri.*

COLLE DI VAL D'ELSA has a
lower and an upper town.
Colle Alta, the upper town, is
of great medieval architectural
interest. Arnolfo di Cambio,
who built the Palazzo Vecchio
in Florence *(see pp78–9)*, was
born here in 1232. In the
modern lower town shops
sell locally-made crystal glass.

🏛 Palazzo Campana
Closed to the public.
This Mannerist palazzo was
built on a viaduct in 1539
by Baccio d'Agnolo, forming
a gateway to Colle Alta.

🏠 Duomo
Piazza del Duomo. **Open** *4–5pm
Mon–Fri, Sun morning (for Mass only).*
📞 *0577 92 01 80.*
The Duomo has a marble
Renaissance pulpit carved
with bas-reliefs of the
Madonna (1465), attributed
to Giuliano da Maiano. The
façade was rebuilt in 1603.

🏛 Museo Archeologico
Palazzo Pretorio, Piazza del Duomo.
📞 *0577 92 29 54.* **Open** *Oct–Mar:
3:30–6:30pm Tue–Sun (also 10am–
noon Sat & Sun); Apr–Sep: 10am–noon
& 5–7pm Tue–Sun.* **Adm charge**.
The museum has a collection
of urns from local Etruscan
tombs. The building was once
a jail: political slogans written
on the walls by Communists
survive from the 1920s.

🏛 Museo d'Arte Sacra
Via del Castello 31. 📞 *0577
92 38 88.* **Open** *see Museo Civico.*
Now incorporated in to the
Museo Civico, the museum
features 14th-century frescoes
of hunting scenes by Bartolo di
Fredi, Sienese paintings and a
collection of Etruscan pottery.

***Sgraffito* cherub, Museo Civico**

🏛 Museo Civico
Via del Castello 31. 📞 *0577 92 38
88.* **Open** *Apr–Oct: 10am–noon, 4–
7pm Tue–Sun; Nov–Mar: 10am–noon,
6:30–8:30pm Sat & Sun.* **Adm charge**.
The museum is in the Palazzo
dei Priori, whose façade is
decorated with *sgraffito* work
scratched in the plaster, incorporating cherubs and Medici
coats of arms. There is a small

collection of Siena School
paintings, Etruscan pottery and
scale models of the old town
of Colle Alta. The chapel next
to the main room has a portico
decorated with frescoes by
Simone Ferri in 1581.

🏠 Santa Maria in Canonica
Via del Castello. **Open** *sporadically.*
The Romanesque church has
a simple belltower and the
stone façade is decorated with
brickwork. The interior was
altered in the 17th century,
and now contains a tabernacle
by Pier Francesco Fiorentino,
showing scenes from the lives
of the Madonna and Child.

⛩ Porta Nova
Via Gracco del Secco. **Open** *daily.*
The Porta Nova is a large
Renaissance fortress, designed
by Giuliano da Sangallo in
the 15th century to guard
against attack from the Volterra
road. There are two heavily
fortified cylindrical towers on
the outside of the building.

Monteriggioni ③

Road map D3. ⛩ *720.* 🚌

MONTERIGGIONI is a gem of
a medieval hilltop town.
It was built in 1203 and ten
years later became a garrison
town. It is totally encircled by
high walls with 14 heavily
fortified towers, built to guard
the northern borders of Siena's
territory against invasion by
Florentine armies.
   Dante was sufficiently
impressed to use the town
as a simile for the abyss at the

Craft shop in the main piazza of Monteriggioni

heart of his *Inferno*, which compares Monteriggioni's "ring-shaped citadel . . . crowned with towers" to giants standing in a moat.

The walls, which are still perfectly preserved, are best viewed from the direction of the Colle di Val d'Elsa road. Within the walls, the sleepy village consists of a large piazza, a pretty Romanesque church, a few houses, a couple of craft shops, restaurants, and shops selling many of the excellent local Castello di Monteriggioni wines.

Siena ❹

See pp 212–19.

Asciano ❺

Road map D3. 🏛 *6,250.*
🚉 🚌 ℹ️ *Corso Matteotti 18 (0577 71 71 04).* 🔷 *Sat.*

THE ROAD from Siena to Asciano passes through the strange Crete landscape of clay hillocks, almost bare of vegetation and looking like massive anthills. Asciano itself is medieval, and retains much of its fortified wall, built in 1351. The main street, Corso Matteotti, is lined with smart shops and Classical *palazzi*. At the top of the street, in Piazza della Basilica, there is a large fountain built in 1472. Facing it is the late 13th-century Romanesque **Basilica di Sant'Agata**.

The Romanesque Basilica di Sant'Agata in Asciano

***Temptation of St Benedict* (1508) by Sodoma in Monte Oliveto Maggiore**

Alongside the church is the **Museo d'Arte Sacra**, which houses a collection of late Siena School masterpieces, including Duccio's *Madonna and Child* and Ambrogio Lorenzetti's unusual *St Michael the Archangel*. The **Museo Archeologico** is in the old San Bernardino church, and displays local Etruscan finds from the **Necropoli di Poggio Pinci**, 5 km (3 miles) east of the village. The artifacts come from tombs built between the 7th and 4th centuries BC. On Via Mameli, the **Museo Amos Cassioli** has a display of portraits by Cassioli, who lived here from 1832–91, and other modern works by local artists.

🔒 **Basilica di Sant'Agata**
Piazza della Basilica. **Open** *daily.*
🏛 **Museo d'Arte Sacra**
Piazza della Basilica.
☎️ *0577 71 82 07.*
Open *by appt.*
🏛 **Museo Archeologico**
Corso Matteotti 46. **Open** *Tue–Sun.*
Adm charge.
🔺 **Necropoli di Poggio Pinci**
Poggio Pinci. ☎️ *0577 71 95 10.*
Open *by appt.*
🏛 **Museo Amos Cassioli**
Via Mameli. *Call tourist information for opening times.* **Adm charge**. ♿

Monte Oliveto Maggiore ❻

Road map D3. ☎️ *0577 70 76 11.*
Open *9:15am–noon, 3:15–5pm daily (to 6pm in the summer).*

THE APPROACH to this abbey is through thick cypresses, with stunning views of eroded cliffs and sheer drops to the valley floor. It was founded in 1313 by the Olivetan order, who were dedicated to restoring the simplicity of Benedictine monastic rule. The 15th-century rose-pink abbey church is a Baroque building with outstanding choir stalls of inlaid wood.

Alongside is the Great Cloister (1427–74), whose walls are covered by a cycle of frescoes on the life of St Benedict, begun by Luca Signorelli, a pupil of Piero della Francesca, in 1495. He completed nine panels; the remaining 27 were finished by Sodoma in 1508. The cycle, which begins on the east wall with Benedict's early life, is considered a masterpiece of fresco painting for its combination of architectural and naturalistic detail.

Street-by-Street: San Gimignano ❶

THE DISTINCTIVE SKYLINE of San Gimignano must have been a welcome sight to the faithful in medieval times, for the town lay on the main pilgrim route from northern Europe to Rome. This gave rise to its great prosperity at that time, when its population was twice what it is today. The plague of 1348, and later the diversion of the pilgrim route, led to its economic decline. However, since World War II it has been recovering rapidly thanks to tourism and local wine production. For a small town, San Gimignano is rich in works of art, and good shops and restaurants.

Sant'Agostino
Here Bartolo di Fredi painted Christ, Man of Sorrows.

To Sant'Agostino

Via San Matteo, in contrast with the more commercial Via San Giovanni, caters mainly for the local residents, selling food and wine, clothes and other typical Tuscan products.

La Buca, Via San Giovanni, selling local wine and wild boar ham

Rocca (1353)

VIA SAN M.

VIA DIACCETO

VIA DI QUERCECCHIO

★ Collegiata
This 11th-century church is covered in delightful frescoes, including The Creation *(1367) by Bartolo di Fredi.*

Museo Ornitologico

Museo d'Arte Sacra
The museum contains religious paintings, sculpture and liturgical objects from the Collegiata.

STAR SIGHTS

★ Collegiata

★ Piazza del Duomo

★ Palazzo del Popolo

KEY

– – – Suggested route

0 metres   250

0 yards   250

★ **Piazza del Duomo**
Among the historic buildings located here is the Palazzo Vecchio del Podestà (1239), whose tower is probably the town's oldest.

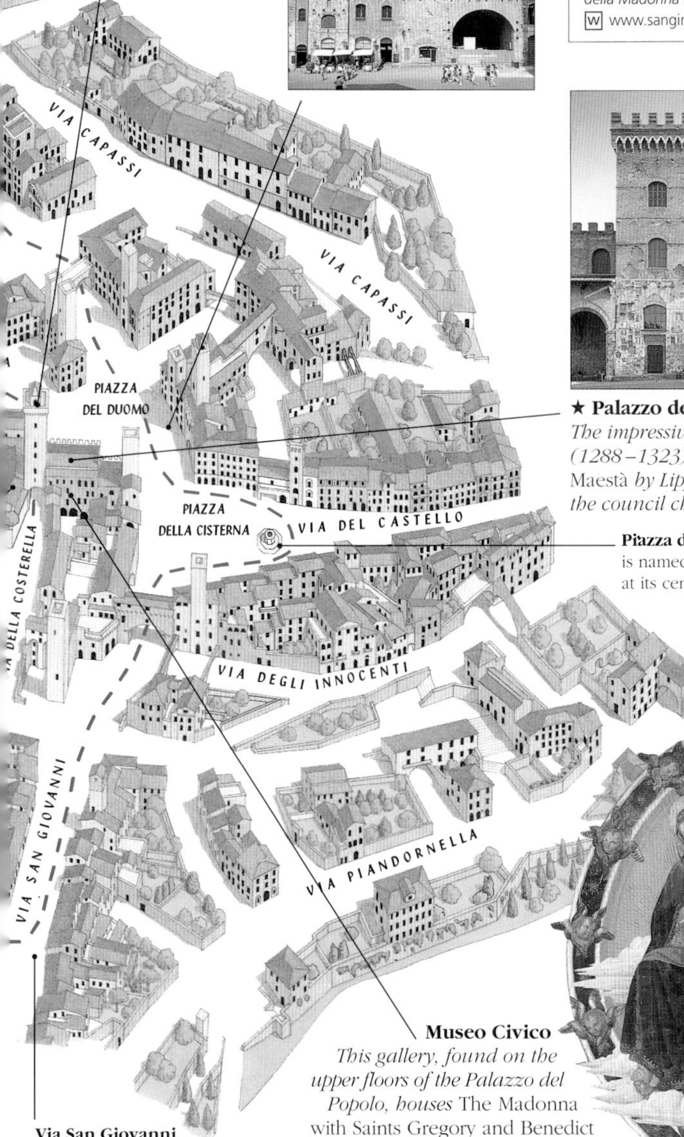

There are spectacular views from the top of the Torre Grossa.

VISITORS' CHECKLIST

Road map C3. 🚍 7,041. 🚌
Porta San Giovanni. ℹ️ *Piazza del Duomo 1 (0577 94 00 08).*
🗓️ *Thu.* **Shops closed** *Mon morning (summer); souvenir shops stay open.* 🎭 *Patron Saints' Festivals: 31 Jan, 12 Mar; Carnival: Feb; Fiera di Santa Fina: 1st week of Aug; Fiera di Sant'Agostino: 29 Aug; Festa della Madonna di Pancole: 8 Sep.*
W www.sangimignano.com

VIA CAPASSI

VIA CAPASSI

PIAZZA DEL DUOMO

PIAZZA DELLA CISTERNA

VIA DEL CASTELLO

LA DELLA COSTERELLA

VIA DEGLI INNOCENTI

VIA SAN GIOVANNI

VIA PIANDORNELLA

★ **Palazzo del Popolo**
The impressive town hall (1288–1323) has a huge Maestà by Lippo Memmi in the council chamber.

Piazza della Cisterna is named after the well at its centre.

Museo Civico
This gallery, found on the upper floors of the Palazzo del Popolo, houses The Madonna with Saints Gregory and Benedict (1511), which was one of the last works to be painted by Pinturicchio.

Via San Giovanni is lined with shops selling local goods.

Exploring San Gimignano

Fresco in Sant'Agostino

THE "CITY OF BEAUTIFUL TOWERS" is one of the best-preserved medieval towns in Tuscany. Its stunning skyline bristles with tall towers dating from the 13th century: 14 of the original 76 have survived. These windowless towers were built to serve both as private fortresses and symbols of their owners' wealth. In the Piazza della Cisterna, ringed by a jumble of unspoilt 13th- and 14th-century *palazzi*, is a wellhead built in 1237. Shops, galleries and jewellers line the two main streets, Via San Matteo and Via San Giovanni, which still retain their medieval feel.

San Gimignano's skyline, almost unchanged since the Middle Ages

⚑ Palazzo Vecchio del Podestà

Piazza del Duomo.
Closed to the public; visitors can observe only from the outside..
The Palazzo Vecchio del Podestà (the old mayor's palace) is in a group of public buildings clustered around the central Piazza del Duomo. It has a vaulted loggia and the 51-m (166-ft) Torre della Rognosa, one of the oldest towers in San Gimignano. A law was passed in 1255 forbidding any citizen to build a higher tower, but the rule was often broken by rival families.

🏛 Museo Civico

Palazzo del Popolo, Piazza del Duomo. **[** 0577 94 03 40.
Museum & tower Open Mar–Oct: 9:30am–7pm daily; Nov–Feb: 10am–5:30pm Tue–Sun. **Adm charge**.
The Museo is on the south side of the Piazza del Duomo, in the Palazzo del Popolo (town hall). Its tower,

finished in 1311, is the tallest in the city, at 54 m (175 ft). This is open to the public and the views from the top are quite stunning. Worn frescoes in the courtyard feature the coats of arms of city mayors and magistrates, as well as a 14th-century *Virgin and Child* by Taddeo di Bartolo. The first public room is the Sala di Dante, where an inscription records the poet's plea to the

12th-century well and medieval *palazzi* in the triangular Piazza della Cisterna

city council in 1300 to support the Guelph (pro-pope) alliance led by Florence. The walls are covered with hunting scenes and a huge *Virgin Enthroned* by Lippo Memmi (1317).
The floor above has a small art collection, which includes Pinturicchio's *Madonna with Saints Gregory and Benedict* (1511) painted against a landscape of blues and greens. The painting of *San Gimignano and his Miracles* by Taddeo di Bartolo shows the saint holding the town – recognizably the same city we see today. The *Wedding Scene* frescoes by Memmo di Filippucci (early 14th-century) show a couple sharing a bath and going to bed – an unusual record of life in a wealthy household in 14th-century Tuscany.

🏛 Museo d'Arte Sacra

Piazza Pecori. **[** 0577 94 22 26.
Open Mar–Oct: 9:30am–7:30pm daily; Nov–Feb: 9:30am–5pm daily.
Adm charge.
The museum is entered from the Piazza Pecori, where buskers play in summer. There is a chapel on the ground floor containing elaborate tomb slabs. The first floor houses paintings, sculpture and liturgical objects from the Collegiata. A marble bust (1493), by Benedetto da Maiano, commemorates the scholar Onofrio di Pietro.

⛪ Collegiata

Piazza del Duomo. **[** 0577 94 03 16.
Open daily.
The plain façade of this 12th-century Romanesque church belies its exotic interior; it is one of the most frescoed churches in Italy. The arches bordering the central aisle are painted in striking blue and white stripes, and the deep blue paint of the vaulted roof is speckled with gold stars. The aisle walls are extensively covered with dramatic fresco cycles of scenes from the Bible. In the north aisle the frescoes are on three levels and comprise 26 episodes

The ceiling of the Collegiata, painted with gold stars

from the Old Testament, including *The Creation of Adam and Eve, Noah and his Ark, Moses Crossing the Red Sea* and *The Afflictions of Job*, finished by Bartolo di Fredi in 1367. On the opposite walls are scenes from the life of Christ, dated 1333–41, now attributed to Lippo Memmi, a pupil of Simone Martini. At the back of the church, on the nave walls, are scenes from *The Last Judgment*, painted by Taddeo di Bartolo (1393–6). They depict the souls of the damned being tortured in hell by devils relishing their task.

The tiny Santa Fina chapel, off the south aisle, is covered with a cycle of frescoes by Ghirlandaio (1475) telling the life story of St Fina; legend has it that she spent most of her short life in prayer. The towers of San Gimignano feature in the background of the funeral scene.

Under an arch to the left of the Collegiata is a courtyard containing the loggia to the Baptistry, frescoed with an *Annunciation* painted in 1482 by Ghirlandaio.

Rocca

Piazza Propositura. **Open** *daily.*
The Rocca, or fortress, was built in 1353. It now has only one surviving tower following its dismantling by Cosimo I de' Medici in the 16th century. It encloses a public garden filled with fig and olive trees, and commands superb views over the vineyards where wine has been produced for hundreds of years.

Sant'Agostino

Piazza Sant'Agostino. **Open** *daily.*
This church was consecrated in 1298 and has a simple façade, contrasting markedly with the heavily decorated Rococo interior (c.1740) by Vanvitelli, architect to the kings of Naples. Above the main altar is the *Coronation of the Virgin* by Piero del Pollaiuolo, dated 1483, and

the choir is entirely covered in a cycle of frescoes of *The Life of St Augustine* (1465), executed by the Florentine artist Benozzo Gozzoli and a group of his assistants.

In the Cappella di San Bartolo, on the right of the main entrance, is an elaborate marble altar completed by Benedetto da Maiano in 1495. The bas-relief carvings show the miracles performed by St Bartholomew, all topped by flying angels and a roundel of the Madonna and Child.

Detail from *The Life of St Augustine*

Museo Ornitologico

Via Quercecchio. 0577 94 13 88.
Open *Apr–Sep: 9:30am–12:30pm, 3–6pm daily.* **Adm charge.**
The museum is in an elaborate 18th-century Baroque church. This is in total contrast to the sturdy cases of stuffed birds that form the collection, put together by a local dignitary.

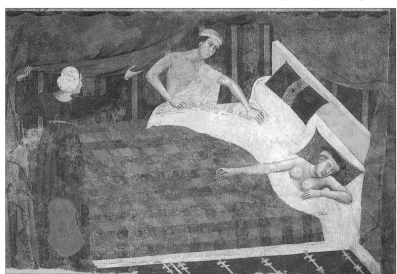

Fresco from the early 14th-century *Wedding Scene* cycle by Memmo di Filippucci in the Museo Civico

Street-by-Street: Siena ❹

Unicorn *contrada*
symbol

T HE PRINCIPAL SIGHTS of Siena are found in
the network of narrow streets and
alleys around the fan-shaped Piazza del
Campo. Scarcely any street is level, as
Siena, like Rome, is built on seven hills.
This adds to the pleasure of exploring:
one minute the city is laid out to view
before you and the next you are in a
warren of medieval houses. Packed into Siena are
the 17 *contrade* (parishes) whose animal symbols are
everywhere on carvings, plaques and car stickers.

Aerial bridges and
corridors linking buildings on
opposite sides of the street
are characteristic of Siena.

Via della Galluzza
leads up to the
house where
St Catherine
was born
in 1347.

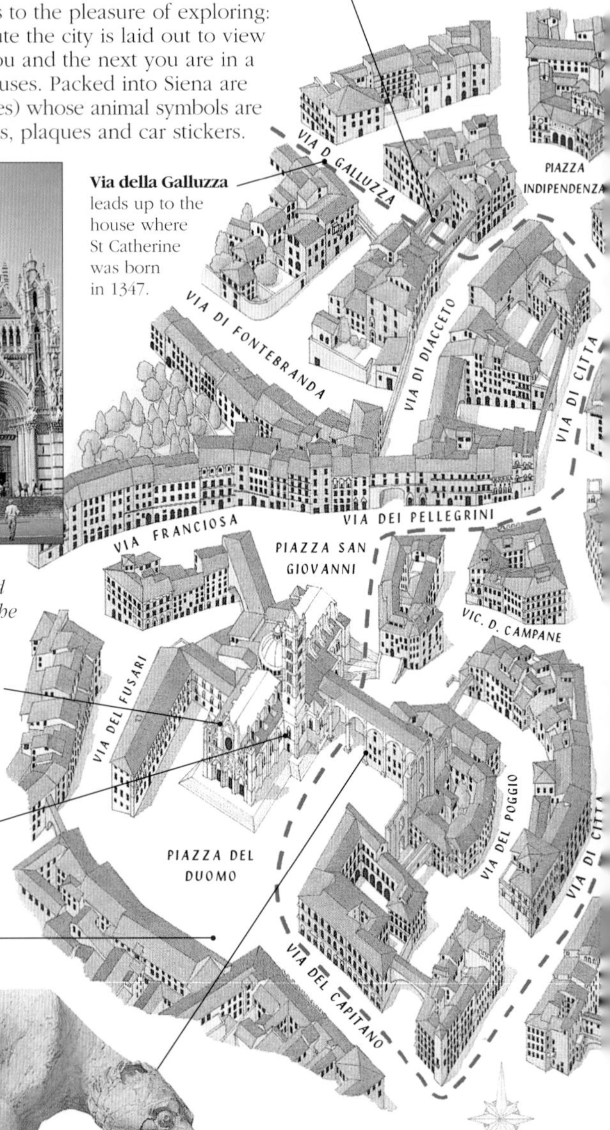

★ Duomo
*Statues of prophets carved
by Giovanni Pisano in the
1290s fill the Gothic
niches of the marble
façade (see pp216–17).*

Each tier of the
Duomo's belltower
has one window
fewer than the
floor above.

Antique shops
line the streets near
the Duomo square.

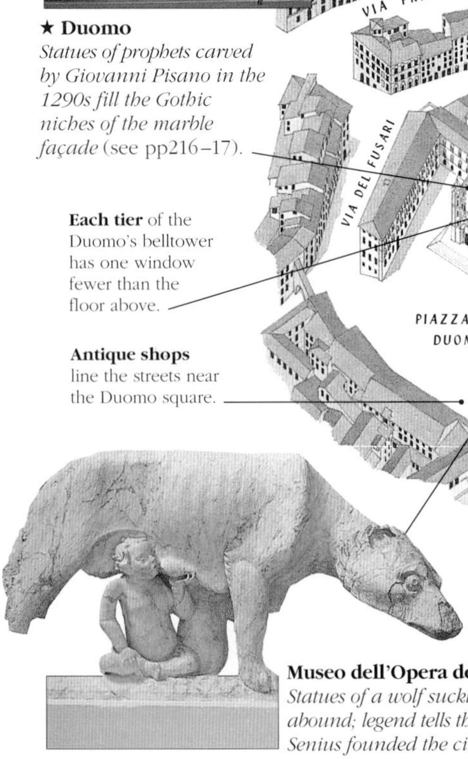

VIA D GALLUZZA

PIAZZA
INDIPENDENZA

VIA DI FONTEBRANDA

VIA DI DIACCETO

VIA DI CITTÀ

VIA DEI PELLEGRINI

VIA FRANCIOSA

PIAZZA SAN
GIOVANNI

VIC. D. CAMPANE

VIA DELL'FUSARI

VIA DEL POGGIO

VIA DI CITTÀ

PIAZZA DEL
DUOMO

VIA DEL CAPITANO

Museo dell'Opera del Duomo
*Statues of a wolf suckling Remus
abound; legend tells that his son
Senius founded the city of Siena.*

KEY

– – – Suggested route

0 metres	300
0 yards	300

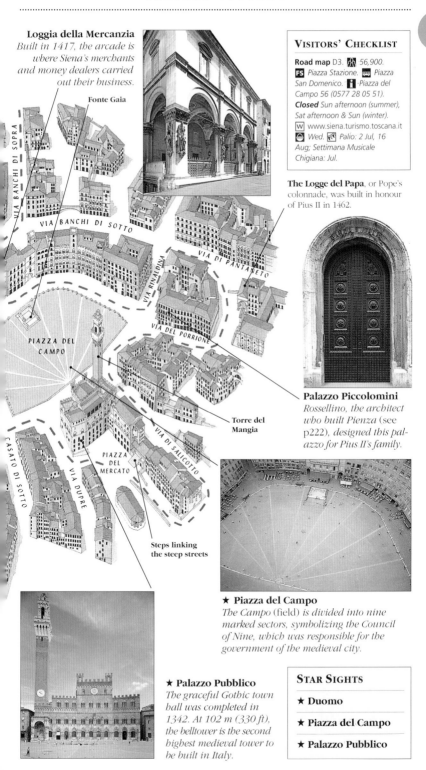

Loggia della Mercanzia
Built in 1417, the arcade is where Siena's merchants and money dealers carried out their business.

Fonte Gaia

VIA BANCHI DI SOPRA

VIA BANCHI DI SOTTO

VIA RINALDINA

VIA DI PANTANETO

VIA DEL PORRIONE

PIAZZA DEL CAMPO

CASATO DI SOTTO

VIA DUPRÉ

PIAZZA DEL MERCATO

VIA DI SALICOTTO

Torre del Mangia

Steps linking the steep streets

VISITORS' CHECKLIST

Road map D3. 56,900.
Piazza Stazione. Piazza San Domenico. Piazza del Campo 56 (0577 28 05 51).
Closed *Sun afternoon (summer), Sat afternoon & Sun (winter).*
www.siena.turismo.toscana.it
Wed. Palio: 2 Jul, 16 Aug; Settimana Musicale Chigiana: Jul.

The Logge del Papa, or Pope's colonnade, was built in honour of Pius II in 1462.

Palazzo Piccolomini
Rossellino, the architect who built Pienza (see p222), designed this palazzo for Pius II's family.

★ **Piazza del Campo**
The Campo (field) is divided into nine marked sectors, symbolizing the Council of Nine, which was responsible for the government of the medieval city.

★ **Palazzo Pubblico**
The graceful Gothic town hall was completed in 1342. At 102 m (330 ft), the belltower is the second highest medieval tower to be built in Italy.

STAR SIGHTS

★ **Duomo**

★ **Piazza del Campo**

★ **Palazzo Pubblico**

Exploring Siena

Siena is a city of steep medieval alleys surrounding the Piazza del Campo. The buildings around the square symbolize the golden age of the city between 1260 and 1348, when wealthy citizens contributed to a major programme of civic building. Siena's decline began in 1348 when the Black Death hit the city, killing a third of the population; 200 years later many more died in an 18-month siege ending in defeat by the Florentines. The victors repressed all further development and building in Siena, which remained frozen in time, crammed with medieval buildings which have recently been renovated.

Aerial view of Siena's Piazza del Campo and surrounding palazzi

🏛 Piazza del Campo

The shell-shaped 12th-century Piazza del Campo is bordered by elegant *palazzi*. It has an elaborate fountain as its focal point, the Fonte Gaia, a rectangular marble basin decorated by statues. The fountain now seen in the square is a 19th-century copy of the original, which was carved by Jacopo della Quercia in 1409–19. This was removed to preserve it from the ravages of the weather.

The reliefs on the fountain depict Adam and Eve, the Madonna and Child, and the Virtues. Water is fed into it by a 25-km (15-mile) aqueduct, which has brought fresh water into the city from the hills since the 14th century.

🏛 Torre del Mangia

Piazza del Campo. **Open** *Nov–mid-Mar: 10am–4pm; mid-Mar–Oct: 10am–7pm (extended hours in summer).* **Adm charge**.

The belltower to the left of the Palazzo Pubblico is the second highest in Italy, at 102 m (330 ft). Built by the brothers Muccio and Francesco di Rinaldo between 1338–48, it is named after the first bell ringer, who was nicknamed *Mangiaguadagni* (literally "eat the profits") because of his great idleness. (It was the bell ringer's responsibility to toll the nightly curfew and warn the citizens of impending danger.) There are 505 steps to the top of the tower, which has views across Tuscany.

🏛 Palazzo Pubblico

Piazza del Campo 1. **📞** *0577 29 22 63.* **Museo Civico open** *mid-Mar–Oct: 10am–7pm daily; Nov–mid-Mar: 10am–5:30pm daily.* **Closed** *1 Jan, 1 May, 1 Dec, 25 Dec.* **Adm charge**.

The Palazzo Pubblico still serves as the town hall, but the medieval state rooms are open to the public. The main council chamber is called the Sala del Mappamondo, named after a map of the world painted by Ambrogio Lorenzetti in the early 14th century. One wall is covered by the *Maestà* (Virgin in Majesty) by Simone Martini. Painted in 1315, it depicts the Virgin Mary as the Queen of Heaven, attended by the Apostles, saints and angels. Opposite is Martini's fresco of the mercenary Guidoriccio da Fogliano (1330).

The walls of the chapel alongside are covered with frescoes of the *Life of the Virgin* (1407) by Taddeo di Bartolo, and the choir stalls (1428) feature wooden panels inlaid with biblical scenes.

The Sala della Pace contains the famous *Allegory of Good and Bad Government*, a pair of frescoes by Ambrogio Lorenzetti, finished in 1338. In *The Good Government (see pp44–5)* civic life flourishes, while *The Bad Government*

Fonte Gaia in Piazza del Campo

Guidoriccio da Fogliano by Simone Martini (1330) in the Palazzo Pubblico

reveals ruins and rubbish-strewn streets.

The Sala del Risorgimento is covered with late 19th-century frescoes illustrating the events leading up to the unification of Italy under King Vittorio Emanuele II *(see pp52–3)*.

🏛 Palazzo Piccolomini

Via Banchi di Sotto 52. **☎** *0577 24 71 45.* **Open** *9am–1pm Mon–Sat.* **Closed** *1st two weeks in Aug.*

This imposing private palazzo was built in the 1460s by Rossellino for the very wealthy Piccolomini family. It contains Sienese state archives and financial records dating back to the 13th century. Other unusual records include a will attributed to Boccaccio and examples of medieval book-binding. Some of these books are illustrated with pictures by artists of the Siena School. Much of the palazzo is not accessible to the public.

🏛 Pinacoteca Nazionale

Via San Pietro 29. **☎** *0577 28 11 61.* **Open** *8am–1:30pm Sun, Mon, 8am–7pm Tue–Sat.* **Closed** *1 Jan, 1 May, 25 Dec.* **Adm charge.** ♿

Housed in the 14th-century Palazzo Buonsignori, this gallery contains a number of important works by the Siena School. Lorenzetti's *Two Views*, painted in the 14th century, are early examples of landscape painting and Pietro da Domenico's *Adoration of the Shepherds* (1510) shows how the art of the Siena School remained stylized long after Renaissance naturalism had influenced the rest of Europe *(see p46)*. There is also a striking *Deposition* (1502) by Sodoma.

🔒 Duomo

See pp216–17.

Cloister of Casa di Santa Caterina

🏛 Museo dell'Opera del Duomo

Piazza del Duomo 8. **☎** *0577 28 30 48.* **Open** *mid-Mar–Oct: 9am–7:30pm; Oct: 9am–6pm; Nov–mid-Mar: 9am–5pm.* **Closed** *1 Jan, 25 Dec.* **Adm charge.**

This museum is built into the unfinished side aisle of the Duomo *(see pp216–17)*. Part of the museum is devoted to the sculpture from the exterior of the Duomo, including Gothic statues by Giovanni Pisano (1250–1314) that had become eroded outside.

Duccio's huge double-sided *Maestà*, one of the best Siena School works, has a room to itself. Painted between 1308–11, it depicts the Madonna and Child on one side and scenes from *The Life of Christ* on the

Pisano's *Simone* (c.1300) in the Museo dell'Opera del Duomo

other. On the top floor, stairs lead off the Sala dei Parati to a loggia with views of the town and countryside.

🏛 Casa di Santa Caterina

Costa di Sant'Antonio. **☎** *0577 441 77.* **Open** *9am–12:30pm, 2:30–6pm daily (3:30–6pm in winter).*

Siena's patron saint, Catherine Benincasa (1347–80), was the daughter of a tradesman. She took the veil at the age of eight, and experienced many visions of God, from whom she also received the stigmata. Her eloquence persuaded Gregory XI to return the seat of the papacy to Rome in 1376, after 67 years of exile in Avignon. She died in Rome and was canonized in 1461. Today, Catherine's house is surrounded by chapels and cloisters. It is decorated with paintings of incidents from her life by artists including Francesco Vanni and Pietro Sorri, both her contemporaries.

Siena Duomo

Siena's Duomo (1136–1382) is one of the most spectacular in Italy, and one of the few to have been built south of the Alps in full Gothic style. Many ordinary citizens helped to cart the black and white stone used in its construction from quarries on the outskirts of the city. In 1339, the Sienese decided to build a new nave to the south with the aim of making it the biggest church in Christendom. This plan came to nothing when plague hit the city soon afterwards, killing off much of the population. The uncompleted nave now contains a museum of Gothic sculpture.

★ Pulpit Panels
Carved by Nicola Pisano in 1265–8, the panels on the octagonal pulpit depict scenes from The Life of Christ.

★ Inlaid Marble Floor
The Massacre of the Innocents is one of a series of scenes in the inlaid marble floor. The marble is usually uncovered during September each year.

Nave
Black and white marble pillars support the vault.

Chapel of St John the Baptist

★ Piccolomini Library
Pinturicchio's frescoes (1509) portray the life of Pope Pius II (see p222). Here he presides at the betrothal of Frederick III to Eleonora of Portugal.

STAR FEATURES

★ Inlaid Marble Floor

★ Piccolomini Library

★ Pulpit Panels by Pisano

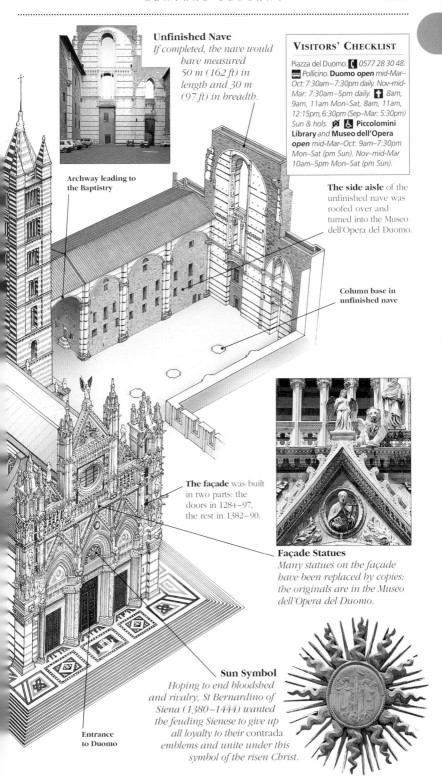

Unfinished Nave
If completed, the nave would have measured 50 m (162 ft) in length and 30 m (97 ft) in breadth.

Archway leading to the Baptistry

VISITORS' CHECKLIST

Piazza del Duomo. ☎ 0577 28 30 48.
🚌 Pollicino. **Duomo open** mid-Mar–Oct: 7:30am–7:30pm daily. Nov–mid-Mar: 7:30am–5pm daily. ✝ 8am, 9am, 11am Mon–Sat, 8am, 11am, 12:15pm, 6:30pm (Sep–Mar: 5:30pm) Sun & hols. 🚫 & **Piccolomini Library** and **Museo dell'Opera open** mid-Mar–Oct: 9am–7:30pm Mon–Sat (pm Sun). Nov–mid-Mar 10am–5pm Mon–Sat (pm Sun).

The side aisle of the unfinished nave was roofed over and turned into the Museo dell'Opera del Duomo.

Column base in unfinished nave

The façade was built in two parts: the doors in 1284–97, the rest in 1382–90.

Façade Statues
Many statues on the façade have been replaced by copies; the originals are in the Museo dell'Opera del Duomo.

Sun Symbol
Hoping to end bloodshed and rivalry, St Bernardino of Siena (1380–1444) wanted the feuding Sienese to give up all loyalty to their contrada emblems and unite under this symbol of the risen Christ.

Entrance to Duomo

The Sienese Palio

**One of the
contrada
symbols**

THE PALIO IS TUSCANY'S most celebrated festival and takes place on 2 July and 16 August each year in the Campo *(see p214)*. It is a bareback horse race and was first recorded in 1283, but may have had its origins in Roman military training. The jockeys represent the 17 *contrade* or districts; the horses are chosen by the drawing of straws and are then blessed at the local *contrada* churches. The races are preceded by heavy betting and pageantry, but only last about 90 seconds each. The winner is awarded a *palio* (banner).

Ringside View
*Huge sums are paid
for a view of the races.*

Flag-Throwing
*The Sienese display their
flag-throwing skills in the
procession and pageantry
before the
race.*

Medieval Knight
*The traditional outfits
worn in the processions
are all hand-made.*

Racing Crowds
*Thousands of people cram
into the piazza to watch the
race, and rivalry is intense
between competitors.*

Galloping towards the finish

**Traditional
drummer
taking part
in pre-race
pageant**

View across the Campo during a race

The façade of San Domenico

🔒 San Domenico

Piazza San Domenico. **Open** daily.
This barn-like Gothic church
was begun in 1226 and its
belltower was added in 1340.
Inside is an exquisite chapel
dedicated to St Catherine (see
p215). It was built in 1460 to
store her preserved head,
which is now kept in a gilded
marble tabernacle on the altar.
This is surrounded by frescoes
showing

Catherine in a state of
religious fervour, painted by
Sodoma in 1526. The marble
pavement is attributed to
Giovanni di Stefano.

Catherine experienced many
of her visions and received
her stigmata in the Cappella
delle Volte at the west end of
the church. Here there is an
authenticated portrait of her
by contemporary Andrea
Vanni, dated around 1380.

🏰 Fortezza Medicea

Viale Maccari. **Fortezza Open** daily.
Enoteca 📞 0577 28 84 97. **Open**
noon–1am Tue–Sat, noon–8pm Mon.
Theatre Open Nov–Apr: performances
only. **Closed** May–Oct.
This huge red-brick fortress
was built for Cosimo I by
Baldassarre Lanci in 1560,
following Siena's defeat by
the Florentines in the 1554–5
war. More than 8,000 Sienese
died either from battle wounds
or through starvation and
disease in the 18-month siege,
reducing the town's population
to a mere 6,000. The town
was repressed by its Florentine
masters, its banking and wool
industries were suppressed
and all building work ended.

The fortress now houses an
open-air theatre, and from the
entrance bastions there are
glorious views of the countryside. The Enoteca Italica, a
wine shop, is in one of the
bastions on the Lizza, the garden fronting the fort. It offers
visitors the chance to taste and
buy from a comprehensive
list of quality Italian wines.

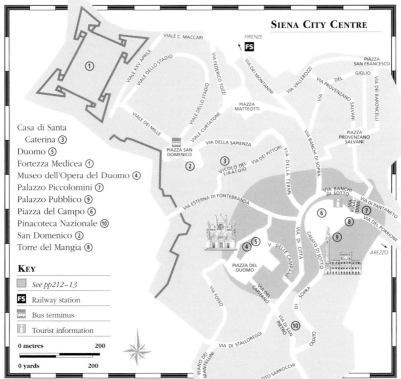

SIENA CITY CENTRE

Casa di Santa
  Caterina ③
Duomo ⑤
Fortezza Medicea ①
Museo dell'Opera del Duomo ④
Palazzo Piccolomini ⑦
Palazzo Pubblico ⑨
Piazza del Campo ⑥
Pinacoteca Nazionale ⑩
San Domenico ②
Torre del Mangia ⑧

KEY

☐ See pp212–13
🚉 Railway station
🚏 Bus terminus
ℹ Tourist information

0 metres   200
0 yards   200

The ruined abbey at San Galgano, surrounded by dense woodland

San Galgano **7**

Road map D4. 🚌 *from Siena.*
📞 *0577 75 66 11.* **Abbey and oratory** *open* daily.

T HE RUINED Cistercian abbey is in dense woodland in a superb setting. It is very remote but well worth the effort of getting there for the beauty of the surroundings and the majesty of the ruined, roofless building. Begun in 1218, the abbey is Gothic in style; unusual in Tuscany, this reflects the French origins of the Cistercian monks who designed and built it.

The monks avoided contact with civilization and divided their lives between prayer and labour, clearing the hills of vegetation to graze their sheep. Despite the Cistercian emphasis on poverty, the monks became wealthy from the sale of wool; by the middle of the 14th century, the abbey was corruptly administered and gradually fell into decline.

In the late 14th century, the English mercenary Sir John Hawkwood sacked the abbey and by 1397 the abbot was the sole occupant. Numbers recovered for a time but the abbey was eventually dissolved in 1652. Empty for many years, the cloister and other monastic buildings alongside the church are now being restored for the Olivetan order of nuns.

On a hill above the abbey is the beehive-shaped chapel of Montesiepi, built on the site of St Galgano's hermitage around 1185, a few years after his death in 1181.

St Galgano's sword stands embedded in a stone just inside the door of the circular oratory. The 14th-century stone walls of the side chapel are covered with frescoes showing scenes from Galgano's life by Ambrogio Lorenzetti (1344); some are now in a poor state of repair.

The shop alongside the chapel sells locally-made herbs, wines, olive oils and toiletries along with books on the history of the region.

Montalcino **8**

Road map D4. 👥 *5,100.* 🚌
ℹ️ *Costa del Municipio 1 (0577 84 93 31).* 🛒 *Fri.*

M ONTALCINO's foremost activity is wine-producing, as is evident from the number of shops where you can both sample and buy the excellent local Brunello wines *(see p256).*

The town, situated on the top of a hill, is of timeless character and the streets are narrow, winding and steep. The highest point is the 14th-century **Fortezza** and its impressive ramparts, built by Cosimo I in 1571.

THE LEGEND OF ST GALGANO

Galgano was born in 1148, the son of noble parents, and grew into a brave but dissolute young knight. He saw his life as futile and turned to God, renouncing the material world. When he tried to break his sword against a rock as a symbol of his rejection of war, it was swallowed by the stone. This he interpreted as a sign of God's approval. He built a hut on the site of today's chapel at Montesiepi, and died a hermit in 1181. In 1185 Pope Urban III declared him a saint and an example to all Christian knights.

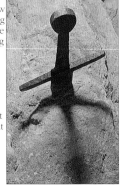

Montalcino's 14th-century Fortezza

Spectacular views over the surrounding countryside are available from the walkway on the ramparts.

There is an Enoteca (wine shop) in the grounds of the Fortezza, where the Brunello red wines are on sale.

Inside the fortress there is an ancient Sienese battle standard, a reminder that the town gave refuge to a band of rebels after Florence conquered Siena in 1555. In remembrance of this, flag-bearers from the village of Montalcino are given the honour of leading the parade before the Palio in Siena every year (see p218).

As you walk down into the town from the Fortezza, the monastery of Sant'Agostino and its 14th-century church, with an attractive rose window, are on the right. Just beyond is the **Palazzo Vescovile**, formerly the bishop's palace. The **Palazzo Comunale** stands on the Piazza del Popolo. Constructed in the 13th and 14th centuries, its tall, slim tower rises above the town.

The Duomo, San Salvatore, was designed in 1818–32 by Agostino Fantastici, and replaced the original Romanesque church building.

♣ **Fortezza**
Piazzale della Fortezza. 📞 *0577 84 92 11.* **Enoteca** *open* Nov–Mar: 9am–6pm Tue–Sun; Apr–Oct: 9am–8pm daily. **Adm charge** for ramparts.
🏛 **Palazzo Vescovile**
Via Spagni 4. 📞 *0577 84 81 68.* **Closed** to the public.
🏛 **Palazzo Comunale**
Costa del Municipio 1. 📞 *0577 84 93 31.* **Closed** to the public.

San Quirico d'Orcia 9

Road map E4. 🚶 *2,390.*
🚌 ℹ️ *Via Dante Alighieri 33 (0577 89 72 11).* 🛒 *2nd & 4th Tue of month.*

Collegiata in San Quirico

STANDING JUST INSIDE the city walls, San Quirico d'Orcia's pride is the **Collegiata**, featuring three ornately carved Romanesque portals built onto an 8th-century structure. Begun in 1080, the capitals and lintels of the portals are carved with details of dragons, mermaids and other mythical beasts.

The church commemorates the 3rd-century martyr St Quiricus, who was killed at the age of five by the Romans for the simple act of declaring himself a Christian. Quiricus is depicted in the elaborate altar piece by Sano di Pietro, along with the Virgin and Child and other saints.

Next to the church is the 17th-century **Palazzo Chigi**, whose frescoed interior has recently been restored. The **Horti Leonini** nearby is a 16th-century garden of box hedges nestling within the town walls. It was intended as a refuge for pilgrims and travellers, and is now used as a public sculpture garden during the summer months.

🔒 **Collegiata**
Via Dante Alighieri. 📞 *0577 89 75 06.* **Open** 8am–8pm daily.
🏛 **Palazzo Chigi**
Piazza Chigi. **Open** 10am–1pm, 4–7pm (Oct–Mar: 3:30–6:30pm) Tue–Sun.
🌿 **Horti Leonini**
Piazza Libertà. 📞 *0577 89 75 06.* **Open** sunrise–sunset daily. 🦽 partial.

Flower-covered house in the pretty town of Montalcino

The Terme di Bagno Vignoni

Bagno Vignoni ⑩

Road map D4. 🏛 *32*. 🚌 *from Siena.*

THIS IS A TINY medieval spa village which consists of a handful of houses built round a huge piazza containing an arcaded, stone-lined pool. Constructed by the Medici, it is full of hot sulphurous water which bubbles up to the surface from the volcanic rocks deep underground. The healing quality of the water has been known since Roman times and, according to legend, famous people who have sought a cure in Bagno Vignoni include St Catherine of Siena *(see p215)* and Lorenzo the Magnificent (to relieve his arthritis). The pool is no longer open for bathing but is still well worth a visit to admire the architecture. Sulphur pools in the grounds of the Posta Marcucci hotel are open for swimming.

Pienza ⑪

Road map E4. 🏛 *1,300*. 🚌 ℹ️ *Corso il Rossellino 59 (0578 74 90 71).* 🗓 *Fri.*

THE CENTRE of Pienza was completely redesigned in Renaissance times by Pope Pius II *(see p47)*. Born here in 1405, when it was called Corsignano, Aeneas Sylvius Piccolomini became known as a leading Humanist scholar and philosopher. He was elected pope in 1458 and in the following year decided to

commission a new centre in Corsignano and rename it Pienza in his own honour. He planned to transform his birthplace into a model Renaissance town, but the grand scheme never progressed beyond the handful of buildings around the Piazza Pio II. The architect Bernardo Rossellino was commissioned to build a Duomo, papal palace and town hall, which were completed in three years. Subsequently Rossellino was caught embezzling papal funds, but Pius II forgave him because he was so delighted with his new buildings.

Away from the grandeur of the main square, Pienza is a quiet agricultural town with shops selling local produce like *pecorino*, cheese made from sheep's milk *(see p255)*.

Coat of arms of Pope Pius II

🔒 Duomo
Piazza Pio II. **Open** *daily.*
The Duomo was built by the architect Rossellino in 1459, and is now suffering from serious subsidence at its eastern end. There are cracks in the walls and floor of the nave, but this does not detract at all from the splendid Classical proportions of this Renaissance church. It is flooded with light from the vast stained-glass windows requested by Pius II; he wanted a *domus vitrea* (literally "a house of glass") which would symbolize the spirit of intellectual enlightenment of the Humanist age.

🏛 Palazzo Piccolomini
Piazza Pio II. ☎ *0578 74 85 03.* **Open** *10am–12:30pm, 3–6pm Tue–Sun (guided tours only).* **Adm charge.**
The palazzo is next door to the Duomo and was home to Pius II's descendants until 1968. Rossellino's design for the building was influenced by Leon Battista Alberti's Palazzo Rucellai in Florence *(see p104).* The apartments open to the public include Pius II's bedroom and library, which are full of his personal possessions. At the rear of the palazzo there is an arcaded courtyard and a triple-tiered loggia. The spectacular view looks across the garden and takes in the wooded slopes of the volcano, Monte Amiata.

Courtyard in Palazzo Piccolomini

🔒 Pieve di Corsignano
Via delle Fonti. ☎ *0578 74 82 03.* **Open** *by appt or through tourist office.*
Pope Pius II was baptized in this 11th-century Romanesque parish church on the outskirts of Pienza. It has an unusual round tower and a doorway decorated with flower motifs.

Pienza's piazza and the town hall, viewed from the steps of the Duomo

The church of Madonna di San Biagio on the outskirts of Montepulciano

Montepulciano ⑫

Road map E4. 🏃 14,000. 🚌
🅘 Via di Gracciano 59 (0578 75 73 41). 🚌 Thu.

MONTEPULCIANO is built along a narrow limestone ridge and, at 605 m (1,950 ft) above sea level, is one of the highest of Tuscany's hilltop towns. The town is encircled by walls and fortifications designed by Antonio da Sangallo the Elder in 1511 for Cosimo I. Inside the walls the streets are crammed with Renaissance-style palazzi and churches, but the town is chiefly known for its good local Vino Nobile wines *(see p256)*. A long winding street called the Corso climbs up into the main square, which crowns the summit of the hill.

On the Corso is the Art Deco Caffè Poliziano, which has an art gallery in the basement. In July the café hosts a jazz festival and the town fills with musicians who perform at the Cantiere Internazionale d'Arte *(see p33)*, an arts festival directed by the German composer Hans Werner Henze.

In August there are two festivals: the Bruscello takes place on the 14th, 15th and 16th, when hordes of actors re-enact scenes from the town's turbulent history. For the Bravio delle Botti, on the last Sunday in August, there is a parade through the streets followed by a barrel race and a banquet to end the day.

🏛 Madonna di San Biagio

Via di San Biagio 14. **Open** daily. 🦽
This beautiful pilgrimage church is on the outskirts of Montepulciano, perched on a platform below the city walls. Built of honey- and cream-coloured travertine, it is Sangallo's masterpiece, a Renaissance gem begun in 1518. The project occupied him until his death in 1534.

🏛 Palazzo Bucelli

Via di Gracciano del Corso 73. **Closed**.
The lower façade of the palazzo (1648) is studded with ancient Etruscan reliefs and funerary urns collected by its 18th-century antiquarian owner, Pietro Bucelli.

🏛 Sant'Agostino

Piazza Michelozzo. **Open** daily.
Michelozzo built the church in 1427, with an elaborate carved portal featuring the Virgin and Child flanked by St John and St Augustine.

🏛 Palazzo Comunale

Piazza Grande 1. 📞 0578 75 70 34.
In the 15th century, Michelozzo added a tower and façade on to the original Gothic town hall. The building is now a smaller version of the Palazzo Vecchio *(see pp78–9)*. The tower is open only during spring and summer months.

🏛 Palazzo Tarugi

Piazza Grande. **Closed**.
The imposing 16th-century palazzo is next to the town hall and currently undergoing restoration to the façade.

🏛 Duomo

Piazza Grande. **Open** daily.
The Duomo was designed between 1592 and 1630 by Ippolito Scalza. The façade is unfinished and plain, but the interior is Classical in proportions. It is the setting for an earlier masterpiece from the Siena School, the *Assumption of the Virgin* triptych painted by Taddeo di Bartolo in 1401. Placed over the High Altar, it is rich in bright, jewel-like colours and heavily embossed with gold leaf.

Taddeo di Bartolo's triptych (1401)

🏛 Santa Maria dei Servi

Via del Poliziano. **Open** by appt. 🦽
The Corso continues from the Piazza up to the Gothic church of Santa Maria dei Servi. The wine bar alongside sells Vino Nobile from medieval storage cellars cut out of the limestone cliffs below the town.

Etruscan frieze in the Museo Nazionale Etrusco in Chiusi

Chiusi ⑬

Road map E4. 🏘 *10,000*. 🚂 🚌
ℹ *Piazza Duomo 1 (0578 22 76 67)*.
📅 *Mon, Tue*.

CHIUSI WAS ONE of the most
powerful cities in the
Etruscan league, reaching the
height of its influence in the
7th and 6th centuries BC *(see
pp40–41)*. There is a large
number of Etruscan tombs in
the surrounding countryside.

🏛 **Museo Nazionale Etrusco**
Via Porsenna 17. 📞 *0578 201 77*.
Open *9am–7:30pm daily*.
Adm charge. ♿
The museum was founded in
1871, and is now packed with
cremation urns, vases decorated with black figures and
Bucchero ware, burnished to
resemble bronze. Most of
these were excavated from
tombs in the area. Arrangements can be made at the
museum to visit local tombs.

🔓 **Duomo**
Piazza del Duomo. **Open** *daily*.
The Romanesque cathedral is
opposite the museum and built
from recycled Roman pillars
and capitals. The decorations
on the nave walls appear to
be mosaics, but in fact were
painted by Arturo Viligiardi in
1887. There is a Roman
mosaic under the High Altar.

🏛 **Museo della Cattedrale**
Piazza del Duomo. 📞 *0578 22 64 90*.
Open *Jun–mid-Oct: 9:30am–12:45pm
4–7pm daily; mid-Oct–May 9:30am–
12:45pm Mon–Sat, 3:30–6:30pm
Sun*. **Adm charge**. ♿ *partial*.
The museum has a display
of Roman, Lombardic and
medieval sculpture. Visits can

be arranged here to the underground galleries beneath the
city, dug by the Etruscans and
used as Christian catacombs
in the 3rd–5th centuries.

Sant'Antimo ⑭

Road map D4. **Custodian** *0577
83 56 59*. **Open** *daily*. ♿

THIS BEAUTIFUL abbey church
(see pp42–3) has inspired
many poets and painters and
enchants everyone who
comes here. The ancient

church, built of creamy
travertine, is set against a
background of tree-clad hills
in the Starcia valley. The very
earliest surviving church on
the site dates back to the 9th
century, but local people
prefer to think the church was
founded by the Holy Roman
Emperor, Charlemagne, in
781. The main part of the
church was built in 1118 in
the French Romanesque style,
and the exterior is decorated
with interlaced blank arcades
carved with the symbols of
the Four Evangelists.

The soft, honey-coloured
alabaster interior has an odd
luminous quality which is
seen to change according to
time of day and season. The
capitals in the nave are carved
with geometric designs, leaf
motifs and biblical scenes.
Recorded plainsong echoes
around the walls, adding to
the eerie atmosphere.

The Augustinian monks
who tend the church sing
Gregorian chant at mass
every Sunday and there are
organ concerts in the church
during July and August.

The beautiful abbey church of Sant'Antimo

A Day Out in Chianti

THIS TOUR TAKES IN the main villages of the Chianti Classico wine region. Castles and wine estates line the route, and vineyards offer tastings and sell direct to the public. Look for signs along the way saying "vendita diretta".

The first stop on leaving Siena is the Castello di Brolio, which has been owned by the Ricasoli family since 1167. From Brolio, drive to Gaiole, diverting to see the 13th-century castle at Meleto. Gaiole is a very quiet agricultural town with a stream running down the main street; wine can be sampled here at the local cooperative. In Badia a Coltibuono there is a restaurant (see p262) and a Romanesque church, and Radda in Chianti offers extensive views over the Parco Naturale della Viriglia. At Castellina in Chianti, there is a 15th-century underground passage built for defence purposes, and the Enoteca Vini Gallo Nero (Via della Rocca 13), which is a showcase for the region's wines (see pp256–7).

Badia a Coltibuono ④
At the crossroads in Gaiole, follow the signs to Montevarchi and divert to the left off the main road before heading right towards the village of Badia.

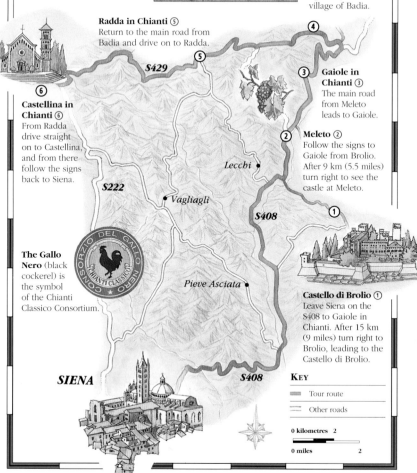

Radda in Chianti ⑤
Return to the main road from Badia and drive on to Radda.

Castellina in Chianti ⑥
From Radda drive straight on to Castellina, and from there follow the signs back to Siena.

Gaiole in Chianti ③
The main road from Meleto leads to Gaiole.

Meleto ②
Follow the signs to Gaiole from Brolio. After 9 km (5.5 miles) turn right to see the castle at Meleto.

The Gallo Nero (black cockerel) is the symbol of the Chianti Classico Consortium.

Castello di Brolio ①
Leave Siena on the S408 to Gaiole in Chianti. After 15 km (9 miles) turn right to Brolio, leading to the Castello di Brolio.

Lecchi

Vagliagli

Pieve Asciata

SIENA

S429

S222

S408

S408

KEY

▬▬ Tour route

═ ═ Other roads

0 kilometres   2

0 miles   2

SOUTHERN TUSCANY

THE SOUTHERNMOST PART *of Tuscany has a very different feel to any other Tuscan region. Thanks to the hotter, drier and sunnier climate, the hills are cloaked in aromatic Mediterranean scrub, known as* macchia. *Palm trees grow in the towns and along the edge of the sandy beaches, and great strands of prickly pear cactus are traditionally used to mark field boundaries in the countryside.*

The coastline, lined with fishing villages and beaches, is very popular in the summer, with numerous holiday villages and caravan sites. Resorts such as Monte Argentario have a much more exclusive image, and are favoured by the wealthy, yacht-owning Italians from Rome and Milan. Inland, the region's wild and unspoiled hills are popular with sportsmen, who come to hunt for wild boar and deer.

The transformation of the marshy coastal strip, known as the Maremma, into a holiday playground is a recent development. The ancient Etruscans, followed by the Romans *(see p40)*, drained its swamps to create richly fertile farming land. After the collapse of the Roman Empire, the drainage channels became choked, turning the Maremma into an inhospitable wilderness of marshland and stagnant pools plagued by malaria-carrying mosquitoes. Re-draining of the land began again in the late 18th century and, with the help of insecticides, the malaria-mosquito was finally eliminated in the 1950s.

LITTLE DEVELOPMENT

The region slumbered from Roman times and for long periods was virtually uninhabited except for farmers and fishermen. Consequently there are few cities or major architectural and artistic monuments. On the other hand, archaeological remains have survived because there were few people here to salvage the stone for new buildings. The relative lack of intensive farming means the region is still rich in wildlife, from butterflies and orchids to tortoises and porcupines.

Detail of Romanesque *tympanum* on the Duomo at Massa Marittima

◁ **The Strada Panoramica at Monte Argentario**

Exploring Southern Tuscany

Away from the coastal resorts, this region remains relatively undiscovered; quiet roads and a lack of tourists only add to the pleasure of exploring rock-cut tombs in Sovana, bathing in hot sulphurous springs at Saturnia or wandering through the Maremma spotting the wildlife. For a busier atmosphere, visit the resorts of Orbetello and Monte Argentario, which have plenty of choice for shopping, restaurants and nightlife.

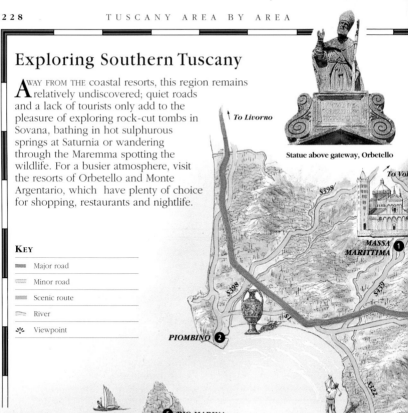

Statue above gateway, Orbetello

To Livorno

To Vol

S398

S398

S439

S1

MASSA MARITTIMA ❶

PIOMBINO ❷

S322

KEY

▬▬ Major road

▭▭ Minor road

▬▬ Scenic route

🝆 River

🌿 Viewpoint

PORTOFERRAIO ❸   ❺ RIO MARINA

MARCIANA ❹

ISOLA D'ELBA

GETTING AROUND

The S1 coastal route cannot cope with the traffic in summer and is best avoided. A busy railway line runs alongside; most trains stop at Grosseto and Orbetello, and buses from Grosseto serve most towns in the area. Vehicle and passenger ferries depart from Piombino to Elba every 30 minutes during the day in summer. Bus services from Portoferraio cover all parts of the island.

View across the rooftops of Massa Marittima to the hills beyond

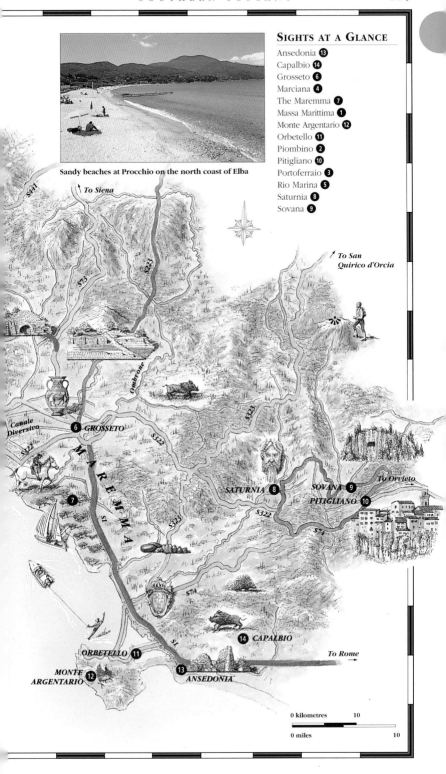

Sandy beaches at Procchio on the north coast of Elba

SIGHTS AT A GLANCE

Ansedonia **13**
Capalbio **14**
Grosseto **6**
Marciana **4**
The Maremma **7**
Massa Marittima **1**
Monte Argentario **12**
Orbetello **11**
Piombino **2**
Pitigliano **10**
Portoferraio **3**
Rio Marina **5**
Saturnia **8**
Sovana **9**

To Siena

To San
Quirico d'Orcia

Canale
Diversivo

6 GROSSETO

To Orvieto

SATURNIA **8**

SOVANA **9**

PITIGLIANO **10**

M A R E M M A

7

14 CAPALBIO

To Rome

ORBETELLO **11**

MONTE
ARGENTARIO **12**

13 ANSEDONIA

Ombrone

0 kilometres   10

0 miles   10

Massa Marittima ❶

Road map C4. 9,469.
ℹ️ *Amatur, Via Norma Parenti 22
(0566 90 27 56).* 🔺 *Wed.*

Sᴇᴛ ɪɴ ᴛʜᴇ Colline Metallifere
(metal-bearing hills), from
which lead, copper and silver
ores were mined, Massa
Marittima is far from being
a grimy industrial town. Its
history is closely associated
with mining and there are
some excellent examples of
Romanesque architecture.

🏠 Duomo

The Romanesque cathedral is
dedicated to St Cerbone, a 6th-
century saint whose story is
told in stone above the door.

The skyline of Massa Marittima

🏛 Museo Archeologico

Palazzo del Podestà, Piazza Garibaldi.
🅒 *0566 90 22 89.* **Open** *Tue – Sun.*
Adm charge.
This 13th-century building
has an archaeological museum
with material from Paleolithic
to Roman times.

🏛 Museo della Miniera

Via Corridoni. 🅒 *0566 90 22 89.*
Open *Mar – Jan: Tue – Sun (guided
tours only).* **Adm charge.**
This museum of mining is
partially located within a
worked-out mine shaft and
has exhibits explaining the
techniques of mining and the
minerals found locally.

Piombino ❷

Road map C4. 36,774. 🚆 🚍
🛳 ℹ️ *Via Ferruccio 4 (0565 22
56 39).* 🔺 *Wed.*

Pɪᴏᴍʙɪɴᴏ is a busy town
dominated by iron and
steel works. It is at the end
of the Massoncello peninsula
and was originally an island.

A Day Out on Elba

Eʟʙᴀ's ᴍᴏsᴛ ꜰᴀᴍᴏᴜs ʀᴇsɪᴅᴇɴᴛ was Napoleon,
who spent nine months here after the fall
of Paris in 1814. Today the island is mainly
populated by holidaymakers, who come by
ferry from Piombino, 10 km (6 miles) away on
the mainland. The main town is Portoferraio,
with an old port and a modern seafront with
smart hotels. The landscape of the island is
varied: on the west coast there are sandy
beaches, suitable for
all water sports; inland,
olive groves and vine-
yards line hillsides,
and vegetation covers
the mountains. The
east coast is more
rugged, with high cliffs
and stony beaches.

Marciana Marina ③
Return to the main road and
follow the coast round, past
Procchio with its long sandy
bays. From here it is 7.5 km
(4.5 miles) to the marina.

Marciana Alta ④
From the marina take
the main road into the
hills to the old medieval
town. After 8 km (5 miles)
turn left on to a minor road
leading to the cable car up
to the top of Monte Capanne.

Marina di Campo ⑤ Stay on the
coast road, round the west end of
the island, until Marina di Campo.

Kᴇʏ

▬▬▬	Tour route
═══	Other roads

0 kilometres   2

0 miles   2

It is the main port for ferries to Elba, which run every half hour in summer and also at fairly frequent intervals in winter. Nearby are the extensive ruins of Etruscan Populonia and the **Museo Etrusco Gasparri**, which contains a collection of bronze and terracotta works found in the surrounding necropolises.

🏛 Museo Etrusco Gasparri
Populonia. 🎔 *0565 294 36.* **Open** *9am–sunset daily.* **Adm charge.** 🚻

Portoferraio ❸

Road map B4. 🏯 *11,500.* 🚌🚆🛥 🛈
Calata Italia 26 (0565 91 46 71). 🚩 *Fri.*

THE FERRY from mainland Piombino arrives here. The town has a pretty harbour but the main sights are Napoleon's two houses. In the centre of Portoferraio is the **Palazzina Napoleonica** (also known as the Villetta dei Mulini), a modest house built around two windmills. **Villa**

San Martino, his country residence, had a Classical façade imposed on it by the Russian emigré, Prince Demidoff, in 1851. Egyptian-style frescoes in the house, painted in 1814, are a reminder of Napoleon's Nile campaigns of 1798–9.

🏯 Palazzina Napoleonica
Villa Napoleonica dei Mulini.
🎔 *0565 91 58 46.* **Open** *9am–7pm Mon, Wed–Sun (to 1pm Sun).* **Closed** *Tue.* **Adm charge.** 🚻

🏯 Villa San Martino
San Martino. 🎔 *0565 91 46 88.* **Open** *9am–7:30pm Tue–Sun (to 1pm Sun).* **Closed** *Mon.* **Adm charge.**

Marciana ❹

Road map B4. 🏯 *3,000.* 🚌
🛈 *Municipio, Marciana Alta (0565 90 12 15).*

ON ELBA'S northwest coast is Marciana Marina, and further inland the well-preserved medieval town of Marciana Alta. The **Museo**

Shady beaches and inlets at Marciana Marina on Elba

Civico Archeologico houses exhibits from Etruscan ships wrecked off Elba. From here, take the cable car up Monte Capanne, Elba's highest peak at 1,018 m (3,300 ft).

🏛 Museo Civico Archeologico
Via del Pretorio, Marciana Alta.
🎔 *0565 90 12 15.* **Open** *Jun–Sep: daily.* **Adm charge.**

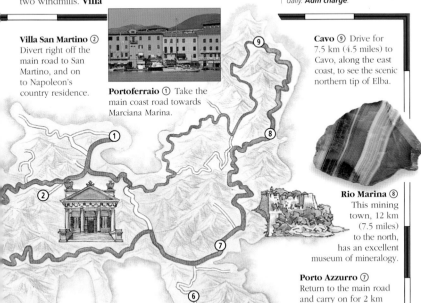

Villa San Martino ② Divert right off the main road to San Martino, and on to Napoleon's country residence.

Portoferraio ① Take the main coast road towards Marciana Marina.

Cavo ⑨ Drive for 7.5 km (4.5 miles) to Cavo, along the east coast, to see the scenic northern tip of Elba.

Rio Marina ⑧ This mining town, 12 km (7.5 miles) to the north, has an excellent museum of mineralogy.

Porto Azzurro ⑦ Return to the main road and carry on for 2 km (1.25 miles) to Elba's second largest port, a fashionable resort over-looking a lovely bay dominated by a 17th-century fortress.

Capoliveri ⑥ Follow the road round the south of the island and divert to the right just before Porto Azzurro to visit this charming old mining village.

The Maremma ❼

Maremma butterfly

T HE ANCIENT ROMANS were the first to cultivate the marshes of the Maremma, but after the collapse of their empire the area went virtually uninhabited until the 18th century. The land has since been reclaimed, the irrigation canals unblocked and farming developed on the fertile soil. The Parco Naturale dell'Uccellina was set up in 1975 to protect the abundant local flora and fauna and prevent more development taking place.

Wildlife
The undergrowth and marshes are home to wild boar and other wildlife.

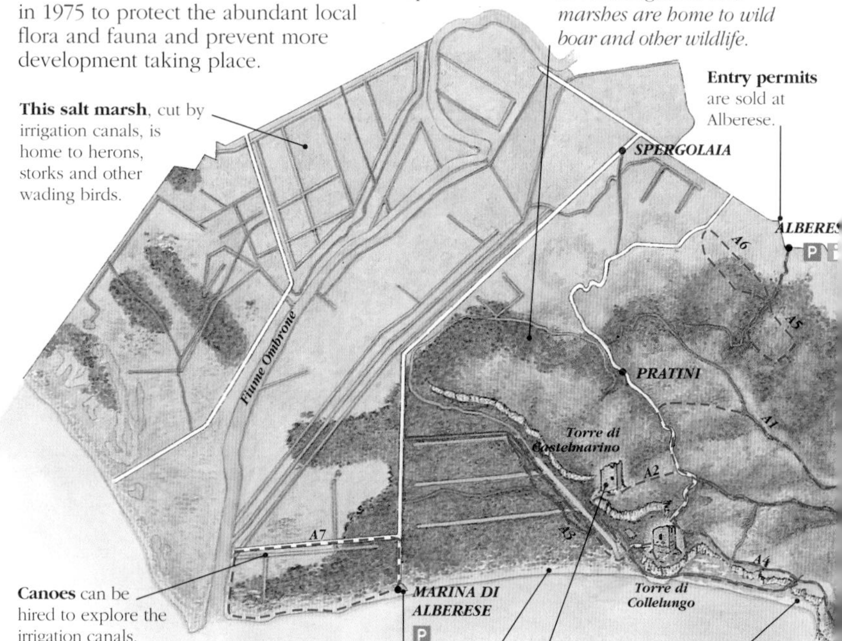

This salt marsh, cut by irrigation canals, is home to herons, storks and other wading birds.

Entry permits are sold at Alberese.

SPERGOLAIA

ALBERESE

PRATINI

Torre di Castelmarino

MARINA DI ALBERESE

Torre di Collelungo

Canoes can be hired to explore the irrigation canals.

There are picnic tables on the beach in the shade of pine trees.

Sea lilies and hollies grow along the sandy shoreline, backed by groves of parasol pines, mastic trees and juniper.

Beaches
The shoreline south of Marina di Alberese has wide, sandy beaches sheltered by steep cliffs.

Torre di Castelmarino
The cliffs are crowned by 16th-century watchtowers, part of a defence system built by the Medici to protect the coastal region from attack.

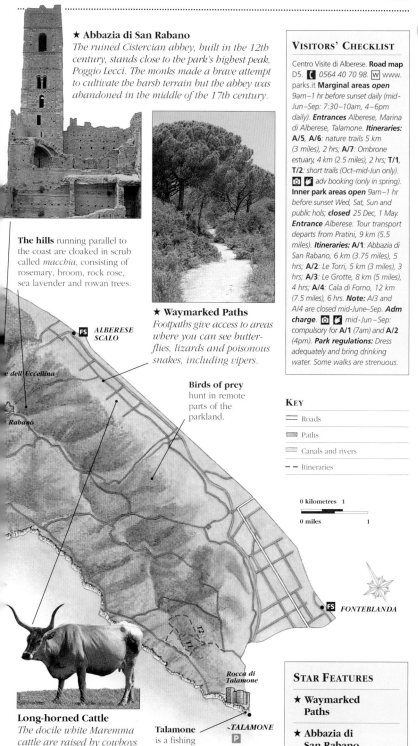

★ Abbazia di San Rabano

The ruined Cistercian abbey, built in the 12th century, stands close to the park's highest peak, Poggio Lecci. The monks made a brave attempt to cultivate the harsh terrain but the abbey was abandoned in the middle of the 17th century.

The hills running parallel to the coast are cloaked in scrub called *macchia*, consisting of rosemary, broom, rock rose, sea lavender and rowan trees.

★ Waymarked Paths

Footpaths give access to areas where you can see butterflies, lizards and poisonous snakes, including vipers.

Birds of prey hunt in remote parts of the parkland.

FS ALBERESE SCALO

e dell'Uccellina

Rabano

VISITORS' CHECKLIST

Centro Visite di Alberese. **Road map** D5. **064 40 70 98.** **W** www. parks.it **Marginal areas open** 9am–1 hr before sunset daily (mid-Jun–Sep: 7:30–10am, 4–6pm daily). **Entrances** Alberese, Marina di Alberese, Talamone. **Itineraries: A/5, A/6:** nature trails 5 km (3 miles), 2 hrs; **A/7:** Ombrone estuary, 4 km (2.5 miles), 2 hrs; **T/1, T/2:** short trails (Oct–mid-Jun only). adv booking (only in spring). **Inner park areas open** 9am–1 hr before sunset Wed, Sat, Sun and public hols; **closed** 25 Dec, 1 May. **Entrance** Alberese. Tour transport departs from Pratini, 9 km (5.5 miles). **Itineraries: A/1:** Abbazia di San Rabano, 6 km (3.75 miles), 5 hrs; **A/2:** Le Torri, 5 km (3 miles), 3 hrs; **A/3:** Le Grotte, 8 km (5 miles), 4 hrs; **A/4:** Cala di Forno, 12 km (7.5 miles), 6 hrs. **Note:** A/3 and A/4 are closed mid-June–Sep. **Adm charge.** mid-Jun–Sep: compulsory for **A/1** (7am) and **A/2** (4pm). **Park regulations:** Dress adequately and bring drinking water. Some walks are strenuous.

Key

— Roads

▬ Paths

▬ Canals and rivers

– – Itineraries

0 kilometres 1

0 miles 1

FS FONTEBLANDA

Rocca di Talamone

Talamone is a fishing village. ~TALAMONE **P**

Long-horned Cattle
The docile white Maremma cattle are raised by cowboys (butteri) who also stage rodeos.

STAR FEATURES

★ **Waymarked Paths**

★ **Abbazia di San Rabano**

Rio Marina ❺

Road map B4. 🏛 *2,038.* 🚌
ℹ *Piazza Salvo d'Acquisto.*
🗓 *Mon.*

Around Rio Marina there are still open-cast mines which extract the ores that attracted the Etruscans to Elba. The **Museo dei Minerali** explains the geology of the island. Shops in the town centre sell jewellery made of local semi-precious stones.

🏛 Museo dei Minerali
Palazzo Comunale. 📞 *0565 96 27 47.* **Open** *Apr–mid-Oct: daily; mid-Oct–Mar: by appt.* **Adm charge**.

Grosseto ❻

Road map D4. 🏛 *71,472.*
🚇 🚌 ℹ *Via Fuccini 43 (0564 46 26 11).* 🗓 *Thu.*

Grosseto is the largest town in southern Tuscany. World War II destroyed many buildings, but the 16th-century walls still stand and several of the bastions are now parks.

🏛 Museo Civico Archeologico e d'Arte della Maremma
Piazza Baccarini 3. **Open** *Oct–Feb: 9am–1pm Tue–Sun (also 4–6pm Sat); Mar–Apr: 9am–1pm, 4–6pm Tue–Sun; May–Sep: 10am–1pm, 5–8pm Tue–Sun.* **Closed** *1 Jan, 1 May, 25 Dec.*
The museum has Etruscan and Roman artifacts from Roselle and Vetulonia. There is also a collection of coins, intaglios (carved stones) and pottery.

Grosseto, a busy town full of narrow streets and shops

Cascate del Gorello, free for all to enjoy in Saturnia

The Maremma ❼

See pp232–3.

Saturnia ❽

Road map D5. 🏛 *550.* 🚌 ℹ *Piazza Vittorio Veneto (0564 60 12 80).*

Holidaymakers come to Saturnia to enjoy the good Maremma food or seek a health cure in the modern spa of Terme di Saturnia. Others prefer to bathe for free in the hot sulphurated waters of the waterfall at Cascate del Gorello on the Montemerano road. This is a pretty spot, with its pools and rocks stained coppery green.

Sovana ❾

Road map E5. 🏛 *100.*

Sovana sits on a ridge high above the Lente valley. Its main street is lined with cafés, restaurants and shops. The 13th-century Romanesque **Rocca Aldobrandesca**, named after the Teutonic family that ruled in the area until 1608, is now in ruins.

The medieval church of **Santa Maria** has frescoes of the late 15th-century Siena School, which were recently discovered under the white-washed walls. The main altar is sheltered by a 9th-century baldacchino that was originally in the Romanesque **Duomo**. This 12th-century building incorporates sculpture from earlier churches built on the same site.

The Etruscans dug tombs nearby in the soft limestone cliffs bordering the river Lente. The most complete set of **Necropoli Etrusca** can be found in a valley just to the west of Sovana.

⚜ **Rocca Aldobrandesca**
Via del Pretorio. **Closed**.
⛪ **Santa Maria**
Piazza del Pretorio. **Open** *daily.*
⛪ **Duomo**
Piazza del Pretorio. **Open** *daily in summer; Sat, Sun only in winter.*
🏛 **Necropoli Etrusca**
Poggio di Sopra Ripa. **Open** *10am–1pm, 3–6pm daily.*

Cafés and shops in Sovana's medieval piazza

Pitigliano ⑩

Road map E5. 🕴 *4,361.* 🚌
🛈 *Piazza Garibaldi 51 (0564 61 71 11).* 🕐 *Wed.*

PITIGLIANO LOOKS spectacular perched on a plateau, high above cliffs carved out by the river Lente. The houses seem to grow out of the cliffs, which are riddled with caves cut out of a soft limestone called tufa. The caves have been used for many years to store locally-made wines and olive oils.

A maze of tiny medieval streets, including Via Zuccarelli, passes through the Jewish ghetto, formed when Jews fleeing from Catholic persecution took refuge here in the 17th century. The Palazzo Orsini in the town centre has its water supply brought in by an aqueduct, built in 1545, that overhangs Via Cavour. The **Museo Palazzo Orsini** in the palazzo has a small exhibition of work by the artist Francesco Zuccarelli (1702–88). He also painted two of the altarpieces in the medieval **Duomo**, whose huge belltower supports a bell which weighs 3 tonnes.

The **Museo Etrusco** contains finds from ancient local settlements.

🏛 Museo Palazzo Orsini
Piazza della Fortezza Orsini.
📞 *0564 61 60 74.* **Open** *10am–1pm, 3–7pm Tue–Sun.* **Closed** *Monday.* **Adm charge.**

🔒 Duomo
Piazza San Gregorio. **Open** *daily.* ♿

🏛 Museo Etrusco
Piazza Fortezza.
📞 *0564 61 40 74.* **Open** *sporadically; call for info.*

Orbetello ⑪

Road map D5. 🕴 *15,455.* 🚉 🚌
🛈 *Piazza del Duomo (0564 86 04 47).* 🕐 *Sat.*

ORBETELLO is a crowded resort bordered by two tidal lagoons. Part of the northernmost lagoon is managed by the Worldwide Fund for Nature as a wildlife park.

The town was the capital of a tiny Spanish state, called the Presidio, from 1557 until 1808, when it was absorbed into the Grand Duchy of Tuscany. The Porta del Soccorso bears the coat of arms of the king of Spain. Inside the gates is the **Polveriera Guzman**, which was originally used as an arsenal. The Duomo, **Santa Maria Assunta**, also has Spanish-style decoration, but the altar in the Cappella di San Biagio is typically Romanesque in design. The Fontone di Talamone, in Piazza della Repubblica, is a terracotta plinth from the Roman-Etruscan era.

Coat of arms on the Porta del Soccorso

🏛 Polveriera Guzman
Viale Mura di Levante. **Closed** *indefinitely.*

🔒 Santa Maria Assunta
Piazza del Duomo. **Open** *daily.*

View over Pitigliano showing soft limestone cliffs and caves bordering the river Lente

Porto Ercole, near Monte Argentario

Monte Argentario ⑫

Road map D5. 🏙 *14,000*. 🚌
ℹ️ *Via Archetto de Palio 1, Porto Santo Stéfano (0564 81 42 08)*. 🛒 *Tue.*

M ONTE ARGENTARIO was an island until the early 18th century, when the shallow waters separating it from the mainland began to silt up, creating two sandy spits of land, known as *tomboli*, that enclose the Orbetello lagoon. Orbetello itself was linked to the island in 1842, when a dyke was constructed linking the mainland to Terrarossa.

The two harbour towns of Porto Ercole and Porto Santo Stéfano are both favoured by wealthy yacht owners. There are good fish restaurants in both towns *(see p263)*, and from the Strada Panoramica there are views over rocky coves, cliffs and bays. Ferries from Porto Santo Stéfano go to the island of Giglio, popular with Italian tourists for its sandy beaches and rich wildlife.

During the summer months the Porto Santo Stéfano ferry also calls at Giannutri, which is a privately-owned island where visitors are not allowed to stay overnight.

Ansedonia ⑬

Road map D5. 🏙 *300*.

A NSEDONIA is a prosperous village of luxurious villas and gardens, high on a hill above the coast. The ruins of the city of Cosa, founded by the Romans in 173 BC, are on the summit of the hill looking over Ansedonia. The **Museo di Cosa**, containing relics from the ancient settlement, is close by. East of Ansedonia is a long stretch of sandy beach and the remains of the Etruscan Canal. The date

An Etruscan Tour

T HE ETRUSCANS GAINED much of their wealth from Tuscany's vast mineral resources, and their monied classes were cultured and worldly. Both their elaborate burial sites and the artifacts found in their tombs give us an insight into their lives *(see pp40 – 41)*. Etruscan burial sites were carved into soft rock or built of huge stone slabs with rock-cut roads leading down to the tombs.

Grosseto ① The Museo Civico Archeologico has a collection of Etruscan artifacts found in local tombs.

ALSO WORTH SEEING

Museo Archeologico, Florence *(see p99)*.

Museo Etrusco, Volterra *(see p162)*.

Vulci and **Tarquinia** These excavated sites, just over the Tuscany border in Lazio, have impressive Etruscan ruins, painted tombs and art collections.

This Etruscan bone brooch, called a *fibula*, was found near Grosseto and is now in the Museo Archeologico in Florence.

Talamone ⑦ Follow the S74 to the S1. Turn right and after 8 km (5 miles) fork off to the left, into the Maremma, for the Etruscan temple, Roman villa and baths.

0 kilometres   5

0 miles   5

Maglie

The Etruscan Canal at Ansedonia

and purpose of the canal are debatable, but it may have been dug in Roman times to keep the harbour free of silt. Alternatively, it may have been part of a canal leading to the Lago di Burano, 5 km (3 miles) down the coast. This lagoon is 4 km (2.5 miles) long and has been turned into a wild-life refuge (*rifugio faunistico*) by the Worldwide Fund for Nature. It is a very important habitat for wading birds.

⚏ Museo di Cosa
Ansedonia. **℡** 0564 88 14 21. **Open** 9am–7pm daily. **Adm charge**.

Capalbio ⓮

Road map D5. **⚟** 4,049. **⚏** **⚏** Wed.

Capalbio is another village which is popular with wealthy Italians. The hilltop town has several restaurants and hotels and is busy all year round. Summer tourists come for the beaches, and winter visitors flock to hunt deer and wild boar in the surrounding woodland, which is now managed as a game reserve. A game festival is held in September each year.

🌺 Giardino dei Tarocchi
Garavicchio, Pescia Fiorentina.
℡ 0564 89 51 22. **Closed** for renovation.
At nearby Pescia Fiorentino, to the southeast of Capalbio, is a modern sculpture garden created by the French artist, Niki de Saint-Phalle in 1982. It was inspired by the figures of the Tarot and has been over ten years in the making. The bigger pieces each represent one card from the Tarot pack. Among the sculptures already finished is *The Tower*, a glittering three-storey edifice made out of broken mirrors.

View across the rooftops of Capalbio

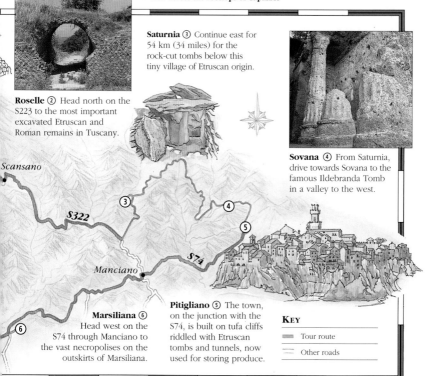

Saturnia ③ Continue east for 54 km (34 miles) for the rock-cut tombs below this tiny village of Etruscan origin.

Roselle ② Head north on the S223 to the most important excavated Etruscan and Roman remains in Tuscany.

Sovana ④ From Saturnia, drive towards Sovana to the famous Ildebranda Tomb in a valley to the west.

Scansano

S322

Manciano

S74

Marsiliana ⑥ Head west on the S74 through Manciano to the vast necropolises on the outskirts of Marsiliana.

Pitigliano ⑤ The town, on the junction with the S74, is built on tufa cliffs riddled with Etruscan tombs and tunnels, now used for storing produce.

KEY

━━ Tour route

= Other roads

TRAVELLERS' NEEDS

WHERE TO STAY

Sign showing hotel rating

O F ALL ITALY'S REGIONS, Tuscany has some of the most charming places to stay. Inland these range from ancient villas to elegant town houses. Smaller, family-run establishments excel in their cuisine and are sometimes filled with antiques. The major cities also offer B&B accommodation. Hotels on the riviera tend to be less distinctive, but the popularity of coastal resorts in summer means that standards are high. Many visitors opt for self-catering holidays. Often the accommodation is a small flat or house on a farm, and the prices can prove very reasonable. Other options include hostels and dormitories and, for walking enthusiasts, there are mountain huts throughout the region. For more information on hotels in Florence and Tuscany see the listings on pages 247–51.

Terrace at Hotel Continental *(see p247)*

WHERE TO LOOK

F LORENCE HAS a wide range of hotels, but prices can be high. The most attractive locations are along the north bank of the Arno, the historic centre and in nearby Fiesole. Parking is a problem in the city centre, so if you have a car it is best to choose a hotel which has parking facilities.

Accommodation in central Pisa is generally sub-standard but there are some lovely Tuscan villa hotels a short drive from the centre.

Though large, Arezzo has relatively few hotels and those in the centre are mostly geared for business people. If you can, stay outside the town and travel in to visit the centre.

The hill towns of central Tuscany offer a number of quality villa hotels, manor houses and even former palaces. The Chianti region is rich in converted villa hotels, with excellent regional restaurants, particularly around Radda and Gaiole. Siena's more attractive options are outside the city, such as the tiny hamlet of Strove.

Street sign showing the direction and location of hotels

HOTEL PRICES

D URING THE LOW season (November to March) prices are cheaper and often negotiable. Florence is less busy than other parts of Tuscany in July and August, but this is the peak holiday season on the coast. Avoid the city during certain weeks of January and July when fashion shows fill the top hotels, raising low-season prices.

Single room rates are higher than individual rates for two people sharing a double room. Prices include tax and service. Bear in mind that accommodation in Florence and Siena is more expensive than elsewhere in the region.

HIDDEN EXTRAS

B EFORE MAKING a reservation, establish whether breakfast is included in the price. Garage parking, laundry and snacks in the hotel or from the minibar may be pricey and telephone charges from your hotel room can be phenomenal. Check the rates first if you are concerned. Some hotels may expect you to take full- or half-board during the high season.

HOTEL GRADINGS AND FACILITIES

H OTELS IN ITALY are classified by a star-rating system, from one to five stars. However, each province sets its own levels for grading; consequently, standards for each category may vary from one area to another. Some hotels may not have a restaurant but those that do will welcome non-residents to stop by and eat.

Some of the converted castles and ancient villas are not air-conditioned, but as the stone walls are thick the

The marvellous gallery entrance of Hotel Villa Villoresi (see p248)

midsummer heat barely penetrates the buildings.

Children are welcome but the smaller hotels generally have limited facilities. Often, the more up-market hotels will arrange a baby-sitting service. Sometimes the proprietor of a smaller hotel, or a member of the family, will mind your children, if they are not busy.

WHAT TO EXPECT

IN FLORENCE, street numbers can be confusing *(see p274)*, so refer to the map references in the listings.

Hotel proprietors are obliged by law to register you with the police, so they will ask for your passport when you arrive. Make sure you take it back, as you will need some form of identification to change money or travellers' cheques.

Even a humble *pensione* should have a reasonably smart bathroom. Rooms without a bathroom will usually have wash basins and towels.

As far as hotel decoration goes, you may sometimes have to sacrifice smart decor for the charm of an old establishment.

The Italian breakfast is light – a cappuccino and a pastry

(brioche). Most hotels serve a continental breakfast of coffee, tea or hot chocolate, bread rolls and jam. However, it may be cheaper to go to a local bar or a *pasticceria*.

Florence can be very noisy. Top-class hotels usually have some form of soundproofing, but ask for a room facing away from the street if you are easily disturbed by noise.

Check-out time is usually noon in four- and five-star hotels and between 10am and noon in other establishments. If you stay longer you will be asked to pay for an extra day. However, many hotels will store your baggage if you plan on leaving the city several hours after check-out time.

BOOKING AND PAYING

BOOK AT LEAST two months in advance if you want to stay in a particular hotel in high season or at Easter. The local tourist office will have listings of all the hotels in the area and will be able to advise you on the best hotels for each category. Most hotels take credit cards, but check which ones when booking. You can usually pay the deposit by credit card, or send an international money order. Confirm your reservation by fax or e-mail including the dates of your stay and your credit card details.

Under Italian law, a booking is valid as soon as the deposit is paid and confirmation is received. As in restaurants, you are required by law to keep your hotel receipt until you leave Italy.

DISABLED TRAVELLERS

FACILITIES FOR the disabled are usually limited. The hotel listings on pages 247–51 indicate which hotels have these facilities.

HOTELS IN HISTORIC BUILDINGS

THE TUSCANY REGIONAL tourist board publishes a leaflet which lists hotels in historic buildings and those of artistic interest. Some of the best are included in the listings here. The booklet is also available from national Italian tourist offices worldwide. **Relais & Châteaux** produces a guide that includes a number of fine Tuscan hotels and hotel restaurants of historic interest, all of high quality.

Villa San Michele, a former monastery, in Fiesole (see p248)

Garden terrace at Villa La Massa *(see p248)*

SELF-CATERING

FARM AND VILLA holiday accommodation abounds in Tuscany. There is an **Agriturist** office in each region with information on self-catering holidays, often on a farm that is still working.

An international agency dealing with self-catering holidays around Florence is the **American Agency**. Other agents include **Casaclub** in Siena, **Cuendet** in Monteriggioni and **Prima Italia** in Grosseto. Solemar and Cuendet have agents throughout the world, such as **Tailor Made Tours** (Solemar) and **International Chapters** (Cuendet).

Prices for self-catering vary enormously depending on the season and location. Generally, a four-person villa within a complex in the low season will cost around €450 per week, while an individual villa in its own grounds can cost as much as €1,750 per week during the peak season.

STAYING IN PRIVATE HOMES

ROOMS IN PRIVATE homes can usually be rented through one of the recreational associations such as **AGAP** (Associazione Gestori Alloggi Privati) in Florence. Meals are not provided but can sometimes be arranged on request.

RESIDENTIAL HOTELS

THROUGHOUT TUSCANY there are former palaces or villas that have been converted into complexes of small apartments, often with facilities

---

DIRECTORY

HISTORIC HOTELS

Relais & Châteaux
Grosvenor Gardens House,
35–37 Grosvenor Gardens,
London SW1W 0BS.
FAX 020 7828 9476.
W www.
relaischateaux.com

SELF-CATERING AGENCIES

Agriturist Ufficio Regionale
Via degli Alfani 6/7,
50122 Florence.
055 28 78 38.
@ agritosc@
confagricoltura.it

American Agency
Via del Ponte Rosso 33r,
50129 Florence.
055 47 50 53.
@ am@americanagency.it

Casaclub
Viale Vittorio Veneto 41,
53100 Siena.
0577 440 41.
@ casaclub@
interbusiness.it

Cuendet
Strada di Strove 17,
53035 Monteriggioni.
0577 57 63 50.
@ internetsales@
cuendet.com

Int. Chapters
47–51 St John's Wood
High St, London NW8 7NJ.
020 7722 9560.
W www.villa-rentals.com

Prima Italia
Viale Tirreno 19,
58046 Principina a Mare
(Grosseto).
0564 300 09.
W www.primaita.it

Tailor Made Tours
22 Church Rise,
London SE23 2UD.
020 8291 9736.

PRIVATE HOMES

AGAP
Piazza San Marco 7,
50122 Florence.
055 28 41 00.
W www.agap.it

RESIDENTIAL HOTELS

Mini Residence
Via Giulio Caccini 20,
50141 Florence.
055 41 08 76.

Palazzo Ricasoli
Via delle Mantellate 2,
50129 Florence.
Map 2 D3.
055 35 21 51.
W www.ricasoli.com

Residence Da-al
Via dell'Ariento 3,
50123 Florence.
Map 1 C4 (5 C1).
055 21 49 79.

La Valle
Via Sanminiatese,
Loc. La Valle, 50050
Montaione (Florence).
0571 69 80 59.
W www.agricolalavalle.it

HOTEL COOPERATIVES

Coopal
Il Prato 2r,
50123 Florence.
Map 1 A4.
055 21 95 25.

Family Hotels
Via Trieste 5,
50139 Florence. Map 2 D1.
055 4620 080.
@ topquark.fi@
mbox.it.net

Florence Promhotels
Viale Alessandro Volta 72,
50100 Florence. Map 2 F2.
055 57 04 81.
@ info@promhotels.it

BUDGET ACCOMMODATION

Associazione Italiana Alberghi per la Gioventù
Viale Augusto Righi 2–4,
50137 Florence.
055 60 03 15.
W www.hostels-aig.org

Europa Villa Camerata
Viale Augusto Righi 2–4,
50137 Florence.
055 60 14 51.

MOUNTAIN REFUGES AND CAMP SITES

Touring Club Italiano
Corso Italia 10, 20122
Milan. 02 852 61.
W www.touringclub.it

Club Alpino Italiano
Via Fonseca Pimental 7,
20127 Milan.
02 205 72 31.

such as swimming pools or bars. The minimum period of stay in these residential hotels is usually a week, but there is more flexibility in low season.

Residential hotels in Florence include **Residence Da-al** and **Palazzo Ricasoli**. The local tourist office keeps a list of others in the region.

Poster (about 1918) for a Pisan hotel

HOTEL COOPERATIVES

THESE ARE NOT chains but consortiums of different hotel types. **Family Hotel** specializes in small, intimate family hotels or *pensioni*, while **Florence Promhotels** provide a wider range of accommodation. **Coopal** only accepts groups of a minimum of 10 people.

BUDGET ACCOMMODATION

ONE- AND TWO-STAR budget hotels have recently increased in price, charging from €25 to €45 per person per night. They are generally small, family-run establishments, which were originally known as *pensioni*. The term is no longer in much use; however, many places retain the name and personal character that has made them so popular with visitors. Most offer breakfast and some have rooms with private bathrooms, but you should not expect particularly high standards of service.

Hostel and dormitory accommodation can often be found in convents and religious institutions. Dormitory accommodation

can be arranged through the local tourist office. The **Associazione Italiana Alberghi per la Gioventù** (Italian Youth Hostel Association) in Rome has lists of youth hostels in Italy. The main youth hostel in Florence is **Europa Villa Camerata**.

Full lists and booking facilities for youth hostels are available through the Italian tourist board (ENIT) worldwide or from the local tourist offices *(see p272)*. Also, log on to www.hostels-aig.org.

MOUNTAIN REFUGES AND CAMP SITES

IF YOU ARE LIKELY to be trekking, backpacking or walking, there are mountain refuges and huts dotted throughout Tuscany. There are also camp sites on the fringes of most towns. A list of camp sites and mountain refuges is available from ENIT *(see p273)* or local tourist offices. **Club Alpino Italiano** in Milan owns most of the huts in the mountain districts of Italy, including Tuscany. The **Touring Club Italiano** publishes a list of camp sites in *Campeggi e Villaggi Turistici in Italia*.

The hotels on pages 247–51 are listed according to area and price category. The symbols summarize the facilities at each hotel.

🛁 all rooms have bath and/or shower unless otherwise indicated
1️⃣ single-rate rooms available
🛏️ rooms for more than two people available, or an extra bed can be put in a double room
📺 television in all rooms
🗒️ air-conditioning in all rooms
🏊 swimming pool in hotel
♿ wheelchair access
🛗 lift
🅿️ car parking available
🍴 restaurant
💳 credit cards accepted

Price categories for a standard double room per night, including breakfast, tax and service:
€ under €55
€€ €55–€85
€€€ €85–€125
€€€€ €125–€175
€€€€€ over €175

Vaulted entrance hall of Hotel Porta Rossa *(see p247)*

Florence's Best Hotels

IN A CITY RENOWNED for its splendid architecture, it is hardly surprising that many of Florence's hotels are favoured by visitors for their charm and individual character. Former palazzi, monasteries such as Villa San Michele, and town villas offer accommodation in all price ranges. Original features are sometimes preserved at the expense of modern comforts: among the older establishments listed on pages 247–8, we try to include those which combine both. The hotels shown here are a selection of the best.

Hotel Tornabuoni Beacci
This family-run former palace is particularly welcoming and furnished with fine antiques. (See p247.)

CITY
CENTRE
WEST

OLTRARNO

Hotel Excelsior
On a 13th-century square near the river Arno, this beautiful hotel epitomizes luxury, with well-appointed bedrooms and 19th-century fittings. (See p248.)

Torre di Bellosguardo
Vast, ancient and individual, this hill-top tower and villa lives up to its name: beautiful view. (See p248.)

Hotel Villa Belvedere
This 1930s hillside hotel is set in 11 acres (4 ha) of landscaped gardens and has excellent views of the city. Inside, the décor is impeccable. (See p247.)

0 metres	1,000
0 yards	1,000

Villa San Michele
This peaceful monastery in Fiesole is said to have been designed by Michelangelo. (See p248.)

Pensione Bencistà
A haven in the hills behind the city, this lovingly kept pensione has luxurious period furniture. (See p248.)

CITY CENTRE NORTH

CITY CENTRE EAST

Hotel Hermitage
The drawing room overlooks the Ponte Vecchio in this comfortable and quiet hotel housed on the top floors of a tall medieval building. (See p247.)

Villa La Massa
Surrounded by parkland, this former country home is one of Florence's most elegant hotels. (See p248.)

Florence and Siena Hotels

THIS CHOOSING CHART is a quick reference to hotels in Florence and Siena, many of which offer charming decor and surroundings even in the lower price categories. These hotels, and others in Tuscany, are listed in more detail on the following pages. For information on other types of accommodation, see pages 242–3.

	Price	Number of Rooms	Family Rooms	Car Parking	Restaurant	Buildings of Historic or Artistic Interest	Attractive Views	Quiet Location
FLORENCE CITY CENTRE *(see pp247–8)*								
Hotel Locanda Orchidea	€	7				▣		
Hotel Casci	€€€	25	●					
Piccolo Hotel	€€€	10						▣
Hotel Aprile	€€€€	28	●			▣		
Hotel Porta Rossa	€€€€	81	●			▣	●	
Hotel Silla	€€€€	36	●			▣	●	▣
Morandi alla Crocetta	€€€€	10	●			▣		
Pensione Annalena	€€€€	20	●			▣		
Splendor	€€€€	31	●					
Grand Hotel Villa Cora	€€€€€	48	●	▣	●	▣		
Hotel Brunelleschi	€€€€€	96	●		●	▣		▣
Hotel Cellai	€€€€€	47	●	▣		▣	●	
Hotel Continental	€€€€€	48	●				●	
Hotel Excelsior	€€€€€	168	●		●	▣		
Hotel Helvetia e Bristol	€€€€€	49	●		●	▣		
Hotel Hermitage	€€€€€	28	●			▣	●	▣
Hotel J and J	€€€€€	18	●			▣		▣
Hotel Loggiato dei Serviti	€€€€€	29	●			▣		
Hotel Monna Lisa	€€€€€	30	●	▣		▣		
Hotel Regency	€€€€€	33			●	▣		▣
Hotel Tornabuoni Beacci	€€€€€	28	●			▣		
Hotel Villa Belvedere	€€€€€	26	●				●	
Rivoli	€€€€€	60	●			▣		
FLORENCE ENVIRONS *(see p248)*								
Hotel Villa Bonelli	€€€	20	●	▣	●		●	▣
Rovezzano Bed & Breakfast	€€€	6		▣			●	▣
Ariele	€€€€	39	●	▣				
Hotel Villa Villoresi	€€€€	28	●	▣	●	▣		
Pensione Bencistà	€€€€	44	●	▣	●	▣	●	▣
Torre di Bellosguardo	€€€€€	16	●	▣		▣	●	▣
Villa La Massa	€€€€€	34	●	▣	●	▣	●	
Villa Le Rondini	€€€€€	40	●	▣	●		●	
Villa San Michele	€€€€€	41		▣	●	▣	●	▣
SIENA *(see p251)*								
Hotel Chiusarelli	€€€	49	●	▣	●			
Pensione Palazzo Ravizza	€€€€	40		▣	●	▣	●	
Santa Caterina	€€€	19	●	▣				
Hotel Certosa di Maggiano	€€€€€	17	●	▣	●	▣		
Villa Patrizia	€€€€€	33	●	▣	●	▣	●	
Villa Scacciapensieri	€€€€€	28	●	▣	●		●	▣

Price categories for a double room per night, including breakfast, tax and service:
€ under €55
€€ €55–85
€€€ €85–125
€€€€ €125–175
€€€€€ over €175.

RESTAURANT
The hotel has a restaurant on the premises serving breakfast, lunch and dinner. Non-residents are usually welcome to use the hotel restaurant, but priority may be given to guests staying at the hotel. Breakfast is served in most of the hotels listed, but it is advisable to check before booking.

CAR PARKING
Hotels with parking facilities. Some hotels will only have limited spaces and there may also be a parking fee.

FAMILY ROOMS
Rooms for more than two people are available, or an extra bed may be put into a double room.

FLORENCE

CITY CENTRE

Hotel Locanda Orchidea

Borgo degli Albizi 11, 50122. **Map** 2 D5 (6 E3). **C** & **FAX** 055 248 03 46. **@** hotelorchidea@yahoo.it **Rooms**: 7. 1 ↑ €

This simple, family-run hotel is on the second floor of a 12th-century building. The rooms are cosy but show some signs of wear.

Hotel Casci

Via Cavour 13, 50129. **Map** 2 D4. **C** 055 21 16 86. **FAX** 055 239 64 61. **@** info@hotelcasci.com **Rooms**: 25. 🛏 1 ♨ TV ↑ 🖥 目 €€€

Housed in a palazzo once owned by the composer Rossini, this family-owned hotel offers clean, quiet rooms conveniently near the Duomo and San Lorenzo.

Piccolo Hotel

Via San Gallo 51, 50129. **Map** 2 D4. **C** 055 47 55 19. **FAX** 055 47 45 15. **W** www.paginegialle.it/piccolofir **Rooms**: 10. 🚹 🛏 TV 🖥 €€€

This charming hotel is close to the main tourist attractions. The rooms are simply decorated, with a few refined touches. It also offers free bikes for its residents.

Hotel Aprile

Via della Scala 6, 50123. **Map** 1 A4 (5 A1). **C** 055 21 62 37. **FAX** 055 28 09 47. **@** info@hotelaprile.com **Rooms**: 28. 🛏 26. 1 ♨ ↑ 🖥 €€€€

Traces of the 16th-century *The Triumph of David* cover the façade of this attractive hotel. In the summer, breakfast is served in the delightful courtyard.

Hotel Porta Rossa

Via Porta Rossa 19, 50123. **Map** 3 C1 (5 C3). **C** 055 28 75 51. **FAX** 055 28 21 79. **Rooms**: 81. 🛏 80. 1 ♨ TV ↑ 🖥 €€€€

Built as a hotel in 1386, this is Italy's second-oldest hotel. The vaulted entrance hall is furnished with leather suites. Some rooms are huge, and all are in different styles.

Hotel Silla

Via dei Renai 5, 50125. **Map** 4 D2 (6 E5). **C** 055 234 28 88. **FAX** 055 234 14 37. **@** hotelsilla@tin.it **Rooms**: 36. 🛏 1 ♨ ↑ P 目 €€€€

This 16th-century hotel is reached through an elegant courtyard with a grand staircase to the first floor and has a relaxing and welcoming ambience.

Morandi alla Crocetta

Via Laura 50, 50121. **Map** 2 E4. **C** 055 234 47 47. **FAX** 0552 48 09 54. **@** welcome@hotelmorandi.it **Rooms**: 10. 🛏 1 ♨ TV 🖥 目 €€€€

Once a convent, this lovely old house is run by Mrs Doyle, an Englishwoman who has lived here since the 1920s. The tasteful interior is decorated with antiques, rugs and an abundance of plants.

Pensione Annalena

Via Romana 34, 50125. **Map** 3 A3. **C** 055 22 24 02. **FAX** 055 22 24 03. **@** annalena@hotelannalena.it **Rooms**: 20. 🛏 1 ♨ TV 🖥 €€€€

Entrance to this 15th-century hotel is through a pleasant courtyard and up some steps. A huge hall houses the reception area and breakfast rooms. The spacious bedrooms are simply but attractively furnished.

Splendor

Via San Gallo 30, 50129. **Map** 2 D4. **C** 055 48 34 27. **FAX** 055 46 12 76. **@** info@hotelsplendor.it **Rooms**: 31. 🛏 25. 1 ♨ TV 🖥 ↑ 🖥 €€€€

The dark-red decor and frescoed, stuccoed ceilings give the impression of a grand mansion, but this family hotel shows signs of wear.

Grand Hotel Villa Cora

Viale Niccolò Machiavelli 18, 50125. **Map** 3 A3. **C** 055 229 84 51. **FAX** 055 22 90 86. **W** www.villacora.com **Rooms**: 48. 🛏 1 ♨ TV 🖥 ♨ ↑ P ⑪ 🖥 €€€€€

Shades of peach and grey windows highlight the Villa Cora's stunning Renaissance-style façades. There are many balustraded terraces segregated by Classical pillars and tall windows. Reception rooms have frescoed ceilings and varnished wooden floors.

Hotel Brunelleschi

Piazza Santa Elisabetta 3, 50122. **Map** 6 D2. **C** 055 273 70. **FAX** 055 21 96 53. **@** info@hotelbrunelleschi.it **Rooms**: 96. 🛏 1 ♨ TV 🖥 ↑ ⑪ P 🖥 €€€€€

Once a prison, this hotel houses a fascinating museum displaying Byzantine ceramics and old stone baths discovered during its reconstruction. The grey brick walls have been retained in the cool, airy reception.

Hotel Cellai

Via XXVII Aprile 14, 50129. **Map** 1 D4. **C** 055 48 92 91. **FAX** 055 47 03 87. **@** info@hotelcellai.it **Rooms**: 47. 🛏 1 ♨ TV 🖥 P 🖥 €€€€€

A beautifully restored 18th-century building houses this family-run hotel in the heart of Florence. The staff will be pleased to organize limousine tours of the trendiest fashion stores (Gucci, Dolce & Gabbana) as well as museum and restaurant bookings.

Hotel Continental

Lungarno degli Acciaiuoli 2, 50123. **Map** 3 C1 (5 C4). **C** 055 272 62. **FAX** 055 28 31 39. **@** continental@lungarnohotels.com **Rooms**: 48. 🛏 1 ♨ TV 🖥 ♨ ↑ 🖥 €€€€€

Decorated with pale grey marble-effect walls throughout, this hotel is in a prime location opposite the Ponte Vecchio. The bar lounge looks over the river, as do the stunning top-floor suites.

Hotel Excelsior

Piazza Ognissanti 3, 50123. **Map** 1 B5 (5 A2). **C** 055 27 151. **FAX** 055 21 02 78. **Rooms**: 168. 🛏 1 ♨ TV 🖥 ♨ ↑ ⑪ P 🖥 €€€€€

The Excelsior has beautiful views over the Arno. Inside it has a feeling of grandeur, style and luxurious opulence, with marble floors and columns, 19th-century staircases, statues, stained-glass windows and oil paintings.

Hotel Helvetia e Bristol

Via de' Pescioni 2, 50123. **Map** 1 C5 (5 C2). **C** 055 28 78 14. **FAX** 055 28 83 53. **W** www.charminghotels.it **Rooms**: 56. 🛏 1 ♨ TV 🖥 ↑ ⑪ P 🖥 €€€€€

This luxurious 18th-century hotel is just a few steps from the Duomo. Beautiful antiques decorate the interior and there is a domed, stained-glass ceiling, evocative of the cathedral itself, as well as a splendid wood and marble bar.

Hotel Hermitage

Vicolo Marzio 1, 50122. **Map** 3 C1 (6 D4). **C** 055 28 72 16. **FAX** 055 21 22 08. **W** www.hermitagehotel.com **Rooms**: 28. 🛏 1 ♨ 目 ↑ €€€€€

On the top floors of a medieval building, this hotel is close to the Ponte Vecchio. Superb views can be enjoyed from the more expensive rooms on the top floor.

For key to symbols see p243

Hotel J and J

Via di Mezzo 20, 50121. **Map** 2 E5.
C 055 26 31 21. **FAX** 055 24 02 82.
@ jandj@dada.it **Rooms**: 18.
TV ▤ **&** ▤ partial.
€€€€€

This pretty, peaceful hotel is set in
a former 16th-century monastery.
The welcoming ground-floor
exterior has full-length glass
windows set between old stone
arches with frescoed ceilings.

Hotel Loggiato dei Serviti

Piazza della SS. Annunziata 3, 50122.
Map 2 D4. **C** 055 28 95 92. **FAX** 055
28 95 95. **@** info@loggiatodeiserviti
hotel.it **Rooms**: 29.
▨ **&** €€€€€

Built in 1527, this hotel has a
reception area with vaulted
ceilings. To reach the entrance
there are steps with no handrail to
climb, and some rooms are small.

Hotel Monna Lisa

Borgo Pinti 27, 50121. **Map** 2 E5
(6 F2). **C** 055 247 97 51. **FAX** 055
247 97 55. **@** monnalis@ats.it
Rooms: 30.
P **&** €€€€€

An impressive stone interior
courtyard leads to the reception
area of this Renaissance palazzo.
Some of the bedrooms are
enormous, with old furniture
and high ceilings. The modern
extension lacks the charm of the
main building.

Hotel Regency

Piazza Massimo d'Azeglio 3, 50121.
Map 2 F5. **C** 055 24 52 47. **FAX** 055
23 46 735. **@** info@regency_hotel.com
Rooms: 33.
P **&** €€€€€

Though well-maintained, this
Florentine town house suggests
little of the grandeur within. The
Classical-style reception and bar
area has wood-panelling decor.
The front bedrooms look on to
the pretty Piazza d'Azeglio.

Hotel Tornabuoni Beacci

Via de' Tornabuoni 3, 50123.
Map 1 C5 (5 C2). **C** 055 21 26 45.
FAX 055 28 35 94. **@** info@bthotel.it
Rooms: 28.
& €€€€€

This former palace is situated on a
busy central street. Wide, carpeted
hallways lead to lounge areas with
antique furniture and tapestries.
The bedrooms are luxurious.

Hotel Villa Belvedere

Via Benedetto Castelli 3, 50124.
Map 3 A5. **C** 055 22 25 01.
FAX 055 22 31 63. **@** reception@
villa-belvedere.com **Rooms**: 26.
& €€€€€

This spacious 1930s villa is set in
landscaped grounds, close to the
Boboli Gardens. All the bedrooms
have a mini-bar, and the first-floor
terraces have lovely garden views.

Rivoli

Via della Scala 33, 50123. **Map** 1 A4
(5 A1). **C** 055 28 28 53. **FAX** 055 29
40 41. **@** info@hotelrivoli.it **Rooms**:
60. **P** €€€€€

The weathered façade gives
a clue to the age of this 15th-
century hotel. It is spacious, cool
and decorated to a high standard,
combining both modern and
Classical styles.

FLORENCE ENVIRONS

Hotel Villa Bonelli

7 km (4.5 miles) NE Florence. Via F
Poeti 1, Fiesole, 50014. **C** 055 595
13. **FAX** 055 59 89 42. **@** info@
hotelvillabonelli.com **Rooms**: 20.
& **P** €€€

This small, friendly hotel is simply
but pleasantly furnished, with
wonderful views of Florence from
the top rooms. All bookings are
half-board, so the price of a room
includes dinner.

Rovezzano Bed & Breakfast

1 km (0.6 mile) E Florence. Via Aretina
417, 50136. **C** 055 69 00 23.
FAX 055 69 10 02. **@** rovezzano@
vigilio.it **Rooms**: 6. **&** €€€

Located within a Renaissance
villa in Rovezzano, this B&B is
immersed in the quiet Florentine
countryside. The villa also hosts
a weaving factory, and each room
is named after the draping fabric
with which it is decorated.

Ariele

500 m (550 yds) from Old Bridge. Via
Magenta 11, 50123. **C** 055 21 15 09.
FAX 055 26 85 21. **@** hotel.ariele@
libero.it **Rooms**: 39. **&**
P €€€€

This homely hotel is located on
a residential side street. It has
extensive lounge and bar areas
with high ceilings, paintings and
antiques. The bedrooms are a little
austere but generally spacious.

Hotel Villa Villoresi

8 km (5 miles) NW Florence. Via Ciampi
2, Colonnata di Sesto Fiorentino,
50019. **C** 055 44 32 12. **FAX** 055 44
20 63. **@** cvillor@tin.it **Rooms**: 34.
P €€€€

Built for military purposes in the
12th century, this villa became a
country house during the 1400s.
The gallery entrance is covered with
murals of Tuscan landscapes interspersed with Egyptian symbols
depicting Napoleon's campaign.

Pensione Bencistà

5 km (2.5 miles) NE Florence. Via
Benedetto da Maiano 4, Fiesole,
50014. **C** 055 591 63. **FAX** 055 591
63. **@** bencista@uol.it **Rooms**: 44.
32. **P** €€€€€

Inside this 14th-century villa are
polished tiles, antique furniture and
cool, airy bedrooms. Watch the sun
set over the Florentine countryside
from the sunlit stone balcony. All
bookings are half-board.

Torre di Bellosguardo

2.5 km (1.5 miles) SW Florence. Via
Roti Michelozzi 2, 50124. **C** 055
229 81 45. **FAX** 055 22 90 08. **@**
torredibellosguardo@dada.it **Rooms**:
16. **P** €€€€€

A long, sweeping road leads to this
14th-century tower and adjoining
16th-century villa with panoramic
views of Florence. Inside, colossal
wooden doors lead to huge
rooms, filled with antiques and
Persian rugs. The bedrooms are
on an equally grand scale.

Villa La Massa

6 km (4 miles) SE Florence. Via la Massa
24, Candeli, 50012. **C** 055 626 11.
FAX 055 63 31 02. **W** www.villalamassa.
com **Rooms**: 34.
P €€€€€

Three 17th-century villas make up
this luxurious hotel with a river-
side restaurant. The formal public
rooms and wonderful bedrooms
are decorated with antique furniture.

Villa Le Rondini

7 km (4 miles) N Florence. Via
Bolognese Vecchia 224, Trespiano,
50139. **C** 055 40 00 81. **FAX** 055
26 82 12. **@** mailbox@villarondini.it
Rooms: 40.
& **P** €€€€€

Set in secluded gardens, this villa
has stunning views of the Arno
valley. The main house has very
traditional furnishings, such as the
beamed ceilings and antique fireplace in the split-level sitting room.

Villa San Michele

8 km (5 miles) NE Florence. Via Doccia 4, Fiesole, 50014. 📞 055 67 82 00. FAX 055 59 87 34. @ reservations@villasanmichele.net **Rooms**: 41. 🛏
1️⃣ TV 🔄 👤 ▤ P 🍴 ⛵
€€€€€

Said to have been designed by Michelangelo, this beautiful villa stands in 15 ha (37 acres) of grounds. The panorama is best seen from the loggia, where you can dine outside. Many of the bedrooms are simple, with an air of elegance.

WESTERN TUSCANY

ARTIMINO

Paggeria Medicea

Road map C2. Viale Papa Giovanni XXIII 3, 50040. 📞 055 87 51 41. FAX 055 875 14 70. @ hotel@artimino.com **Rooms**: 37. 🛏 1️⃣ 🔄 TV ▤
🔄 P 🍴 ⛵ €€€€€

Ferdinand I de' Medici built this marvellous hilltop villa. The eclectically designed hotel is housed in the former servants' quarters.

PISA

Rest Hotel Primavère

Road map B2. Via Aurelia km 342 & 750, Migliarino Pisano, 56010.
📞 050 80 33 10. FAX 050 80 33 15.
Rooms: 62. 🛏 1️⃣ 🔄 TV ▤ 👤
🔄 P 🍴 ⛵ €€€

This functional hotel is convenient for drivers. It is clean, in excellent decorative order and has extensive lawns. Four rooms are specially equipped for disabled guests.

Royal Victoria Hotel

Road map B2. Lungarno Pacinotti 12, 56126. 📞 050 94 01 11. FAX 050 94 01 80. @ rvh@csinfo.it **Rooms**: 48. 🛏 40. 1️⃣ 🔄 🔄 P ⛵ €€€

This dignified hotel was built in the 19th century. Original features still remain, including *trompe-l'œil* drapery and wood-panelled doors.

Hotel d'Azeglio

Road map B2. Piazza Vittorio Emanuele II 18b, 56125. 📞 050 50 03 10. FAX 050 280 17. **Rooms**: 29. 🛏
1️⃣ TV 🔄 P ⛵ €€€€€

The attraction of this tall, modern block is the view from the seventh-floor breakfast room and coffee bar. Windows on all sides look over Pisa to the mountains beyond.

RIGOLI

Hotel Villa di Corliano

Road map B2. Via Statale del Brennero 50, 56010. 📞 050 81 81 93. FAX 050 81 88 97. **Rooms**: 12. 🛏 🔄 🍴 ⛵ €€€ **Closed** in winter.

Two sweeping driveways lead on either side of parkland to this magnificent late-Renaissance mansion. An architectural delight inside and out, it features restored Classical murals on the walls and ceilings. The enormous stately bedrooms lead off the central hall.

VOLTERRA

Albergo Villa Nencini

Road map C3. Borgo Santo Stefano 55, 56048. 📞 0588 863 86. FAX 0588 806 01. W www.villanencini.it
Rooms: 32. 🛏 1️⃣ 🔄 🔄 ⛵ €€

This stone country hotel is situated in a small park, a few minutes' drive from the town. Bedrooms are cool and light, though not very large. There is a smart breakfast room and basement taverna, as well as a lounge bar and terrace.

NORTHERN TUSCANY

BALBANO

Villa Casanova

Road map B2. Via di Casanova, 55050. 📞 0583 54 84 29. FAX 0583 36 89 55. **Rooms**: 40. 🛏 1️⃣ 🔄
🔄 🍴 €€€ **Closed** in winter.

Overlooking the valley, this huge 17th-century Tuscan farmhouse is perched on a small hill. The rooms are comfortably furnished. There is a tennis court and the hotel lies close to a stable. This hotel is in an excellent location for walkers, cyclists and those wishing to get away from it all. There are also reduced charges for children.

LUCCA

Piccolo Hotel Puccini

Road map C2. Via di Poggio 9, 55100. 📞 0583 554 21. FAX 0583 534 87. @ hotelpuccini@onenet.it
Rooms: 14. 🛏 1️⃣ 🔄 TV ⛵ €€

This attractive, old stone building is a few steps from the Piazza San Michele. Inside it is small but smart, and there is a bar with tables beside a full-length window looking on to the pretty, narrow street.

Hotel Universo

Road map C2. Piazza del Giglio 1, 55100. 📞 0583 49 36 78. FAX 0583 95 48 54. @ info@hoteluniversolucca.it
Rooms: 60. 🛏 1️⃣ 🔄 TV ▤ ⛵
€€€€

Built in the 19th century, this big, slightly worn hotel has a cosy wood-panelled bar and a marble reception area. The comfortable bedrooms have luxurious marble bathrooms; some rooms have pleasant views on to the square.

Locanda L'Elisa

Road map C2. Via Nuova per Pisa 1952, 55050. 📞 0583 37 97 37. FAX 0583 37 90 19. @ locanda.elisa@lunet.it **Rooms**: 10. 🛏 1️⃣ TV ▤ 🔄
🔄 👤 🍴 ⛵ €€€€€

This stately home imitates 18th-century Parisian style. The beautiful bedrooms have a mix of reproduction and genuine antique furniture, and each room is fitted with a safe. Free alcoholic drinks are kept out on a table in the smaller of the two drawing rooms. This hotel is suitable for individuals or couples wanting luxury and peaceful surroundings, rather than families with children.

PISTOIA

Hotel Piccolo Ritz

Road map C2. Via A Vannucci 67, 51100. 📞 0573 267 75. FAX 0573 277 98. **Rooms**: 21. 🛏 1️⃣ 🔄 TV
👤 ⛵ €€

Close to the station on the Piazza Dante Alighieri, and in the historic centre of Pistoia, the Piccolo Ritz lives up to its name. Inside it is smart, but rather small. It has a pleasant café-style bar with an original frescoed ceiling.

Albergo Patria

Road map C2. Via F Crispi 8, 51100. 📞 0573 251 87. FAX 0573 36 81 68. **Rooms**: 28. 🛏 23. 1️⃣ 🔄 TV ⛵
€€€

Set in the centre of Pistoia, this ancient hotel has a dark, modern interior. There are good-sized 1970s-style rooms, with fair-sized bathrooms, a rather worn TV lounge and a pleasant bar and restaurant. The top bedrooms have views of the Romanesque Duomo.

PONTENUOVO

Il Convento

Road map C2. Via San Quirico 33, 51030. 📞 0573 45 26 51. FAX 0573 45 35 78. **Rooms**: 24. 🛏 1️⃣ 🔄 TV
🔄 🍴 P ⛵ €€€

For key to symbols see p243

A pretty pathway leads to the reception and rather worn lounge area of this former convent. The tables in the intimate dining areas are set with crisp linen cloths. The main dining area still has the old wooden benches on which the nuns sat. The bedrooms are simple but comfortable.

VIAREGGIO

Hotel President

Road map B2. Viale Carducci 5, 55049. 📞 0584 96 27 12. **FAX** 0584 96 36 58. @ info@hotelpresident.it
Rooms: 37. 🛏 1 ♨ TV 🖥 ↕
🍴 🅿 €€€€€

The President is an elegant villa-style hotel on the beach front. Newly refurbished, the bedrooms of this hotel are particularly attractive. Dine in the lovely roof-top restaurant and enjoy stunning sea views.

EASTERN TUSCANY

AREZZO

Castello di Gargonza

Road map E3. Gargonza, Monte San Savino, 52048. 📞 0575 84 70 21. **FAX** 0575 84 70 54.
W www.gargonza.it *Rooms*: 7.
🛏 ♨ 🍴 🅿 €€€€€

More of a medieval "castle-cum-village", this guesthouse also has 25 self-catering apartments. A tree-lined driveway curves around the castle walls to the entrance. There is a tiny garden and a pretty frescoed chapel where services are held once a week.

CORTONA

Hotel San Luca

Road map E3. Piazzale Garibaldi 2, 52044. 📞 0575 63 04 60. **FAX** 0575 63 01 05. W www.sanlucacortona. com *Rooms*: 60. 🛏 1 ♨ TV 🖥
🅿 €€€

Built into the hillside, the San Luca enjoys an all-round panorama over the valleys below. The reception area is large, light and comfortably furnished, but the bedrooms are simple.

Hotel San Michele

Road map E3. Via Guelfa 15, 52044. 📞 0575 60 43 48. **FAX** 0575 63 01 47. @ sanmichele@ats.it *Rooms*: 40. 🛏 1 ♨ TV 🖥 ↕ 🅿 🅿 €€€€€

The San Michele is a beautifully restored Renaissance palazzo, fronting on to a narrow town street. It retains the original tall, heavy wooden doors outside. A maze of corridors lead to the comfortable, homely bedrooms and there is a superb attic suite.

CENTRAL TUSCANY

CASTELLINA IN CHIANTI

Salivolpi

Road map D3. Via Fiorentina 89, 53011. 📞 0577 74 04 84. **FAX** 0577 74 09 98. @ info@hotelsalivolpi.com
Rooms: 19. 🛏 ♨ 🅿 🅿 €€€

This restored country farmhouse has a smart rustic interior with whitewashed walls and warm terracotta floors. The bedrooms in the main farmhouse have low windows, beamed ceilings and gleaming bathrooms.

Tenuta di Ricavo

Road map D3. Località Ricavo, 53011. 📞 0577 74 02 21. **FAX** 0577 74 10 14. @ ricavo@ricavo.com
Rooms: 23. 🛏 1 ♨ 🅿 🍴
closed Tue. 🅿 €€€€€

This charming hotel occupies the entire 1,000-year-old hamlet of Ricavo. Many of the rooms are in old country houses, half with their own terrace. The sitting rooms are styled in a harmonious blend of antique and peasant furniture. Discounts are available for long stays.

GAIOLE IN CHIANTI

Castello di Spaltenna

Road map D3. Spaltenna 53013. 📞 0577 74 94 83. **FAX** 0577 74 92 69. *Rooms*: 37. 🛏 ♨ TV 🖥 ↕ 🍴 🅿
€€€€€ *Closed* Jan–Feb.

Sitting on a hill, the Castello di Spaltenna is in a beautiful, fortified former monastery. The owners take pride in their restaurant (*see p262*), where the food is cooked in a wood-burning oven. Spacious rooms overlook the courtyard and some have the luxury of a Jacuzzi.

PANZANO IN CHIANTI

Villa le Barone

Road map D3. Via San Leolino 19, 50020. 📞 055 85 26 21. **FAX** 055 85 22 77. W www.villalebarone.it
Rooms: 14. 🛏 1 ♨ ♨ 🅿 🍴
🅿 €€€€€

This 16th-century family house used to belong to the della Robbia family, famous for their ceramics. Fresh flowers brighten the sitting rooms and antiques furnish the bedrooms.

RADDA IN CHIANTI

Relais Fattoria Vignale

Road map D3. Via Pianigiani 9, 53017. 📞 0577 73 83 00. **FAX** 0577 73 85 92. W www.vignale.it *Rooms*: 34. 🛏 1 ♨ 🖥 ♨ 🅿 🍴 🅿
€€€€€ *Closed* in winter.

Inside this superb manor are attractive lounges with terracotta floors, murals, stone fireplaces, antiques and rugs. Bedrooms to the rear overlook the valley below.

SAN GIMIGNANO

Albergo Leon Bianco

Road map C3. Piazza della Cisterna 13, 53037. 📞 0577 94 12 94. **FAX** 0577 94 21 23. @ leonbianco@ iol.it *Rooms*: 25. 🛏 1 ♨ TV 🅿
🅿 €€€

Parts of the original stone wall remain in this former palazzo. The rooms are airy with pleasant views and have terracotta floors.

Hotel Villa Belvedere

Road map C3. Via Dante 14, 53037. 📞 0577 94 05 39. **FAX** 0577 94 03 27. *Rooms*: 15. 🛏 1 TV ♨ 🅿
🅿 €€€

A pretty villa with modern bedrooms painted in soothing pastel shades. The garden has a hammock slung between cypress trees.

La Cisterna

Road map C3. Piazza della Cisterna 24, 53037. 📞 0577 94 03 28. **FAX** 0577 94 20 80. @ lacisterna@ iol.it *Rooms*: 47. 🛏 1 ♨ TV 🅿
🍴 🅿 €€€

Situated in a 14th-century palazzo, La Cisterna offers rooms furnished in traditional Florentine style and views over the Tuscan countryside.

Villa San Paolo

Road map C3. Strada per Certaldo, 53037. 📞 0577 95 51 00. **FAX** 0577 95 51 13. @ sanpaolo@ iol.it
Rooms: 18. 🛏 ♨ ♨ ↕ 🅿
€€€€ *Closed* 10 Jan–5 Mar.

This attractive hillside villa is set in spacious terraced gardens, which include a tennis court. Inside, there are intimate lounges and pretty bedrooms.

SAN GUSMÉ

Villa Arceno

Road map D3. Castelnuovo Berardenga, 53010. (0577 35 92 92. **FAX** 0577 35 92 76. **Rooms**: 16. 🛏 1 🎱 📶 📺
🗏 ♨ ♓ P 📶 🗏 €€€€€
Closed mid-Nov–mid-Feb.

Large bedrooms feature in this 17th-century villa, set in beautiful woodland. The bedrooms are spacious and the vaulted public rooms are furnished with light, reproduction "antiques".

SIENA

Hotel Chiusarelli

Road map D3. Viale Curtatone 15, 53100. (0577 28 05 62. **FAX** 0577 27 11 77. @ info@chiusarelli.com
Rooms: 49. 🛏 1 🎱 📺 P 📶
🗏 €€€

This pretty villa shows some signs of wear and tear, but the interior has recently undergone extensive restoration. Outside, the pleasant garden is filled with palm trees.

Pensione Palazzo Ravizza

Road map D3. Pian dei Mantellini 34, 53100. (0577 28 04 62.
FAX 0577 22 15 97. @ bureau@ palazzoravizza.it **Rooms**: 40. 🛏 1
🎱 ♨ P 📶 🗏 €€€€

Within the city walls, this is a charming base. The rooms have excellent views over the Tuscan landscape. The restaurant is only open in summer and at Christmas, and guests must take half-board at these times.

Santa Caterina

Road map D3. Via Enea Silvio Piccolomini 7, 53100. (0577 22 11 05.
FAX 0577 27 10 87. @ hsc@ sienanet.it **Rooms**: 19. 🛏 1 🎱 📺
🗏 ♿ P 🗏 €€€€

This 18th-century house is one of Siena's most economical options. It is pleasantly furnished in rustic style and in keeping with its age. The bedrooms differ in style and size, and are decorated with a variety of interesting antiques.

Hotel Certosa di Maggiano

Road map D3. Strada di Certosa 82, 53100. (0577 28 81 80. **FAX** 0577 28 81 89. @ certosa@relaischateaux.fr
Rooms: 17. 🛏 🎱 🗏 📺 ♨ P
📶 🗏 €€€€€

Built in 1314, this former Carthusian monastery was the oldest in Tuscany. This amazing hotel – its rooms adorned with antique paintings – makes an exclusive, homely and peaceful retreat.

Villa Patrizia

Road map D3. Via Fiorentina 58, 53100. (0577 504 31. **FAX** 0577 504 42. @ info@villapatrizia.it
Rooms: 33. 🛏 1 🎱 📺 ♨
♨ P 📶 🗏 €€€€€

This rambling old villa is on the northern outskirts of the city. The bedrooms are simply furnished, and comfortable.

Villa Scacciapensieri

Road map D3. Via di Scacciapensieri 10, 53100. (0577 414 41. **FAX** 0577 27 08 54. @ villasca@tin.it **Rooms**: 28.
🛏 1 🎱 🗏 📺 ♨ ♿ P 📶 🗏
€€€€€

Set in attractive grounds, this villa has an antiquated lounge with a huge stone fireplace. The spacious bedrooms have views of Siena and the Tuscan hills. The hotel has a tennis court and bikes for hire.

SINALUNGA

Locanda dell'Amorosa

Road map E3. Località Amorosa, 53048. (0577 67 94 97.
FAX 0577 63 20 01. @ locanda@ amorosa.it **Rooms**: 20. 🛏 1 🎱 🗏
♨ P 📶 🗏 €€€€€

This idyllic 14th-century villa is part of an estate with its own vineyard and farmland. Inside, the bedrooms are cool and airy.

STROVE

Albergo Casalta

Road map D3. Comune di Monteriggioni, 53035. (& **FAX** 0577 30 10 02. @ casalta@chiantiturismo.it
Rooms: 10. 🛏 📶 closed Wed.
€€ **Closed** in winter.

A tiny hamlet is home to this hotel in a 1,000-year-old stone building. The central hearth in the reception gives a warm and welcoming feel and there is an elegant restaurant.

San Luigi Residence

Road map D3. Via della Cerreta 38, 53035. (0577 30 10 55.
FAX 0577 30 11 67. **Rooms**: 64. 🛏
1 🎱 ♨ P 📶 🗏 €€€€€

These beautifully restored farm buildings lie in an expansive park. Sporting facilities include tennis courts, a volley ball court and a children's play area.

SOUTHERN TUSCANY

ELBA

Capo Sud

Road map B4. Località Lacona, 57037. (0565 96 40 21. **FAX** 0565 96 42 63. @ info@caposud.it **Rooms**: 39. 🛏 1 🎱 📺 on request.
🗏 🎱 P 📶 €€€

A small resort with views of the bay. The rooms are in a complex of villas around the hotel grounds. The restaurant serves produce from its own vineyard and orchard.

GIGLIO PORTO

Castello Monticello

Road map C5. Via Provinciale, 58013. (0564 80 92 52. **FAX** 0564 80 94 73.
@ info@hotelcastellomonticello.com
Rooms: 29. 🛏 1 🎱 📺 🗏 P
📶 🗏 €€€ **Closed** Oct–Easter.

This castle hotel on the island of Giglio was originally built as a private house. It sits on a hill and enjoys superb views.

PUNTA ALA

Piccolo Hotel Alleluja

Road map C4. Via del Porto, 58040. (0564 92 20 50. **FAX** 0564 92 07 34.
Rooms: 38. 🛏 📺 🗏 🎱 P
📶 🗏 €€€€€ **Closed** mid-Oct–Mar.

A small seaside hotel with a stylish, simple interior. Some bedrooms have their own sitting rooms. There are tennis courts and a card room.

PORTO ERCOLE

Il Pellicano

Road map D5. Località San Barcatello, 58018. (0564 85 81 11. **FAX** 0564 83 34 18. @ info@pellicanohotel.com
Rooms: 41. 🛏 🗏 📺 🗏 🎱 P 📶
🗏 €€€€€ **Closed** mid-Oct–Mar.

Luxurious and exclusive with its own rocky beach area, this old-style villa is elegantly furnished.

For key to symbols *see p243*

RESTAURANTS, CAFÉS AND BARS

FOOD IS ONE of the great Italian passions, and eating out on a balmy summer's evening can be a memorable experience. Few restaurants in Tuscany serve anything but Italian food, and most concentrate on the robust fare that typifies the region's cuisine. Most Tuscans take their lunch *(pranzo)* around 1pm, and have dinner *(cena)* from 8pm. Restaurants may shut for several weeks during the winter and also during the holiday season in summer. If in doubt, phone first to check that the restaurant is open. Finding the restaurants in Florence can be confusing due to the dual numbering of the streets *(see p274)*, so use the map references. The restaurants listed on pages 258–263 have been selected from the best the city and region can offer across all price ranges.

Italian waiter at your service

TYPES OF RESTAURANTS AND BARS

ITALIAN RESTAURANTS have a bewildering variety of names, but in practice there's little difference between a *trattoria, osteria* or *ristorante* in terms of price, cooking or ambience. Both a *birreria* and *spaghetteria* are more downmarket establishments, and sell beer, pasta dishes and snacks. A *pizzeria* is a cheap, informal restaurant with pasta, meat and fish on the menu as well as pizzas. It is usually open only in the evening, especially if it has wood-fired ovens.

At lunchtime you could visit a *tavola calda*, one of the increasingly rare places selling a limited range of hot snacks. A *rosticceria* offers spit-roast chicken to take away, often with other fast foods. Most bars sell filled rolls *(panini)* and sandwiches *(tramezzini)* and small pizza bars sell slices of pizza *(pizza taglia)* to eat on the street.

Old-fashioned wine bars *(vinaii or fiaschetterie)* are a dying breed, but they are atmospheric places to grab a snack or a glass of wine. Ice-cream parlours *(gelaterie)*, by contrast, are thriving, and Florence has some of the best in Italy.

VEGETARIAN FOOD

MOST ITALIANS find it hard to understand vegetarianism, and Florence boasts only a couple of vegetarian restaurants. However, in the wake of mad-cow disease,

Outside Palle d'Oro (see p258)

restaurants are offering a wider vegetarian selection and you should have no trouble assembling a meat-free meal, particularly if you eat fish and seafood. Starters *(antipasti)* will usually include some suitable dishes. There are also vegetable-based soups and pasta sauces, but check that they have been cooked with vegetable stock *(brodo vegetariano)*.

HOW MUCH TO PAY

PRICES ARE OFTEN higher in Florence than elsewhere. In the cheaper eating establishments and pizzerias you can have a two-course or a fixed-price *(menù turistico)* meal with half a litre of wine for around €9–€12. Average prices for a three-course meal are €13–€26, and in up-market restaurants you could easily pay as much as €45–€55.

Nearly all restaurants have a cover charge *(pane e coperto)*, usually about €3. Many also add a 10 per cent service charge *(servizio)* to the bill *(il conto)*, so always establish whether or not this is the case. Where leaving a tip is a matter of your own discretion, 12–15 per cent is acceptable.

Restaurants are obliged by law to give you a receipt *(una ricevuta)*. Scraps of paper with an illegible scrawl are illegal, and you are perfectly within your rights to ask for a proper bill.

Inside the long-established Le Fonticine in Florence (see p259)

Cash is the preferred form of payment in most cafés and bars, but many restaurants, particularly the more expensive, will accept major credit cards. Check which cards are accepted when booking.

MAKING RESERVATIONS

FLORENCE'S BEST restaurants in all price ranges are well patronized. It is therefore advisable to try and reserve a table, even in the more down-market places. Where restaurants do not accept bookings, try to arrive early to avoid queuing.

DRESS CODE

ITALIANS ARE RELAXED about eating out, but nevertheless like to dress up to dine. The restaurant listings indicate where formal dress is required.

Trattoria Angiolino *(see p258)*

READING THE MENU

A MEAL IN A RESTAURANT will usually start with *antipasti*, or hors d'œuvres (hams, olives, salamis, crostini), followed by *primi* (soups, pasta or rice). Main courses – *secondi* – will be meat or fish, either served alone or accompanied by vegetables *(contorni)* or a salad *(insalata)*.

To finish, there will probably be a choice of fruit *(frutta)*, cheese *(formaggio)*, puddings *(dolci)*, or a combination of all three. Coffee – always espresso, never cappuccino – is ordered right at the end of a meal, often with a *digestivo* *(see p257)*. In cheaper restaurants, the menu *(il menù* or *la lista)* may be

The 11th-century Badia a Coltibuono in Gaiole in Chianti *(see p262)*

written on a blackboard and in many establishments the waiter *(cameriere)* will recite the chef's daily specials at your table.

CHOICE OF WINE

H OUSE WINES will usually be Chiantis or some close cousin. The cheaper establishments usually have only house wine, or a small choice of other Tuscan wines. Those in the €40–€55 price range will have a fuller selection of regional wines, as well as wines from other parts of Italy. At the top of the scale, there should be a wide range of Italian and local wines, and, as at the Enoteca Pinchiorri *(see p259)*, a selection of French and other foreign vintages. *(See also pp256–7.)*

CHILDREN

C HILDREN ARE GENERALLY welcome in restaurants, but less so in the evening and in more up-market places.

Outside dining at the popular Rivoire café *(see p265)*

Special facilities such as high chairs are not commonly provided. Check the menu for the option of a small portion *(una porzione piccola)*: most restaurants will prepare a half portion *(mezza porzione)* if requested and some charge less for these smaller portions.

SMOKING

I TALIANS STILL SMOKE more than most. Few restaurants and virtually none of the bars or cafés set aside space for non-smokers.

WHEELCHAIR ACCESS

F EW RESTAURANTS make special provision for wheelchairs, though a word when you are booking should ensure a conveniently situated table and assistance on arrival.

USING THE LISTINGS

Key to the symbols in the listings on pp258–63.

🍽️ fixed-price menu
👔 jacket and tie required
🪑 tables outside
🌬️ air-conditioning
🍷 good wine list
★ highly recommended
💳 credit cards accepted. Check which cards are accepted when booking.

Price categories for a three-course meal for one including a half-bottle of house wine, cover charge, tax and service.
€ under €15
€€ €15–€25
€€€ €25–€40
€€€€ €40–€55
€€€€€ over €55

What to Eat in Florence and Tuscany

Plum tomato

Tuscan cuisine still has its roots in peasant cooking, relying on basic staples such as olive oil, for which the region is renowned, tomatoes, beans, hams and salamis. Chewy, saltless bread or thick vegetable soups such as *ribollita* often take the place of pasta, followed by grilled or roast meats, the great stand-bys of rustic cuisine. Sheep's milk cheeses are common, especially *pecorino* and the creamy *ricotta*. Fruit or ice cream round off many meals, or try Siena's nougat-like *panforte* or the famous *cantucci* accompanied by *vin santo*.

Maritozzi
These soft buns with raisins and candied peel can be filled with whipped cream.

Panzanella
Basil, tomatoes, parsley, garlic and oil-soaked bread make up this summer salad.

Liver paste   Tomato paste

Olive paste   Anchovy paste

Crostini
Pieces of toasted bread are rubbed with garlic and olive oil. Chopped tomatoes, mushrooms or liver paste can be added to make a delicious snack.

Ribollita
This thickened soup is a rich broth of cabbage, herbs, beans and vegetables.

Fagioli all'Uccelletto
A classic combination of beans in a tomato sauce, this is one of the most popular vegetable dishes in Tuscany.

Salame di Cinghiale
This is a strongly flavoured salami made from wild boar.

Pappardelle alla Lepre
Typically Tuscan, these broad noodles are covered in a hare sauce. The hare is often cooked in its own blood, or in a rich beef stock.

Trippa alla Fiorentina
Tripe and a parmesan-topped tomato sauce are used to make this dish.

Bistecca alla Fiorentina
Grilled over an open fire, this large, tender steak can be seasoned with oil and herbs.

Baccalà
This is dried salt cod, most often prepared with garlic, parsley and tomatoes.

Scottiglia di Cinghiale
Prepared with wild boar chops, this dish is particularly popular in the Maremma.

Arrosto Misto
This common rural dish is a mixture of roast meats, such as lamb, pork, chicken, liver and spicy sausages (salsicce).

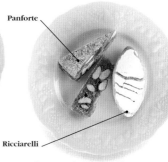

Panforte

Ricciarelli

Castagne Ubriache
Chestnuts are covered in red wine sauce and often served with baked custard.

Torta di Riso
Rice cakes can be served with a simple fruit sauce.

Panforte and Ricciarelli
Panforte is a dense, dark cake spiced with cloves and cinnamon. Ricciarelli *are made from ground almonds, candied orange peel and honey.*

Pecorino
This sheep's cheese can either be fresh and sweet, or well-matured and hard.

Olive oil

Ricotta
Made from sheep's milk whey, ricotta can be eaten with olive oil or honey.

Cantucci
These sweet biscuits taste best dipped in vin santo, a delicious dessert wine.

What to Drink in Florence and Tuscany

Medieval engraving of a grape crusher

TUSCANY IS A MAJOR wine-producing region whose wines make ideal partners for the robust local food. Both reds and whites are made here, ranging from light, house wine (*vino della casa*) to the very best Europe can produce. The most famous reds, notably Brunello di Montalcino, Vino Nobile di Montepulciano and Chianti, are made from the Sangiovese grape and are produced inland, on the hills of Tuscany. A number of estates, particularly in Chianti Classico, also experiment with non-Italian grape varieties with considerable success. Throughout Tuscany, bars and cafés are open all day serving drinks from wine to beer and coffee. See also *A Day Out in Chianti* on page 225.

Il Poggione is an excellent producer of Brunello di Montalcino.

RED WINE

CHIANTI IS MADE in seven defined zones, but the best wines generally come from the hilly areas of Classico and Rufina. Brunello, from further south, needs ageing and can be expensive but Rosso di Montalcino, made for younger drinking, often offers better value. Tuscan table wine can be cheap or expensive – the top-priced wines may not fit the traditional Chianti regulations, but are likely to be extremely good. Sassicaia, made from the French Cabernet Sauvignon grape, is an example. Other fine reds include Fontalloro, Cepparello and Solaia.

Tuscan table wine

Chianti produced by Ruffino

Carmignano, a good dry red, is made north of Florence.

Sassicaia is made from Cabernet Sauvignon grapes.

WHITE WINE

Galestro

TUSCANY'S WHITE WINES are less interesting than the reds, although some producers are experimenting with a handful of quality whites from grapes such as Chardonnay and Sauvignon. Most Tuscan white wine is made from the Trebbiano grape, at its lightest in the spritzy style called Galestro, but usually sold as plain dry Bianco della Toscana. Vernaccia di San Gimignano, from the Vernaccia grape, is sometimes good and Montecarlo, from near Lucca, a blend of grapes, offers more interesting drinking. Most Tuscan whites need to be drunk young.

VIN SANTO

Vin Santo

VIN SANTO, or "Holy Wine", is a traditional wine once made on farms throughout the region and now seeing a revival of interest from modern producers. The best versions are sweet, though it can be found as a dry wine. It is often offered with *cantucci*, small almond biscuits, in Tuscan restaurants and homes. Vin Santo is made from Trebbiano and Malvasia grapes which are semi-dried, made into wine and then aged in small barrels for a number of years before bottling. The best are very concentrated in flavour. Quality varies, but superb versions are made by Avignonesi and Isole e Olena.

How Chianti is Made

Chianti is made as soon as possible after the October harvest. The quality of the wine can be very high, as wineries have combined the best of traditional and modern techniques.

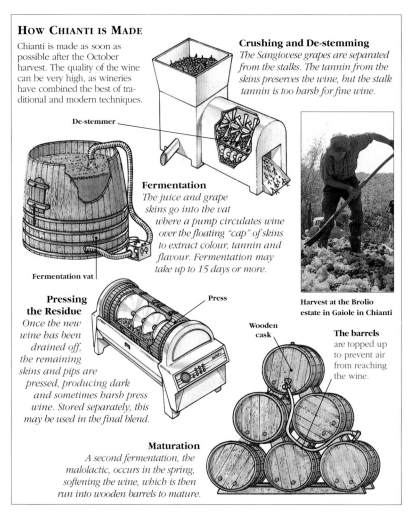

Crushing and De-stemming
The Sangiovese grapes are separated from the stalks. The tannin from the skins preserves the wine, but the stalk tannin is too harsh for fine wine.

De-stemmer

Fermentation
The juice and grape skins go into the vat where a pump circulates wine over the floating "cap" of skins to extract colour, tannin and flavour. Fermentation may take up to 15 days or more.

Fermentation vat

Harvest at the Brolio estate in Gaiole in Chianti

Pressing the Residue
Once the new wine has been drained off, the remaining skins and pips are pressed, producing dark and sometimes harsh press wine. Stored separately, this may be used in the final blend.

Press

Wooden cask

The barrels
are topped up to prevent air from reaching the wine.

Maturation
A second fermentation, the malolactic, occurs in the spring, softening the wine, which is then run into wooden barrels to mature.

Cinzano, a popular early evening *aperitivo*

Aperitifs and Digestifs

PRE- AND POST-MEAL tipples include Campari, Cinzano and the artichoke-based Cynar, as well as Crodino, the best-known of several non-alcoholic drinks. The herb-flavoured *amaro* or a *grappa* commonly round off a meal; otherwise try a *limoncello*, a sweet, lemon-based liqueur, the aniseed-scented Sambuca or almond-flavoured Amaretto.

Beer

BEER CAN BE a great thirst-quencher, especially in the summer heat. Draught beer (*birra alla spina*) is less expensive than bottled beer, and is sold by the measure. Good Italian lager-style beers include Peroni and Moretti.

Other Drinks

FRUIT JUICES are sold in small bottles (*succo di frutta*) or freshly squeezed (*spremuta*). In summer, iced tea or coffee can be refreshing. Italian coffee is drunk with frothy milk for breakfast (*cappuccino*) or black after meals (*espresso*). An *espresso* with a spot of milk is called a *macchiato*.

Espresso

Cappuccino

FLORENCE

CITY CENTRE

Trattoria Mario

Via Rosina 2r. **Map** 1 C4. 055 21 85 50. **Open** noon–2:30pm Mon–Sat.

This lively trattoria is always packed with a broad mix of business people and visitors from the centre who know where to get good, traditional homestyle food at very reasonable prices. The daily handwritten menu is posted near the kitchen area, and features one or two soups, different types of pasta with sauce, and a number of meat and side dishes. Mario's serves fresh fish on Friday.

Acquacotta

Via de' Pilastri 51r. **Map** 2 E5. 055 24 29 07. **Open** 12:30–2pm, 7–10pm Thu–Mon, 12:30–2pm Tue. **Closed** Wed, Aug.

This inexpensive, three-roomed restaurant is named for the house speciality, *acquacotta*, which literally means cooked water. It is in fact a Florentine vegetable soup served over toast with a poached egg on top. The food in this establishment is very traditional, homestyle cuisine, including dishes that may require quite a strong stomach, such as pigs' trotters and *bollito misto e salsa verde* (boiled meat with a green sauce).

Da Pennello

Via Dante Alighieri 4r. **Map** 4 D1 (6 E3). 055 29 48 48. **Open** noon–3pm, 7–10pm Tue–Sat.

You will need to book well ahead unless you are prepared to wait for some time to sit at the tables in the charming summer garden or in the bright dining room. This is a restaurant that has been well and truly discovered, and rightly so. It is best known for its wide variety of *antipasti*, which could easily constitute a meal in itself. It also offers a "light lunch" menu.

Osteria dei Macci

Via de' Macci 77r. **Map** 4 E1. 055 24 12 26. **Open** 7:30pm–1am Tue–Sun.

This restaurant's slightly outlying position on the edge of the Sant'Ambrogio market – but close to Santa Croce – means it sees far fewer tourists than some. It is a basic trattoria of the old school.

Palle d'Oro

Via Sant'Antonino 43r. **Map** 1 C5 (5 C1). 055 28 83 83. **Open** noon–2:30pm, 6:30–9:45pm Mon–Sat.

This sparse, spotlessly clean trattoria is as simple as they come. There are wooden booths and tables at the rear, and a take-away sandwich bar at the front.

Paoli

Via dei Tavolini 12r. **Map** 4 D1 (6 D3). 055 21 62 15. **Open** noon–2:30pm, 7–10:30pm Wed–Mon. **Closed** 3 wks in Aug.

The food here is not exceptional, but the ambience is scarcely bettered anywhere in the city. The dining area is a single, vaulted hall completely smothered in medieval frescoes. This, and its position just off Via dei Calzaiuoli, means it is invariably full, so be sure to book or arrive early.

San Zanobi

Via San Zanobi 33r. **Map** 1 C4. 055 47 52 86. **Open** noon–2:30pm, 7–10pm Mon–Sat.

Dedicated cooking is evident in San Zanobi in everything, from the delicacy and inventiveness of the food to the scrupulous attention to detail in the refined dining room. The dishes, based on a traditional Florentine theme, are light and superbly presented. The new lunchtime menu includes a hearty plate of pasta at a reasonable price.

Trattoria Angiolino

Via di Santo Spirito 36r. **Map** 3 B1 (5 A4). 055 239 89 76. **Open** noon–2:30pm, 7:15–10:30pm daily (Nov–Mar: closed Mon).

This good-looking restaurant in Oltrarno has a typically bustling Florentine atmosphere. However, the quality of the food – which can be excellent – and service is not always consistent. Particularly charming is the iron stove in the middle of the restaurant, which is lit in the winter months. Specialities on the menu include *penne ai funghi* (mushroom). Be sure to ask for the daily specials.

Alle Murate

Via Ghibellina 52r. **Map** 4 E1. 055 24 06 18. **Open** 8–11:30pm Tue–Sun. **Closed** 15 days in Dec.

This increasingly popular restaurant is buoyed by the delicate cooking of a young female chef who, with dishes such as *ravioli di gamberi* (pasta stuffed with prawns), combines basic Italian staples with a dash of more far-flung Mediterranean cuisines. Desserts are light and innovative, and the wine cellar is among the best in the city.

Buca dell'Orafo

Volta de' Girolami 28r. **Map** 6 D4. 055 21 36 19. **Open** 12:30–2:30pm, 7:30–10:30pm Tue–Sat, 12:30–2:30pm Mon. **Closed** Aug.

Packed with visitors during lunch and early evening and with locals later on, this friendly hole-in-the-wall is a longtime favourite with Florentines looking for homely cooking. The pasta is home-made and daily specials always feature *baccalà* on Friday, *pasta e fagioli* on Saturday and *ribollita* on Thursday, Friday and Saturday. The house *dolce*, a sponge cake oozing cream and topped with almonds and meringue, is renowned.

Buca Mario

Piazza degli Ottaviani 16r. **Map** 1 B5 (5 B2). 055 21 41 79. **Open** 12:30–2:30pm, 7:30–10:30pm Fri–Tue, 7:30–10pm Thu. **Closed** 3 wks in Aug.

This large restaurant is a staple among foreign tourists, who often form a little knot outside. They wait patiently for a table down below in the cellar and a chance to enjoy home-made pastas and grilled meats at premium prices.

Cafaggi

Via Guelfa 35r. **Map** 1 C4. 055 29 49 89. **Open** 12:30–3pm, 7–10pm Mon–Sat.

This classic Tuscan trattoria, with just two simply furnished rooms, has been in the Cafaggi family for more than 80 years. The oil and several of the wines come from the family farm in Chianti and complement the fresh, well-prepared dishes. The *crostini*, rustic *zuppa di farro* (wheat berry soup), *involtini* (veal rolled with ham and sage leaves) and crème caramel are particularly good. Stick to one of the three fixed-price menus for a reasonably priced meal – you can take your choice between the *turistico*, *leggero* (light) or *vegetariano* (vegetarian).

Da Ganino

Piazza dei Cimatori 4r. **Map** 6 E3. 055 21 41 25. **Open** 12:30–2:45pm, 7:30–10:30pm Mon–Sat.

Uncrowded restaurants are in short supply close to the Duomo and Via dei Calzaiuoli. This small restaurant, however, is friendly and popular with locals and tourists, and offers all the basics at a reasonable price. It has an old-fashioned interior and a few tables outside on a tiny piazza. If the tables are full, try the Birreria Centrale next door (see p265).

Dino

Via Ghibellina 51r. **Map** 4 D1 (6 E3). **(** 055 24 14 52. **Open** noon–2:30pm, 7:30–10:30pm Tue–Sat, 12:30–2:30pm Sun. ▤ ▢ ▢ €€€

This well-regarded restaurant is situated on the edge of the Santa Croce district in a beautiful 14th-century palazzo. This restaurant has one of Florence's best wine cellars and its decorous and refined setting complements a long menu and excellent seasonal cooking. Dishes on the menu, which can be adventurous, include *tagliatelle all'erba limoncella* (pasta with herbs), several types of *baccalà* as well as the famous *filettino di maiale al cartoccio* (pork fillets baked in paper).

Le Fonticine

Via Nazionale 79r. **Map** 1 C4. **(** 055 28 21 06. **Open** noon–2:30pm, 7–10pm Tue–Sat. ▢ ▢ €€€

The owners of this long-established and well-known restaurant come from the neighbouring Emilia Romagna region, which is famed for the excellence of its cuisine. They give a refined twist to solid Tuscan dishes such as *trippa*, *ossobuco* (veal) and *cinghiale*. Meats are generally of the highest quality and the pasta is home-made.

I' Francescano

Largo Bargellini 16r. **Map** 4 E1. **(** 055 24 16 05. **Open** 12:30–2:30pm, 7:30–10:30pm Wed–Mon (daily in summer). ▢ ▢ €€€

A rustic atmosphere fills this restaurant, which serves simple Tuscan dishes refined for a modern palate. The clientele, consisting of mainly young Florentines, have a choice of dishes such as *pappa al pomodoro* or *ribollita* – both soups – and various meat dishes. The choice of wines and desserts on offer is impressive.

LOBS

Via Faenza 75r.
Map 1 C4 (5 C1). **(** 055 21 24 78. **Open** noon–2:30pm, 7:30–10:30pm daily. ▤ ▢ ▢ €€€

Located in the heart of San Lorenzo, near the central market, LOBS is a small and informal fish restaurant, with a warm and welcoming atmosphere. Pasta dishes, such as spaghetti with clams and vegetable *gnocchi* with shrimp, are served for lunch, while a variety of platters of assorted fish with vegetables are available for dinner.

Le Mossacce

Via del Proconsolo 55r.
Map 2 D5 (6 E2). **(** 055 29 43 61. **Open** noon–2:30pm, 7–9:30pm Mon–Fri. ▢ ▢ €€€

Multilingual menus and a chaotic lunchtime air shouldn't put you off this 100-year-old restaurant, located between the Bargello and the Duomo. Nor should the name, which, when translated into English, means "discourteous".

Tiny wooden tables and paper tablecloths are complemented by suitably robust Tuscan food, with barely a nod to dishes from outside the region. The fixed-price menu, even without a dessert, is good value. Unfortunately, you cannot reserve a table here.

La Taverna del Bronzino

Via delle Ruote 25–27r. **Map** 2 D3. **(** 055 49 52 20. **Open** 12:30–2:30pm, 7:30–10:30pm Mon–Sat. **Closed** Aug. ▤ ▢ ▢ €€€

The 15th-century palazzo that houses this restaurant has connections with the Florentine painter Bronzino, hence the name.

Well-heeled businessmen on expense account lunches make up the major part of the restaurant's clientele. The atmosphere is reserved without being stuffy and the surroundings are airy and beautifully finished. The *antipasti* and wide choice of pastas are characteristically Tuscan, while the main courses are more ambitiously Florentine. All the cooking is of the highest quality.

Trattoria Zà Zà

Piazza del Mercato Centrale 26r. **Map** 1 C4. **(** 055 21 54 11. **Open** noon–3pm, 7–11pm Mon–Sat. ▢ ▦ ▢ €€€

Both the upper and lower rooms of this canteen-like restaurant are packed with customers perched on stools, elbow-to-elbow at wooden trestle tables. Yellowing posters of 1950s film stars provide the decoration, shadowed by shelves of precariously stacked bottles of Chianti. The service is amiable and the food is robust. The hot *antipasti* are consistently excellent. Soups such as *ribollita*, *pomodoro* (tomato) and *passato di fagioli* (bean purée) make good

primi, while *arista* (roast pork) and *scaloppine* (veal) are dependable main courses. To finish off, try the house speciality, *torta di mele alla zà zà* (apple tart).

Cibrèo

Via Andrea del Verrocchio 8r. **Map** 4 E1. **(** 055 234 11 00. **Open** 12:50–2:30pm, 7–11:15pm Tue–Sat. **Closed** 1 wk in Jan, Aug. ▤ ▢ ★ ▢ €€€€

Under the guiding hand of Fabio and Benedetta Picchi Cibrèo, this restaurant offers superbly prepared traditional Tuscan food in an unstuffy atmosphere. Cibrèo does not serve pasta so choose from thoroughly Florentine dishes such as tripe, sheep's brains, cockscombs and kidneys, or go for more palatable items such as duck stuffed with sultanas and pine nuts or lamb with artichokes. Try also the delicious selection of desserts.

Enoteca Pinchiorri

Via Ghibellina 87. **Map** 4 D1 (6 E3). **(** 055 24 27 77. **Open** 12:30–2pm, 7:30–10pm Tue, Thu–Sat, 7:30–10pm Wed. ▢ ▦ ▢ ▢ ★ ▢ €€€€

The Pinchiorri is frequently described as Italy's finest restaurant, and also boasts that many have called the greatest wine cellar in Europe (over 80,000 bottles of French and Italian vintages).

The restaurant's setting, on the ground floor of the 15th-century Palazzo Ciofi-Iacometti, matches the excellence of the award-winning cooking, a mixture of Tuscan and French-inspired *cucina nuova*. The set-price *menù degustazione* includes glasses of wine appropriate to each course, thus allowing you to sample the cellar without having to buy whole bottles. Not everyone, will be comfortable with the ceremony and seriousness which is attached to eating and drinking at the Pinchiorri.

Sabatini

Via Panzani 9a. **Map** 1 C5 (5 C1). **(** 055 21 15 59. **Open** 12:30–2:30pm, 7:30–11pm Tue–Sun. ▦ ▤ ▢ ▢ €€€€

Once Florence's most eminent restaurant, Sabatini's glory days are now long gone. However, the critical backlash that flayed its reputation has done a disservice to the cooking – a mixture of Italian and international – which is always reliable and occasionally superlative. The ambience and service are as fine as ever, though neither the food nor the excellent selection of wines comes cheap.

FLORENCE ENVIRONS

Caffè Concerto

2 km (1.25 miles) E Florence. Lungarno Cristoforo Colombo 7. 055 67 73 77. **Open** *12:30–2:30pm, 7:30–11pm Mon–Sat.* **Closed** *Aug.* €€€€

Gabriele Tarchiani's eclectic decor and *cucina nuova* aren't to all tastes. However, the view over the Arno from the veranda is almost reason enough to sample some of the innovative dishes. The menu is changed seasonally.

WESTERN TUSCANY

ARTIMINO

Da Delfina

Road map C2. Via della Chiesa 1. 055 871 80 74. **Open** *12:30–2:30pm, 8–10pm Tue–Sat; 12:30–2:30pm Sun.* **Closed** *Aug.* ★ €€€

A restaurant "for people who take eating seriously". Carlo Cioni has continued the authentic culinary traditions of his mother, Delfina, in this lovely restaurant, located in a walled medieval village just 22 km (14 miles) west of Florence. Game is a particular speciality of this restaurant. Pork with wild fennel and black Tuscan cabbage is just one of numerous outstanding local dishes.

LIVORNO

La Barcarola

Road map B3. Viale Carducci 39. 0586 40 23 67. **Open** *noon–2:45pm, 8–10:15pm Mon–Sat.* €€€€

Livorno may not be Tuscany's prettiest city, but it is undoubtedly the best place to eat fish. The one dish not to miss at this lively restaurant is *cacciucco*, the traditional Livornese fish soup. Other specialities include *zuppa di pesce* and *penne* with scampi.

La Chiave

Road map B3. Scali delle Cantine 52. 0586 88 86 09. **Open** *8–10pm Thu–Tue.* €€€€

La Chiave offers refined and elegant dining. The fish menu changes often and includes traditional local fare and Italian specialities from as far afield as Naples and Sicily.

PISA

Al Ristoro dei Vecchi Macelli

Road map B2. Via Volturno 49. 050 204 24. **Open** *12:30–2:30pm, 8–10pm Thu–Tue.* **Closed** *Sun lunch.* €€€€€

Traditional bean soup with seafood is one of several innovative dishes in this pleasant, intimate restaurant that serves light Tuscan food with a twist. Fish, seafood and game specialities are delicately prepared and the home-made desserts are sensational. For the indecisive, there are three tasting menus.

VOLTERRA

Etruria

Road map C3. Piazza dei Priori 6–8. 0588 860 64. **Open** *Aug & Sep: noon–3:30pm, 7–10:30pm daily; Oct–Jul: noon–2:30pm, 7–10:30pm Wed–Mon.* €€€

In a town not generally blessed with good restaurants, the Etruria, on Volterra's main square, is your best bet. Try the game and roast boar specialities when in season, generally in the autumn.

NORTHERN TUSCANY

BAGNI DI LUCCA

La Ruota

Road map C2. Via Giovanni XXIII 29b. 0583 80 56 27. **Open** *noon–2:30pm, 7–10pm Wed–Sun, noon–2:30pm Mon.* **Closed** *Tue.* €€€

La Ruota has an extensive menu, which includes grilled meats and fish and a number of local and national specialities.

LUCCA

Giulio in Pelleria

Road map C2. Via delle Conce 47. 0583 559 48. **Open** *noon–2:30pm, 7–10pm Tue–Sat.* €€€

You must book ahead and enter into the spirit of this bright, boisterous and extremely busy neighbourhood restaurant. Here the hearty local dishes offer few surprises, but the prices are extremely reasonable.

Buca di Sant'Antonio

Road map C2. Via della Cervia 3. 0583 558 81. **Open** *12:30–3pm, 7:30–10:30pm Tue–Sat, 12:30–3pm Sun.* €€€€

This, Lucca's most famous restaurant, was once graced with compliments. The heavy rustic cooking no longer excels, but the variety of dishes from the Garfagnana region make it reliable and well priced.

Solferino

Road map C2. Via delle Gavine 50, San Macario in Piano. 0583 591 18. **Open** *7:30–10:30pm Mon–Tue & Thu–Sat, noon–2:30pm, 7:30–10:30pm Sun & public hols.* €€€

Solferino has been in the same family for generations and is among the most famous and highly regarded restaurants in Tuscany. The menu is mainly Tuscan, but cooks Edema and Giampiero regularly come up with innovative interpretations. The wines are superb.

Vipore

Road map C2. Pieve Santo Stefano. 0583 39 40 65. **Open** *Apr–Oct: 12:30–3pm, 7:45–10:30pm Tue–Sun.* **Closed** *Jan* €€€€

Situated on a hilltop, this restaurant has magnificent views. The chef produces food of unusual originality, using seasonal vegetables and game, dressed with herbs and local olive oil. The *maccheroncini* is particularly good.

MONTECATINI TERME

Enoteca Giovanni

Road map C2. Via Garibaldi 27. 0572 716 95. **Open** *12:30–2:30pm, 8–11pm Tue–Sun.* **Closed** *Jul.* **Closed** *Jul.* €€€€€

Giovanni Rotti's "new Tuscan" cuisine earns high praise with dishes such as pigeon with grapes and pine nuts. Fine local wines match the standard of cooking. Superb service and a friendly ambience add to a pleasurable dining experience.

PESCIA

Cecco

Road map C2. Via Francesco Forti 96–98. 0572 47 79 55. **Open** *12:15–2:30pm, 7:45–10:20pm Tue–Sun.* €€€€

This quiet, easy-going restaurant is the best place to sample Pescia's famous *asparagi* (asparagus). Other examples of traditional fare include *pollo al mattone* (chicken) and *fagioli al fiasco* (beans). On cold days, try the pudding – *ciancia* – a delicious house speciality.

PISTOIA

La Bottegaia

Road map D2. Via del Lastrone 4.
[0573 36 56 02. **Open**
12:30–2:30pm, 7:30–10:15pm
Tue–Sat, 7:30– 10:15pm Sun.
Closed Aug. 🅰 €€€

Close to Piazza del Duomo, this restaurant offers a wide assortment of locally produced cold meats and traditional dishes such as *pappa al pomodoro*, *ribollita* and stewed veal. The friendly waiters will be able to help you with your wine selection.

PRATO

Osvaldo Baroncelli

Road map D2. Via Fra' Bartolomeo 13.
[0574 238 10. **Open** 12:30–
2:30pm, 7:30–10:15pm Mon–Fri,
7:30–10:15pm Sat. 🅰 €€€

Forty years of experience on the part of the eponymous Osvaldo ensure a high standard in dishes such as small tarts of potato and *porcini* mushrooms. The chicken stuffed with pistachios and the tasty sweet rolls laced with honey and Calvados are delicious. The menu changes according to what is in season.

Il Pirana

Road map D2. Via Valentini 110.
[0574 257 46. **Open** 12:30–
2:30pm, 8–10:30pm Mon–Fri,
8–10:30pm Sat. 🇪 🅰 €€€€

Many rate this as one of the best fish restaurants in Italy, certainly in Tuscany. Do not be put off by the over-precious modern interior or by the factory-dotted location of this place, ten minutes' drive from the centre of Prato.

VIAREGGIO

Romano

Road map B2. Via Mazzini 120. **[**
0584 313 82. **Open** 12:30– 2:30pm,
7:30–10pm Tue–Sun. **Closed** Jan.
🍴 🇪 🚻 ★ 🅰 €€€€€

Romano is one of Tuscany's best fish restaurants. Although expensive, few other places give such value for money. Wines

are fairly priced and the fixed-price menu has ten full courses. Romano at the front of house is unfailingly courteous, and his wife, Franca, prepares simple, often inventive and always immaculately presented food.

EASTERN TUSCANY

AREZZO

Buca di San Francesco

Road map E3. Via San Francesco 1.
[0575 232 71. **Open** noon–
2:30pm, 7–9:30pm Wed–Sun,
noon–2:30pm Mon. 🅰 €€€€

The food in the Buca di San Francesco is nothing to write home about. However, its medieval ambience and position alongside the church of San Francesco, with Piero della Francesca's fresco cycle, make it popular with visitors to Arezzo.

CAMALDOLI

Il Cedro

Road map E2. Via di Camaldoli 20,
Moggiona. **[** 0575 55 60 80.
Open Jul–Aug: 12:30–2pm,
7:30–9pm daily. **Closed** Mon from
Sep–Jun. €€

Finely cooked specialities such as venison, boar and fried vegetables combine with the lovely location overlooking the Casentino forests and mountains. This small restaurant is one of the most popular and appealing in the region. For dinner, it is advisable to book a table.

CASTELNUOVO BERARDENGA

La Bottega del Trenta

Road map D3. Villa a Sesta, Via Santa Caterina 2. **[** 0577 35 92 26. **Open**
8pm Thu–Mon (one sitting only,
reservation required). **Closed** Sun in
Jul & Aug. 🍴 🚻 €€€€

This is a serious and tasteful restaurant run by lively patron Franco Cameilia and his French wife, Hélène. The menu includes a renowned *petto di anatra con il finocchio selvatico* (breast of duck with wild fennel). Pastas may be too adventurous if you are used to simple Tuscan cooking, but the desserts are excellent and the choice of wine extensive.

CORTONA

Locanda nel Loggiato

Road map E3. Piazza di Pescheria 3.
[0575 63 05 75. **Open** 12:30–
2:30pm, 7:30–10:30pm Thu–Tue
(Jun–Sep: daily). 🅰 €€€

The Locanda nel Loggiato sits in the centre of Cortona, looking down over a small square from its medieval loggia. Inside, the atmosphere is cool and sedate, with scrubbed stone medieval walls. Be sure to try the home-made *cannelloni* with spinach and ricotta cheese.

SANSEPOLCRO

Il Fiorentino

Road map E3. Via Luca Pacioli 60.
[0575 74 20 33. **Open** 12:30–
2:30pm, 7:30–10pm Sat–Thu. 🅰
€€€

This central, amiable and unfussy hotel restaurant is dedicated to the regional cuisines of nearby Umbria and Marche. Pigeon with olives, a classic local dish, is an excellent choice, as are several of the herb-flavoured pasta sauces. Try the assortment of local cheeses.

Paola e Marco Mercati

Road map E3. Via Palmiro Togliatti 68.
[0575 73 48 75. **Open** 7–10:30pm
Mon–Sat. 🍴 🅰 €€€€€

This is a new and dignified restaurant whose fixed-price menu is particularly good value. Dishes include Tuscan black cabbage cooked with white truffles, vegetable ravioli and truffles, roast pigeon, *gnocchi* (dumplings) in a sauce of tomatoes, and seafood.

CENTRAL TUSCANY

COLLE DI VAL D'ELSA

Antica Trattoria

Road map C3. Piazza Arnolfo 23.
[0577 92 37 47. **Open** 12:30–
2:30pm, 8–10:30pm Wed–Mon.
🔲 ★ 🅰 €€€€

The Antica Trattoria is the more homely and relaxed of Colle's two excellent restaurants. It is a family-run concern dedicated to *cucina creativa toscana* – innovative regional cuisine. The setting is medieval and the service, under the eye of owner Enrico Paradisi, is lively and attentive.

Arnolfo

Road map C3. Via XX Settembre
50–52. [C] *0577 92 05 49.* **Open** *1–
2:30pm, 8–10pm Wed–Mon.* **Closed**
*Tue, Wed lunch, 10 Jan–10 Feb, 1–10
Aug.* [icons] €€€€€

French-trained chefs have earned
this intimate three-roomed restaurant one of Tuscany's few Michelin
stars. The wines, food and service
are all impeccable, but the dignified,
reverential atmosphere is a little too
solemn for an Italian restaurant.
Typical dishes include pigeon
cooked with wine, prunes and
pine nuts, a sublime *ribollita* and
an asparagus and onion tart.

GAIOLE IN CHIANTI

Badia a Coltibuono

Road map D3. Badia a Coltibuono.
[C] *0577 74 94 24.* **Open** *Easter–Oct:
noon–2:30pm, 7:30–9:30pm daily
(Nov–Feb: closed; Mar–Easter: closed
Mon).* [icons] €€€€

The Badia, an 11th-century abbey,
forms the heart of an eminent vineyard where wines and oils are used
in the distinguished adjoining restaurant. The menu offers meats
roasted on a spit and delicious
desserts. Visitors can take a tour
around the estate and there are also
cookery courses available.

Castello di Spaltenna

Road map D3. Via Spaltenna 13.
[C] *0577 74 94 83.* **Open** *12:30–
2:30pm daily.*
[icons] ★ €€€€
See also **Where to Stay**, *p250.*

This lovely stone-walled and
flower-filled restaurant forms part
of a peaceful hotel situated in a
castle just outside Gaiole in
Chianti. Popular with expatriates,
it offers refined versions of Tuscan
classics such as pigeon cooked in
Chianti, fresh *porcini* mushrooms,
chickpea soup and the occasional
more offbeat innovation.

MONTALCINO

Taverna e Fattoria
dei Barbi

Road map D4. Località Podernovi. [C]
0577 84 12 00. **Open** *12:30– 2:30pm,
7:30–9:30pm (May–mid-Jul: Thu–Tue;
mid-Jul–Sep: daily; Oct–Apr: Thu–Mon
& Tue lunch).* [icons] ★ €€€€

Magnificent Brunello wines
from the surrounding vineyards
complement the superb country

cooking of this renowned restaurant south of Montalcino. Try to
get a table outside, where you can
admire the lovely views over the
surrounding hills.

MONTEPULCIANO

Il Cantuccio

Road map E4. Via delle Cantine 1/2.
[C] *0578 75 78 70.* **Open** *1–2pm,
7:30–9pm Tue–Sun.* [icons] €€€

For a successful combination of
traditional food and great atmosphere, try Il Cantuccio, located in
a beautiful 13th-century palace.
Do not miss the house speciality:
pici alla nana, pasta with a duck,
tomato and red wine sauce.

MONTERIGGIONI

Il Pozzo

Road map D3. Piazza Roma 2.
[C] *0577 30 41 27.* **Open** *12:15–
2:40pm, 7:45–10pm Tue –Sat,
12:15– 2:40pm Sun.* [icons] €€€

The old stone-walled ambience
of this restaurant is what you
would expect from a village
as thoroughly medieval as
Monteriggioni. This is an ideal
place for lunch, and the food is
rigorously Tuscan, simple and
enthusiastically prepared. The
home-made desserts of the owner,
Lucia, are widely renowned.

PIENZA

Da Falco

Road map D4. Piazza Dante
Alighieri 3. [C] *0578 74 85 51.*
Open *12–3pm, 7–10pm Sat–Thu.*
[icons] €€€

This friendly restaurant is among
the best of Pienza's handful of
places to eat. The *antipasti* are
excellent and there is a vast choice
of *primi* and *secondi* on a long
menu of regional specialities.

SAN GIMIGNANO

Le Terrazze

Road map C3. Albergo La Cisterna,
Piazza della Cisterna 24. [C] *0577
94 03 28.* **Open** *12:30–2:30pm, 7:30–
9:30pm Thu –Mon, 7–9:30pm Wed.*
Closed *10 Jan–10 Mar.* [icons] €€€

The Terrazze's selling point, as
its name suggests, is a terrace
with views over the rolling hills

of southern Tuscany. The dining
room is medieval, with low
ceilings and wooden beams, and
forms part of a 13th-century
palazzo, mostly occupied by the
adjoining hotel *(see p250)*. This
is a good place for regional
specialities, though the menu also
boasts the occasional novelty.

SIENA

La Torre

Road map D3. Via Salicotto 7–9.
[C] *0577 28 75 48.* **Open** *noon–
3pm, 7–10pm Fri –Wed.* €€

Despite its position immediately
off the Campo, this tiny old-
fashioned trattoria remained all
but unknown for years. Now it
has been discovered, so arrive
early to grab one of the handful
of tables in the narrow, noisy
stone-arched dining room.

Il Campo

Road map D3. Piazza del Campo 50.
[C] *0577 28 07 25.* **Open** *noon–
10pm Wed–Mon.* [icons] €€€

Most of the restaurants that ring
Piazza del Campo tend to be
expensive and slipshod tourist
traps. The most expensive,
however, Il Campo, is the
exception, and the place to
come if you're going to treat
yourself to a meal in arguably
Italy's loveliest piazza.

Al Marsili

Road map D3. Via del Castoro 3.
[C] *0577 471 54.* **Open** *12:30–
2:30pm, 7:30–10pm Tue –Sun.*
[icons] €€€

Standards in this long-term rival to
Osteria Le Logge *(see below)* for
the title of Siena's best restaurant
have been erratic. However, with
Le Logge's prices now edging
towards excessive, the Marsili's
equally elegant and central setting
once again looks tempting.

Osteria Le Logge

Road map D3. Via del Porrione 33.
[C] *0577 480 13.* **Open** *noon– 3pm,
7–10:30pm Mon–Sat.*
[icons] €€€€

Siena's prettiest, and often full,
restaurant has a dark wood and
marble interior. The tables are
laid with crisp linen cloths and
decorated with plants. Home-
produced oils and Montalcino
wines accompany dishes which
wander slightly from mainstream
Tuscan cooking. More exotic
primi include stuffed guinea fowl
(faraona), chicken with lemon,

duck and fennel, and meats stuffed with rabbit and capers. Book or arrive early to avoid waiting for a table.

Ristorante Certosa di Maggiano

Road map D3. Via di Certosa 82.
[0577 28 81 80. **Open** 1–2pm, 8–10:30pm daily. 🍴 🅿
€€€€€
See also **Where to Stay**, p251.

The Hotel Certosa di Maggiano, a restored 14th-century abbey, is the perfect place for a honeymoon. While the food in the restaurant doesn't quite live up to the idyllic surroundings, it's still a fine place to escape the city and enjoy – at quite a considerable price – a rarefied and delicate Italian cooking. Meals are served in the dining room or in the quiet 14th-century cloisters.

SOUTHERN TUSCANY

CAPALBIO

Da Maria

Road map D5. Via Nuova 3. **[** 0564 89 60 14. **Open** summer: noon–2:30pm & 7:30–10pm daily; winter: noon–2:30pm & 7:30–10pm Wed–Mon.
Closed 7 Jan–7 Feb. 🍴 🅿 €€€

Capalbio's holiday population of Roman politicians and media types sit down with locals and visitors to enjoy Maurizio Rossi's variety of soundly cooked, authentic Maremman cuisine. Dishes include *cinghiale alla cacciatora* (wild boar in a rich "hunter's" sauce), *acquacotta*, *tortelli tartufati* (stuffed pasta with truffles), *fritto misto vegetale* (mixed deep-fried vegetables) and many more.

ELBA

Rendez-Vous da Marcello

Road map B4. Piazza della Vittoria 1, Marciana Marina. **[** 0565 992 51.
Open Jul–Oct: noon–2:30pm, 7–10pm daily; Mar–Jun: noon–2:30pm, 7–10pm Thu–Tue (closed Nov–Feb). 📷 🍽 🍴 🅿 €€€

Outdoor tables on the harbourfront at this noted fish restaurant make a pleasant retreat from the summer crowds of Marciana Marina. Most dishes are pleasantly

simple but the menu may, at times, include the fashionable culinary fads of the moment.

Publius

Road map B4. Piazza del Castagneto, Poggio Marciana. **[** 0565 992 08.
Open Apr–Oct: 12:30–2:30pm, 7–10:30pm, Tue–Sun (mid-Jun–mid-Sep: daily); Nov–Mar: only by appt.
🍴 ★ 🅿 €€€

Not only does this pleasant and historic trattoria have perhaps the best wine cellar on the island, but it also provides a respite from the unfailing diet of fish and seafood that dominates most Elban restaurants. Here, in addition to fish, you can eat poultry, game, wild boar, lamb roasted in herbs and a wide choice of *pecorino* and other cheeses. There are fantastic views of the island from the restaurant.

MASSA MARITTIMA

Bracali

Road map C4. Via Pietro Sarcoli, Frazione Ghirlanda. **[** 0566 90 23 18. **Open** 1– 2:30pm, 8–10:30pm Wed–Sun. 🅿 €€€€€

For such a popular tourist town, Massa Marittima has few good central eating places. However, it is worth a few minutes' drive on the main road north out of town to sample Maremman cooking in a family restaurant that is not afraid to search further afield for the best ingredients. Among the mouthwatering *secondi* are *brasato* of wild boar (thin cut slices), pigeon with honey, cold duck with balsamic vinegar and blackcurrants and guinea fowl with white grapes.

ORBETELLO

Osteria del Lupacante

Road map D5. Corso Italia 103.
[0564 86 76 18. **Open** 12:30–3pm, 7:30–midnight Wed–Mon (Jun–Sep daily). 🍽 🍴 🅿
€€€

This pleasant *osteria* sticks to old ways in a place increasingly overrun by visitors and affluent out-of-towners. The cooking, which focuses on fish and seafood, has a light touch but can nonetheless be adventurous. Dishes include house speciality *zuppa di pesce* (fish soup), *cozze in salsa di Marsala* (mussels in a Marsala sauce), *risotto con gamberi e pinoli* (risotto with prawns and pine nuts) and sole with almonds and onions.

PORTO ERCOLE

Bacco in Toscana

Road map D5. Via San Paolo 6.
[0564 83 30 78. **Open** 8pm–midnight Thu–Tue (Aug daily).
Closed Nov. 🍴 🅿 €€€€

This rather intimate restaurant serves excellent seafood dishes. Favourites are scampi with lemon, *spaghetti alle vongole* (clams) and *cozze* (mussels) with potato.

PORTO SANTO STEFANO

La Bussola

Road map C5. Viale Marconi.
[0564 81 42 25. **Open** 12:30–2:30pm, 7:30–10:30pm Thu–Tue.
Closed Nov. 🍴 📷 🍽 🍴 🅿 €€€

This restaurant serves adventurous first course dishes, often a seafood pasta. The traditional main course is less fancy and will usually include grilled fish. Dine on the terrace where there are lovely views across the peninsula.

SATURNIA

I Due Cippi da Michele

Road map D5. Piazza Vittorio Veneto 26a. **[** 0564 60 10 74. **Open** Oct–Jun: 12:30–2:30pm, 7:30–10:30pm Wed–Mon (Jul–Sep daily). **Closed** 10–25 Jan, 15–26 Dec. 🍴 €€€

This is one of the region's most popular restaurants and a touchstone for Maremman cuisine. Its more traditional offerings remain unbeatable at the price. Next door, the proprietors have opened a wine shop and *degustazione*, where local jams and sweets can be sampled and bought.

SOVANA

Taverna Etrusca

Road map E5. Piazza del Pretorio 16.
[0564 61 61 83. **Open** 12:30–2:30pm, 7:30–9:30pm Thu–Tue.
Closed Jan. 📷 🍴 🅿 €€€

The Etrusca's popularity is due, perhaps, to the exacting standards set by its two owners. This small restaurant has a medieval dining area which is beautifully presented, and the food – Tuscan with sophisticated cosmopolitan touches – is excellent.

For key to symbols see p253

Light Meals and Snacks in Florence

THE TRADITIONAL PAVEMENT CAFÉ is not as much a part of local life in Florence as in other Italian cities. However, small, hole-in-the-wall bars can be found on most of the city's streets. Here, you can have alcoholic and soft drinks, as well as a range of tempting breakfast and lunch-time snacks. Old-fashioned wine bars provide alternative eating and drinking venues, and the city has plenty of take-away establishments, especially near Santa Maria Novella station, if you want to eat on the move.

Sitting down at a bar or café can be expensive, as there is a charge for taking a table. If you only want a quick snack, it may be cheaper to eat at the stand-up counter. It is also worth noting that some cafés and bars may close during August.

Bars

LOCALS GENERALLY use bars as stop-offs for a coffee, quick snack, an early morning apéritif, to make a phone call or to use the toilet (il bagno). Some bars may stay open late, particularly during the summer, but most are busiest during the day. Most of them have a stand-up counter rather than tables.

Some bars also double as a pastry shop (pasticceria) and virtually all serve filled rolls (panini) or sandwiches (tramezzini) for lunch.

Breakfast is usually un caffè (a short espresso) or un cappuccino (milky coffee) with a plain jam or custard-filled croissant (una brioche or un cornetto).

The cheapest way to buy beer at a bar is from the keg (una birra alla spina) either as a piccola, media or grande measure. Italian bottled beers such as Peroni are also reasonably priced but foreign beers are expensive. Other drinks available are freshly squeezed fruit juice (una spremuta), grappa and wine by the glass (un bicchiere di vino).

Once you have chosen what to eat or drink, you must first pay at the cash desk (la cassa), and then take your receipt (lo scontrino) to the bar, where you will be served. A small tip on the counter will usually ensure quicker service.

There are numerous bars dotted around Florence, and many are convenient for the sights. For example, Caffè is opposite the Palazzo Pitti, or go to Gran Caffè San Marco on the Piazza San Marco.

Wine Cellars

ONCE A FLORENTINE institution, wine cellars (vinaii or fiaschetterie) are now a dying breed. Locals meet in these wonderfully old-fashioned places to eat and drink.

Many wine bars offer crostini, antipasti or a light meal as an accompaniment.

Cafés

FOUR OF FLORENCE'S handful of old-world cafés stand around the dour perimeter of Piazza della Repubblica. Gilli, renowned for its cocktails, dates back to 1733. It has two rear panelled rooms still redolent of an earlier age. Giubbe Rosse, once the haunt of the city's turn-of-the-century literati, also evokes its former glory with dazzling chandeliers. However, like the neighbouring cafés, it is overpriced and likely to be filled with wealthy foreigners rather than elegant Florentines. Instead, locals head for the Rivoire, also expensive, but with more genuine class and a beautiful marble interior. Bars which offer Manaresi, a locally roasted coffee, are usually worth a stop. This coffee is considered by many to be the best in Italy.

The younger set hang out at Giacosa, the birthplace of the Negroni cocktail (Martini, gin and Campari), or at Procacci, renowned for its delicious truffle rolls (tartufati).

Take-Away Food

TRADITIONAL STREET food includes tripe and lampredotto (pig's intestines) sandwiches, sold from the stalls at the Mercato Centrale (see p88), around the Mercato Nuovo behind the Porcellino statue (see p112), as well as in the Piazza dei Cimatori. The Mercato Centrale is a great place to buy picnic provisions if you are planning a day's excursion out of the city.

In the same areas you will also find vans selling porchetta, crispy slices of suckling pig in round rolls known as rosette. Small shops selling pizza by weight or slice (pizza taglia) are found all over the city, especially on the streets around Santa Maria Novella station.

Bars offer other take-away options including panini, tramezzini and ice cream. Some vinaii or fiaschetterie, notably in Via dei Cimatori and Piazza dell'Olio, serve crostini and sandwiches to eat out on the pavement.

Snack bars, such as Gastronomia Vera, selling burgers, chips and flavoured milk shakes, are becoming increasingly popular.

Ice-Cream Parlours

FLORENTINES OFTEN round off a meal or the evening passeggiata (walk) with an ice cream (gelato). No day in the city is complete without at least one visit to an ice-cream parlour (gelateria). You can choose between a cone (un cono) and a cup (una coppa) and pay by size, usually starting at €1 and working up in 50-cent stages to enormous multi-scoop offerings at €3.

Generally, it's best to avoid bars where the selection is limited and the ice cream is made off the premises. Make instead for Bar Vivoli Gelateria (see p71), thought by many to produce the best ice cream in Italy, or to the more outlying Badiani famed for its egg-rich Buontalenti. Locals also favour Frilli.

DIRECTORY

CITY CENTRE EAST

Bars and Cafés

Bar 16
Via del Proconsolo 51.
Map 2 D5 (6 E2).

Caffè Caruso
Via Lambertesca 14–16r.
Map 6 D4.

Caffè Meseta
Via Pietrapiana 69.
Map 4 E1.

Chiaroscuro
Via del Corso, 36r.
Map 4 E1.

Dolci Dolcezze
Piazza Cesare Beccaria 8r.
Map 4 F1.

Fantasy Snack Bar
Via de' Cerchi 15.
Map 6 D3.

Galleria degli Uffizi
Piazzale degli Uffizi 6.
Map 6 D4.

Red Garter
Via de' Benci 33.
Map 4 D2 (6 E4).

Rivoire
Piazza della Signoria 5.
Map 4 D1 (6 D3).

Robiglio
Via de' Tosinghi 11.
Map 6 D2.

Scudieri
Piazza di San Giovanni 19.
Map 1 C5 (6 D2).

Trattoria Santa Croce
Borgo Santa Croce 31r.
Map 4 D1 (6 F4).

Wine Cellars

Bottiglieria Torrini
Piazza dell'Olio, 15r.
Map 6 D2

Enoteca Baldovino
Via San Guiseppe, 18r.
Map 4 E1.

Fiaschetteria Balducci
Via de' Neri 2r.
Map 4 D1 (6 E4).

I Fratellini
Piazza dei Cimatori 38r.
Map 6 D3.

Vini del Chianti
Via dei Cimatori.
Map 4 D1 (6 D3).

Vini e Panini
Via dei Cimatori 38r.
Map 4 D1 (6 D3).

Take-Away Food

Cantinetta del Verrazzano
Via dei Tavolini 18–20r.
Map 4 D1 (6 D3).

Fiaschetteria Baldwin
Via de' Neri 2r.
Map 4 D1 (6 E4).

Giovacchino
Via de' Tosinghi 34r.
Map 6 D2.

Italy & Italy
Piazza della Stazione 25.
Map 1 B5 (5 B1).

Ice-Cream Parlours

Bar Vivoli Gelateria
Via Isola delle Stinche 7r.
Map 6 F3.

Gelateria Valentino
Via del Corso 75r.
Map 2 D5 (6 D3).

Gelateria Veneta
Piazza Cesare Beccaria.
Map 4 F1.

Perchè No!
Via dei Tavolini 19r.
Map 4 D1 (6 D3).

CITY CENTRE NORTH

Bars and Cafés

Da Nerbone
Mercato Centrale.
Map 1 C4 (5C1).

Gran Caffè San Marco
Piazza San Marco.
Map 2 D4.

Robiglio
Via dei Servi 112.
Map 2 D5 (6 E2).

Rex Café
Via Fiesolana 23–25r.
Map 2 E5.

Wine Cellars

Casa del Vino
Via dell'Ariento.
Map 1 C4.

Ice-Cream Parlours

Badiani
Via dei Mille 20.
Map 2 F2.

Carabè
Via Ricasoli, 60r.
Map 2 D5.

CITY CENTRE WEST

Bars and Cafés

Alimentari
Via Parione 12r.
Map 3 B1 (5 B3).

Caffè Amerini
Via della Vigna Nuova 61–63.
Map 3 B1 (5 B3).

Caffè Strozzi
Piazza degli Strozzi 16r.
Map 3 C1 (5 C3).

Caffè Voltaire
Via della Scala 9r.
Map 1 A4 (5 A1).

Donnini
Piazza della Repubblica 15r.
Map 1 C5 (6 D3).

Giacosa
Via della Spada.
Map 5 B2.

Gilli
Piazza della Repubblica 39r.
Map 1 C5 (6 D3).

Giubbe Rosse
Piazza della Repubblica 13–14r.
Map 1 C5 (6 D3).

Il Barretto Piano Bar
Via Parione 50r.
Map 3 B1 (5 B3).

La Vigna
Via della Vigna Nuova 88.
Map 3 B1 (5 B3).

Paszkowski
Piazza della Repubblica 6r.
Map 1 C5 (6 D3).

Procacci
Via de' Tornabuoni 64r.
Map 1 C5 (5 C2).

Rose's Bar
Via Parione 3.
Map 3 B1 (5 B3).

Ice-Cream Parlours

Banchi
Via dei Banchi 14r.
Map 1 C5 (5 C2).

OLTRARNO

Bars and Cafés

Bar Ricchi
Piazza di Santo Spirito 9r.
Map 3 B2 (5 A5).

Bar Tabbucchin
Piazza di Santo Spirito.
Map 3 B2 (5 A5).

Caffè
Piazza de' Pitti 11–12r.
Map 3 B2 (5 B5).

Caffè Santa Trìnita
Via Maggio 2r.
Map 3 B2 (5 B5).

Caffeteria Henry
Via dei Renai 27a.
Map 4 D2 (6 E5).

Cennini
Borgo San Jacopo 51r.
Map 3 C1 (5 C4).

Dolce Vita
Piazza del Carmine.
Map 3 A1 (5 A4).

Gastronomia Vera
Piazza de' Frescobaldi 3r.
Map 3 B1 (5 B4).

Il Rifrullo
Via di San Niccolò 55r.
Map 4 D2.

La Loggia
Piazzale Michelangelo 1.
Map 4 E3.

Marino
Piazza Nazario Sauro 19r.
Map 3 B1 (5 A3).

Pasticceria Maioli
Via de' Guicciardini 43r.
Map 3 C2 (5 C5).

Tiratoio
Piazza de' Nerli.
Map 3 A1.

Wine Cellars

Cantinone del Gallo Nero
Via di Santa Spirito 5–6r.
Map 3 B1 (5 A4).

Take-Away Food

Gastronomia Vera
Piazza de' Frescobaldi 3r.
Map 3 B1 (5 B4).

Ice-Cream Parlours

Frilli
Via San Miniato 5r.
Map 4 E2.

Il Innocenti
Piazza Sauro 25r.
Map 3 B1 (5 A3).

SHOPS AND MARKETS

SHOPPING IN FLORENCE can be a unique experience as you wander through its ancient and medieval streets, exploring the city's renowned tradition of crafts and family-run businesses. Few cities of comparable size can boast such a profusion and variety of high-quality goods. Walking around the city you will find shops selling fashionable clothes,

Protective bag with designer label

antiques and jewellery as well as typical Florentine crafts. Tuscany is dwarfed by Florence when it comes to shopping possibilities. However, the rich traditions of many outlying towns and villages boast a variety of local crafts and specialities. These range from ceramics and hand-woven materials to the region's many gastronomic delicacies. *(See also pp28–9.)*

A colourful shop display of elegant handbags

WHEN TO SHOP

GENERALLY, SHOPS OPEN around 9am and close at 1pm. In the afternoon they are open from 3:30pm to 7:30pm in winter, and 4pm to 8pm in summer. In Florence, Siena and Arezzo, shops close on Monday morning in winter, and on Saturday afternoon in summer; in Pisa and Lucca they are shut on Monday morning throughout the year.

Bear in mind that shops and markets close by the score for two or three weeks around 15 August, the national holiday *(ferragosto)*.

HOW TO PAY

MAJOR CREDIT CARDS are usually accepted in larger shops, but smaller shops prefer cash. Travellers' cheques are also widely accepted for payment of goods, though the rate is less favourable than at a bank.

Shopkeepers and market stallholders should by law give you a receipt *(ricevuta fiscale)*. If a purchased item is defective, most shops will change the article or give you a credit note, as long as you show the till receipt. Cash refunds are uncommon.

VAT EXEMPTION

VISITORS FROM non-EU countries can reclaim the 19 per cent sales tax (IVA) on purchases from the same shop exceeding €160. Ask for an invoice *(la fattura)* when you buy the goods and inform the shop of your intention to reclaim the tax. The invoice must be stamped at customs as you leave the country. The shop will reimburse the tax in euros, once they have received the stamped invoice.

SHOPPING IN FLORENCE

THE CENTRE OF FLORENCE is packed with shops selling everything from designer clothes to second-hand books. The best time for bargains is during the January and July sales. Also explore the streets

Window shopping in the Via de' Tornabuoni, Florence

away from the centre around Piazza di Santa Croce, Piazza dei Ciompi and Piazza di Santo Spirito, where craftsmen are busy at work.

DEPARTMENT STORES

THE MAIN CHAIN STORE in Florence is **Coin**, which is also in Montecatini Terme and Livorno. Another possibility is **Rinascente** in the Piazza della Repubblica and also found in towns throughout Tuscany.

FASHION AND ACCESSORIES

IN FLORENCE, the big names in Italian fashion are mostly found in Via de' Tornabuoni *(see p105)*, such as **Gucci**, **Giorgio Armani**, **Prada** and **Enrico Coveri**, or Via della Vigna Nuova *(see p105)*, where you'll find **Versace**, **Dolce & Gabbana** and **Valentino**. Make an appointment to visit the showroom at **Emilio Pucci**'s family palace *(see p88)*, famous for his extravagant 1960s clothes. Alternatively, visit the shop in Via della Vigna Nuova. **Principe** sells classic menswear as well as women's and children's clothes. **Eredi Chiarini** has more casual styles.

Florence abounds in shoe and leather shops. The classic styles and refined finishing of **Ferragamo's** shoes are sought-after by Hollywood stars. Alternatively, try the more affordable **Cresti** for a range of fashionable and comfortable footwear, or stroll down Via de' Cerretani. Across the Arno is the tiny shop **Francesco**, selling simple, hand-made shoes and sandals at modest prices. Piazza di Santa Croce and the adjoining streets are lined with leather shops. Elegant leather bags are sold at **Bojola** in Via de' Cerretani.

There are opulent fabrics at **Valli** and fine silks at **Lisio – Arte della Seta**. Embroidered linen can be found at **Taf**.

TOILETRIES

TOILETRIES AND BEAUTY products can be bought at a *profumeria*, while an *erboristeria* (herbalist) dispenses natural remedies and a range of natural products. A typical example of the latter in Florence is **Erboristeria** (Palazzo Vecchio) *(see p75)*. Also well worth a visit is the **Farmacia di Santa Maria Novella**, a frescoed apothecary shop on Via della Scala selling products from the elixirs of the Camaldoli monks to herbal remedies and soaps.

Typical antiques shop in Florence

ART, ANTIQUES AND INTERIOR DESIGN

FLORENCE HAS ALWAYS been noted for its craftsmen, especially gold and silver-smiths. Go to **Torrini**, whose family has produced jewellery in Florence for six centuries, and to **Buccellati**, renowned for its diamond-encrusted wedding rings.

For lovers of Art Nouveau and Art Deco furnishings there is **Fallani Best**. For top-quality antiques go to **Neri**. **Romanelli** has bronze statuary and works encrusted in semi-precious stones, from

Alessi kitchenware at Rebus

small boxes to large urns. For modern art objects and gifts go to **Armando Poggi**. **Ugo Poggi** has a selection of household objects including elegant porcelain, while **Rebus** sells Alessi kitchenware.

BOOKS AND GIFTS

THE MAIN BOOKSHOPS in Florence include **Seeber**, which sells publications in various languages, and **Feltrinelli**. **The Paperback Exchange** has the widest range of titles in English. For a selection of maps and guidebooks, try **Il Viaggio**.

Typically Florentine crafts include hand-made marbled paper, used to decorate a variety of objects. These are available at **Giulio Giannini** or **Il Torchio**.

Go to **Ugolini** and **Mosaico di Pitti** for tables and framed pictures made with the old technique of marble inlay. For terracotta and decorative glazed ceramics visit **Sbigoli**, and **Arredamenti Castorina** for an astonishing selection of intricate intarsias. Via de' Guicciardini is packed with shops selling books, silver and other objects bound in coloured leather hide.

FOOD AND WINE

SHOPPING FOR FOOD should not pose too much of a problem. **Pegna**, a mini-supermarket in the heart of Florence, stocks fresh foods and a vast selection of delicacies. For typically British items such as teas, gentleman's relish and whiskies go to **Old England Stores**.

For wines, one of the best-stocked shops is the **Enoteca Bonatti** where you'll find a vast selection of Italian wines, and olive oil from Fiesole, bottled on the premises from a huge terracotta vase. Another place to buy wine is **Zanobini**, where you can join with the locals and have a *bicchiere*.

FLORENCE'S MARKETS

FLORENCE'S CENTRAL street market is the **Mercato di San Lorenzo**, which caters mostly for tourists *(see p88)*. Nearby, in Via dell'Ariento, is **Mercato Centrale**, the city's main food market *(see p88)*.

In the city centre, beneath the 16th-century Loggia del Porcellino, is the **Mercato Nuovo**, or Straw Market, which sells leather goods and souvenirs *(see p112)*.

On Tuesday mornings, there is an enormous market at the **Parco delle Cascine**. Clothing, shoes, housewares and food are available at cheap prices.

The **Mercato delle Pulci** is a Flea Market, selling a range of antiques and bric-à-brac.

Flower enthusiasts might want to check out the small **Mercato delle Piante**, selling herbs and ornamental plants.

Fresh vegetables at a Florentine market stall

SHOPPING IN TUSCANY

SMALL TOWNS throughout Tuscany have a multitude of shops selling a range of handicrafts, foods and some of the best wine in Italy. These are invariably displayed in small shops or at the frequent markets, seasonal fairs and local celebrations (see pp32–7) which are such an integral part of Tuscan rural life.

Display of local pottery

GIFTS AND SOUVENIRS

CHARACTERISTIC CERAMICS are found throughout the region, from the famed raw terracotta of Impruneta to the decorated glazed pottery of Montelupo and Siena. In San Gimignano, look out for shops selling artistic ceramics (see p28) and hand-woven fabrics.

The best in marble can be found in Pietrasanta and Carrara (see p168). The world-famous white marble of the Alpi Apuane continues to serve local craftsmen, who make busts and reproductions of sculpted works of art, as in Michelangelo's day.

The Etruscans mastered the art of working alabaster, and today the tradition lives on in Volterra, where many shops sell a range of souvenirs (see p162). The Etruscans also had knowledge of the

minerals and precious stones characteristic of the volcanic Colline Metallifere, Maremma and the island of Elba, the latter famous for its quartz and opals (see pp230–1).

For textiles, Lucca lays claim to a rich tradition of silk manufacture, as well as embroidery and hand-woven fabrics, reflecting the strong rural craft tradition of the nearby Garfagnana area. Rustic crafts are common in the Mugello and Casentino.

FOOD AND WINE

EXCURSIONS INTO Tuscany should be accompanied by visits to a local vineyard where wine is sold directly from the cellars. The Chianti region is studded with castles and farms producing their own wines (see p225). Greve has several good wine outlets, and during the third week of September there is the annual wine festival, the Rassegna del Chianti Classico (see p36).

The excellent Vernaccia, a white wine, is typical of the San Gimignano area. The vineyards around Montalcino produce some of the best wine in Italy (see p220).

Tuscany's rich gastronomic tradition is reflected in the profusion of local products. The main streets of towns such as Greve, Montalcino, San Gimignano and Pienza have a range of food shops.

Sheep's cheese (pecorino), produced around the area of Crete, can be bought directly from the farm or from shops in local towns. In Pienza, shop shelves are laden with local

A Tuscan delicatessen

cheeses (see p222), cured meats, wines and grappas. In Grosseto you will find truffles.

Siena is renowned for its *panforte*, a dark cake spiced with cloves and cinnamon, which has been produced since the Middle Ages. Biscuits include *cavallucci* (ground walnuts and aniseed) and *ricciarelli* (ground almonds, candied orange peel and honey) (see p255).

MARKETS IN TUSCANY

MARKETS are plentiful throughout the region. Particularly famous is the Mercato dell'Antiquariato, which sells goods from antique furniture to bric-à-brac. It is a sprawling affair which takes place in Arezzo on the Piazza Grande on the first weekend of each month, in Pisa on the Ponte di Mezzo on the second weekend, and in Lucca in Piazza San Martino on the third weekend.

The Mercato dell'Antiquariato on the Piazza Grande in Arezzo

FLORENCE DIRECTORY

DEPARTMENT STORES

Coin
Via dei Calzaiuoli 56r.
Map 6 D3.
055 28 05 31.

Rinascente
Piazza della Repubblica 1.
Map 1 C5 (6 D3).
055 21 91 13.

FASHION AND ACCESSORIES

Bojola
Via de' Rondinelli 25r.
Map 5 C2.
055 21 11 55.

Cresti
Via Roma 9r.
Map 1 C5 (6 D2).
055 29 23 77.

Emilio Pucci
Via della Vigna
Nuova 97r.
Map 3 B1 (5 B3).
055 29 40 28.

Enrico Coveri
Via de' Tornabuoni, 81r.
Map 1 C5 (5 C2).
055 21 12 63.

Eredi Chiarini
Via de' Tosinghi 12r.
Map 1 C5 (6 D2).
055 21 55 57.

Ferragamo
Via de' Tornabuoni 14r.
Map 1 C5 (5 C2).
055 29 21 23.

Francesco
Via di Santo Spirito 62r.
Map 3 B1 (5 A4).
055 21 24 28.

Giorgio Armani
Via de' Tornabuoni
48/50r.
Map 1 C5 (5 C2).
055 21 90 41.

Gucci
Via de' Tornabuoni 73r.
Map 1 C5 (5 C2).
055 26 40 11.

Lisio – Arte della Seta
Via dei Fossi 45r.
Map 1 B5 (5 B3).
055 21 24 30.

Prada
Via de' Tornabuoni 67r.
Map 1 C5 (5 C2).
055 28 34 39.

Principe
Piazza Strozzi 1.
Map 1 C5 (5 C3).
055 29 27 64.

Taf
Via Por Santa Maria 22r.
Map 6 D4.
055 21 31 90.

Valentino
Via della Vigna Nuova 47r.
Map 3 B1 (5 B3).
055 29 31 42.

Valli
Via degli Strozzi 4–6r.
Map 1 C5 (5 C3).
055 28 24 85.

Versace-Versus Boutique
Via Vigna Nuova 36/38r.
Map 1 C5 (5 C2).
055 217 619.

ART, ANTIQUES AND INTERIOR DESIGN

Armando Poggi
Via dei Calzaiuoli
103–116r.
Map 6 D3.
055 21 65 28.

Buccellati
Via de' Tornabuoni 71r.
Map 1 C5 (5 C2).
055 239 65 79.

Fallani Best
Via della Fonderia 5r.
055 22 37 46.

Neri
Via dei Fossi 55–57r.
Map 1 B5 (5 B3).
055 29 21 36.

Rebus
Borgo Ognissanti 114r.
Map 1 A5 (5 A2).
055 28 39 11.

Romanelli
Lungarno degli
Acciaiuoli 74r.
Map 3 C1 (5 C4).
055 239 66 62.

Torrini
Piazza del Duomo 10r.
Map 2 D5 (6 D2).
055 230 24 01.

Ugo Poggi
Via degli Strozzi 26r.
Map 1 C5 (5 C3).
055 21 67 41.

BOOKS AND GIFTS

Arredamenti Castorina
Via di Santo Spirito 15r.
Map 3 B1 (5 A4).
055 21 28 85.

Feltrinelli
Via de' Cerretani 30–32r.
Map 5 C2.
055 238 26 52.

Feltrinelli International
Via Cavour 12–20r.
Map 2 D4.
055 21 95 24.

Giulio Giannini
Piazza de' Pitti 37r.
Map 3 B2 (5 B5).
055 21 26 21.

Il Torchio
Via de' Bardi 17.
Map 3 C2 (6 D4).
055 234 28 62.

Il Viaggio
Borgo degli Albizi 41r.
Map 4 D1 (6 E3).
055 24 04 89.

Mosaico di Pitti
Piazza de' Pitti 16–18r.
Map 3 B2 (5 B5).
055 28 21 27.

Paperback Exchange
Via Fiesolana 31r.
Map 2 E5.
055 247 81 54.

Salimbeni
Via M Palmieri 14–16r.
Map 4 E1 (6 F3).
055 234 09 04.

Seeber
Via de' Tornabuoni 68r.
Map 1 C5 (5 C2).
055 21 56 97.

Ugolini
Lungarno degli
Acciaiuoli 66–70r.
Map 3 C1 (5 C4).
055 28 49 69.

FOOD AND WINE

Enoteca Bonatti
Via Vincenzo Gioberti
66–68r (off Piazza C
Beccaria). **Map** 4 F1.
055 66 00 50.

Old England Stores
Via de' Vecchietti 28r.
Map 1 C5 (5 C2).
055 21 19 83.

Pegna
Via dello Studio 26r. **Map**
6 E2. 055 28 27 01.

Zanobini
Via Sant'Antonino 47r.
Map 1 C5 (5 C1).
055 239 68 50.

TOILETRIES

Erboristeria
Via Vaccherreccia 9r.
Map 3 C1 (6 D3).
055 239 60 55.

Farmacia di Santa Maria Novella
Via della Scala 16.
Map 1 A4 (5 A1).
055 21 62 76.

MARKETS

Mercato Centrale
See p88.

Mercato delle Piante
Via Pellicceria. **Map** 6 D3.
Open Thu am.

Mercato delle Pulci
Piazza dei Ciompi. **Map** 4
E1. **Open** 8am–7:30pm
daily (Nov–Mar: Mon–Sat).

Mercato di San Lorenzo
Piazza di San Lorenzo.
Map 1 C5 (6 D1).
Open 8am–8pm daily
(Nov–Mar: Mon–Sat).

Mercato Nuovo
See p112.

SURVIVAL
GUIDE

PRACTICAL INFORMATION

VISITORS HAVE BEEN coming to Tuscany for centuries, drawn by its magnificent art and architecture, landscape and cuisine. These may all seem overwhelming at first, so try to plan your stay to make the most of this beautiful region. Start your day early and take time over lunch: most sights and shops close for several hours and reopen in the late afternoon.

ENTE NAZIONALE ITALIANO PER IL TURISMO
Tourist board logo

Try to have a relaxed attitude to your sightseeing – opening hours can be erratic and may vary depending on the season. Bear in mind that most Italians take their holiday in August, so some places may be shut. If your stay in Florence is limited, you could take a city tour. You can also combine your stay with a study course, offered throughout the year by colleges.

MUSEUMS AND MONUMENTS

MUSEUMS IN ITALY often have irregular opening times, so it may be worth your while to plan ahead by visiting a few relevant websites (see p273) prior to your trip. Most museums open in the morning and close all day Monday. Privately owned museums have various opening hours and often open later in the afternoon. There is usually an admission charge but some museums offer concessions. In Florence, on most evenings (9–11pm) between June and September, a different museum is open free of charge. Ask at the tourist office for details. Visitors should note that many ticket offices often close half an hour before the closing time of the museum. The booklet *Florence and its Surroundings*, available at most tourist offices, lists the different museums.

In Florence, there is an entry ticket which allows you to visit several museums,

Evening concert in Piazza del Campo in Siena

including the Palazzo Vecchio and Museo di Firenze com'era. It is valid for six months and can be bought from any one of their ticket booths.

TOURIST INFORMATION

FLORENCE, PISA and Siena have several **Ufficio Informazioni Turistiche** (tourist offices), and most small towns have at least one. However, most offices only have details on their particular town. Travel agents such as **CIT Viaggi** and **American Express** have information on local tours and offer guidance on rail and coach travel in Italy. If you want to plan ahead, it may be worth contacting **ENIT** (the Italian Tourist Board) in your country before you leave for Italy.

Sign for tourist information

ENTERTAINMENT INFORMATION

THE BEST GUIDE for entertainment is the daily *La Nazione*. It has a supplement for Florence, Siena, Pisa and Empoli. In Florence, the monthly magazines *Firenze Spettacolo* and *Florence Today* have restaurant and café guides, as well as details of concerts, exhibitions, museums and sporting events. Another useful booklet is *Concierge Information*, which is written in Italian and English and is available from most hotels. Tourist offices often have a selection of leaflets on local entertainment and events.

During the summer evenings, fêtes with local bands are often held

A busker with an accordion entertaining outside the Uffizi

Listings magazines for Florence

throughout Tuscany. Most of the nightspots are found in the cities and beach resorts, although you are likely to find a bar just about anywhere you go.

GUIDED TOURS

Tours AROUND Florence can be arranged through a number of travel agents including **CIT Viaggi** and **American Express**. For guided walks around the city, contact **Walking Tours of Florence**. Guides for private groups can be hired from the **Tourist Guide Association**.

Tourist offices and travel agents throughout Tuscany have lists of authorized guides for both city and regional tours.

A guided tour of Florence

ETIQUETTE

Efforts TO SPEAK a few words of Italian will be appreciated, although most of the big hotels have multilingual staff.

Italians drink in moderation, but smoking is common everywhere, except in cinemas and on public transport.

VISITING CHURCHES

Italians ARE STRICT on dress code in churches and you may be refused entry if you are wearing shorts or if your upper arms are bare. Some churches charge an entrance fee. Most are dark, so make sure you carry plenty of small change for the automatic metered lighting.

TIPPING

Service IN RESTAURANTS is included in the price, unless otherwise stated (see p252). However, foreigners are expected to tip. Keep a few euros handy for taxi drivers, porters, doormen and sacristans.

DISABLED TRAVELLERS

Facilities FOR the disabled traveller in Tuscany are limited. If you book a package tour, representatives can assist in organizing help at airports and ensure the most convenient hotel room.

Some intercity trains have special facilities for wheelchair users. There is a lift at some stations, such as Santa Maria Novella, to help those with wheelchairs on and off trains, but it must be booked 24 hours in advance.

WCs

There ARE FEW public toilets in Tuscany. Many galleries and museums have toilets, otherwise most bar and café owners will let you use theirs.

USEFUL ADDRESSES

American Express
Via Dante Alighieri 22r,
Florence. **Map** 4 D1 (6 E3).
📞 055 509 81.
@ amexfi@tin.it

CIT Viaggi
Piazza della Stazione 51r,
Florence.
Map 1 B5 (5 B1).
📞 055 28 41 45.

ENIT UK
1 Princes Street,
London W1R 8AY.
📞 020 7408 1254.
🌐 www.enit.it

**Tourist Guide
Association for
Florence and Provence**
Via Roma 4, Florence.
Map 1 C5.
📞 055 230 22 83.
@ caftours@tin.it

**Ufficio Informazioni
Turistiche**
Via Cavour 1r,
Florence.
Map 2 D4 (6 D1).
📞 055 29 08 32.
🌐 www.firenze.turismo.toscana.it
Via Carlo Cammeo 2, Siena.
📞 0577 28 05 51.
🌐 www.siena.turismo.toscana.it
Piazza del Duomo, Pisa.
📞 050 56 04 64.

**Walking Tours
of Florence**
Piazza Santo Stefano 2,
Florence.
📞 055 264 50 33.
🌐 www.artviva.com

HORSE-DRAWN CARRIAGES

This is a very pleasant way to spend an hour seeing the historic part of Florence. Carriages carry up to five people and can be hired in Piazza della Signoria and Piazza del Duomo. They can be expensive so try to negotiate a price depending on the duration of the ride. Establish whether the price is per person, or for the whole carriage.

Carriage at the Piazza della Signoria

IMMIGRATION AND CUSTOMS

EUROPEAN UNION (EU) residents and visitors from the US, Canada, Australia and New Zealand do not need visas for stays of up to three months. However, all visitors need to bring a full passport. A visa is needed for stays longer than three months. However, it is advisable to check with the Italian consulate before departure. Vaccination certificates are not necessary.

All visitors to Italy should by law register with the police within three days of arrival. Most hotels will register visitors when they check in. If in doubt, contact a local police department or phone the **Questura**.

Duty-free allowances are as follows: non-EU residents can bring in either 400 cigarettes, 100 cigars, 200 cigarillos or 500 grams of tobacco; 1 litre of spirits and 2 litres of wine; 50 grams of perfume. Goods such as watches and cameras may be imported as long as they are for personal or professional use. EU residents no longer have to declare goods, but random checks are often made to guard against any drugs traffickers.

The refund system for Valued Added Tax (IVA in Italy) for non-EU residents is complicated and slow and is only worth reclaiming if you have spent at least €160 in a single establishment *(see p266)*.

SELF-CATERING HOLIDAYS

IF YOU ARE TRAVELLING with a family, self-catering accommodation is usually cheaper than hotels *(see p242)*, but be prepared for the odd hiccup, such as a shortage of water.

Italy has retained the small shops culture, so you may have to go to several different shops to get your necessities. Fortunately, even the smallest

Student relaxing in the sun in Gaiole in Chianti

village usually has a grocery store *(alimentari)*. Shops may shut for a couple of hours at lunchtime *(see p266)*. Launderettes *(lavanderie)* will offer service washes.

ADDRESSES

FLORENCE HAS a confusing dual address system. Each street has a double set of numbers: a red number indicates a shop, restaurant or business, while a blue or black number refers to a hotel or domestic residence. When writing to a business, insert an "r" after the number to distinguish it from a residential address. Each set of numbers has its own sequence, so business premises at, say, No. 10r may well be next to a residential address at No. 23.

Red street number

Blue street number

STUDENT INFORMATION

AN INTERNATIONAL STUDENT Identity Card (ISIC) or a YIEE (Youth International Educational Exchange Card) will usually get reductions on museum and other charges. For discount travel go to the **Centro Turistico Studentesco (CTS)**. **Villa Europa Camerata** youth hostel provides listings of hostels in Tuscany.

Discount air and rail tickets, such as the Transalpino/BIJ rail tickets for those under 26, can be bought from **Wasteels**, at Santa Maria Novella station in Florence, the CTS or any travel agent displaying the green Transalpino sign.

EDUCATIONAL COURSES

THERE ARE NUMEROUS language and art schools in Tuscany. **The British Institute** in Florence is one of the better known, as is the **Centro di Cultura per Stranieri dell'Università di Firenze**. The **Istituto per l'Arte e il Restauro** offers courses on art, restoration, upholstery, ceramics, drawing and painting. The **Centro Internazionale Dante Alighieri** or the **Università per Stranieri** in Siena has courses on Italian culture, history and cooking. A list of schools in Tuscany is available from the **Ufficio Promozione Turistica, Turismo Sociale e Sport**.

NEWSPAPERS, TV, RADIO

TUSCANY'S MAIN newspaper is *La Nazione*, with regional supplements. European and American newspapers and magazines are also available, and *USA Today* and the *International Herald Tribune* are available on the day of issue.

Newspaper stall selling national and international publications

La Nazione with supplement

The state TV channels are RAI Uno, RAI Due and RAI Tre. Satellite and cable TV transmit European channels in many languages, as well as CNN news in English. BBC World Service is broadcast on radio on 15.070 MHz (short wave) in the mornings and 648 KHz (medium wave) at night.

EMBASSIES AND CONSULATES

If you lose your passport or need other help, contact your national embassy or consulate as listed below.

ELECTRICAL ADAPTORS

Electrical current in Italy is 220V AC, with two-pin, round-pronged plugs. It is probably better to buy an adaptor before leaving for Italy. Most hotels with three stars and above have electrical points for shavers and hair-dryers in all bedrooms.

Standard Italian plug

TUSCAN TIME

Tuscany is one hour ahead of Greenwich Mean Time (GMT). The time difference between Tuscany and other cities is as follows: London: -1 hour; New York: -6 hours; Perth: +7 hours; Auckland: +11 hours; Tokyo: +8 hours.

These figures may vary for brief periods in the summer with local changes. For all official purposes the Italians use the 24-hour clock (eg 10pm = 22.00 hrs).

RELIGIOUS SERVICES

The florence duomo has a mass in English at 5:30pm every Saturday *(see pp64–5)*. See below for other services.

CONVERSION TABLE

Imperial to Metric
1 inch = 2.54 centimetres
1 foot = 30 centimetres
1 mile = 1.6 kilometres
1 ounce = 28 grams
1 pound = 454 grams
1 pint = 0.6 litres
1 gallon = 4.6 litres

Metric to Imperial
1 centimetre = 0.4 inches
1 metre = 3 feet, 3 inches
1 kilometre = 0.6 miles
1 gram = 0.04 ounces
1 kilogram = 2.2 pounds
1 litre = 1.8 pints

DIRECTORY

IMMIGRATION INFORMATION

Questura
Via Zara 2, Florence.
Map 2 D3.
📞 055 497 71.

Via del Castoro, Siena.
📞 0577 20 11 11.

Via Lalli 4, Pisa.
📞 050 58 35 11.

STUDENT INFORMATION

Centro Turistico Studentesco
Via de' Ginori 25r,
Florence. **Map** 2 D4 (6 D1).
📞 055 28 95 70.
🌐 www.cts.it

Via Bandini 21, Siena.
📞 0577 28 50 08.

Villa Europa Camerata
Viale Augusto Righi 2–4,
Florence.
📞 055 60 14 51.

Wasteels
Santa Maria Novella
Station (platform 16),
Florence. **Map** 1 B4 (5 B1).
📞 055 28 06 83.

EDUCATIONAL COURSES

Centro di Cultura per Stranieri dell' Università di Firenze
Via Vittorio Emanuele II 64,
50134 Florence. **Map** 1 C1.
📞 055 47 21 39.

Centro Internazionale Dante Alighieri
Via Tommaso Pendola 36,
53100 Siena.
📞 0577 495 33.

Istituto per l'Arte e il Restauro
Palazzo Spinelli Borgo
Santa Croce 10, 50122
Florence. **Map** 4 D1 (6 F4).
📞 055 24 60 01.
🌐 www.spinelli.it

The British Institute Library
Lungarno Guicciardini 9,
50125 Florence.

Map 3 B1 (5 B3).
📞 055 267 78 270.

Ufficio Promozione Turistica, Turismo Sociale e Sport
Via di Novoli 26
50127 Florence.
📞 055 438 21 11.
🌐 www.turismo.toscana.it

Università per Stranieri
Piazzetta Grassi 2 53100
Siena. 📞 0577 492 60.

EMBASSIES AND CONSULATES

Australia
Via Alessandria 215,
Rome.
📞 06 85 27 21. 🌐 www.
australian-embassy.it

New Zealand
Via Zara 28, Rome.
📞 06 441 71 71.
@ nzemb.rome@
flashnet.it

UK
Lungarno Corsini 2
Florence. **Map** 3 B1 (5 B3).
📞 055 28 41 33.
🌐 www.britain.it

US
Lungarno Amerigo
Vespucci 38, Florence.
Map 1 A5 (5 A2).
📞 055 239 82 76.
🌐 www.italyemb.it

RELIGIOUS SERVICES

American Episcopal
Via Bernardo Rucellai 9,
Florence. **Map** 1 A4.
📞 055 29 44 17.

Chiesa Evangelica Valdese
Study Centre, Via Manzoni
21, Florence. **Map** 2 D3.
📞 055 247 78 00.

Church of England
Via Maggio 16, Florence.
Map 3 B2 (5 B5).
📞 055 29 47 64.

Jewish
Tempio Israelitico
Via Luigi Farini 4, Florence.
Map 2 F5.
📞 055 24 52 52.

Methodist
Via de' Benci 9, Florence.
Map 4 D2 (6 E4).
📞 055 28 81 43.

Personal Security and Health

Tuscany and its cities are generally safe as long as a few simple precautions are taken. As in many European cities, pickpockets are a common problem, especially around Florence and Pisa. Take extra care in crowded areas, particularly around popular tourist spots, and on buses. Leave valuables and any important documents in the hotel safe, and carry only the minimum amount of money necessary for the day. Make sure you take out adequate travel insurance before leaving for Italy, as it is very difficult to obtain once you are in the country.

Florentine policewoman helping a tourist with directions

Looking After Your Property

Travellers' cheques are the safest way to carry large sums of money. Try to keep your receipts and travellers' cheques separate, together with a photocopy of vital documents, in case of loss.

Be wary of pickpockets, especially around the Duomo and Santa Maria Novella in Florence, and around the Leaning Tower in Pisa. They are mainly children, operating in small groups, usually carrying newspapers or cardboard as a cover for their hands. "Bum bags" or money belts are their favourite target, so try to keep them hidden. Thefts from cars are particularly common.

Buses are notorious for pickpockets. Be aware if someone bumps into you – they may be trying to distract you while somebody else takes your wallet. Buses No. 12/13 to Piazzale Michelangelo in Florence and No. 7 to Fiesole are prime targets, as are the buses to and from Pisa station.

To make an insurance claim you must report the theft to the police within 24 hours and obtain a statement (denuncia).

Personal Safety

Although there is a fair amount of petty crime in the cities, such as pickpocketing and car theft, violent crime is rare. The streets are busy until late evening and women travelling alone are rarely harassed, and usually not very persistently. However, try to avoid badly lit areas late at night. Always use the official taxis, with the licence number clearly displayed. When you call for a taxi, make sure you are given the code name of the driver, for example, Napoli 37.

Police

The vigili urbani, or municipal police, wear blue uniforms in winter and white during the summer. They are most often seen in the streets regulating the traffic. The carabinieri are the military police. They dress in red striped trousers and

Municipal policeman

A team of carabinieri in traffic police uniform

deal with a variety of offences from theft to speeding. La polizia (the state police) wear blue uniforms, with white belts and berets. They specialize in serious crimes. Any of these should be able to help you.

Personal Precautions

Visitors from the European Union (EU) are officially entitled to reciprocal state medical care in Italy. Before you travel, pick up form E111 from the post office, which covers you for emergency medical treatment. You may want to take out additional medical insurance, as E111 does not cover repatriation costs or additional expenses, such as accommodation, food and flights for anyone travelling with you. Visitors from outside the EU should take out a comprehensive travel insurance policy which covers against emergency medical treatment.

Inoculations are not necessary for Tuscany, but take mosquito repellent, especially for the rural areas. One effective solution to rid mosquitos is a small electrical machine which burns a tablet on a tiny hotplate. It repels insects for up to 12 hours and is available from most department stores, such as UPIM (see p269). Also, do not underestimate the strength of the sun – drink plenty of water and use a high factor sunscreen. You can drink the water from the taps but most Italians prefer bottled water.

MEDICAL TREATMENT

Outside a Florentine pharmacy with green cross sign

I̶F YOU ARE IN NEED of urgent medical attention, go to the *Pronto Soccorso* (outpatients) department of the nearest main hospital. Patients ̄staying in hospitals are expected to supply their own cutlery, crockery, towels and toilet paper, but not bed linen. The nursing staff will also expect either friends or

A volunteer for the Misericordia dressed in traditional black cassock

relatives to help feed and wash hospital patients.

In Florence and Siena, the **Associazione Volontari Ospedalieri** has volunteer interpreters on call who can help with medical matters. The service is free and available in French, German and English. The **Tourist Medical Centre** in Florence has English- and French-speaking doctors and specialists.

Dentists are expensive in Italy. You can find the nearest one in the yellow pages (pagine gialle), or ask for a recommendation at your hotel.

Pharmacies in Tuscany have a night rota (servizio notturno) and Sunday opening rota posted on their doors. The **Farmacia Comunale 13** at Florence's Santa Maria Novella station stays open 24 hours a day, as does the **Farmacia Molteni** in Via dei Calzaiuoli.

In Tuscany, the Misericordia (see p193) is one of the oldest charitable lay institutions in the world. It is responsible for a large part of the ambulance services. Most of the staff are trained volunteers, but there is also a team of fully qualified medical staff. Volunteers do not wear the traditional black cassock when out on a medical emergency.

Ambulance run by the Misericordia, on the streets of Florence

USEFUL INFORMATION

Associazione Volontari Ospedalieri
Florence 🅲 055 234 45 67.
Siena 🅲 0577 58 63 62.

Tourist Medical Centre
Via Lorenzo Il Magnifico 59, Florence.
Map 1 C3.
🅲 055 47 54 11.

Farmacia Comunale 13
Santa Maria Novella station, Florence.
Map 1 B4 (5 B1).
🅲 055 21 67 61.

Farmacia Molteni
Via dei Calzaiuoli 7r, Florence.
Map 6 D3.
🅲 055 21 54 72.

Florence Hospital
Arcispedale di Santa Maria Nuova.
Piazza di Santa Maria Nuova 1.
Map 6 F2.
🅲 055 275 81.

Siena Hospital
Policlinico Le Scotte,
Viale Bracci 16.
🅲 0577 58 61 11.

Pisa Hospital
Ospedale di Santa Chiara.
Via Roma 67.
🅲 050 99 21 11.

Questura (Police Offices)
Via Zara 2, Florence.
Map 2 D3.
🅲 055 497 71.
Via del Castoro, Siena.
🅲 0577 20 11 11.
Via Lalli, Pisa.
🅲 050 58 35 11.

Missing Credit Cards
American Express.
🅲 06 722 82.
Diners Club.
🅲 800 86 40 64 (freephone).
VISA.
🅲 800 87 72 32 (freephone).

Missing Travellers' Cheques
American Express.
🅲 800 87 20 00 (freephone).
Thomas Cook.
🅲 800 87 20 50 (freephone).
VISA.
🅲 800 87 41 55 (freephone).

Banking and Local Currency

VISITORS TO TUSCANY have a number of options available to them for changing money. Banks tend to give more favourable rates than bureaux de change, hotels and travel agents, but the paperwork is usually more time consuming. Alternatively, credit cards can be used for purchasing goods. When changing money you will need to show some form of identification, such as a passport. Try to keep a few coins in reserve for telephones, tips and for coin-operated lights which illuminate works of art in churches.

Exchange office at one of the Italian national banks

CHANGING MONEY

BANKING HOURS can be erratic, especially the day before a bank holiday, so bring some euros with you. Exchange rates will vary from place to place, so you may want to shop around. Main post offices exchange currency commission free.

For the best rates, change money at a bank (look for the sign *cambio*). Hotels tend to give poor rates, even if they charge modest commissions. The American Express office (*see p273*) offers good rates.

A convenient way to change money is to use electronic exchange machines. These are found at Florence and Pisa airports, in Florence and Siena, as well as in some smaller towns, such as San Gimignano. There are multilingual instructions and the exchange rate is displayed on the screen. You simply feed in notes of the same foreign currency, and you will get euros back.

CREDIT CARDS

CREDIT CARDS are widely accepted throughout Italy, and it is worth bringing one with you. VISA and Access (MasterCard) are the most popular, followed by American Express and Diners Card.

Most banks and cash dispensers in Florence and throughout Tuscany accept VISA or Access cards for cash advances, but be aware that interest is payable as soon as the money is withdrawn.

Some restaurants, cafés or shops may require a minimum expenditure to accept credit card payment. Always make sure you have some cash in case your credit card is not accepted.

TRAVELLERS' CHEQUES

TRAVELLERS' CHEQUES are probably the safest way to carry large sums of money. Choose a well-known, reputable name such as Thomas Cook, American Express or cheques issued through a major bank. There is a minimum commission charge, which may make changing small sums of money uneconomical. Some establishments will charge you for each cheque.

You should check the exchange rates before you travel and decide whether sterling, dollar or euro travellers' cheques are more appropriate for your trip. Bear in mind that it may be more difficult to cash euro travellers' cheques, especially in hotels, because it is not very profitable for the exchanger.

BANKING HOURS

BANKS ARE USUALLY open between 8:30am–1:20pm, Mon–Fri. Most branches also open for an hour in the afternoon from about 2:45pm till 4pm. They close at weekends and for public holidays (*see p35*), and they also close early the day before a major holiday. Exchange offices stay open longer but in general the rates are less favourable.

In Florence, the exchange office behind the station is open from 8am till late evening, depending on the season. In Pisa, the exchange offices in Piazza del Duomo and at the railway station stay open until the evening and at weekends.

USING BANKS

CHANGING MONEY at a bank can at times be a frustrating process, as it inevitably involves endless form-filling and queuing. You must apply first at the window displaying the *cambio* sign, then go to the *cassa* to obtain your euros. It is a good idea to take some form of identification with you, such as a passport.

For security reasons, most Italian banks have electronic double doors. Press the button to open the outer door, then wait for it to close behind you. The inner door then opens automatically. Metal objects may set off emergency detectors as you enter.

Entering and leaving a bank through an electronic double door

THE EURO

TWELVE COUNTRIES have replaced their traditional currencies, such as the Italian lire, with the euro. Austria, Belgium, Finland, France, Germany, Greece, Ireland, Italy, Luxembourg, Netherlands, Portugal and Spain chose to join the new currency; the UK, Denmark and Sweden stayed out, with an option to review their situation. The euro was introduced on 1 January 1999, but only for banking purposes. Notes and coins came into circulation on 1 January 2002. A transition period allowed euros and lire to be used simultaneously, and the lire was phased out on 28 February 2002. All euro notes and coins can be used anywhere inside the participating member states.

Banknotes

Euro banknotes have seven denominations. The 5-euro note (grey in colour) is the smallest, followed by the 10-euro note (pink), 20-euro note (blue), 50-euro note (orange), 100-euro note (green), 200-euro note (yellow) and 500-euro note (purple). All notes show the stars of the European Union.

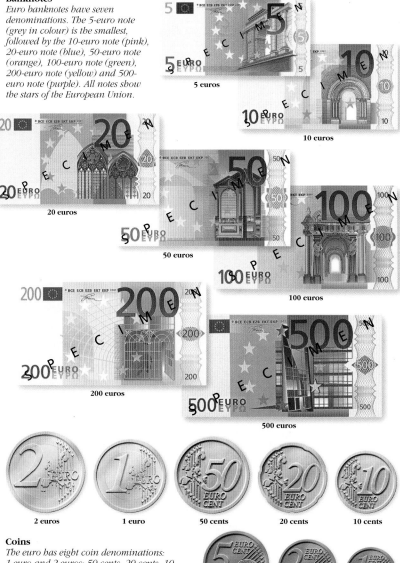

5 euros

10 euros

20 euros

50 euros

100 euros

200 euros

500 euros

2 euros   1 euro   50 cents   20 cents   10 cents

Coins

The euro has eight coin denominations: 1 euro and 2 euros; 50 cents, 20 cents, 10 cents, 5 cents, 2 cents and 1 cent. The 2- and 1-euro coins are both silver and gold in colour. The 50-, 20- and 10-cent coins are gold. The 5-, 2- and 1-cent coins are bronze.

5 cents   2 cents   1 cent

Using Tuscany's Telephones

THERE ARE PLENTY of public phones throughout Tuscany but telephoning, especially abroad, can at times be frustrating. Do not be surprised if you get a crossed line or if you get cut off in mid-conversation. There are phone kiosks on the streets of all main towns, and public phones can also be found in bars, tobacconists and post offices.

Telephone company logo

PUBLIC TELEPHONES

THE GROWING USE of mobile phones in Italy has caused a cutback in certain public telephone services. Florence has a single telephone office (*Telefono*) centre run by Telecom Italia at via Cavour 21/r. Here you can buy phonecards from a machine and use the directories covering the whole of Italy. The centre is open daily until 11pm, and there is no attendant on duty. Similar services are at Pisa train station, open until 9:45pm, and at Pisa airport. The Telecom Italia office in Siena is at Via dei Termini 40. Telecom Italia phone boxes can still be

Telephone sign

found in train stations, airports, and in restaurants and bars displaying a telephone sign.

Privately operated phone centres offering economical rates are springing up, especially around the train station in Florence. These centres also sell international phonecards that can be used with any telephone. International faxes can be sent from post offices.

CALL CHARGES

CALLS WITHIN ITALY are cheapest between 10pm and 8am from Monday to Saturday and all day Sunday. They are also cheap between 6:30pm and 10pm weekdays and after

1pm on Saturdays. Calls within Europe are cheapest between 10pm and 8am and all day Sunday. Calls to Canada and the US are cheapest from 11pm to 8am weekdays, and 11pm to 2pm at weekends. For Australia, call between 11pm and 8am Monday to Saturday and all day Sunday.

Hotels will charge a higher rate to call from your room. Also, calls from Italy cost more than the equivalent call from the US or the UK.

E-MAIL

ACCESS TO E-MAIL and the Internet is very convenient in Florence, and is expanding throughout Italy. Privately run Internet points are proliferating around Florence and can be found in the most popular areas of town. These offer particularly

USING A TELECOM ITALIA CARD TELEPHONE

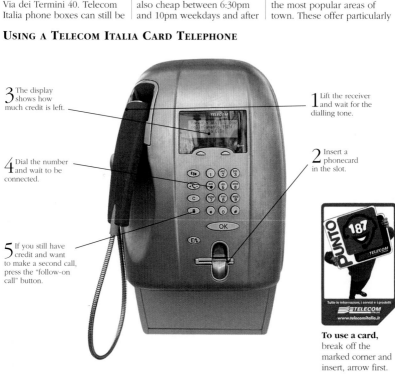

3 The display shows how much credit is left.

4 Dial the number and wait to be connected.

5 If you still have credit and want to make a second call, press the "follow-on call" button.

1 Lift the receiver and wait for the dialling tone.

2 Insert a phonecard in the slot.

To use a card, break off the marked corner and insert, arrow first.

good deals for tourists, selling Internet time in 15- and 30-minute segments. The most widely established of these services is **Internet Train**, which has 13 centres operating in Florence. Internet Train issues a magnetic card on which clients place credit and which can be used in any Internet Train centre in any of the 22 Italian cities in which the company is located.

Internet Train
Borgo S. Jacopo 30/r, Florence.
Map 3 C1 (5 C4).
[C] 055 265 79 35.
[W] www.internettrain.it

USING PUBLIC TELEPHONES

Y OU CAN MAKE long-distance and international calls from Telecom Italia telephones. When making long-distance calls, have plenty of change ready. If you don't put enough coins in to start with, the telephone disconnects you and retains your money. Coin-operated telephones are being phased out and replaced with phones that take pre-paid phonecards (*carta* or *scheda*

REACHING THE RIGHT NUMBER

• Dialling codes are:
Florence 055;
Siena 0577;
Pisa 050;
Viareggio 0584;
Arezzo 0575;
Lucca 0583; and
Pistoia 0573.
• International directory enquiries are on 176.
• International operator assistance is on 170. You can place reverse charge and credit card calls on this number.
• With the Italcable service you can dial directly to an operator in your own country to place a collect or credit card call. Dial 172 followed by: 0044 for UK; 1061 for Telstra, Australia; 1161 for Optus, Australia; 1011 for AT&T, US; 1022 for MCI, US; 1877 for US Sprint; 1001 for Canada.
• *See also* Emergency Numbers, *p276*.

---

telefonica). You can buy these from bars, newsagents and tobacconists displaying the black-and-white T sign.

Some older-style phones in remote villages only accept tokens (*gettoni*), which are now being withdrawn from circulation. Find a metered phone for long-distance calls; ask a bar owner if you can use the phone and the meter will be set. You pay when you have finished your call.

When dialling local numbers always remember to include the area code, such as 055 for Florence or 050 for Pisa.

Telephone cards and stamps are available from here

Sending Letters

L ETTERS CAN BE SENT either by ordinary post or by priority mail. The ordinary post is the most economical, with a fixed rate for letters sent within Italy and the rest of Europe. Postcards inside a regular stamped envelope arrive faster than a stamped postcard. *Poste priorità*, priority mail, requires a special stamp and an adhesive sticker. Letters sent priority mail should be placed in the blue collection boxes, or in traditional red boxes marked *poste priorità*. You can buy stamps (*francobolli*) and stickers from any tobacconist with the black-and-white T

City letters   Other destinations

Italian post box

Post Office sign

sign as well as from post offices. Sub-post office hours are usually 8:30am–2pm, Mon–Fri and 8:30am–noon on Saturday and the last day of the month. Main offices stay open until early evening.

SENDING PARCELS

C ERTAIN RULES MUST be adhered to when sending parcels. The package must be placed in a rigid box, wrapped in brown paper and bound with string and a lead seal. You may also need to fill in a simple customs declaration form. Often a stationery or gift shop in the major towns will, for a fee, wrap your package. Very few post offices offer this service. Parcels sent inter-nationally arrive most quickly

---

if mailed via *postacelere*, available at most major post offices.

POSTE RESTANTE

L ETTERS AND PARCELS should be sent care of (c/o) Fermo Posta, Ufficio Postale Principale, then the name of the town in which you wish to pick them up. Print the surname clearly in block capitals and underline it to make sure the letters are filed correctly. To collect your post you need to show some form of identity (such as a passport) and pay a small fee.

MAIN POST OFFICES

Pellicceria 3, Florence. **Map** 6 D3.
[C] 055 277 41.

Piazza Matteotti 37, Siena.
[C] 0577 20 22 73.

Piazza Vittorio Emanuele II, Pisa.
[C] 050 450 80.

TRAVEL INFORMATION

Tuscany is most easily reached by air, but although planes arrive from European airports, there are no direct intercontinental flights, and visitors from outside Europe have to transfer. The nearest intercontinental airports are Milan and Rome. Tuscany's main airport is in Pisa; it receives both domestic and European flights as well as most charter traffic. Florence's airport is smaller and is located slightly north of

Alitalia aircraft

the city, a short bus ride away from the centre. Almost exclusively, it deals with scheduled flights. Florence is also the main arrival point for the far-reaching European train and coach network, and Pisa has good international rail connections. However, overland travel to Tuscany is much slower than flying, and the savings on cost are negligible. It is only worthwhile if you have particular reasons for doing so.

The main entrance hall at Pisa airport

ARRIVING BY AIR

DAILY FLIGHTS between London and Pisa are operated by **Alitalia**, **British Airways** and low-cost airline **Ryanair** (from Stansted). Pisa also serves Florence from Munich and Frankfurt.

There are no direct intercontinental flights to Pisa or Florence, but it is easy to fly direct to Rome or Milan and connect to these cities from there. Alitalia has good connections from Los Angeles, Vancouver, and Sydney and many other airlines can offer good worldwide connections via Rome and other European capitals. Transfers to Pisa and Florence from Milan and Rome can also easily be made by road or rail.

Italian airline **Meridiana** serves Florence with direct flights from Amsterdam, Barcelona, Paris and London Gatwick, and has a wide

range of domestic flights to Pisa and Florence from points all over Italy.

Generally speaking, the further you are able to book your ticket in advance, the lower will be the available fare. However, many of the best fares are non-refundable so it is vital to take out the necessary travel insurance at or before the time of booking. Also, remember that the lowest fares are often only

The train station at Pisa's Galileo Galilei airport

made available on the Internet, so check the airlines' websites.

The Italian travel agency **CIT Viaggi** has offices worldwide; to book or change flights during your stay in Tuscany, try their local office or the **American Express** office in Florence.

USEFUL NUMBERS

Alitalia
National Flights
🔲 8488 65 641.
International Flights
🔲 8488 65 642.
Information
🔲 8488 65 643.
🔲 www.alitalia.it

British Airways
📞 8488 12 266.
🔲 www.britishairways.com

Meridiana
📞 0552 30 23 34.
🔲 www.meridiana.it

Ryanair
📞 119 114 114.
🔲 www.ryanair.com

CIT Viaggi
Florence 📞 055 28 41 45.
London 📞 020 8686 0677.
Sydney 📞 (2) 267 12 55.

American Express
Via Dante Alighieri 22r,
Florence 📞 055 509 81.

Airport Information
Florence 📞 055 306 15.
🔲 www.safnet.it
Pisa 📞 050 50 07 07.
🔲 www.pisa-airport.com

PACKAGE HOLIDAYS

PACKAGE HOLIDAYS are almost always cheaper than travelling independently, unless you are travelling on a very tight budget and prefer camping and youth hostels. Florence is often offered as part of a two- or three-centre holiday with Rome and Venice, or with a stay in the Tuscan countryside. Different tour operators may use the same hotels in Florence, so it is worth looking around for the best deal. Transfer from the airport on arrival is usually included in the holiday price, and saves both money and effort.

PISA AIRPORT

Sign to the trains at Pisa airport

TRAINS RUN DIRECTLY from Pisa's Galileo Galilei airport to Florence's Santa Maria Novella station. To reach the trains, turn left as you leave the airport arrivals hall. Train tickets can be bought from the information kiosk at the airport. The journey to Florence takes an hour and the service runs once an hour, but is less regular or frequent in the early morning and late evening. There is also an infrequent train serving Lucca and Montecatini.

The through train to Florence stops at Pisa Centrale, and Empoli, where you

Trolley attendant at Pisa airport

can change on to the local line that serves Siena.

The No. 7 bus runs from Pisa airport to the town centre. Buy tickets before you get on the bus from the airport information kiosk. There is also a taxi rank at the front of the airport.

There are baggage trolleys at the airport, but you must have cash ready to hand over to the attendant. Buy some euros before landing, as there are no facilities available for changing money in the baggage reclaim hall.

FLORENCE AIRPORT

FLORENCE'S Amerigo Vespucci airport, often known as Peretola, is very small. The SITA bus *(see p287)* travels to and from the airport every 30 minutes between 9:40am and 10:30pm. The SITA bus to the city centre leaves from the front of the airport building, while the bus to the

airport departs from the SITA station (Via di Santa Caterina di Siena 15r). The journey takes 20 minutes. Buy tickets before you get on, from the bar at the airport.

Only take a taxi from the official rank. They will charge a supplement for coming from the airport plus a supplement for the luggage. There is also an extra charge on Sundays and holidays. Most drivers are honest, but check that the meter is switched on and showing the minimum fare before you begin your journey.

CAR RENTAL

ALL THE MAJOR car rental firms have rental offices at both airports. However, it is wise to make rental arrangements before your departure *(see p290)*, as it will cost you far less than renting after you arrive in Italy.

Leaving Pisa airport by car, it is straightforward to get on to the dual carriageway linking Pisa and Florence. At Florence airport, it might be easier to take public transport into the centre and pick up your car there *(see p291)*.

AIRPORT CAR RENTAL

Avis
Florence Airport 📞 055 31 55 88.
Pisa Airport 📞 050 420 28.

Hertz
Florence Airport 📞 055 30 73 70.
Pisa Airport 📞 050 432 20.

Maggiore
Florence Airport 📞 055 31 12 56.
Pisa Airport 📞 050 425 74.

Florence's Amerigo Vespucci airport, which has only recently started accepting international flights

Travelling by Train

Travelling overland can be a very pleasurable way of getting to and travelling around Tuscany. Italy's state railway (Ferrovie dello Stato, or FS) has a train for every type of journey, from the quaintly, maddeningly slow *locali* (stopping trains) through various levels of rapid intercity service to the luxurious, superfast Eurostar, which rushes between Italian cities at a speed to match its ticket price. The network between large cities is very good, but journeys to towns on branch lines may be quicker by coach (bus) *(see p287)*.

An FS train at Florence station

Arriving by Train

Florence and Pisa are the main arrival points for trains from Europe. The Galilei from Paris and the Italia Express from Frankfurt travel direct to Florence. Passengers from London have to change in Paris or Lille.

From Florence, there is also a direct Alitalia train link with Pisa's Galileo Galilei airport, which can be very useful.

Europe-wide train passes, such as EurRail (US) or Inter-Rail for those under 26 (Europe), are accepted on the FS network. You may have to pay a supplement, however, to travel on fast trains. Always check first before using any private rail lines.

Eurostar high-speed train

Train Travel in Italy

Trains from all over Italy arrive at and depart from Pisa Centrale and Florence's Santa Maria Novella station *(see p286)*, while the Eurostar uses Florence's Rifredi station. If you are planning to travel around, there are passes which allow unlimited travel on the FS network for a determined period of time, such as the Italy Rail Card and the Italy Flexi Rail Card. Available only to non-residents, the cards can be purchased from the station. The *biglietto chilometrico* allows 20 trips totalling no

more than 3,000 km (1,865 miles) for up to five people. This is available from international and Italian **CIT** offices *(see p282)*, and from any travel agent selling train tickets. There are facilities for disabled travellers on some intercity services *(see p273)*.

Booking and Reservations

Booking is obligatory on the Eurostar and on some other intercity services, indicated on the timetable by a black R on a white background. The booking office is at the front of Florence station. Alternatively you can book on the FS website (www.fs-on-line.com). Users must first register on the site, then follow the instructions on how to book and pay for seats. Tickets booked online can be delivered by courier for an additional charge, or picked up for free at a self-service ticket machine in stations offering this service. Do not forget to bring the booking code (PNR) you receive via e-mail after completing the transaction

online. Travel agents can book your railway tickets free of charge.

Booking is advisable if you wish to travel at busy times: during the high season or at weekends. Buying your intercity ticket at least five hours before travelling entitles you to a free seat reservation. For a small fee, you can reserve a seat on any train, except local trains.

Booking Agents

CIT Viaggi
Piazza della Stazione 51r, Florence.
Map 1 B5 (5 B1). **⟨** *055 28 41 45.*

Palio Viaggi
Piazza Gramsci, Siena.
⟨ *0577 28 08 28.*

Tickets

Always buy a ticket before you travel. You can also purchase your ticket on the train, but you will be

Ticket machines at Florence's Santa Maria Novella station

surcharged a percentage of the ticket price. You can upgrade to first class or sleeper by paying the conductor.

If the ticket office is busy, try one of the self-service ticket machines found at most stations. They accept coins, notes and credit cards. The instructions are easy to follow and come in six European languages.

If you are travelling no more than 200 km (124 miles), you can buy a short-range ticket *(biglietto a fasce chilometriche)* from a station newsstand. The name of your station of departure will usually be stamped on the ticket, but if it is not, write it on the back. You must then validate the ticket by stamping it in one of the gold-coloured machines situated at the entrance to most platforms. These machines must also be used to timestamp the return portion of a ticket.

Both the outward and return portions of a return (round-trip) ticket must be used within three days of purchase. Singles (one-way tickets) are issued in 200-km (124-mile) bands and are valid according to band: for example, a ticket for 200 km lasts for a day, a ticket for 400 km (248 miles) lasts for two days, and so on.

All intercity trains charge a supplementary fee *(supplemento)* even if you have an InterRail card. This includes the Eurostar and Eurocity services. The cost depends on how far you are travelling.

Stamp ticket here

Machine for validating tickets

MACHINES FOR FS RAIL TICKETS

These machines are easy to use, and most have instructions on screen in a choice of six languages. They accept coins, notes and credit cards.

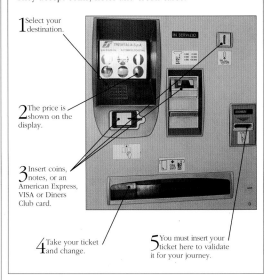

1 Select your destination.

2 The price is shown on the display.

3 Insert coins, notes, or an American Express, VISA or Diners Club card.

4 Take your ticket and change.

5 You must insert your ticket here to validate it for your journey.

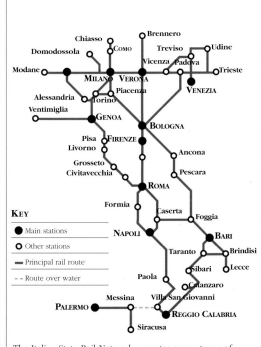

KEY

● Main stations
○ Other stations
— Principal rail route
- - Route over water

The Italian State Rail Network operates seven types of service. Study a timetable before buying your ticket and choose a service to suit both your pocket and agenda.

Santa Maria Novella Station, Florence

Santa Maria Novella station is Florence's central railway station, although the Eurostar *(see p284)* uses Firenze Rifredi. Santa Maria Novella is always busy, and like most major termini attracts some unsavoury characters; it is not a place to linger. There is a taxi rank at the front, and local buses *(see p288)* depart from the side of the station.

In summer, long queues form at the main ticket office, so it is worth tackling the self-service machines *(see p285)* or booking a ticket through a travel agent.

The left luggage office *(deposito bagagli)* is on platform 16, as is a Wasteels student travel office *(see p274)*, and the *Polfer*, the railway police.

To get information about timetables, you will need to queue at the staffed information booths. Take a ticket and wait for your number to be shown. There are usually some staff available who speak French and English.

Other facilities in the foyer include a 24-hour pharmacy, an office with a hotel booking service and some tourist information, and stalls selling international magazines, newspapers and city bus tickets. The international telephone office is near platform 5. There is a bank and a bureau de change inside the station and, in the foyer of the ticket office, there is also an automatic currency exchange machine. There is a tourist information office located in Piazza della Stazione 4, which is run by the city of Florence, and one at Via Cavour, 1r.

View of Santa Maria Novella railway station, Florence

This is operated by a different public entity and tends to have more complete information on the entire province.

Entrance to Santa Maria Novella station, with departure board

Siena Station

Situated outside the city walls on Piazzale Carlo Roselli, Siena station is quite small and is about a 20-minute walk from the centre. Any bus from opposite the station goes to the city centre.

Train information is available at the ticket office and there are also automatic help points with information available in English, French

and German. Other facilities include a left luggage office, a snack bar and a newspaper stand. In addition to services leaving from the city centre, the TRA-IN bus company runs coaches to Montepulciano, Montalcino and Buonconvento. These depart from the front of the station. Tickets must be bought from the bus ticket window or self-service machines in the station foyer before you board.

Pisa Centrale

Pisa's central station is quite large, with most facilities situated either in the foyer or on platform 1: a restaurant and bar, newspaper kiosks which sell bus tickets and telephone cards, and several self-service information and ticket machines.

An exchange booth, open until 7pm, is on the left of the foyer, along with the train information and booking office. The international telephone office, which is open until 9:45pm, is on the right. The left luggage office and the *Polfer* (railway police) are on platform 1.

Tourist information is at the front of the station, near the Banca Nazionale del Lavoro. Most local buses, including that for the Campo dei Miracoli *(see pp154–5)* and that for the airport, stop in front of the station. A bus information and ticket office are close to the bus stops, on your right as you leave the station. There is also a machine selling tickets.

There is another station at Pisa airport *(see p283)*.

Concourse of Santa Maria Novella station

Travelling by Coach (Bus)

Lazzi coach, for travel all over Italy

FLORENCE IS LINKED by coach (bus) to most major European cities and local companies operate an extensive network of services within Tuscany. Coaches are quicker where there is no direct train link, particularly in the countryside. Although the train is faster for long journeys, the coach may be cheaper. To plan trips by coach, maps and timetables are available from all the coach companies' offices, which are usually situated near city railway stations.

ARRIVING BY COACH (BUS)

SANTA MARIA NOVELLA railway station in Florence is Tuscany's main arrival and departure point for all long-distance coach (bus) journeys, and the hub of the extensive local coach network. The **Lazzi** company runs coach links with major European cities from Florence and sells tickets for Eurolines coaches (buses). Book tickets at their office by Santa Maria Novella station. Express services to Rome are run by Lazzi from Florence and **TRA-IN** from Siena.

FLORENCE

FLORENCE HAS FOUR main coach (bus) companies. **Lazzi** serves the region north and west of Florence and **SITA** serves the southern and eastern region. The **COPIT** bus company connects the city with the Abetone/Pistoia region and **CAP** links it to the Mugello area north of the city. All these have ticket and information offices near Santa Maria Novella railway station.

SIENA

SIENA'S MAIN BUS and coach company is TRA-IN, which runs urban, local and regional services. Local services leave from Piazza Antonio Gramsci and regional buses from Piazza San Domenico. There is an information/ticket office in both squares. TRA-IN runs buses to most of Tuscany, including a direct coach to Rome twice daily.

Lazzi office in Florence

PISA

THE CITY BUS COMPANY **CPT** also serves the surrounding area, including the towns of Volterra, Livorno, San Miniato and Pontedera. These buses leave from Piazza Sant'Antonio. **Lazzi** runs a service to Viareggio, Lucca and Florence from Pisa, departing from Piazza Vittorio Emanuele II, which has a Lazzi ticket office.

A Florence coach (bus) line

SITA coach arriving at the station in Florence

Getting Around on Foot and by Bus

Pedestrian zone sign

Tuscan cities are compact enough to get around reasonably comfortably on foot, and the city buses are relatively cheap, regular and wide-ranging. A one-way ticket takes you 15 km (10 miles) out of town, making the bus ideal for trips from the city centre to outlying areas of Florence, Pisa or Siena. The buses get very hot in the summer and are popular with pickpockets (especially Florence's No. 7 bus), so take care when they're crowded.

Bus stop displaying the route

One of Florence's ATAF buses, heading back to depot

WALKING

SIGHTSEEING ON FOOT in Tuscan cities is made all the more pleasurable by the fact that there are plenty of squares in which to rest and watch the world go by, or cool churches to pop into when the heat gets too much. Moreover, there are limited-traffic zones in the centre of most towns, which makes life slightly easier for pedestrians.

Signs for sights and landmarks are usually quite clear, especially those in Siena. In Florence it is easy to pick out the Duomo and the river and orientate yourself in relation to them. A gentle stroll around the main sights of Florence can take just a couple of hours. The Duomo, Santa Maria Novella, Ponte Vecchio and the Accademia are all within ten minutes' walk of each other. The main sights in Pisa are all in the same square. Siena is also compact but hilly, so be sure to wear comfortable shoes.

The cities can, however, be unbearably hot in summer. Plan your day so that you are inside for the hottest part. Recuperate Italian-style with a

Stay on the pavement at all costs

It is marginally less dangerous to cross

leisurely lunch followed by a siesta. Shopping is more pleasant in the early evening when it is cooler, and the streets start to come alive.

CROSSING ROADS

USE THE *sottopassaggio* (underpass) wherever possible. The busiest roads also have signals to help you cross: the green *avanti* sign gives you right of way, in theory, but *never* expect drivers to recognize this as a matter of course. Seize your opportunity and walk out slowly and confidently, glaring at the traffic and maintaining a determined pace: the traffic should stop, or at least swerve. Take extra care at night: traffic lights are switched to flashing amber and crossings become free-for-alls.

CITY BUSES

FLORENCE'S CITY BUS company is called **ATAF**, Pisa's is **CPT**, and Siena's **TRA-IN**. All the buses are bright orange. Most lines run until at least 9:30pm, with the most popular running until midnight or 1am in Florence.

In Pisa and Florence, buses run near all the main sights. Among the most useful Florentine routes for visitors are the No. 12 and No. 13, which make hour-long clockwise/anticlockwise circuits of the city, the No. 7 to Fiesole, and the new "eco-routes" A, B, C and D which are electric or eco-diesel fuelled minibuses.

USING LOCAL SERVICES

FLORENCE DOES NOT HAVE a main terminus, but most buses can be picked up alongside Santa Maria Novella station. In Pisa, most buses stop at the railway station and Piazza Vittorio Emanuele II; in Siena, at Piazza Antonio Gramsci and Piazza San Domenico. There are bus information kiosks at all these points, but they are not always open. Tourist information offices can usually help.

Enter the bus at the front or back and get off through the middle doors. The four low seats at the front of the bus are meant for the elderly, the disabled and people with children. Fare dodging is common, but so are inspectors. The fine is at least 50 times the cost of a ticket. To validate a ticket, feed it through a ticket machine on the bus.

BUS TICKETS

TICKETS FOR CITY BUSES must be bought before you travel, from newsstands, bars displaying the bus company sign (ATAF, APT, TRA-IN) or tobacconists, or at the bus termini. If you are likely to make a few trips, buy several tickets at once; they become valid when you timestamp them in

Signposting for pedestrian routes to sights in Florence

the machine at the front or rear of the bus. There are also ticket vending machines in the streets which take coins and low-value notes.

Ticket prices and validity vary from town to town. You can usually buy a ticket valid for one, two or sometimes four hours' unlimited travel. The time limit starts when you stamp your ticket on the first bus. You can also buy daily passes, or a ticket for *quattro corsi*, valid for four trips. You must stamp the ticket for each of the four trips. A *quattro corsi* is slightly cheaper than the same number of single tickets. You just stamp it as and when needed until you have made the permitted number of trips.

LONG-TERM PASSES

IF YOU ARE STAYING for a long time in one town, a monthly pass for unlimited travel is a good idea. You will need an identity card with your photograph. These are available for a small charge from the **ATAF Ufficio Abbonamenti** located in Piazza della Stazione and at most newsstands. In Siena, photocards are available from the TRA-IN office in Piazza San Domenico. Monthly passes can be bought wherever bus tickets are on sale.

In Florence, the best bus ticket is the *plurigiornale*, available from the ATAF office, bars, newsstands and tobacconists. These are valid for 2, 3 or 7 days. The ATAF

Main bus stop at Florence's Santa Maria Novella station

also sells a ticket called an *abbonamento plurigiornaliero*, valid for between 2–25 days. These are non-transferable.

You can also buy a *carta arancio*, valid for 7 days on trains and bus lines within the province of Florence. You can buy it from any train, coach or bus company ticket office.

USEFUL ADDRESSES

ATAF
Ufficio Informazioni & Abbonamenti, Piazza della Stazione, Florence.
Map 1 B5 (5 B1). 800 424 500.
W www.ataf.net

CPT
Ufficio Informazioni,
Piazza Sant'Antonio 1, Pisa.
050 505 511. W www.cpt.pisa.it

TRA-IN
Piazza Antonio Gramsci, Siena.
0577 20 42 46.

Stamping machine

Ticket inserted here

Ticket valid for 4 rides of 1 hour

Ticket valid for 1 hour

Ticket valid for 3 days

Validating Tickets
Bus tickets are bought in advance and only become valid when stamped in special machines on the bus.

TAXIS IN TUSCANY

Official taxis are white in Tuscan cities, with a "Taxi" sign on the roof. Only take taxis at official ranks, not offers from touts at the stations. There are supplements for baggage, for rides between 10pm and 7am, on Sundays and on public holidays, and for journeys to and from the airport. If you phone for a taxi, the meter starts to run from the moment you book the taxi; by the time it arrives there could already be several euros clocked up. Generally, travelling by taxi is costly. Taxi drivers are usually honest, but make sure you know what any supplements are for. Italians give very small tips or nothing at all, but 10 per cent is expected from visitors.

In Florence, there are ranks at Via Pellicceria, Piazza di Santa Maria Novella and Piazza di San Marco. In Siena, taxis can be found in Piazza Matteotti and Piazza della Stazione, and in Pisa at the Piazza del Duomo, Piazza Garibaldi and Piazza della Stazione.

BOOKING NUMBERS

Florence Radiotaxi
055 47 98 or 055 42 42 or 055 43 90.

Siena Radiotaxi
0577 492 22.

Pisa Radiotaxi
050 54 16 00.

Taxi waiting for a fare at an official rank in Florence

Motoring in Florence and Tuscany

The classic Fiat 500

Amotoring tour through Tuscany makes a memorable holiday, if you are prepared for high fuel costs and erratic Italian driving. But if you are staying in Siena or Florence, with no plans to travel around, there is little point in having a car: both cities are small enough to walk around and parking can be difficult and expensive. If you are staying in the countryside and visiting towns by car, it is best to park on the outskirts and walk or take a bus into the centre.

ARRIVING BY CAR

Drivers from Britain need a Green Card for insurance purposes and the vehicle's registration document. EU nationals who intend to stay for more than six months and do not have the standard pink licence will need an Italian translation of their licence, available from most motoring organizations and Italian tourist offices.

The **ACI (Automobile Club d'Italia)** provides excellent maps and invaluable help. It will tow anyone free, and offers free repairs to members of affiliated associations, such as the AA or RAC in Britain, the ADAC in Germany, the AIT in France, the RACE in Spain and ANWB in Holland. SOS columns on motorways allow instant, round-the-clock access to the emergency services.

CAR RENTAL

Car rental in Italy is expensive and, ideally, should be organized through a tour operator before leaving for Tuscany. Cars can be pre-booked through any rental firm with branches in Italy. If you rent a car when in Tuscany, a local firm such as **Maggiore** may be cheaper. Book in advance, especially for weekend outings.

To rent a car you must be over 21, and have held a licence for at least a year. Visitors from outside the EU need an international licence. Make sure the rental package includes collision damage waiver, breakdown service and insurance against theft.

Getting around Florence by scooter

BIKE AND MOPED RENTAL

A day spent cycling in the countryside can be a healthy and relaxing pastime, and a moped or scooter makes

Rules of the Road
Drive on the right and, generally, give way to the right. Seat belts are compulsory in the front and back, and children should be properly restrained. You must also carry a warning triangle in case of breakdown. In town centres, the speed limit is 50 km/h (30 mph); on ordinary roads 90 km/h (55 mph); and on motorways 110 km/h (70 mph) for cars up to 1099cc, and 130 km/h (80 mph) for more powerful cars. Penalties for speeding include spot fines and licence points, and there are drink-driving laws as elsewhere in the EU.

One-way street

swifter work of the Tuscan hills. Bicycles can be rented for around €3 per hour; moped prices start at about €25 per day. Helmets are mandatory on mopeds. Bicycles can be rented from the main paid parking areas of Florence for a cheaper price.

DRIVING IN TOWN

City centres are usually fraught with one-way systems, limited traffic zones and erratic drivers, and are only recommended to the confident driver. In Lucca, Siena and San Gimignano, only residents and taxis may drive inside the city walls. Visitors may go in to unload at their hotel but must then park outside the walls.

Pisa has limited traffic zones around the Arno, and the rule for tourists unloading also applies in Florence, with its *zona traffico limitato* or *zona blu*, which covers most of the centre. There is a pedestrian zone around the Duomo, although pedestrians here should be prepared, nevertheless, to step aside for taxis, mopeds and bicycles. The latter two often do not comply with traffic light instructions.

Speed limit (on minor road)	**End of speed restriction**

Pedestrianized street – no traffic	**Give way to oncoming traffic**

Give way 320 m (350 yd) ahead	**Danger (often with description)**

Automatic tollbooths on the motorway outside Florence

PARKING

OFFICIAL PARKING AREAS are marked by blue lines, usually with meters or an attendant nearby. There are two large underground car parks in Florence: at Santa Maria Novella station, open daily 6:30am until 1am; and on the northeast side of Piazza della Libertà. The *disco orario* system allows free parking for a fixed period, mainly outside city centres. Set the disc to your time of arrival and you then have one or two hours *(un'ora* or *due ore)*. Rental cars have discs, and fuel stations sell them.

If you park illegally, your car could be towed away. In Tuscany, one day a week is set aside for street cleaning, when parking is forbidden. This is indicated by signs saying *zona rimozione* with the day and time. Beware of residents-only parking areas,

Parking disc

marked *riservato ai residenti*. If your car is towed away, phone the **Vigili**, the municipal police, to find out where it has been taken.

DRIVING IN THE COUNTRYSIDE

DRIVING ON the quiet Tuscan country roads can be a pleasure. However, distances can be deceptive. What may look like a short trip on the map, could actually take much longer because of winding roads. Some back roads may not be surfaced, so beware of punctures. You may also find driving at night disorientating as roads and signs are generally poorly lit.

TOLLS AND FUEL

TOLLS OPERATE on all motorways, although there are some free dual carriageways. Tollbooths take cash or prepaid magnetic "swipe" cards called Viacards, available from tobacconists and ACI.

Motorway service stations occur at irregular intervals, and there are fewer fuel stations in the countryside than in the cities. Hardly any outside the cities take credit cards. Many close at noon and reopen about 3:30pm until about 7:30pm; few open on Sundays. Many in the countryside close in August.

At fuel stations with self-service pumps, put notes or credit cards in the machine. Lead-free fuel is *senza piombo*.

Official parking area patrolled by attendant

General Index

Acknowledgments

DORLING KINDERSLEY would like to thank the following people whose contributions and help have made the preparation of this book possible.

MAIN CONTRIBUTOR
Christopher Catling has been visiting Florence and Tuscany since his first archaeological dig there as a student at Cambridge University 25 years ago. He is the author of several guide books on the city and region.

ADDITIONAL PHOTOGRAPHY
Jane Burton, Philip Dowell, Neil Fletcher, Steve Gorton, Frank Greenaway, Neil Mersh, Poppy, Clive Streeter.

ADDITIONAL ILLUSTRATIONS
Gillie Newman, Chris D Orr, Sue Sharples, Ann Winterbotham, John Woodcock, Martin Woodward.

CARTOGRAPHY
Colourmap Scannning Limited; Contour Publishing; Cosmographics; European Map Graphics. Street Finder maps: ERA Maptech Ltd (Dublin), adapted with permission from original survey and mapping by Shobunsha (Japan).

CARTOGRAPHIC RESEARCH
Caroline Bowie, Peter Winfield, Claudine Zante.

DESIGN AND EDITORIAL ASSISTANCE
Louise Abbott, Gaye Allen, Douglas Amrine, Sam Atkinson, Rosemary Bailey, Hilary Bird, Lucia Bronzin, Ann-Marie Bulat, Jacob Cameron, Cooling Brown, Vanessa Courtier, Felicity Crowe, Joy FitzSimmons, Natalie Godwin, Jackie Gordon, Annette Jacobs, Steve Knowlden, David Lamb, Neil Lockley, Siri Lowe, Georgina Matthews, Helen Partington, Alice Peebles, Sands Editorial, Andrew Szudek, Dawn Terrey, Tracy Timson, Daphne Trotter, Glenda Tyrrell, Nick Turpin, Janis Utton, Alastair Wardle, Lynda Warrington, Fiona Wild, Stewart J. Wild (proofreader).

SPECIAL ASSISTANCE
Antonio Carluccio; Sam Cole; Julian Fox, University of East London; Simon Groom; Signor Tucci at the Ministero dei Beni Culturali e Ambientali; Museo dell'Opificio delle Pietre Dure; Signora Pelliconi at the Soprintendenza per i Beni Artistici e Storici delle Province di Firenze e Pistoia; Prof. Francesco Villari, Direttore, Istituto Italiano di Cultura, London.

For special assistance in supplying the computer-generated image of the Gozzoli frescoes in the Palazzo Medici Riccardi: Dr Cristina Acidini, Head of Restoration, and the restorers at Consorzio Pegasus, Firenze; Ancilla Antonini of Index, Firenze; and Galileo Siscam SpA, Firenze, producers of the CAD Orthomap graphic programme.

PHOTOGRAPHIC REFERENCE
Camisa I & Son, Carluccio's, Gucci Ltd.

PHOTOGRAPHY PERMISSIONS
DORLING KINDERSLEY would like to thank the following for their permission to photograph:
FLORENCE: Badia Fiorentina; Biblioteca Mediceo-Laurenziana; Biblioteca Riccardiana; Centro Mostra di Firenze; Comune di Firenze; Duomo; Hotel Continental; Hotel Hermitage; Hotel Villa Belvedere; Le Fonticine; Museo Bardini; Museo di Firenze com'era; Museo Horne; Museo Marino Marini; Museo dell'Opera del Duomo di Firenze; Ognissanti; Palazzo Vecchio; Pensione Bencistà; Rebus; Santi Apostoli; Santa Croce; San Lorenzo; Santa Maria Novella; Santa Trinità; Soprintendenza per i Beni Ambientali e Architettonici delle Province di Firenze e Pistoia; Tempio Israelitico; Trattoria Angiolino; Ufficio Occupazioni Suolo Pubblico di Firenze; Villa La Massa; Villa Villoresi.
TUSCANY: Campo dei Miracoli, Pisa; Collegiata, San Gimignano; Comune di Empoli; Comune di San Gimignano; Comune di Vinci; Duomo, Siena; Duomo, Volterra; Museo della Collegiata di Sant' Andrea, Empoli; Museo Diocesano di Cortona; Museo Etrusco Guarnacci, Volterra; Museo Leonardiano, Vinci; Museo dell'Opera del Duomo, Pisa; Museo dell'Opera del Duomo, Siena; Museo delle Sinopie, Pisa; Opera della Metropolitana di Siena; Opera Primaziale Pisana, Pisa; Soprintendenza per i Beni Ambientali e Architettonici di Siena; Soprintendenza per i Beni Artistici e Storici di Siena; Soprintendenza per i Beni Ambientali, Architettonici, Artistici e Storici di Pisa.

PICTURE CREDITS
t = top; tl = top left; tc = top centre; tr = top right; cla = centre left above; ca = centre above; cra = centre right above; cl = centre left; c = centre; cr = centre right; clb = centre left below; cb = centre below; crb = centre right below; bl = bottom left; b = bottom; bc = bottom centre; br = bottom right; (d) = detail.

Every effort has been made to trace the copyright holders and we apologize in advance for any unintentional omissions. We would be pleased to insert the appropriate acknowledgments in any subsequent edition of this publication.

The publisher would like to thank the following individuals, companies and picture libraries for permission to reproduce their photographs:

AGENZIA PER IL TURISMO, FIRENZE: 72tr; ARCHIVI ALINARI, FIRENZE: 104b; THE ANCIENT ART AND ARCHITECTURE COLLECTION: 77tl; ARCHIVIO FOTOGRAFICO ENCICLOPEDICO, ROMA: Giuseppe Carfagna 36t, 37b, 199t, 199c; Luciano Casadei 36b; Cellai/Focus Team 36c; Claudio Cerquetti 31bl; B. Kortenhorst/K & B News Foto 19t; B. Mariotti 37c; S. Paderno 21t, 37t; G. Veggi 32c.

THE BRIDGEMAN ART LIBRARY, LONDON: Archivo dello Stato, Siena 45clb; Bargello, Firenze 68t, 69t; Biblioteca di San Marco, Firenze/K & B News Foto 97t; Biblioteca Marciana, Venezia 42br; Galleria dell'Accademia, Firenze 94b; Galleria degli Uffizi, Firenze 25br, 43b, 45cla, 80b, 81tl, 81tr, 83t, 83b; Musée du Louvre, Paris/Lauros-Giraudon, 105t; Museo di San Marco, Firenze 50tl, 51t, 97cb; Museo Civico, Prato 184t; Palazzo Pitti, Firenze 121tr; Sant'Apollonia, Firenze 89t (d), 92c (d); Santa Croce, Firenze 72b; Santa Maria del Carmine, Firenze 127bl (d); Santa Maria Novella, Firenze 111cr; © THE BRITISH MUSEUM: 40b.
BRUCE COLEMAN: N. G. Blake 31br, Hans Reinhard

31cla, 31cra; Joe Cornish: 30–31, 34t, 35, 129t, 201t, 223t; Giancarlo Costa, Milano: 32t, 43t, 53clb, 54ca, 54bl, 145 (inset), 256tl.

Mary Evans Picture Library: 44t, 46b, 48bl (Explorer), 53b, 54br, 74c, 175c, 192c.

Ferrovia dello Stato: B Di Giulio 284cl.

Jackie Gordon: 55cb, 267cl, 285, 290c.

Robert Harding Picture Library: 56–7; Alison Harris: Museo dell'Opera del Duomo, Firenze 25bl, 67t, 67c; Palazzo Vecchio, Firenze/Comune di Roma/Direzione dei Musei 4t, 50cb (Sala di Gigli), 51clb, 79t; San Lorenzo, Firenze/ Soprintendenza per i Beni Artistici 91c; Santa Felicità, Firenze 119t (d); Santo Spirito, Firenze 118b; 116; Hotel Porta Rossa, Firenze: 179b; Pippa Hurst: 179cr.

The Image Bank: 58t; C. Place 100, 108t; Guido Alberto Rossi 11t, 11b; Impact Photos: Piers Cavendish 5b; Brian Harris 17b; Index, Firenze: 182t (d), 182b, 182c (d), 183t; Biblioteca Nazionale, Firenze 9 (inset); Biblioteca Riccardiana, Firenze 57 (inset), 239 (inset) 271 (inset); Galileo Siscam, S.p.A, Firenze 54–5; P. Tosi, 66cr; Istituto e Museo di Storia della Scienza di Firenze: 74b, 75t.

Frank Lane Picture Agency: R. Wilmshurst 31crb.

The Mansell Collection: 45b; Museo dell'Opificio delle Pietre Dure, Firenze: 95c.

Marka: F Pizzochero 29cla; Roberto Benzi 276cla; M Motta 277cl.

Grazia Neri, Milano: R. Bettini 34b; Carlo Lannutti 55b; Peter Noble: 5t, 16, 168b, 218tr, 218cra, 276c.

Oxford Scientific Films: Stan Osolinski 232tr.

Roger Phillips: 198cra, 198crb; Andrea Pistolesi, Firenze: 220b, 277t; Emilio Pucci S.R.L, Firenze: 55cla.

Retrograph Archive, London: © Martin Breese 169c, 180b, 243t, 257bl; Royal Collection: © Her Majesty Queen Elizabeth II: 53t (d).

Scala, Firenze: Abbazia, Monte Oliveto Maggiore 207t; Galleria dell'Accademia, Firenze 92b, 94t, 95t; Badia, Fiesole 47clb; Badia, Firenze 70b; Bargello, Firenze 39t, 42bl, 44b, 47cla, 47b, 49cr, 52br, 66tr, 68b, 69cla, 69cra, 69clb, 108c; Battistero, Pisa 154b; Biblioteca Laurenziana, Firenze 90c; Camposanto, Pisa 152b; Cappella dei Principi, Firenze 48tl, 90t; Cappelle Medicee, Firenze 51crb, 91t; Casa del Vasari, Arezzo 195t (d); Chiesa del Carmine, Firenze

126–7, (126t, 126b, 127br all details); Cimitero, Monterchi 26c; Collegiata, San Gimignano 208cb; Corridoio Vasariano, Firenze 106t; Duomo, Lucca 176b; Duomo, Pisa 155t; Duomo, Prato 26t (d), 27t (d) 27c (d), 27b (d), 26–7; Galleria Comunale, Prato 184b; Galleria d'Arte Moderna, Firenze 52cb, 121tl; Galleria Palatina, Firenze 53crb, 122–3; Galleria degli Uffizi, Firenze 17t, 41cla, 41br, 46c, 48c, 48br, 49t, 49cl, 49b, 50cl, 50b (Collezione Giovanna), 80t, 81ca, 81cb, 81b, 82t, 82b, 83c (d); Loggia dei Lanzi, Firenze 77tr; Musée Bonnat, Bayonne 69b; Musei Civici, San Gimignano 38, 209b, 211b; Museo Archeologico, Arezzo 195c; Museo Archeologico, Firenze 40ca, 41clb, 41bl, 93cb, 99t, 99b, 236b; Museo Archeologico, Grosseto 236c; Museo Civico, Bologna 46tr; Museo degli Argenti, Firenze 51b, 52t, 52ca, 120b; Museo dell'Accademia Etrusca, Cortona 41t, 42ca; Museo dell'Opera del Duomo, Firenze 45t, 63t (d); Museo dell'Opera Metropolitana, Siena 24t; Museo di Firenze com'era, Firenze 71t, 125t, 161b; Museo Diocesano, Cortona 200b; Museo Etrusco Guarnacci, Volterra 40t; Museo di San Marco, Firenze 59t, 84, 96t (d), 96c, 96b, 97ca, 97b; Museo Mediceo, Firenze 48tr; Museo Nazionale di San Matteo, Pisa 153t; Necropoli, Sovana 237crb; Palazzo Davanzati, Firenze 103c (Sala dei Pappagalli); Palazzo Medici Riccardi, Firenze 2–3; Palazzo Pitti, Firenze 120c, 121bl; Palazzo Pubblico, Siena 44–5, 215t; Palazzo Vecchio, Firenze 50–51 (Sàla di Clemente VII), 78t (Sala dei Gigli); Pinacoteca Comunale, Sansepolcro 193b; Pinacoteca Comunale, Volterra 162cr; San Francesco, Arezzo 196–7 (196t, 196b, 197t, 197b, 197cl all details); San Lorenzo, Firenze 25t; Santa Maria Novella, Firenze 24b, 44c (d), 47t (d), 110b; Santa Trinità, Firenze 102t; Santissima Annunziata, Firenze 98b; Tomba del Colle, Chiusi 40cb, 224t; Tribuna di Galileo, Firenze 52–3; Vaticano 39b (Galleria Carte Geographica); Sygma: G. Giansanti 218cla, 218 crb, 218bl; Keystone 55t.

The Travel Library: Philip Enticknap 94cr, 214t, 272c.

Jacket
Front – Corbis: Mark L. Stephenson clb; DK Picture Library: John Heseltine crb; David Murray bc; Getty Images: Michael John O'Neill main image. Back - DK Picture Library: Philip Enticknap b, John Heseltine t. Spine - Getty Images: Michael John O'Neill.

Front Endpaper: The Image Bank: tl; Scala, Firenze: tr.

All other images © Dorling Kindersley. For further information see **www.dkimages.com**

Dorling Kindersley Special Editions

Phrase Book

IN AN EMERGENCY

Help!	**Aiuto!**	*eye-yoo-toh*
Stop!	**Fermate!**	*fair-mah-teh*
Call a	**Chiama un**	*kee-ah-mah oon*
doctor.	**medico**	*meh-dee-koh*
Call an	**Chiama un'**	*kee-ah-mah oon*
ambulance.	**ambulanza**	*am-boo-lan-tsa*
Call the	**Chiama la**	*kee-ah-mah lah*
police.	**polizia**	*pol-ee-tsee-ah*
Call the fire	**Chiama i**	*kee-ah-mah ee*
brigade.	**pompieri**	*pom-pee-air-ee*
Where is the	**Dov'è il telefono?**	*dov-eh eel teh-leh-*
telephone?		*foh-noh?*
The nearest	**L'ospedale**	*loss-peh-dah-leh pee-*
hospital?	**più vicino?**	*oovee-chee-noh?*

COMMUNICATION ESSENTIALS

Yes/No	**Sì/No**	*see/noh*
Please	**Per favore**	*pair fah-vor-eh*
Thank you	**Grazie**	*grah-tsee-eh*
Excuse me	**Mi scusi**	*mee skoo-zee*
Hello	**Buon giorno**	*bwon jor-noh*
Good bye	**Arrivederci**	*ah-ree-veh-dair-chee*
Good evening	**Buona sera**	*bwon-ah sair-ah*
morning	**la mattina**	*lah mah-tee-nah*
afternoon	**il pomeriggio**	*eel poh-meh-ree-joh*
evening	**la sera**	*lah sair-ah*
yesterday	**ieri**	*ee-air-ee*
today	**oggi**	*oh-jee*
tomorrow	**domani**	*doh-mah-nee*
here	**qui**	*kwee*
there	**la**	*lah*
What?	**Quale?**	*kwah-leh?*
When?	**Quando?**	*kwan-doh?*
Why?	**Perché?**	*pair-keh?*
Where?	**Dove?**	*doh-veh*

USEFUL PHRASES

How are you?	**Come sta?**	*koh-meh stah?*
Very well,	**Molto bene,**	*moll-toh beh-neh*
thank you.	**grazie.**	*grah-tsee-eh*
Pleased to	**Piacere di**	*pee-ah-chair-eh dee*
meet you.	**conoscerla.**	*coh-noh-shair-lah*
See you soon.	**A più tardi.**	*ah pee-oo tar-dee*
That's fine.	**Va bene.**	*va beh-neh*
Where is/are ...?	**Dov'è/Dove sono ...?**	*dov-eh/doveh soh-noh?*
How long does	**Quanto tempo ci**	*kwan-toh tem-poh*
it take to get to ...?	**vuole per**	*chee voo-oh-leh pair*
	andare a ...?	*an-dar-eh ah...?*
How do I	**Come faccio per**	*koh-meh fah-choh*
get to ...?	**arrivare a ...?**	*pair arri-var-eh ah...?*
Do you speak	**Parla inglese?**	*par-lah een-gleh-zeh?*
English?		
I don't	**Non capisco.**	*non ka-pee-skoh*
understand.		
Could you speak	**Può parlare**	*pwoh par-lah-reh*
more slowly,	**più lentamente,**	*pee-oo len-ta-men-teh*
please?	**per favore?**	*pair fah-vor-eh*
I'm sorry.	**Mi dispiace.**	*mee dee-spee-ah-cheh*

USEFUL WORDS

big	**grande**	*gran-deh*
small	**piccolo**	*pee-koh-loh*
hot	**caldo**	*kal-doh*
cold	**freddo**	*fred-doh*
good	**buono**	*bwoh-noh*
bad	**cattivo**	*kat-tee-voh*
enough	**basta**	*bas-tah*
well	**bene**	*beh-neh*
open	**aperto**	*ah-pair-toh*
closed	**chiuso**	*kee-oo-zoh*
left	**a sinistra**	*ah see-nee-strah*
right	**a destra**	*ah dess-trah*
straight on	**sempre dritto**	*sem-preh dree-toh*
near	**vicino**	*vee-chee-noh*
far	**lontano**	*lon-tah-noh*
up	**su**	*soo*
down	**giù**	*joo*
early	**presto**	*press-toh*
late	**tardi**	*tar-dee*
entrance	**entrata**	*en-trah-tah*
exit	**uscita**	*oo-shee-ta*
toilet	**il gabinetto**	*eel gab-bee-net-toh*
free, unoccupied	**libero**	*lee-bair-oh*
free, no charge	**gratuito**	*grah-too-ee-toh*

MAKING A TELEPHONE CALL

I'd like to place a	**Vorrei fare**	*vor-ray far-eh oona*
long-distance call.	**una interurbana.**	*in-tair-oor-bah-nah*
I'd like to make	**Vorrei fare una**	*vor-ray far-eh oona*
a reverse-charge	**telefonata a carico**	*teh-leh-fon-ah-tah ah*
call.	**del destinatario.**	*kar-ee-koh dell dess-*
		tee-nah-tar-ree-oh
I'll try again later.	**Ritelefono più**	*ree-teh-leh-foh-noh*
	tardi.	*pee-oo tar-dee*
Can I leave a	**Posso lasciare**	*poss-oh lash-ah-reh*
message?	**un messaggio?**	*oon mess-sah-joh?*
Hold on.	**Un attimo,**	*oon ah-tee-moh,*
	per favore	*pair fah-vor-eh*
Could you speak	**Può parlare più**	*pwoh par-lah-reh*
up a little please?	**forte, per favore?**	*pee-oo for-teh, pair*
		fah-vor-eh?
local call	**la telefonata**	*lah teh-leh-fon-ah-ta*
	locale	*loh-kah-leh*

SHOPPING

How much	**Quant'è,**	*kwan-teh*
does this cost?	**per favore?**	*pair fah-vor-eh?*
I would like ...	**Vorrei ...**	*vor-ray*
Do you have ...?	**Avete ...?**	*ah-veh-teh.. ?*
I'm just looking.	**Sto soltanto**	*stoh sol-tan-toh*
	guardando.	*gwar-dan-doh*
Do you take	**Accettate**	*ah-chet-tah-teh kar-teh*
credit cards?	**carte di credito?**	*dee creh-dee-toh?*
What time do	**A che ora apre/**	*ah keh or-ah*
you open/close?	**chiude?**	*ah-preh/kee-oo-deh?*
this one	**questo**	*kweh-stoh*
that one	**quello**	*kwell-oh*
expensive	**caro**	*kar-oh*
cheap	**a buon prezzo**	*ah buon pret-soh*
size, clothes	**la taglia**	*lah tah-lee-ah*
size, shoes	**il numero**	*eel noo-mair-oh*
white	**bianco**	*bee-ang-koh*
black	**nero**	*neh-roh*
red	**rosso**	*ross-oh*
yellow	**giallo**	*jal-loh*
green	**verde**	*vair-deh*
blue	**blu**	*bloo*
brown	**marrone**	*mar-roh-neh*

TYPES OF SHOP

antique dealer	**l'antiquario**	*lan-tee-kwah-ree-oh*
bakery	**la panetteria**	*lah pah-net-tair-ree-ah*
bank	**la banca**	*lah bang-kah*
bookshop	**la libreria**	*lah lee-breh-ree-ah*
butcher's	**la macelleria**	*lah mah-chell-eh-ree-ah*
cake shop	**la pasticceria**	*lah pas-tee-chair-ee-ah*
chemist's	**la farmacia**	*lah far-mah-chee-ah*
delicatessen	**la salumeria**	*lah sah-loo-meh-ree-ah*
department store	**il grande**	*eel gran-deh*
	magazzino	*mag-gad-zee-noh*
fishmonger's	**la pescheria**	*lah pess-keh-ree-ah*
florist	**il fioraio**	*eel fee-or-eye-oh*
greengrocer	**il fruttivendolo**	*eel froo-tee-ven-doh-loh*
grocery	**alimentari**	*ah-lee-men-tah-ree*
hairdresser	**il parrucchiere**	*eel par-oo-kee-air-eh*
ice-cream parlour	**la gelateria**	*lah jel-lah-tair-ree-ah*
market	**il mercato**	*eel mair-kah-toh*
news-stand	**l'edicola**	*leh-dee-koh-lah*
post office	**l'ufficio postale**	*loo-fee-choh pos-tah-leh*
shoe shop	**il negozio di**	*eel neh-goh-tsioh dee*
	scarpe	*skar-peh*
supermarket	**il supermercato**	*su-pair-mair-kah-toh*
tobacconist	**il tabaccaio**	*eel tab-bak-eye-oh*
travel agency	**l'agenzia di viaggi**	*lah-jen-tsee-ah dee*
		vee-ad-jee

SIGHTSEEING

art gallery	**la pinacoteca**	*lah peena-koh-teh-kah*
bus stop	**la fermata**	*lah fair-mah-tah*
	dell'autobus	*dell ow-toh-booss*
church	**la chiesa**	*lah kee-eh-zah*
	la basilica	*lah bah-seel-i-kah*
closed for the	**chiuso per la**	*kee-oo-zoh pair lah*
public holiday	**festa**	*fess-tah*
garden	**il giardino**	*eel jar-dee-no*
library	**la biblioteca**	*lah beeb-lee-oh-teh-kah*
museum	**il museo**	*eel moo-zeh-oh*
railway station	**la stazione**	*lah stah-tsee-oh-neh*
tourist	**l'ufficio**	*loo-fee-choh*
information	**turistico**	*too-ree-stee-koh*

STAYING IN A HOTEL

Do you have any vacant rooms?	**Avete camere libere?**	*ah-veh-teh kah-mair-eh lee-bair-eh?*
double room	**una camera doppia**	*oona kah-mair-ah dob-pee-ah*
with double bed	**con letto matrimoniale**	*kon let-toh mah-tree-moh-nee-ah-leh*
twin room	**una camera con due letti**	*oona kah-mair-ah kon doo-eh let-tee*
single room	**una camera singola**	*oona kah-mair-ah sing-goh-lah*
room with a bath, shower	**una camera con bagno, con doccia**	*oona kah-mair-ah kon ban-yoh, kon dot-chah*
porter	**il facchino**	*eel fah-kee-noh*
key	**la chiave**	*lah kee-ah-veh*
I have a reservation.	**Ho fatto una prenotazione.**	*oh fat-toh oona preh-noh-tah-tsee-oh-neh*

EATING OUT

Have you got a table for ...?	**Avete una tavola per ... ?**	*ah-veh-teh oona tah-voh-lah pair ...?*
I'd like to reserve a table.	**Vorrei riservare una tavola.**	*vor-ray ree-sair-vah-reh oona tah-voh-lah*
breakfast	**colazione**	*koh-lah-tsee-oh-neh*
lunch	**pranzo**	*pran-tsoh*
dinner	**cena**	*cheh-nah*
Enjoy your meal.	**Buon appetito.**	*bwon ah-peh-tee-toh*
The bill, please.	**Il conto, per favore.**	*eel kon-toh pair fah-vor-eh*
I am a vegetarian.	**Sono vegetariano/a.**	*soh-noh veh-jeh-tar-ee-ah-noh/nah*
waitress	**cameriera**	*kah-mair-ee-air-ah*
waiter	**cameriere**	*kah-mair-ee-air-eh*
fixed price menu	**il menù a prezzo fisso**	*eel meh-noo ah pret-soh fee-soh*
dish of the day	**piatto del giorno**	*pee-ah-toh dell jor-no*
starter	**antipasto**	*an-tee-pass-toh*
first course	**il primo**	*eel pree-moh*
main course	**il secondo**	*eel seh-kon-doh*
vegetables	**il contorno**	*eel kon-tor-noh*
dessert	**il dolce**	*eel doll-cheh*
cover charge	**il coperto**	*eel koh-pair-toh*
wine list	**la lista dei vini**	*lah lee-stah day vee-nee*
rare	**al sangue**	*al sang-gweh*
medium	**al puntino**	*al poon-tee-noh*
well done	**ben cotto**	*ben kot-toh*
glass	**il bicchiere**	*eel bee-kee-air-eh*
bottle	**la bottiglia**	*lah bot-teel-yah*
knife	**il coltello**	*eel kol-tell-oh*
fork	**la forchetta**	*lah for-ket-tah*
spoon	**il cucchiaio**	*eel koo-kee-eye-oh*

MENU DECODER

l'abbacchio	*lah-back-kee-oh*	lamb
l'aceto	*lah-cheh-toh*	vinegar
l'acqua	*lah-kwah*	water
l'acqua minerale gasata/naturale	*lah-kwah mee-nair-ah-leh gab-zah-tah/ nah-too-rah-leh*	mineral water fizzy/still
l'aglio	*labl-yoh*	garlic
al forno	*al for-noh*	baked
alla griglia	*ah-lah greel-yah*	grilled
l'anatra	*lah-nah-trah*	duck
l'aragosta	*lah-rah-goss-tah*	lobster
l'arancia	*lah-ran-chah*	orange
arrosto	*ar-ross-toh*	roast
la birra	*lah beer-rah*	beer
la bistecca	*lah bee-stek-kah*	steak
il brodo	*eel broh-doh*	broth
il burro	*eel boor-oh*	butter
il caffè	*eel kah-feh*	coffee
il carciofo	*eel kar-choff-oh*	artichoke
la carne	*la kar-neh*	meat
carne di maiale	*kar-neh dee mah-yah-leh*	pork
la cipolla	*lah chee-poll-ah*	onion
i fagioli	*ee fah-job-lee*	beans
il formaggio	*eel for-mad-joh*	cheese
le fragole	*leh frah-goh-leh*	strawberries
frutta fresca	*froo-tah fress-kah*	fresh fruit
frutti di mare	*froo-tee dee mah-reh*	seafood
i funghi	*ee foon-gee*	mushrooms
i gamberi	*ee gam-bair-ee*	prawns
il gelato	*eel jel-lah-toh*	ice cream
l'insalata	*leen-sah-lah-tah*	salad
il latte	*eel laht-teh*	milk
i legumi	*ee leh-goo-mee*	vegetables

lesso	*less-oh*	boiled
il manzo	*eel man-tsoh*	beef
la mela	*lah meh-lah*	apple
la melanzana	*lah meh-lan-tsah-nah*	aubergine
la minestra	*lah mee-ness-trah*	soup
l'olio	*loll-yoh*	oil
l'oliva	*lob-lee-vah*	olive
il pane	*eel pah-neh*	bread
il panino	*eel pah-nee-noh*	roll
le patate	*leh pah-tah-teh*	potatoes
patatine fritte	*pah-tah-teen-eh free-teh*	chips
il pepe	*eel peh-peh*	pepper
la pesca	*lah pess-kah*	peach
il pesce	*eel pesh-eh*	fish
il pollo	*eel poll-oh*	chicken
il pomodoro	*eel poh-moh-dor-oh*	tomato
il prosciutto cotto/crudo	*eel pro-shoo-toh kot-toh/kroo-doh*	ham cooked/cured
il riso	*eel ree-zoh*	rice
il sale	*eel sah-leh*	salt
la salsiccia	*lah sal-see-chah*	sausage
secco	*sek-koh*	dry
succo d'arancia/ di limone	*soo-koh dah-ran-chah/ dee lee-moh-neh*	orange/lemon juice
il tè	*eel teh*	tea
la tisana	*lah tee-zah-nah*	herb tea
il tonno	*ton-noh*	tuna
la torta	*lah tor-tah*	cake
l'uovo	*loo-oh-voh*	egg
l'uva	*loo-vah*	grapes
vino bianco	*vee-noh bee-ang-koh*	white wine
vino rosso	*vee-noh ross-oh*	red wine
il vitello	*eel vee-tell-oh*	veal
le vongole	*leh von-goh-leh*	baby clams
lo zucchero	*lob zoo-kair-oh*	sugar
gli zucchini	*lyee dzo-kee-nee*	courgettes
la zuppa	*lah tsoo-pah*	soup

NUMBERS

1	**uno**	*oo-noh*
2	**due**	*doo-eh*
3	**tre**	*treh*
4	**quattro**	*kwat-roh*
5	**cinque**	*ching-kweh*
6	**sei**	*say-ee*
7	**sette**	*set-teh*
8	**otto**	*ot-toh*
9	**nove**	*nob-veh*
10	**dieci**	*dee-eh-chee*
11	**undici**	*oon-dee-chee*
12	**dodici**	*dob-dee-chee*
13	**tredici**	*tray-dee-chee*
14	**quattordici**	*kwat-tor-dee-chee*
15	**quindici**	*kwin-dee-chee*
16	**sedici**	*say-dee-chee*
17	**diciassette**	*dee-chah-set-teh*
18	**diciotto**	*dee-chot-toh*
19	**diciannove**	*dee-chah-nob-veh*
20	**venti**	*ven-tee*
30	**trenta**	*tren-tah*
40	**quaranta**	*kwah-ran-tah*
50	**cinquanta**	*ching-kwan-tah*
60	**sessanta**	*sess-an-tah*
70	**settanta**	*set-tan-tah*
80	**ottanta**	*ot-tan-tah*
90	**novanta**	*nob-van-tah*
100	**cento**	*chen-toh*
1,000	**mille**	*mee-leh*
2,000	**duemila**	*doo-eh mee-lah*
5,000	**cinquemila**	*ching-kweh mee-lah*
1,000,000	**un milione**	*oon meel-yoh-neh*

TIME

one minute	**un minuto**	*oon mee-noo-toh*
one hour	**un'ora**	*oon or-ah*
half an hour	**mezz'ora**	*medz-or-ah*
a day	**un giorno**	*oon jor-noh*
a week	**una settimana**	*oona set-tee-mah-nah*
Monday	**lunedì**	*loo-neh-dee*
Tuesday	**martedì**	*mar-teh-dee*
Wednesday	**mercoledì**	*mair-koh-leh-dee*
Thursday	**giovedì**	*joh-veh-dee*
Friday	**venerdì**	*ven-air-dee*
Saturday	**sabato**	*sab-bah-toh*
Sunday	**domenica**	*dob-meh-nee-kah*

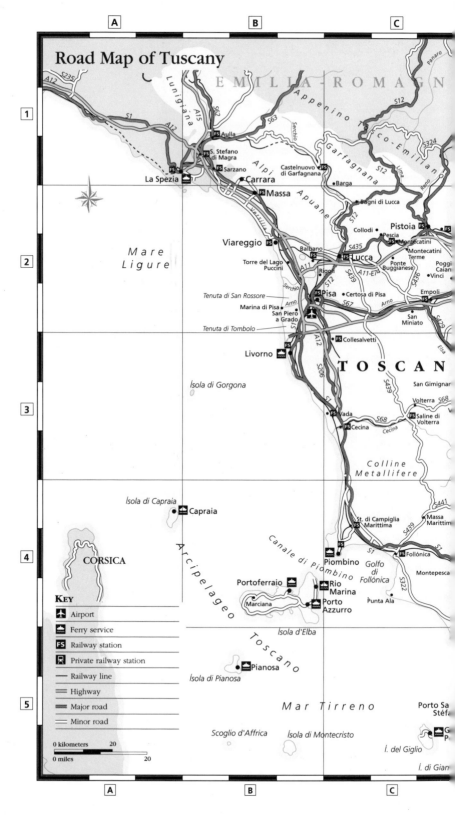